THE
BLONDELIAN SYNTHESIS

STUDIES IN THE HISTORY OF

CHRISTIAN THOUGHT

EDITED BY

HEIKO A. OBERMAN, Tübingen

IN COOPERATION WITH

HENRY CHADWICK, Oxford
EDWARD A. DOWEY, Princeton, N.J.
JAROSLAV PELIKAN, New Haven, Conn.
BRIAN TIERNEY, Ithaca, N.Y.

VOLUME I

JOHN J. McNEILL s.j.

THE BLONDELIAN SYNTHESIS

LEIDEN
E. J. BRILL
1966

THE
BLONDELIAN SYNTHESIS

A STUDY OF THE INFLUENCE
OF GERMAN PHILOSOPHICAL SOURCES
ON THE FORMATION OF BLONDEL'S METHOD
AND THOUGHT

BY

JOHN J. McNEILL s.j.

Le Moyne College, Syracuse, N.Y.

LEIDEN
E. J. BRILL
1966

TABLE OF CONTENTS

PREFACE

Dear Father McNeill:

Ever since our first conversations at the Blondel Archives in Aix-en-Provence I have followed the development of your study of Maurice Blondel's philosophical thought with the greatest of interest. I remember agreeing enthusiastically with the project you outlined to me at that time; and I was delighted to be able to assist you in any way I could in your study of the unedited manuscripts. I had the impression that from the beginning you were in complete harmony with Blondel's thought. I recall telling you that you seemed quite naturally to have parachuted down, as it were, into the very center of that difficult philosophy, but a philosophy whose inexhaustible richness and fecundity you had already intuited in your previous studies.

Today, after reading the completed work entitled *The Blondelian Synthesis,* I am pleased to be able to communicate to you the pleasure and the profit which I have derived from it. I am most grateful to you both for having written this study and also for the privilege you extended to me of reading it in manuscript. This is the first time that a work of this nature has been undertaken concerning Blondel's philosophy. I must compliment you both for your impressive erudition and for the manner in which you succeeded in dominating so complex and so rich a subject matter. It will be a wonderful help to all Blondel scholars and I am sure that its publication will stimulate further studies in the same spirit and with the same method. I dare even to hope that your work will be published subsequently in a French translation as well as in other languages.

There is a special reason why I am so pleased with your effort to bring out the influence of the history of philosophical thought on Blondel. He himself constantly repeated to me what importance he attached to a serious knowledge of the history of philosophical thought in order to successfully affront any philosophical problem whatsoever. The years which he had spent at the Ecole Normal Supérieur had made a deep impression on him in this regard. The formation in the history of philosophical thought was held in great honor there at that time and was a primary center of enthusiastic interest for both professors and students alike. Blondel always claimed to have been deeply formed in that discipline by assisting at the lectures of his professors and by means of the interminable discussions of his fellow students. All his life he continued to cultivate that study with the greatest of pleasure. I should never finish adding details concerning this subject if I were to call back to mind Blondel, the professor at the University of Aix-Marseille at the time when I prepared my university studies under his direction, or Blondel, the philosopher-writer, when for eighteen years I was his hands and his eyes. (A visual infirmity deprived him of the power of reading and of writing, yet he remained eager for intellectual contact.)

You have pointed out quite justly that he was above all else an original genius, a creator, quite capable of absorbing and transforming all his sources and the influences he had received in order to construct a vast "synthesis". Blondel loved to contemplate the great systems of the past; he was intolerant of those who attempted to impose a blanket condemnation of these systems. He was convinced that every doctrine contributed some important lesson to the over-all current of philosophical thought and he excelled at discovering what it was from each doctrine of the past which could be assimilated with profit by the present-day thinker. Consequently he recommended constantly that one read both the ancient and modern authors and that one go directly to the original texts and the living sources of each thinker. However it was not Blondel's objective in demanding this return to sources that they be used purely as a means of erudition. Rather he hoped that each one would be capable of stimulating and nourishing his own personal thought by means of this contact.

This, it seems to me, is exactly what you have done yourself in relation to Blondel. In his own interpretation of the philosophers of the past Blondel was always particularly interested in uncovering the religious inspiration, open or secret, which animated their intentions. Yet he was no less scrupulous in his respect for the text and in his effort to explain each philosopher in his own terms, that is to say, by the letter of his writings as well as the spirit. His correspondence with Victor Delbos gives ample evidence of this and his own historical writings are its proof.

This is why I find that your study fulfills exactly the lesson which Blondel himself gave. You have noted, at times even in detail, Blondel's reactions to the works of his predecessors. Your work concentrates primarily on the German philosophers. (It would have been impossible to include all the philosophers who inspired Blondel, who sought inspiration from such various sources as Saint Thomas, Pascal,

Descartes, Maine de Biran etc.) You have succeeded in situating each one in his proper context and, what is more, in function of what Blondel himself thought of each one, keeping in mind the state of historical knowledge at his time. As a result you permit the reader to participate in a sort of dialogue between Blondel and Spinoza, Blondel and Kant, Blondel and Fichte, Schelling and Hegel etc. I am convinced that this will prove extremely profitable to all those who are interested in the history of ideas. At the same time you forcibly underline how Blondel, who as a sincere believer was obliged to pose the religious problem in philosophical terms, was equally obliged to find other ways and other methods from those of his most illustrious predecessors in order to resolve that problem. In other words you explain to what point he was aware of the past and yet inevitably led to a true independence of the past. This also should serve as an example for all our present-day philosophers as well as those yet to come. There is a philosophical technique which is apprehended only at the price of inserting oneself in a tradition; but there is also a personal option which obliges us finally to confide ourselves to a Master other than human teachers.

I am especially joyous to see that at present Maurice Blondel has awakened prolonged echos in the new world as in the old. You have well appreciated all that he is capable of conveying of openness and enrichment of spirit for your America whose youth, dynamism and generosity Blondel (as he frequently told me) always admired and loved. The true philosophers will recognize him as one of their own. Religious spirits will be attentive to his witness. To the one and to the other you have brought a new sustenance and a new stimulation. For this I am infinitely grateful to you.

Aix-en-Provence, February, 1965   N. PANIS

INTRODUCTION

Maurice Blondel was above all else an original philosopher. This is the primary fact which one must keep in mind in the very process of searching out and appraising the various historical affinities and ties of his first and most important work, *Action*, published in 1893.[1] The synthesis which he achieved in his philosophy of action is unquestionably the work of a highly independent and creative thinker; it is nonetheless a synthesis—a conscious assimilation of all that was vital and significant in the past into a higher, more comprehensive unity. No major philosopher can be properly and accurately understood without a least some reference to those other philosophers who served as his inspiration. Thus the first logical step towards a just comprehension of Blondel's originality should be that of establishing the various historical sources—those philosophers and their ideas—which factually provided the challenge and the materials for his original synthesis.

The purpose of this work is to serve as an introduction and a beginning for such an understanding of Blondel in terms of his historical sources; it represents for all practical purposes a beginning because until the present no major study has been published which attempts to place Blondel's thought within the context of the major currents of philosophical tradition beginning with the viewpoint of Blondel himself. For the most part, Blondel's commentators have shied away from an investigation of the historical sources which had an influence on his thought in *Action* as if it were the exclusive product of his personal thought without any significant relation to previous philosophical tradition. A few have been satisfied to indicate exterior resemblances and differences. For example, attention has been called in particular to the relation between Blondel's method and Kantian criticism.[2] One major work has been dedicated to an objective comparative study of the relation of Blondel's *Action* and Hegel's *Phenome-*

---

[1] Maurice Blondel, *L'Action: Essai d'une Critique de la Vie et d'une Science de la Pratique* ("Bibliothèque de Philosophie Contemporaine," Paris: Félix Alcan, 1893). This first book of Blondel was reedited under the same title in the series "Les Premiers Ecrits de Maurice Blondel" (Paris: Presses Universitaires de France, 1950). The pagination is identical in both editions. This book is always referred to as *Action*.

[2] The most detailed analysis of the relation between Blondel's and Kant's methodology is to be found in Henry Dumery's recent work, *Raison et Religion*

nology of the Spirit.[1] Another compares Blondel's problematic with that of existentialist thought.[2] All these works are indeed helpful for an understanding and appreciation of the importance and originality of Blondel's philosophy. But the fact remains that, as yet, no major attempt has been made to render explicit that vision of the history of philosophical thought which is intrinsic to *Action* and which served as the frame of reference interior to the Blondelian system itself.

The exact nature of that interior frame of reference is by no means open to an arbitrary choice. On several occasions in his published works and letters, as we shall see, Blondel explicitly placed his idea of a philosophy of action within the framework of a specific historical tradition. He himself describes that tradition as an evolution of moral philosophy beginning with Spinoza's *Ethics*, passing through Kantian criticism and the idealist efforts at synthesis of Fichte, the early Schelling, Hegel, and ending with the philosophy of religion of the final Schelling. Blondel attributes to each of these philosophers the inspiration for an important element in his own philosophy of action. From Spinoza he claimed that he derived his problem and the essential principle of his methodology; from Kant, the synthetic a priori and his concept of criticism; from Fichte and the early Schelling, the unity and the continuity of the rational and the practical in subjective consciousness; from Hegel, a logic capable of embracing the total phenomenon of subjective life and action; from the final Schelling, the legitimate role of a philosophy of religion. Blondel insists further that without an understanding and appreciation of these major steps in the evolution of modern thought one cannot hope to understand what he tried to accomplish in *Action*.[3]

Following out this admonition of Blondel, what we propose to do is to retrace the process of evolution represented by these five philosophers as Blondel himself understood it. We cannot hope to achieve an exhaustive study of the inspiration Blondel drew from any one of these philosophers. However, by using Blondel's own published

---

dans la Philosophie de l' Action (Paris: Editions du Seuil, 1963), pp. 441-473. Dumery also gives some brief indications of the influence of Hegel (pp. 473-476) and of Fichte (p. 476, footnote 93).

[1] Peter Henrici, *Hegel und Blondel*, (Pullach, Verlag Berchmanskolleg, 1958).

[2] Albert Cartier, *Existence et Vérité: Philosophie Blondélienne de l'Action et Problé-matique Existentielle*, ("Nouvelle Recherche", Paris: Presses Universitaires de France, 1955).

[3] Confer below, Chapter I, pp. 5-10, for Blondel's statements concerning the relation of *Action* to this tradition.

writings and, on occasions, his unpublished notes we will try to establish what he saw as the key contribution of each one of these philosophers in that evolution, what he rejected as deficient and why; and how he tried to assimilate all these various contributions into a new synthesis. By this means we hope to arrive at a clearer understanding of *Action* itself and to disengage more precisely what was original and creative in its philosophical synthesis.

Before we embark on this study of the role of philosophical tradition in Blondel's thought, a preliminary caution is in order. Blondel himself was by no means a professional historian of philosophy. What interested him in past philosophical thought was those ideas which he considered as still vital and of contemporary consequence. But he was not personally involved in the specifically historical task of a faithful objective reconstitution of past thought. For his understanding of German thought and, in particular, those works which were not available to him in French translations, he depended on indirect sources. The two most important of these sources were, as we shall see, Emile Boutroux, who as Blondel's professor at the Ecole Normale and as director of his thesis, introduced him to the major ideas of post-Kantian thought, and his friend Victor Delbos, the future historian of modern philosophy at the Sorbonne, with whom Blondel worked in close collaboration under the direction of Boutroux during the years that both of them prepared their doctoral dissertations.[1] Without doubt Broutoux and Delbos represent two of the French philosophers of that period who had the most advanced critical understanding of post-Kantian German thought. Hence Blondel's interpretation of his German sources, derived in great part from these men, was frequently in advance of the ordinary critical understanding of his time.

However, Blondel's primary interest was his own creative effort to find a new synthesis; he consciously used ideas from others systems only in so far as they served his project. He defined philosophy as life itself insofar as it achieves a clear reflexive consciousness of itself. Hence he could truthfully claim that life itself, insofar as it revealed its meaning from within consciousness, was his one and only true source. If he made use of a particular historical tradition, he did so because he wished to enter into communication with his contemporaries in terms of their problems and idioms, and because he judged that particular tradition to be the most advanced and most fruitful.

---

[1] Confer below, Chapter I, pp. 5-10, for a discussion of the influence of Emile Boutroux and Victor Delbos on Blondel.

Hence what is of primary importance in Blondel's thought is not his interpretation of other philosophers but his own project. If one wishes to judge Blondel as a philosopher one must confront his finished work with that project in order to examine how well he realized it. Did he remain faithful to his point of departure and to his method? Is his system of reference coherent, and his technical vocabulary rigorous? Are his hypotheses confirmed by his analysis? From this point of view, which is the point of view of this study, what is of importance is not so much the objective validity of the expression Blondel gives to the history of philosophy as an attempt to understand that expression as the interior frame of reference of his own thought.

Thus when Blondel speaks of Spinoza, for example, as a "realist" or of Kant as an "idealist" or of both as "rationalists", even granting that these designations are unjust as concerns the objective reality of the thought of these philosophers, yet nonetheless they represent a certain definition of philosophy which Blondel wished to make for his own purpose. And we must try to understand what Blondel meant by this "realism", "idealism" or "rationalism" if we wish to understand how and by what means he intended to transcend these viewpoints. This is the only means by which one can hope to formulate a just verdict on the result of his creative effort and appreciate whether he succeeded or not in fulfilling his original project.

For this reason we have limited our objective primarily to an exposé of Blondel's interpretation of his sources without attempting a thorough objective criticism of that interpretation. However, there are moments when Blondel seems to accept as objective historical fact his own interpretation of previous philosophers. These moments could lead a hasty reader to the conclusion that Blondel did not realize his objective because he misunderstood Spinoza, or Kant, or Hegel, etc. But these two questions remain independent. Even if we grant that Blondel did not fully understand the historical sources that he used, yet he did nevertheless create a true philosophical work which represents a genuine contribution to the history of thought and an original and profound response to the problems of our times. Further, even these faulty historical judgments can help the judicious reader to a better appreciation of Blondel's genius as an original philosopher; for in many instances where his judgment of past thought could be judged deficient, the understanding he manifests of the resulting difficulty and the means he proposes to overcome it correspond remarkably with the deeper meaning presented in more recent critical appraisals of the philosopher himself whom Blondel criticizes.[1]

A second and final caution to the reader is also in order. As we have noted, the five philosophers dealt with in this study represent, according to Blondel himself, the five major steps in the evolution of that tradition in which he places his *Action*. However, in dealing with the influence of these particular philosophers we have no intention of denying or limiting in any way the influence of other thinkers and other traditions. Before he wrote the final version of *Action*, Blondel had acquired a profound and thorough philosophical culture; he had passed fifteen years almost exclusively in philosophical studies and reading, under the direction of some of the outstanding professors of philosophy of that day. His own notes and publications manifest an interest in and an understanding of nearly every major philosophical current in the Occident.

Consequently for a complete understanding of the historical influences which helped to form Blondel's thought another fundamental question can and should be posed. From precisely what sources did Blondel draw those elements in his thought and method which distinguish him from the specific historical tradition to which he relates himself? In order to answer this question one must study the influence of at least two other currents of thought which had a profound impact on Blondel's thought. The first is Leibnitz, whose theory of the *Vinculum Substantiale* served as the subject of Blondel's latin thesis which, he claimed, contained a "key" to the understanding of *Action*. The second is Maine de Biran, whose writings Blondel studied intensively; and with Maine de Biran the entire influence of specifically French philosophical tradition and thought, passing through Ravaisson, Lachelier, Boutroux and Ollé-Leprune. However, within the limited context of this study we have been obliged to limit the recognition of these influences to some passing references.

One final introductory point, the title of this study speaks of the influence of "German" philosophical sources on the formation of Blondel's method and thought. But the first philosopher whose in-

---

[1] If, for example, Blondel can be said to have exaggerated the dualism of Kant's distinction of pure and practical reason, and not to have taken sufficient account of the *Critique of Judgment*, yet the solution he searched for in *Action* as a means of overcoming that dualism is remarkably close to the solution Eric Weil maintains Kant himself sought in his final Critique. The interpretation that Weil gives of Kant's thought in his recent work *Problèmes Kantiens*, (Paris: Vrin, 1963) bears a remarkable resemblance to Blondel's concept of a philosophy of action.

fluence we deal with is Spinoza who was by no means a German. Despite this fact, we have retained the title because, although Blondel understood Spinoza's *Ethics* as the point of departure of the tradition to which his *Action* belongs, yet every major step in the evolution of that tradition was the work of a German philosopher.

PART ONE

SPINOZAN REALISM AND KANTIAN CRITICISM: THE THESIS AND ANTITHESIS OF BLONDEL'S METHOD

Before composing *Action* Blondel himself defined his project as an attempt to redefine the relation between the rational and the practical orders in such a way as to reconcile and transcend the realist and critical position. In the course of this study it will become evident that Blondel understood Spinoza's *Ethics* as containing the definitive expression in the context of modern thought of the classical realist position, and Kant's *Critique of Practical Reason* as the definitive expression of the criticist position. Blondel saw these two works as constituting, as it were, the thesis and antithesis of a possible philosophical synthesis which had yet to be established.

The first part of our study of the influence of his sources on Blondel's method and thought will be an attempt to establish what Blondel himself understood as the primary positive contribution of Spinoza and Kant to his own philosophy of action, and the limitations of that contribution. In the first introductory chapter we discuss Blondel's method in using his historical sources, the nature of Blondel's contact with German philosophical tradition and, finally, his personal idea of the overall evolution of modern thought leading to his philosophy of action. In chapter two we discuss the influence of Spinoza's thought on Blondel's problem and method. In chapter three, four and five we discuss the three major themes of Kantian influence.

CHAPTER ONE

BLONDEL'S HISTORICAL METHOD

BLONDEL'S USE OF HISTORICAL SOURCES

Blondel did not consider himself the disciple of any given philosopher or any school of philosophers. As we noted, what philosophy as such meant to him was "life itself in so far as that life assumes consciousness and undertakes direction of itself."[1] Thus the only ultimate source from which Blondel drew his philosophy was that vital life-force in so far as it revealed itself to him in his own consciousness.

Further, Blondel himself believed that the method and the doctrinal synthesis which he had achieved in *Action* had an original value. For that reason he feared that if his readers were to associate his doctrine too closely with past philosophical systems, there was a danger that precisely what was original in his contribution to philosophical thought would be lost. He found that fear justified by the attitude of those critics who tried to dismiss his thought by reducing it to being "nothing more than a form of Neo-Kantianism." What Blondel wished to avoid on all accounts was an attitude of "historicism" which would lead to a judgment of the ultimate value of his thought in terms of its conformity with previous philosophical systems. His own consciousness of life was his one ultimate source; his reader's consciousness of life should be the only ultimate norm of judgment concerning the value of his ideas.

In order to deter his readers from this tendency to historical reduction Blondel's first reaction was to deny any direct historical affiliation with the past. For example, when Adolf Lasson, professor at the University of Berlin wrote to Blondel in 1894 calling attention to the remarkable parallel between *Action* and the thought of Fichte and Hegel, Blondel answered:

---

[1] Bernard Aimant (Maurice Blondel), "Une des Sources de la Pensée Moderne: L'Evolution du Spinozisme, "*Annales de Philosophie Chrétienne*, Tome 64 (Juin, 1894), I, 261. A second part of this article was published in the same magazine in July of the same year. All future references will be to "L'Evolution du Spinozisme," I or II.

Wishing to compose a book in which I could freely express my most cherished thoughts, I requested a leave of absence, which I employed in solitude with no other master than that interior master whose voice you know. This is the entire history of *Action*...[1]

It would be a mistake, however, to conclude from this and similar protestations of Blondel himself to the absence of any influence of past philosophical thought on *Action* or the impossibility of tracing these influences. For, as we shall see, Blondel in still another context is quite explicit in acknowledging and identifying the tradition in which *Action* is to be placed. But these protestations should serve as an indication that the manner in which he used his sources was highly independent and free of any major concern for fidelity to objective historical norms.

Blondel was never interested in an accurate reconstitution of an historical system as such. He was inclined to use all previous philosophical doctrines as means by which he could "pull out what was still vital" and "gather up the seeds of his own personal thought". In his own use of sources it is evident that Blondel himself followed the advice which he sent to his friend, Victor Delbos, in 1889:

> I do not consider your subject as properly historical; and you do not treat it as such. At base it represents the most vital and up-to-date part of contemporary preoccupations. I must admit that in my judgment there is no purely historical subject which merits to be the subject of a thesis... One can, indeed, study ancient and forgotten doctrines, but only in order to pull out what is still vital and gather up the seeds of one's personal thought. In dealing with the successive forms of dialectical pantheism you ought, then, to consider these doctrines... in so far as they form the various levels of your own intellectual evolution and the source of your own synthesis.[2]

In his own study, Blondel tells us, he sought "...not a faithful restitution of dead doctrine, but to sense above all the uninterrupted work of life, ...the continuity of the great and main effort which human reason has tried and which it continues to pursue..."[3]

As these texts indicate Blondel understood the creative process of philosophical thinking as necessarily a highly personal process, and he wished to avoid an overconcern with literal historical fidelity as inimical to that process. He was also aware, however, that by con-

---

[1] Blondel, *Lettres Philosophiques* ("Editions Montaigne," Paris: Aubier, 1961), pp. 71-72.
[2] *Ibid.*, p. 16.
[3] *Ibid.*, "L'Evolution du Spinozisme," I, 261.

sciously employing his sources only in so far as they served his personal project, he ran the risk of distorting their meaning in relation to their original context. Hence on frequent occasions when he undertook to criticize an idea which he received from another philosopher, he adds a characteristic reservation as a caution to his reader. For example, in criticizing the shortcomings of various logical systems of the past, he cautions: "I do not wish this introduction to take on a properly historical character. I do not speak of Hegel or of Aristotle... in themselves. Rather I am only trying to render an account from my own actual viewpoint of the manner in which I understand each of these types of logic."[1] On still another occasion Blondel acknowledges that the idea he is criticizing is popularly ascribed to Henri Bergson, but he does not intend to faithfully represent that particular author's doctrine and, therefore, he refrains from attributing to Bergson the idea which he presents.

> In order to put us on guard against certain false interpretations, I have borrowed here some recently coined expressions. But since I have isolated them in order to criticize them as if they formed a total thought in themselves, while without doubt they probably do not serve except to emphasize a single aspect of a much more complex doctrine, I must remark that my concern is not with the intention of their authors, but rather with the tendencies which they could serve to transmit.[2]

For this reason Blondel seldom names the philosopher whose ideas he employs, nor does he normally give any references to their works.

Blondel's attitude towards his philosophical sources is, however, highly complex; and to isolate this one tendency would result in a distorted view of his attitude. For he also had a profound respect for the work of the great philosophers of the past; and he was keenly aware that no genuine progress could be made in philosophy without first penetrating and mastering the accomplishment of past philosophers. Any attempt to advance philosophical thought, Blondel himself maintained, if it is to be meaningful, must satisfy the exigencies which Hegel formulated.

---

[1] *Ibid.*, "Ebauche de Logique Générale," *Revue de Métaphysique et de Morale*, Tome 65, No. 1 (Janvier-Mars, 1960), 10-11.

[2] *Ibid.*, "Le Point de Départ de la Recherche Philosophique," *Annales de Philosophie Chrétienne*, Tome 151 (Janvier, 1906), 353, footnote 1; Tome 152 (Juin, 1906), 243, footnote 1.

Science cannot be judged except according to the very idea on which it is based, and any judgment which one can bring to bear on that idea will not be so much a judgment as a development and progress which becomes one with the object it judges. Thus the last philosophy in time, if it is a true philosophy, is the result of all the earlier ones; nothing is lost; all principles are preserved.[1]

Thus, although Blondel believed that a too great enslavement to literal historical objectivity spelled the end of original creative thought, at the same time he believed that no real advance could be made in philosophical thinking except at the price of a profound positive understanding and appreciation from within of the essential contributions of past philosophers. In his own words "... in order to discuss a great philosophy the most efficacious means is not to react against it from without but by entering fearlessly into it to push its analysis further along than it had gone before."[2] In Blondel's judgment the only use of historical sources which represented a true fidelity to the past was to undertake a personal project which remained faithful to the spirit of the past rather than its letter.

The Nature of Blondel's Contact with German Philosophical Tradition

From what we have already seen of Blondel's method in making use of his sources it is evident a priori that the task of determining the exact nature the influence these sources had will be a difficult one. Some commentators have been inclined to accept Blondel's various protestations of independence as a denial of any major influence of past philosophers on his thought. This is especially true of Kant and Hegel. A detailed discussion of the evidence for Blondel's direct and indirect contacts with the thought of each of the five philosophical sources treated in this study will be reserved until we deal with each of these sources in particular. At this point, however, it will be helpful to undertake a general discussion of Blondel's contact with the German philosophical tradition which he claimed served as the frame of reference of *Action*.

Blondel was a voracious reader of philosophical literature. In fact,

---

[1] *Ibid.*, "L'Evolution du Spinozisme," II, 336. In one of his rare source-references Blondel refers his reader to Vera's French translation of Hegel's *Logic*, Tome I, pp. 173-200.

[2] *Ibid.*, I, 263.

his near blindness in the last period of his life was due to this continual reading day by day. Despite his own protestation to Adolf Lasson that he had "read very little as yet", we have ample evidence of the extensive reading in philosophy which he undertook during the period in which he prepared his thesis. Among the works to be found in Blondel's personal library at Aix, which date from this same period, are nearly all the works of the five philosophers we shall study here which had been translated into French. And there is further evidence that Blondel went out of his way to borrow (probably from Boutroux) and read those translated texts of which he did not possess a personal copy. For example in March 1890 he wrote to his friend Maurice Lena:

> I've brought back a pile of books from Paris, books fit to make your head swim; the *Transcendental Idealism* of Schelling, the theological writings of Boehme, the speculative mysticism of Master Eckhart, etc.; and since it was necessary to return them as quickly as possible I devoured them.[1]

Blondel seems to have limited himself in his direct contact with German philosophy for the most part to translated sources. However, this limitation was a matter of choice rather than necessity. Blondel was capable of reading and understanding German. During the years in which he prepared his thesis he made several trips to Germany primarily in order to consult unpublished manuscripts of Leibnitz' works in the library at Hanover. He also published a review of an untranslated German work in 1897.[2] However, in harmony with his method of using his sources as a stimulant for his own thought, it would seem Blondel preferred to read these authors in his own language. For the same reason his reading was seldom systematic, in the sense that he preferred to read a variety of authors concerning a specific problem, but did not attempt a systematic mastery of the thought and works of any one author as would become a disciple or an historian.

The most important clue to an understanding of the influence of the German philosophers on Blondel's thought is not to be found by answering the question what he had read or not read by this or that author. Rather it lies in the special relationship which bound him to his

---

[1] *Ibid.*, *Lettres Philosophiques*, p. 20. This particular letter will prove important later in this work, because it connects in time the study of Schelling's *Transcendental Idealism* with Blondel's next redaction of his thesis, the manuscript of 1890 entitled "Projet de Thèse." This was the first redaction in which certain key ideas appeared.

[2] Blondel, "Compte Rendu de P. Shanz, Apologie du Christianisme...," *Bulletin Critique de Littérature* (Paris: 1897) Tome 18, 391-396.

professor and director, Emile Boutroux and to his classmate, friend and collaborator: the historian of German philosophical thought, Victor Delbos. As we noted previously, Blondel considered that true fidelity to the past was a question of fidelity to its spirit rather than to its letter. For his understanding of the essential spirit of the great German philosophers he depended more on the living interpretation of these two men than on his own reading:

In the same letter to Adolf Lasson quoted above, Blondel added:

> If the choice of my subject, the nature of my method and the sense itself of my conclusions imposed themselves bit by bit on me without intermediaries nor exterior interventions, yet I owe very much to two masters whom I had at the Ecole Normale, Emile Boutroux and Léon Ollé-Laprune. The second gave me something of the matter, and the first something of the form of my philosophical convictions.[1]

The "matter" which Blondel attributes here to Ollé-Laprune was his apologetic concern to defend the philosophical validity of his religious belief. However, Blondel tended to find Ollé-Laprune's apologetic efforts philosophically wanting. He was much more impressed by the critical and logical rigor of Boutroux. With his friend Delbos he followed Boutroux' courses on Kantian and post-Kantian idealist philosophy in the years 1882-1883, and subsequently, it was Boutroux who directed both their theses.[2] Evidently Boutroux' lectures on idealist thought at that period evoked an enthusiastic response from his students. In the preface of his work, *The Philosophy of Fichte*, Xavier Léon, another of Blondel's friends, describes the profound impression Boutroux' lectures had made.[3] As the correspondence between Blondel and Delbos manifests, Boutroux was also the inspiration behind their effort to achieve a critical understanding of German thought from Kant through to Hegel.

But even more important for Blondel was the relation with his friend and collaborator Victor Delbos. The exchange of ideas and

---

[1] *Ibid., Lettres Philosophiques*, p. 73.

[2] The primary influence of Boutroux on Blondel and Delbos had more to do with his critical lectures on Kantian and post-Kantian German thought rather than his own published works. However Maréchal claimed to find a connection between Boutroux' personal thought and that of Blondel. In a text of 1917 he called attention to the "finalist epistemology of Boutroux as a preparation for the philosophy of action of Blondel." Confer "Un Texte Inédit du P. Maréchal, S.J.: L'Action de Maurice Blondel," présenté et commenté par André Hayen, S.J. *Convivium Estudios Filosoficos*, Num. 4 (Ano II, Fasc. 2, Julio-Diciembre, 1957) pp. 5-41.

[3] Xavier Léon, *La Philosophie de Fichte* (Paris: Félic Alcan, 1902) PP. III-IV. Emile Boutroux himself contributed the preface to this work.

inspiration between these two young men, especially during the period
when both were preparing their doctoral dissertation, was so close
that, to borrow a phrase of Léon Brunschvicg, we could call that relation "a sort of reciprocal causality".[1] The evidence of that "reciprocal
causality" it so be found primarily in Blondel's *Action* and in Delbos'
thesis, *The Moral Problem in the Philosophy of Spinoza and in the History of
Spinozism*, published in the same year and dedicated to the same master,
Léon Ollé-Laprune.[2] The series of letters exchanged between Blondel
and Delbos during the period of over five years preceding the publication of their theses leaves no doubt that there was a constant mutual
influence during the writing of these two works.[3] In April, 1892
Delbos in a letter to Ollé-Laprune indicated to what extent he felt
indebted to Blondel for the help he had contributed in the composition
of his book on Spinoza:

> Despite his fatigue, despite the worry of his thesis, Blondel was most
> willing to read the pages of my work which I sent to him, give me his
> impressions, indicate the passages to be revised and corrected. He will
> not believe to what point his remarks were fruitful to me...; he was
> truly my *conscience*.[4]

---

[1] Léon Brunschvicg, "Sur la Philosophie Religieuse au XVIII Siècle," *Pour un
Cinquantenaire Hommage à Maurice Blondel* ("La Nouvelle Journée, 12" Bloud et Gay,
1945), p. 186. Brunschvicg uses this phrase in reference to the relation of Delbos
and Spinoza but, as the article itself implies, it is applicable in a different and truer
sense to the relation of Delbos and Blondel.

[2] Victor Delbos, *Le Problème Moral dans la Philosophie de Spinoza et dans l'Histoire
du Spinozisme* (Paris: Félix Alcan, 1893).

[3] Among the letters sent by Blondel to Delbos, we call attention to the following
published in *Lettres Philosophiques*: 1, pp. 13-15, no date given; a discussion of
certain ideas contained in the *Mémoire* of Delbos' thesis on Spinoza - 2, pp. 15-19,
the 6th of May, 1889, which contains a discussion of the Hegelian dialectic. 3,
pp. 23-27 the 1st of April, 1892; Blondel's comment on the first chapter of Delbos'
book dealing with the relation of Spinoza to Descartes. 4, pp. 61-64, the 23rd of
September, 1894; the letter concerns the article which Delbos was to publish in
the *Revue Philosophique* of December 1894 on Blondel's *Action*. 5, pp. 64-67, 25th of
September, 1894; on the final chapter of *Action* which Blondel added after the
defence of his thesis because of Delbos' insistence and advice. Unfortunately many
of the letters which Blondel wrote to Delbos without recopying were destroyed
at the time of Delbos' early death in 1916. All of Delbos' correspondence with
Blondel can be found in the Archives of Blondel, 15 rue Roux-Alphéran, at
Aix-en-Provence.

[4] Confer *Lettres Philosophiques*, p. 25, footnote 1. As early as the fifth of September, 1887 Delbos had sent a complete outline of his thesis to Blondel. An indication
of Delbos' primary interests among the many philosophers he treats can be found
in the note he added:

> There are many parts which interest me and others which leave me cold.
> I intend to write at once the chapters on Spinoza and on Schelling; the latter

A few months after the publication of his own thesis Blondel, under the assumed name, Bernard Aimant, published an article in the *Annales de Philosophie Chrétienne* entitled: "One of the Sources of Modern Thought: the Evolution of Spinozism".[1] This article was his review of his friend Delbos' book. Calling attention to this article in 1932, Blondel stated that his purpose in writing it was to link Delbos' critical historical study to his own philosophy of action.

> Two centuries of history were called to witness to establish that the method and the conclusions of the thesis published a few months before on *Action*, far from being an isolated effort against the tides, had been prepared and even demanded by a speculative effort which was thoroughly in accord with the exigencies of reason.[2]

Thus Blondel himself leaves us without doubt as to the most important philosophical tradition in which we must place *Action*. He himself considered his work as the critical continuation in an evolution of moral philosophy which had its beginnings with Spinoza's *Ethics* and continued through the development of thought contained in the works of Kant, Fichte, Schelling and Hegel, as that evolution was exposed and interpreted in Delbos' book on the Spinozan tradition in German philosophical thought. This book in manuscript form was on Blondel's desk during those very months when he was composing *Action* and was the subject of his critical reflection and appraisal. Further it expressed that philosophical tradition which Blondel acknowledged as the frame of reference interior to his *Action*. Consequently we will consider Delbos' book, together with Blondel's article interpreting

---

is one of those who interest me the most. I shall have to consult you on many points...

As we shall note, this preference for Schelling manifests itself both in Delbos' book and in Blondel's concept of the evolution of modern thought. The text of this unpublished letter is to be found at the Blondelian Archives at Aix-en-Provence. By the second of June, 1889, Delbos had forwarded everything to Blondel up to and including the final chapter on Hegel.

[1] Confer page 2, footnote 1, above, Blondel probably used an assumed name because he did not wish his readers to be prejudiced against the objective validity of his appraisal of his friend's work. A further motive probably was connected with his effort in this article, as we shall see, to connect his own idea of a philosophy of action to the historical evolution which Delbos describes.

[2] Blondel, "L'Evolution du Spinozisme et l'Accès qu'elle ouvre à la Transcendence," Anno XI, Fasc. IV (Décembre, 1932) 1-2. Delbos in his turn published the most penetrating review of *Action* in the *Revue Philosophique de la France et de l'Etranger*, Tome 38 (Décembre, 1894) 634-641.

that book, as companion pieces with *Action*, a sort of historical commentary which represents "the various levels of Blondel's own intellectual evolution and the source of his own synthesis."

BLONDEL'S IDEA OF THE "EVOLUTION OF MODERN THOUGHT"

After the publication of *Action* Blondel wrote a series of articles which represent reflections on various aspects of his philosophy of action. Each of these articles confirms anew the importance of the influence of the historical tradition contained in Delbos' book on his own personal thought. The article, "The Idealist Illusion", for example, treats that same evolution of modern thought from an epistemological viewpoint and sees it as leading inevitably to a philosophy of action as the only means of escaping the impasse of "intellectualism."

> The purpose of this study is to show that..., if from the viewpoint of action all the traditional problems seem to be transposed, that change is neither arbitrary nor optional; nor is it to be detached from the evolution of human thought. The philosophy of action is not just another doctrine simply juxtaposed or substituted for the others, but an extension and utilization of philosophical tradition. From the viewpoint of action the oppositions of the majority of previous systems can be reduced to the common note of intellectualism.[1]

Or again the same vision of the evolution of modern thought occurs in Blondel's article on "The Point of Departure of Philosophical Research", on this occasion from the viewpoint of philosophical method.[2]

But the best confirmation of the importance of this historical tradition in the formation of Blondel's thought is to be found in the famous article "Letter on the exigencies of contemporary thought in matters of apologetics and the method of philosophy in the study of the religious problem", which Blondel published in the *Annales de Philosophie Chrétienne* in January and July of 1896.[3] Blondel's major purpose in the

---

[1] Blondel, "L'Illusion Idéaliste," *Les Premiers Ecrits de Maurice Blondel* ("Bibliothèque de Philosophie Contemporaine," Paris: Presses Universitaires de France, 1956), p. 99. This article was republished from the *Revue de Métaphysique et de Morale*, Tome 6 (Novembre, 1898) 727-746.

[2] Confer above page 4, footnote 2, for bibliographical information concerning this article.

[3] Blondel, "Lettre sur les Exigences de la Pensée Contemporaine en matière d'Apologétique et sur la Méthode de la Philosophie dans l'Etude du Problème Religieux," *Les Premiers Ecrits de Maurice Blondel*. This letter appeared originally

Letter of 1896 was to defend the philosophical and rational nature of *Action* against a charge of psychologism. Once again he tries to show that his *Action* formed a part of, and was, as it were, the most recent step in the evolution of thought beginning with the rationalism of the seventeenth century.

The *Letter of 1896*, in contrast to the articles on the evolution of Spinoza's thought published two years previously, deals explicitly with the problem of method in the philosophy of religion. Whereas the previous articles were addressed mainly to the professional philosophers of the Universities, the *Letter of 1896* is directed primarily to Catholic philosophers and theologians. Blondel seeks to convince them that the contemporary trend in philosophical method, rather than being opposed to the establishment of a true philosophy of religion, is perhaps the first philosophical tradition in the history of the West which renders a true Christian philosophy of religion possible. Consequently, Blondel pleads with the Catholic intelligentsia to forsake an attitude of hostility and to enter intrepidly into the movement of contemporary thought.

> There are two ways to take into consideration philosophical ideas either, while remaining apart from the general current of ideas which preoccupy the intellectual world, one excludes radically everything which contradicts the system which one has adopted for reasons which one judges valid by the highest of motives; and the result is to separate oneself from that living thought which alone is fruitful,—or, indeed, in searching to comprehend that process of birth with which humanity is perpetually in labor, one strives to profit from that immense effort to clarify it, to help it succeed,... to refuse to believe easily that there is nothing salutary for us, even in those doctrines which are the most opposite to our own; ... and this is the means of discovering the source of intellectual fruitfulness.[1]

Blondel frankly admits that what he proposed to establish in *Action* was a philosophy in complete accord with the Catholic faith.

> A slow and laborious evolution of thought was necessary in order to disengage the true perspective, to give birth to the only method which permits the erection of an integral philosophy within the context of an integral Christianity ... perhaps it is time now, after so many superficial efforts and overhasty attempts, for the precisely Catholic idea to reveal

---

in the *Annales de Philosophie Chrétienne* in January and July of 1896. It will be referred to from here on as *Lettre (1896)*.

[1] Blondel, *Lettre (1896)*, p. 29.

its efficacy and give rise to a philosophy which will be wholly appropriate to it, but only in so far as that philosophy will be autonomous.[1]

Blondel was convinced that as yet, such a philosophy of religion was inexistent. "As yet there has never existed a Christian philosophy in the strict sense. Those systems which have that name do not deserve it, neither from the viewpoint of philosophy nor that of Christianity. If it is possible to possess a philosophy which fully merits that name, it has yet to be constituted."[2] The Scholastic tradition had achieved a provisional and unstable equilibrium between faith and reason, a subordination of the objects of faith and reason without any intrinsic and dynamic unity. "Thomism appears to many as an exact description but, if I may speak so, as *static*, as a superposition of elements, but without power to provoke from within us a movement which raises us from the one to the other; an inventory, but not a discovery capable of justifying by the dynamism which it engenders the ascending movement of thought."[3] This instability as we shall see later was attributed to the presence of the Aristotelian concept of the divinity of reason in the Thomistic effort at synthesis.[4] It was precisely this idea of the absolute sovereignty of speculative reason, according to Blondel, which served as the middle ground, the meeting place between reason and the objects of faith.[5] But one had no idea as yet to criticize what we could call "the subjective possibility or formal compatibility of these two orders."[6]

---

[1] *Ibid.*, pp. 92-94.

[2] *Ibid.*, p. 64.

[3] *Ibid.*, p. 27. What Blondel criticized in Scholasticism, as he understood it, was not the "theological use of reason": "It is in that sense that one ought to admit that Scholasticism... proposes an objective rationalism in which we have nothing to attack, because it represents the most authentic organization of truths of which the Church is custodian. ... So that after criticizing the pseudo-philosophy of scholasticism, one cannot praise sufficiently its theological rationalism." *Ibid.*, p. 77.

[4] Blondel's understanding of what was meant by Scholastic realism will be discussed later under the title "The Realist Tradition", confer pp. 36-39.

[5] "At the point of departure, that is, for the Scholastics, the natural and supernatural orders were subordinated in an ascending hierarchy. *They were superimposed* as touching each other. There were, so to speak, three areas or stages; below, that where reason was entirely at home, *mundus traditur disputationibus hominum*; above, that where faith alone revealed the mysteries of divine life...; between, a place of meeting or mutual encounter, where reason discovered empirically what faith clarified and confirmed concerning the most important natural truths. And it was here, thanks to that community of known *objects*, that the two movements issuing from mediately different origins flowed together and mixed their streams without confounding them." *Ibid.*, p. 29.

[6] *Ibid.*, pp. 29-30.

The Protestant revolt destroyed that provisional synthesis achieved by the Scholastics. The result was the rise in the seventeenth century of autonomous rational philosophy. Having separated faith from reason, Luther, by a sort of reverse process, freed reason to press its ancient claim to be everything or nothing. This modern rationalism gave the impression at first of returning to the free spirit of Greek thought and to the pagan concept of the divinity of human reason. That appearance, however, was deceptive. What was destroyed in this process was neither the Christian idea nor the philosophical idea; what was destroyed was the middle term which Scholasticism had used to bring them together." ... It was the ancient concept of the divinity of our reason, that realism of thought, ontological and intellectual at the same time, which claimed to dominate and be all, the doctrine of the sufficiency of metaphysics, the belief in the intrinsic consistency of objects apart from mediating action, and such as they are apprehended by the mind; in brief, it was a false philosophy which tried to convince us a priori that the rational order contained eminently all the rest."[1]

Thus the continued presence in philosophical consciousness of the Christian idea made impossible any complacent return to pagan rationalism. Its hidden and, at times, contradictory persuasion forced the new rationalism to widen its horizons far beyond anything conceived by classical thought. At the same time it forced philosophy to undertake a process of self-criticism and development according to its own inner law. "This evolution, which in appearance was spontaneous and continually more autonomous... led philosophy to define its own limits and convert itself in precisely that way which Christianity could have hoped; because in fact, it was the Christian idea which invisibly prepared that evolution."[2] The end result of that slow and laborious evolution was a philosophy which Blondel believed was finally apt to serve as a valid philosophy of religion. Philosophy had achieved a sober and realistic appraisal of both its limits and its competence.

> At present one sees philosophy tend more and more to specify, criticize, and limit itself... It no longer accepts knowledge as the total substitute for effective existence. Thought, even when adequate to reality or identical with being, is not considered sufficient in itself to achieve our fulfillment. ... It understands that even if every speculative system can be made absolute by a progress in speculation, the only doctrine which contains, at its core, a definitive truth is that which does not search for

---

[1] *Ibid.*, pp. 91-92.
[2] *Ibid.*, p. 55.

its own sufficiency in itself. Finally, it realizes that theoretical solutions
cannot be satisfying except in so far as they require something else
which they themselves do not supply, i.e. by manifesting the necessity
and defining the conditions of a life and a thought fully consequent to
their own internal laws.[1]

Consequently philosophy could now serve as a fit instrument for a
philosophy of religion which would not be a substitution of philosophy for religion. It is this task that Blondel set himself in *Action*:
"I have tried to accomplish for the Catholic form of religious thought
what the German philosophers have done long ago and continue to do
for the Protestant form whose philosophy, it is true, was much more
easily derived."[2] But Blondel insists, in his *Letter of 1896 on the Exigencies of Contemporary Thought*, that the most recent stage in the evolution
of modern thought (whose description fits perfectly his own *Action*)
cannot be understood and appreciated unless one is willing to enter
into and follow out that process of evolution: "... without considering
these successive steps, one is incapable of an exact understanding of
the meaning or of the importance of this transformation."[3] In the
brief outline of the steps of that evolution which Blondel gives us in
the *Letter of 1896* we find among others, the same key philosophical
doctrines which appear in Delbos' book on the evolution of Spinozism
and in Blondel's earlier commentary on that book. There are references to Spinoza, Kant, Fichte, Schelling and Hegel.

Blondel insists over and over again in the *Letter of 1896* on the importance of a thorough understanding of this evolution of thought.
One can practically detect frustration on his part especially with those
critics whom he felt misunderstood and misinterpreted his method in
Action, precisely because they condemned out of hand, or were
ignorant of contemporary philosophy.

> Let no one reproach me with having exaggerated the importance of
> these doctrines which have filled the history of ideas since the Renais-
> sance. One cannot exaggerate it. Nor can one hope successfully to ignore
> these doctrines. For we cannot hide the fact that it is precisely these
> ideas which have life and fruitfulness in them. The advantages of this
> philosophical movement... ought to appear as singularly precious to us,
> if it is true that they have succeeded in specifying the science of philoso-
> phy, in maintaining its sovereignty within its domain while maintaining

---

[1] *Ibid.*, p. 59.

[2] Blondel, *Lettres Philosophiques*, p. 34. The excerpt is from a letter to Georges
Perrot, director of the *Ecole Normale*, the 20th of October, 1893.

[3] Blondel, *Lettre (1896)*, p. 60.

its compatibility with theology with which until now it could not collaborate without compromise. They will have even greater value in our eyes if we realize that they are the end result of the hidden virtues and, as it were, of the constraint of the Christian idea.[1]

Following out this admonition of Blondel, what we propose to do is to retrace this process of evolution in contemporary thought as Blondel himself understood it. The majority of the published works on Blondel's *Action* have concentrated almost exclusively on his treatment of the apologetic problem, the question of the compatibility of Blondel's approach to the intellectual justification of belief with Catholic theology. As a result, the philosophical originality of Blondel and his position within the context of major philosophical trends has been relatively overlooked. One can demand as a consequence how Blondel's contribution to the philosophy of religion can be accurately understood without a profound study of that historical background which he himself thought was essential to understand properly what he was trying to do.

By using primarily his own published writings and unedited notes, we wish to establish exactly what he saw as the major contribution of each of the key figures in that evolution, and what he rejected as outmoded, and why; and finally how he tried to assimilate all these various contributions into a new synthesis. By this means we hope to arrive at a clearer understanding of the place of *Action* in the history of philosophy and to disengage more precisely what was original and creative in its philosophical synthesis.[2]

---

[1] *Ibid.*, pp. 68-69.

[2] The unedited works of Blondel, his correspondence, journals, notes for conferences and classes, manuscript copies and earlier redactions of his published works etc., can be found at the *Archives Blondel* in his former home in Aix-en-Provence.

CHAPTER TWO

THE CONTRIBUTION OF SPINOZA'S *ETHICS*
TO THE PHILOSOPHY OF ACTION

The importance of Spinoza's philosophy, the ultimate reason why, for Blondel, it was "a source of modern thought" has a great deal more to do with the problem Spinoza posed and the methodological principle he inaugurated than with the specific content of his doctrine.[1] Blondel maintained that the problem of human destiny which was his point of departure in *Action* was introduced into modern thought by Spinoza. However, his method in dealing with that problem represented an explication of the order of discovery which was presupposed in Spinoza's *Ethics* as well as a reversal of the process of demonstration; with the result that the order of discovery and process of demonstration, while divergent in Spinoza's *Ethics*, are one and the same in his *Action*. Further, what Blondel particularly admired in Spinoza's problematic and claimed to imitate, was his effort to resolve the specific problem of human destiny within the context of a "total philosophy", an effort which in Blondel's judgment opened the way for the constitution of a valid philosophy of religion. How exactly Blondel understood Spinoza's problem and the relation of that problem to total philosophy will be the first object of our research.

The second object has to do with what Blondel understood as Spinoza's "method of immanence". We will deal with the three aspects of that method: immanence of the norm of truth, of value judgment and, finally, of the norm of being or total explanation. In the course

---

[1] Blondel published three articles on Spinoza. His first article is the most important and the primary source for this chapter: "Une des Sources de la Pensée Moderne: l'Evolution du Spinozisme," (Confer above Chapter I, footnote 1). In 1921 Blondel published the second article as a tribute to his friend Victor Delbos; "Un Interprète de Spinoza: Victor Delbos, 1862-1916." *Chronicon Spinozanum*, Tomus Primus (Hague Comitis, 1921), 290-300. This article adds important details concerning Delbos' and Blondel's interpretation of Spinoza's influence in the development of modern philosophy of religion. In 1932 Blondel published a third article which was more or less a synthesis of the previous two articles: "L'Evolution du Spinozisme et l'accès qu'elle ouvre à la Transcendance," *L'Archivo di Filosofia*, XI (Décembre, 1932), Fasc. IV, 3-12.

Blondel also lists a bibliography of the most important works concerning Spinoza published in France between the years 1888 and 1894 on page 260 of his first article, "L'Evolution du Spinozisme."

of this study parallels will be indicated between certain aspects of Spinoza's and Blondel's thought, for example, between Spinoza's distinction between *natura naturans* and *natura naturata* and Blondel's distinction between will-willing (volonté voulante) and will-willed (volonté voulue). Obviously, Spinoza's distinction has to do with a structure within the absolute, *Deus seu Natura*, whereas Blondel's distinction is expressly anthropological. However, a complete discussion of the relation of these ideas and justification of their affiliation must await the presentation of Blondel's idea of the evolution and transformation of Spinoza's thought within the idealist school and, especially, in Schelling's final philosophy.

Finally, we will present Blondel's criticism of Spinoza's thought, especially as concerns his treatment of the problem of becoming, and Blondel's idea of the "realist illusion" which he believed was at the root of Spinoza's problem.

SPINOZA'S PROBLEM

"The *primum movens* of Spinoza's investigation," Blondel writes, "was the intention of resolving the problem of human happiness, and to resolve that problem solely by means of human reason."[1] Spinoza was "the first philosopher in modern times to pose in its radical form that principle: that the mind can find in itself alone and by itself alone all truth necessary for life."[2]

Spinoza's major work, *Ethics*, has all the appearances of being a book of metaphysics, beginning, as it does, with a tract *De Deo* and proceeding by a deductive process modeled on geometric principles (ordine geometrico demonstrata) to its conclusions. But it was not without reason, Blondel maintains, that he entitled this work *Ethics*. The title points out very well his dominant interest. "An infinity of things," he writes, "result necessarily from the divine essence and continue infinitely to modify themselves." But he proposes to explain "only those things which can lead us by the hand to the knowledge of the human mind and its supreme happiness."[3] Again he writes, "I wish to direct

---

[1] Blondel, "L'Evolution du Spinozisme," I, 263-264.

[2] *Ibid.*, I, 262.

[3] Spinoza, *Ethica*, Part II, Praefatio: Transeo jam ad ea explicanda, quae ex Deo, ... necessario debuerunt sequi. Non quidem omnia; infinita enim infinitis modis ex ipsa debere sequi demonstravimus: sed ea solummodo, quae nos ad Mentis humanae, ejusque summae beatitudinis cognitionem, quasi manu, ducere possunt. *Spinoza Opera*, Carl Gebhardt ed. (Heidelberg: Carl Winters) Tome II, p. 84.

all sciences in one direction or to one end, namely, to attain the greatest possible human perfection and thus everything in the sciences which does not promote this endeavor must be rejected as useless; that is, in a word, all our endeavors and thoughts must be directed to this end."[1]

The opening line of *Action* establishes the similarity between Blondel's problematic and that of Spinoza's *Ethics*: "Yes or no, does human life have a sense and does man have a destiny?"[2] The problem which serves as the inspiration of both works is fundamentally the same; it is "the problem of human destiny and eternal life." Blondel was quite consciously accepting the problematic of Spinoza; what he was proposing in the opening line of *Action* was a moral philosophy, an ethics, in the tradition of Spinoza's *Ethics*, which has as its purpose "to unify all the sciences to one unique end and purpose, in order that one can arrive at the perfection of man."

For Blondel, an ethics is above all a "science of practice" (Une Science de la Pratique), a science of action. Granted the dominant ethical preoccupation of Spinoza, it would seem to follow that his *Ethics* should also take the form of a science of action, a problem of moral progress, a study of being in the process of becoming. In fact the very manner in which Spinoza formulates his problem seems to emphasize its dynamic aspect: "All our endeavors and thought must be directed to this end." Yet to all appearances Spinoza's *Ethics* begins with a speculative metaphysical doctrine which by definition rules out all becoming. Substance or Infinite Object, which embraces all thought and all reality, because it is necessarily one and total, is posed as an indisputable affirmation at the very outset.[3] After this affirmation the ethical problem becomes a matter of integrating all the apparent negations which would seem to divide in some way this necessary and absolute unity. There is question of eliminating all the "illusions" by which we persuade ourselves that we are existing things capable of free action, and that our existence has a substantial reality apart from this infinite totality.[4] We are faced with the paradox that, after having posed a problem of becoming, Spinoza begins his philosophy by affirming a necessarily static universe and thus a priori eliminating his

---

[1] Spinoza *Tractatus de Intellectus Emendatione*, *loc. cit.*, p. 9.

[2] Blondel, *L'Action*, Introduction, p. 1.

[3] Spinoza, *Ethica*, Part I, De Deo; Propositio XIV: Praeter Deum nulla dari neque concipi potest substantia. *loc. cit.*, p. 156. Also confer Corallarium I.

[4] Blondel, "L'Evolution du Spinozisme," I. 265. Also confer Spinoza, *op. cit.* Part IV, De Servitute Humana, Praefatio, pp. 205-209.

problem as an illusion. By what process did Spinoza arrive at this seemingly contradictory point of departure?

In calling attention to this discrepancy between problem and method Blondel remarks that very frequently the method of exposition and demonstration of a constituted system does not always retain the trace of its method of discovery. "Particularly in this case, if from the beginning the doctrine follows a deductive and synthetic development in the manner of a geometric morality, yet it does not presuppose any the less for all that a previous work of regressive analysis."[1] This remark of Blondel is very significant and can be of considerable help to understand how he conceived the similarity and diversity of his *Action* with Spinoza's *Ethics*. In the final chapter of *Action*, entitled "The Connection of Knowledge and Action in Being" (Le Lien de la Connaissance et de l'Action dans l'Etre) we find the following passage: "Thus up to this point what, by means of a regressive analysis has appeared as a series of necessary conditions and successive means required in order to constitute action step by step, from this point on, by means of a *synthetic* view, will be revealed as a system of real truths and beings simultaneously coordinated."[2] How did Blondel understand the relation between that implicit regressive analysis which he claimed was the real method of discovery in Spinoza's *Ethics* and his own explicit regressive analysis? It would seem, at a first reading, that when Blondel says in the last chapter of *Action* that he would now pass from a "regressive analysis" to a "synthetic view" one could conclude that the entire development of *Action* up to the last chapter was an explicit development of that which was implicit in Spinoza's *Ethics*. According to this interpretation Blondel would have merely tried to explicitate Spinoza's method of discovery. Thus the entire development of *Action* could, so to speak, be inserted into Spinoza's *Ethics* between the opening title, *Ethics*, and the heading of part one, *De Deo*, as an introduction to that properly metaphysical tract which would, in turn, correspond in its objective and structure to the final synthetic chapter of *Action*.

Such a literal interpretation, however, would be certainly misleading. As Blondel will remark later in his article on Spinoza, the most damaging limitation of Spinoza's method was precisely to propose "to resolve the problem of human happiness exclusively by means of human reason." In contrast, Blondel understood the dialectic of his

---

[1] Blondel, *op. cit.* I, 263.
[2] Blondel, *L'Action*, p. 245. Italics added.

final chapter as passing beyond the range of pure reason whether it be analytical or synthetic into a "dialectic of knowledge and action in being."

To establish the true relation it is necessary to consider the two levels of meaning which Blondel sees in the word reason.

> The term reason has evolved in two different directions, which has resulted in not only differentiating but in actually opposing the meanings which it conveys in philosophical terminology with the resulting confusions against which we must be on our guard. Reason, depending on whether one envisages primarily the analytic character of its operations, or the clear evidence of its assertions, refers in the first case to the essentially discursive faculty which, by its capacity to organize expressions or proofs, establishes their demonstration. In the second case, it refers to the faculty by means of which we affirm the absolute; we know and, so to speak, capture being as it is; we furnish the principles and reach those truths necessary and sufficient for both thought and life. According to the first sense reason is simply an instrument which serves, aids, or mimics the work of a higher faculty of intuition. According to the second sense, reason assumes the primary role; it pretends more or less deliberately to attribute a realistic value to the discursive effort of the spirit and to reconstitute the real by means of the artificial fragments of the analysis.[1]

From this distinction it is clear that when Blondel refers to the method of reflexive analysis which he employed in *Action*, he is referring to reasoning in the first meaning. Parting from an initial datum analytical reflection attempts to establish step by step "the series of necessary conditions and successive means" required in order to constitute the datum. We have here, as we shall see, something similar to Kant's transcendental method adapted to an analysis of human action. Blondel calls the entire reasoning process or reflexive analysis which occupies all but the last chapter of his book "the phenomenon of Action" (Le Phénomène de l'Action).[2] What he intends to convey by this appellation is, in fact, that he does not consider the reasoning employed in his reflexive analysis as capable of "affirming the absolute or knowing and capturing being as it is." The phenomenology of Blondel consists, rather, of putting aside provisionally the ontological problem and of refusing at each step of the dialectic to pronounce concerning the absolute reality of the order of things. He is content to determine the development of inter-locked relations in human con-

---

[1] Blondel, "Reason," *Vocabulaire Technique et Critique de la Philosophie*, ed. André Lalande, II (1926) 669-670; II (1947) 858-859.

[2] Blondel, *L'Action*, p. 43.

sciousness under the influence of practical necessity. "Even when it became necessary to introduce the idea of God ... there was no question of concluding to the existence of God; there was only question of ascertaining that the necessary concept of a real God led in turn to the necessity of the supreme alternative."[1] Thus Blondel affirms that the entire rational process of the reflexive analysis in *Action* remained in the phenomenal order. Consequently the rational necessity which compels us to introduce an idea into that process in no way justifies a metaphysical affirmation of the being to which the idea corresponds. The famous axiom of Spinoza: "the order and connection of ideas is identical to the order and connection of things" is thereby implicitly rejected.[2] It is probably this axiom, and the ontological pretensions of human reason which it contains, to which Blondel refers when he speaks of a second meaning of reason as the faculty which "pretends more or less deliberately to attribute a realistic value to the discursive effort of the mind." In his critique of Spinoza's doctrine this is exactly the charge Blondel makes against him.

> But who does not remark that that conception of truth, wherein the necessary and methodological connection between facts is constitutive of their contingent reality, is applicable to phenomena and to their determined scientific laws? It is only concerning the phenomena and scientific laws that it is true to say that being and knowing coincide: the a posteriori data are thus penetrated and, so to speak, reconstructed by the initiative of reason which renders them intelligible.[3]

We can conclude then that Blondel understood Spinoza's *Ethics* to be, in reality, a study of phenomenon which mistook itself for a metaphysics. But Spinoza's phenomenal moral investigation differs from *Action* because it reverses the order of procedure. Blondel begins with a methodological doubt: ... "that indirect route which alone is scientific, because, beginning with doubt, it eliminates scientifically all chance of error and every cause of illusion."[4] He ends with the affirmation of the necessary idea of God. In other words, he employs a reflexive analysis in which the order of discovery and the process of demonstration are one. On the contrary, Spinoza begins where Blondel ended, with the affirmation of the necessary idea of God, and proceeds by a synthetic deductive process under what Blondel believed was the

---

[1] *Ibid.*, p. 426.
[2] Spinoza, *Ethica*, Part II, Propositio VII: *loc. cit.*, p. 89.
[3] Blondel, "L'Evolution du Spinozisme," II, 332.
[4] Blondel, *L'Action*, Introduction, p. XVIII.

false illusion that the order and connection of ideas is identical to the order and connection of things. When he arrives at the end of his phenomenal dialectic of action, in the chapter entitled "The Uniquely Necessary" (L'Unique Nécessaire) Blondel makes this comment on Spinoza's initial ontological proof for the existence of God: "In order to find Him we must not begin from Him, where we are not; we must begin with ourselves, where He is."[1]

TOTAL PHILOSOPHY

We have seen that Blondel accepted the problem posed in Spinoza's *Ethics* as his own, while rejecting its ontological and geometric pretensions. There is another aspect of Spinoza's approach to philosophy, closely associated with his problem, which Blondel admired and imitated; it was the former's effort to create a "total philosophy". In an address to a Spinozan Congress at The Hague in 1921, in a memorial to his friend Delbos, Blondel underlined this contribution of Spinoza to modern thought:

> By his manner of posing his problem Spinoza was, perhaps, the first modern to embrace the domain of total philosophy by including not only the problem of science and the organisation of the present life, but also the question of destiny and of eternal life understood in the full and precise sense of Christian tradition. By this method, Spinoza, thrusting to the end and to the heights of reason, introduced into the competence of philosophical investigation those ideas which, although they have had a specific and positive religious character historically and theologically, have no less a rational aspect, a reality which is immanent in man. Thanks to the new elements of the controversy which he had thus introduced, Spinoza is and rests one of the principal sources of modern thought.[2]

Blondel, in the same address, attributes this insight into the significance of Spinoza's contribution to his friend Delbos. In his book, *The Moral Problem in the Philosophy of Spinoza*, Delbos inquires into the influence of Descartes on Spinoza. He advances the theory of Lucas that Spinoza's principle of immanence was based on the maxim of Descartes that "one should never accept anything as true except for good and solid reasons." But Spinoza's originality lay in the use he made of that maxim. "Without doubt this maxim, in so far as it gave Spinoza's tendencies a precise formulation, gave them in addition a

---

[1] *Ibid.*, p. 344.
[2] Blondel, "Un Interprète de Spinoza: Victor Delbos, 1862-1916," p. 299.

new force. But the moral problem, whose solution would be determined by this principle was precisely one of those problems which Cartesian philosophy had neglected or, even, in the end eliminated."[1]

In Delbos' opinion, it was primarily this opening of the moral problem as such to rational investigation which separates Spinoza from the Cartesian tradition.

> ... It was the truths of faith which guaranteed his provisional morality in Descartes' eyes. But, more important still, it was the truths of faith which dispensed him from the need of making a rational examinaton of the moral problem. A sincere believer, he found in the teachings of religion sufficient guides for the conduct of life. ... Moral truths, inseparable from religious truths, are derived exclusively from the resources of the will (Rules for the Direction of the Mind, Rule III), and it is religious belief which provides them with their certainty and protects them against any critical attack, even against the curiosity of the understanding.[2]

Such a position was, in fact, impossible for Spinoza. The historical circumstances of his life, his expulsion from the synagogue, for example, in conjunction with his own consequent rejection of established religion, made it impossible for him to share Descartes' belief in and dependence on revealed truth in the area of morality. Rather, he was obliged to seek a rational reconstruction of morality.

Blondel, after having read Delbos' portrayal of the relation between Descartes' philosophy and that of Spinoza in the manuscript copy of his book, wrote to his friend congratulating him especially for this portrayal.[3] On several occasions in his subsequent writings Blondel returns to the problem of Descartes' "relative agnosticism". Blondel held that the central thesis of Descartes is that all necessary and eternal truths depend on a free voluntary act of God.[4] Because the free will-act

---

[1] Delbos, *Le Problème Moral dans la Philosophie de Spinoza*, p. 4.

[2] *Ibid.*, p. 7.

[3] In a letter dated the first of April 1892, Blondel wrote to Delbos, "... the relations between Descartes and Spinoza are superbly delimitated..." *Lettres Philosophiques*, pp. 23-24.

[4] Blondel, "Le Christianisme de Descartes," *Revue de Métaphysique et de Morale*, No. 4 (Juillet, 1896) 6-9, (tiré à part). This article is the principle one of three which Blondel published on Descartes. It was an effort to explain the nature and origin of Descartes' concept of a "separated philosophy." In 1916, Blondel published a comparative study of Descartes' separated philosophy with the effort to integrate philosophy and religion undertaken by Malebranche: "L'Anti-Cartésianisme de Malebranche," *Revue de Métaphysique et de Morale*, Tome XXIII (Janvier, 1916), I-26. (tiré à part). In 1937, Blondel published a third article concerning the paradoxical use that Descartes made of his ontological proof for God's existence, namely, to guarantee the certitude of positive scientific truth while

of God is at least logically prior to His intellect, any logical continuity
or any purely intellectual necessity is excluded from His nature. Consequently any operation of God, either natural or supernatural, is an
expression of the "creative originality of his omnipotence" or the
"paradoxical marvel" of His love and grace. These operations can
never be reduced to any intellectual process. The consequence of this
thesis was to eliminate from the competence of our thought anything
which had to do with the infinite or the eternal, and reserve these
themes to God alone. Such things become accessible to us only by
means of revelation and, when revealed, are exclusively objects for
the human will.¹

However, what Descartes truly sought, Blondel maintains, was not
this negative restriction on reason; rather, it was to leave all the rest,
all human science, exclusively within the domain of positive knowledge. It is true that Descartes' ontological proof for the existence of
God in his *Meditations* is the "keystone" of his philosophy. But, in
contrast to Spinoza, this proof is not introduced to help solve the
problem of human destiny. On the contrary, it is introduced to avoid
any need to deal with that problem. This proof is undertaken only
to guarantee the certainty by which mathematical ideas can be applied
to the conquest of physical reality.²

> The profound flaw in his (Descartes) christianity was to put to one side
> the absolute mystery which the will alone could attain by means of
> grace, and to the other the absolute clarity of thought which is totally
> sovereign in its domain. The result was to suppress all rational prepara-
> tion for the faith, to establish a basic heterogeneity between divine
> reason and human reason, between our reason and our will.³

---

freeing philosophy from any further need to deal with moral or religious problems,
"La Clef de Voûte du Système Cartésien," *Revista di Filosofia Neoscholastica*,
Supplemento, Vol. XXIX (Luglio, 1937), 69-77.

¹ Blondel, "L'Anti-Cartésianisme de Malebranche," p. 8.

² "Historically, it was the purpose of rendering legitimate the application of
mathematics to physics ... which led Descartes to interrupt his mathematical
studies and to fit into his intellectual life a properly metaphysical period, that of
the nine months during which he wrote the *Meditations*. ... These metaphysical
truths were such in his eyes, that he believed that he had established and confirmed
them in such a way that no one need return to them again. Man had nothing more
to do except develop the infinite chain of pragmatic truths." "La Clef de Voûte
du Système Cartésien," p. 75.

³ Blondel, "Le Christianisme de Descartes," p. 16. In another context, Blondel
gives a different and more positive interpretation of Descartes' motivation for this
separation of faith and science. In a letter to J. Wehrlé, 12 July 1904, he has this
to say of Descartes: "Descartes had a strong intuition that Christianity is bound

Blondel has, obviously, many reservations concerning the exclusive speculative effort to resolve the problem of human destiny, "... that knowledge, even supposing it to be the most adequate possible could supply for faith and practice." Nonetheless he leaves no doubt that philosophically he prefers the intellectual audacity of Spinoza to the weak fideism and relative agnosticism of Descartes. He is in accord with Delbos in attributing three principal positive results to Spinoza's effort at synthesis. First, by the very manner in which he understood human beatitude, Spinoza introduced into philosophy "... the idea which corresponds to what religious consciousness calls salvation. The destiny of man appears as an alternative between eternal life and death."[1] Further, his philosophical doctrine "... overturned the external and conventional order of relations by which, until then, philosophy and religion had been brought together, in order to establish a philosophy which was religiously inspired, not by accident, but by nature; without, however, being so by prejudice."[2] Finally, Spinoza had a lively sentiment of the necessity of divine aid and support, of a divine *concursus*. This sentiment is expressed in Spinoza's teaching that "the intellectual love of God, the act by which reason brings our being back to its source, is impossible without the cooperation of that source itself."[3] Because of these results Blondel is in full accord with Delbos in attributing to Spinoza the primary effort to establish a philosophy of religion in modern times. "The Spinozan doctrine is certainly the

---

to a philosophy of will and of love and that, in effect, the divine will realizes those things which the understanding cannot conceive," (*Lettres Philosophiques*, p. 237.) Still later, Blondel seems to have reconsidered his earlier judgment on Descartes volontarism and somewhat revised that judgment:

"One is wrong when one attributes to him (Descartes) the concept of an arbitrary will either in us or in God. As concerns ourselves, he forcibly affirmed that perfect liberty cannot be separated from certain knowledge, without which choice would be more revelatory of imperfection than power. As concerns God, he did not admit any priority between intellect and will. And if he did insist on the absolute sovereignty of God, it was in order to react against a residue of classical thought which seemed to subject God to his own nature as a condition which would enslave him once again to Styx and to the Destinies; and also his purpose was to render fully evident the entire gratuity of creation and the whole created order." "La Clef de Voûte du Système Cartésien," p. 72.

[1] Blondel, "Un Interprète de Spinoza: Victor Delbos, 1862-1916," p. 294.
[2] *Ibid.*, p. 294. This citation of Delbos is quoted from the preface he wrote to the book, *Le Problème Relifieux dans la Philosophie de l'Action*, by Thomas Cramer (Paris: Alcan, 1912), p. XIII.
[3] Blondel, "Un Interprète de Spinoza: Victor Delbos, 1862-1916," p. 294.

most powerful effort which has been undertaken until recently to
establish an accord between certain theological ideas and the tendencies of modern thought."[1]

SPINOZA'S METHOD OF IMMANENCE

Apart from the problem which Spinoza posed, it was his "principle
of immanence" which caused Blondel to link his *Action* to Spinoza's
Ethics. Normally one presumes that the method of immanence had
Kantian criticism as its primary source. But Blondel is quite explicit
in ascribing the principal source of his own method to Spinoza.

> In the formation of that method which is called "immanent criticism"
> ... the part which Spinoza played is far more considerable than that of
> Kantianism itself. Without doubt, Kant contributed to dispossessing
> reason of the pretention to impose an absolute rule, a judgment based
> on being, on the objects of knowledge. But it is scarcely in this nega-
> tive restriction that the essence of immanent criticism consists.[2]

Exactly what is the "essence" of the immanent criticism whose formation Blondel attributes to Spinoza? We can distinguish three main
elements in Spinoza's concept of a method of immanence, the immanence of a norm of truth, the immanence of a norm of value, and,
most important for Blondel, immanence as a norm of being or "total
explanation".

THE IMMANENT NORM OF TRUTH

We have already seen the influence that Descartes' doctrine of clear
and distinct ideas had on Spinoza's concept of the norm of truth. Like
Descartes, Spinoza understood the relation between the understanding
and its object according to the geometric model of the relation which
unites the consequence to its principle. Now it is the peculiar property
of this mathematical type of relation that it is entirely immanent to the
mind. The principle, for example, the idea of a triangle, is a construction of the mind and, as such, is necessarily perfectly clear and distinct
to the mind constructing it. So too, any conclusion drawn from such a
mathematical construction also remains totally immanent to the constructed principle. As Blondel notes, "... the law of human intelligence
is to propose always a term exterior to itself and to be directed to an

---

[1] *Ibid.*
[2] Blondel, "L'Evolution du Spinozisme," II, 332.

end; but Spinoza considered intelligibility primarily under the form of an internal relation and of a geometric synthesis which is exclusive of all finality."[1] Because he had thus reduced all philosophical truth to a mathematical model, Spinoza was able to eliminate the classical finalist concept of truth as a conformity of the mind to its object. For Spinoza:

> ... the truth of a true idea is not an extrinsic and accidental quality, but interior to the true itself; it is an inherent and constitutive property. Just as the deductive constructions of mathematics, although they are formed by a progressive synthesis, are entirely immanent to their premises, so the truth is constituted by the reflection of idea on idea. The unique norm of truth is, then, the truth itself; and the method, far from being an exterior instrument, is nothing other than the act of understanding itself.[2]

It is interesting to note how this elimination of finality from the norm of truth will serve Spinoza's pantheistic purposes. According to his mathematical principle all truth is immanent to the mind. Further, "nothing can be conceived or exist apart from the divine substance."[3] Consequently the mind is also immanent in the divine substance. Finally, since divine causality is necessarily immanent and not transient, it will follow that "the order and connection of ideas is identical to the order and connection of things." The immanent process by which the human mind derives true propositions from a clear and distinct first principle is transformed into the very process by which the divine being acts. Truth for us becomes truth in itself, and the mind's identity with itself in true knowledge becomes the identity of the infinite substance with its own being. What would appear at first glance as an imprisonment of the mind within itself becomes an identification of our thought with divine life.

NORM OF VALUE JUDGMENT

If the use of the principle of immanence as an epistemological norm is not original in Spinoza's thought but derived from Descartes, yet as Delbos noted "the moral problem whose solution would be determined by this principle was precisely one of those problems which Cartesian philosophy had neglected, or even, in the end, eliminated." Descartes' ethical norm, Blondel held, was purely extrinsic, a question of blind

---

[1] *Ibid.*, I. 268,
[2] *Ibid.*, II, 331.
[3] Spinoza, *Ethica*, Part I, Propositio XIV, p. 56.

assent of the will to an ultimately unintelligible divine caprice. The originality of Spinoza was his effort to construct an ethics based on an immanent principle. He proposed "... to resolve the problem of human beatitude and to resolve that problem by the sole resources of thought."[1] Consequently he was obliged to transform the principle of immanence from an epistemological norm into an ethical norm, a norm of value. Because of the pantheistic premise of Spinoza's system, such a transformation, Blondel argues, became simply a question of affirming the identity of the two norms. If the method whereby the mind proceeds from a principle to a conclusion is identical with the immanent causality of the divine substance, then truth is being, *bonum et verum convertuntur*, and the same norm which permits the judgment, this is true; also justifies the judgment, this is good. The moral process, in imitation of the pure identity of the divine substance, becomes a searching of identity of the mind with itself.

We shall consider later to what extent Blondel accepted Spinoza's concept of immanence. Suffice it here to note that nothing could be more radically opposed to Blondel's doctrine on the relation of truth and being than this total identity which Spinoza affirms. For Blondel, the necessary knowledge of the truth is only a means either of acquiring or of losing possession of reality.[2] But it is important here to remark how this immanent ethical norm is applied concretely by Spinoza to judge the value of human emotion and conduct.

In the Introduction to Part III of his *Ethics*, Spinoza remarks that traditionally those who have written on the emotions and human conduct have considered man as "a kingdom within a kingdom". Spinoza, however, intends to treat man as a part of nature, and "to regard human actions and desires exactly as if it were dealing with lines, planes and bodies."[3] The full meaning of this statement becomes clear when we recall that for Spinoza nature is identical with God, *Deus seu Natura*.[4] The basic dynamic factor by which Nature (or God) manifests itself in every individual being is what Spinoza calls endeavor, *conatus*, the tendency to persist in its own being. "The endeavor wherewith a thing endeavors to persist in its being is nothing else than the actual essence of the thing."[5] This tendency, or essence, when it is referred

---

[1] Blondel, *op. cit.*, I, 264.
[2] Blondel, *L'Action*, p. 406.
[3] Spinoza, *Ethica*, Part III, Praefatio, p. 137.
[4] *Ibid.*, Part IV, Praefatio, p. 206.
[5] *Ibid.*, Part III, Propositio VII; Conatus, quo unaquaeque res in suo esse perseverare conatur, nihil est praeter ipsius rei actualem essentiam. p. 146.

to the mind is called will (voluntas). Since man has consciousness of this tendency, the conscious tendency is called desire (cupiditas).

Although we are dealing here with a metaphysical structure in man, Spinoza holds that the basic tendency to self-preservation and self-perfection, which "is nothing else than the actual essence of that thing", is reflected in consciousness as desire. He also maintains that there is a reflection in consciousness of a transition to a state of greater or lesser perfection which he calls respectively pleasure (laetitia) and pain (tristitia). The immanent norm by which man can formulate value judgments follows from these definitions: "The knowledge of good and evil is nothing other than the affection of pleasure and pain in so far as we have consciousness of it."[1] In the dynamic order this tendency to greater or lesser perfection becomes "that which increases or diminishes, helps or reduces our power to act."[2] Spinoza argues that the mind is fully active and, consequently, most perfect only in so far as it knows.[3] But the supreme object which the mind can know is God. Thus it follows that the supreme virtue of the mind is to have a clear and certain knowledge of God. "The supreme good of the mind is the knowledge of God and the supreme virtue of the mind is to know God."[4]

There is a striking similarity here with Blondel's quotation from Saint John of the Cross: "The action which encloses and perfects all the others is to think truly of God".[5] But to avoid confusion of meaning we must keep in mind the distinction Blondel makes between thought as act or commitment, and thought as a matter of content, of clear and distinct concepts, of which Blondel says "it is only a means either of acquiring or of losing possession of reality". Whereas Spinoza tends to dissolve all finite reality into the concept of infinite object, Blondel seeks the concretization of all thought into the affirmation of act.

But apart from this all-important difference in their conception of the function of thought, Blondel himself sees a parallel between

---

[1] *Ibid.*, Part IV, Propositio VIII; Cognitio boni, et mali nihil aliud est, quam Laetitiae, vel Tristiae affectus, quatenus enim sumus conscii. p. 215.

[2] *Ibid.*, Part IV, Propositio VIII, Demonstratio: Id bonum aut malum vocamus ... quod nostram agendi potentiam auget, vel minuit, juvat vel coercet. p. 215.

[3] *Ibid.*, Part iv, Propositio XXVIII, Demonstratio: Est igitur mentis absoluta virtus intelligere, p. 228.

[4] *Ibid.*, Part IV, Propositio XXVIII: Summum mentis bonum est Dei cognitio, et summae mentis virtus Deum cognoscere, p. 228.

[5] Blondel, "Action," *Vocabulaire Technique et Critique de la Philosophie*, André Lalande ed., I (1926) 17; I (1947) 21.

Spinoza's immanent ethical norm and the norm he applied in *Action*. In the criticism of Spinoza's morality, which Delbos inaugurates in the final chapter of his book, we find that this idea of Spinoza has already undergone a first transformation which helps indicate the connection it has with the ethical or value norm in *Action*. For example, the "tendency to persist in being" becomes the "radical will to be" which is immanent in every action but never absorbed totally by any given action. "Behind the motives of our consciousness which seem to be the most adequate to explain our actions, there is always a force which flows over, which, although immanent to every one of them, is never exhausted by any one of them. That force is the radical will to be, or, as Spinoza says, the tendency to preserve our being."[1] This will is described by Delbos as an antecedent will which must be developed by all our consequent partial acts of will. He maintains that there is an entire original development of the will implicit in this position which Spinoza tends to ignore:

> It is already a fact of primary importance that the will-which-wills cannot remain one, because it must be at the same time the will-which-wills (volonté qui veut) and the will-willed (volonté voulue). But the will-willed does not derive directly from the will-which-wills; for in the will-which-wills there is a potential infinite which cannot be contented with anything finite.[2]

In these two lines Delbos gives us a brief summary of one of the central ideas of *Action*, the metaphysical composition of will, which is, as we shall see, the source of Blondel's dialectical dynamism. Without doubt we have to do here with the reciprocal relation between Blondel, the philosopher, and Delbos, his historian. What is significant is the parallel of this couplet, will-willing and will-willed, to Spinoza's distinction between *natura naturans and natura naturata*.[3] On one occasion Spinoza himself applies this distinction to the intellect and the will: "The intellect in act ... as also the will ... must be referred to *natura naturata* and not to the *naturans*."[4] Thus according to Spinoza

---

[1] Delbos, *Le Problème Moral dans la Philosophie de Spinoza*, p. 533.

[2] *Ibid.*, p. 549.

[3] Spinoza, *Ethica*, Part I, Propositio XXIX, Scholion: Per naturam naturantem nobis intelligendum est id, quod in se est, et per se concipitur, sive talia substantia attributa, quod aeternam et infinitam essentiam exprimunt; hoc est Deus, quatenus, ut causa libera, consideratur. Per naturatem autem intelligo id omne, quod ex necessitate Dei naturae, sive uniuscujusque Dei attributorum sequitur; hoc est omnes Dei attributorum modos, quatenus considerantur, ut res quae in Deo sunt, et quae sine Deo nec esse, nec concipi possunt. p. 71.

[4] *Ibid.*, Part I, Propositio XXXI: Intellectus actu, sive in finitis sit sive infinitis,

himself will as action must be referred to *natura naturata* and, therefore, can be called will-willed (volonté voulue). Whereas will as "the essence of the divine attribute of mind" should be called will-willing (volonté voulante). Thus the activity of the mind in so far as that activity is immanent in Nature or God must, within Spinoza's system, be logically distinguished into the same double will or, rather, metaphysical structure of will which, as we shall see, Schelling would later employ in his final philosophy.[1]

There is also a parallel in the use made of this distinction in Blondel's argument for freedom. According to Spinoza the *natura naturans* is identified with God "in so far as He is regarded as free cause"; whereas *natura naturata* is said to be "that which follows by necessity from the nature of God." Delbos, in the same passage mentioned above, argues from the infinite potential of the will-willing to the existence of freedom in human action. Blondel employs an analogous argument to establish human freedom.

> ... In order to act it is necessary to participate in an infinite power; in order to have consciousness of acting, it is necessary that one have the idea of that infinite power. Now it is in the rational act that there is a synthesis of the power and the idea of the infinite; and this synthesis is what one calls liberty.[2]

Yet, even while indicating these parallels between Blondel's doctrine and that of Spinoza, we must continually keep in mind the basic, all-important difference: Spinoza's pantheistic postulate which permitted him, in Blondel's judgment, to identify the human mind and will with the divine. Spinoza's norm of value judgment is a reflection in consciousness of a transition to a greater or lesser state of perfection; that is, to the identity of *natura naturans* and *natura naturata*, to the

---

ut et voluntas ... ad naturam naturatam, non vero ad naturantem referri debent, p. 71.

[1] Spinoza defined endeavor (conatus) as "nothing else than the actual essence of that thing," and this essence, when it refers to mind is called the will (voluntas). As we shall see later, Blondel was aware of the influence Spinoza's concept of a double nature had on the transcendental idealists and the transformation of it Schelling introduced in terms of a double will.

[2] Blondel, *L'Action*, p. 121. Blondel defined the word "infinite" as used in this context as "... that which transcends all distinct representations, and all delimited motives; that which cannot be measured by the object of knowledge nor by the stimulants of spontaneity." (Confer *L'Action*, p. 118). We will discuss Blondel's concept of the infinite later. However, we must keep in mind that Blondel makes his own, while transposing it, a remark of Leibnitz: "There are many degrees of infinitude."

absolute identity of the divine substance with itself. The norm of judgment for Blondel, as we will see, is the progressive identity of self with self, of the will-willing (volonté voulante) and will-willed (volonté voulue). If this dialectic must pass through the supreme option in face of the uniquely necessary (l'unique nécessaire), it is not a problem of identity but of participation which is in question. Granted this reservation, it is increasingly clear why Blondel should consider *Action* as a continuation of a philosophical tradition inaugurated by Spinoza's *Ethics*.

THE NORM OF TOTAL EXPLANATION

So far we have examined Spinoza's principle of immanence as a norm of truth and of value judgment. We have seen that Blondel also ascribes to Spinoza a more considerable part than Kant in the formation of immanent criticism:

> ... it is scarcely in this negative restriction (of Kant) that the essence of immanent criticism consists. The essence of immanent criticism, the idea which is its foundation, is that every act, every work of man or nature, has its value as well as its reality *determined by the whole of which it is part*, ... there is only one way to judge, that is to understand and to understand everything, to explain everything. It is to incorporate the contingent and even the irrational into the chain of necessity and reason. It is, in a sense, to justify everything.[1]

The point that Blondel wishes to make here is that, if one accepts the principle of immanence as a norm of truth and value, then one must be consistent. This principle cannot be applied legitimately only to an isolated problem, as did Descartes, for, as Blondel remarks, "... every fact is not isolated or limited; rather it is indefinite; nothing terminates in itself but forms part of a totality; everything in the universe touches and is interlinked; ... to know truly, is to understand under the form of unity and the absolute."[2] The principle of immanence must be acknowledged as a failure if, by using it, we cannot arrive at a satisfactory explanation of the entire universe, a total philosophy, a philosophy of being. Spinoza was quite aware of this exigency. When he resolved to solve the ethical problem using the principle of immanence, he was fully conscious that if he separated this problem from

---

[1] Blondel, "L'Evolution du Spinozisme," II, 332-333. Italics added.
[2] *Ibid.*, II, 334.

the total philosophical problem of being, it would ultimately be insoluble.

> Having posed the moral problem, Spinoza pretends to show that it cannot conserve the character of a special problem as is commonly thought, if it is to be resolved. For it is nothing other than a particular form of the problem of being and of the absolute. Thus only a metaphysics is capable of discovering the meaning of life by leading us to understand ourselves as part of a Unity and to be as part of Being.[1]

If the ethical problem is incapable of solution apart from the universal problem of being, then it follows logically that the norm which is applied for the solution of the ethical problem must be equally applicable to the universal problem of being. We have seen how Spinoza, after posing the ethical problem, solved it within a metaphysical framework by taking as his point of departure, infinite substance. Because our mind is immanent to this infinite substance, and since the immanent processes of our mind are identical to the processes of immanent causality within this unique substance, the principle of immanence becomes simultaneously a method capable of solving the particular problem of human beatitude and the universal problem of being.

Whatever judgment we make concerning the legitimacy of Spinoza's procedure, we must admit the consistency of his method and the legitimacy of his inspiration. If our initial postulate of method demands that we remain interior to a fact or idea, then to know really that fact or idea it is not enough to remain on the level of positivistic explanation or psychological description. "Above all else the method of immanence is based on this idea, that in each state of the mind the infinite is present; that is to say that without going outside that fact we must determine in it the internal relations which constitute its truth and are its law."[2] This, for Blondel, is the essence of immanent criticism: working from within to find this infinity, to trace the pattern of necessary relations which go *ad infinitum*, that is, to understand the inner structure which unites this fact to the one and the absolute. Blondel was convinced, as we shall see, that a consistent and thorough application of this principle, understood in this sense, would "give access to the transcendent".[3]

---

[1] *Ibid.*, II, 329.

[2] *Ibid.*, II, 334.

[3] The title of Blondel's third article concerning Spinoza in 1932 was: "L'Evolution du Spinozisme et l'Accès qu'elle ouvre à la Transcendence."

SPINOZA'S DIFFICULTY: THE PROBLEM OF BECOMING

Once Spinoza postulated his pantheistic principle that only the infinite substance exists and nothing exists nor can be conceived of apart from it, he found a means, in Blondel's estimation, to resolve the ethical problem within the framework of a metaphysics of being.[1] Everything which is, is true and good in so far as it is; everything which is becomes false or evil in so far as we detach it from the absolute in order to confer on it an imaginary and isolated existence. However, this illusion is capable of being understood, and the moment that it is explained it disappears without leaving a trace. Further, the movement which dissipates the error and suppresses passion is itself the effect of a necessity, that of a necessary development or *fieri* in being.[2] Thus Blondel finds a paradoxical consequence of Spinoza's pantheistic postulate. Grant that the basis of all illusion and error is to attribute to the individual a reality independent of Being, then one is forced to the conclusion that the illusion of the reality of the individual is founded in a development, a becoming within Being itself.

This necessary consequence explains the apparent contradiction in Spinoza's *Ethics* between God, as he is defined in the first book, as infinite substance or total object, whose infinite and eternally actual perfection would seem to exclude any process of becoming; and God, as he is presented in the fifth book, where we read, "... the intellectual love of the mind towards God is a part of the infinite love by which God loves himself." This apparent contradiction is resolved, Blondel maintains, when we recall that between the first and the fifth book of the *Ethics* Spinoza inserts the entire development of human life as an expression of divine activity, "... not in so far as He (God) is infinite, but in so far as He can comprehend Himself by means of the essence of human mind considered under the form of eternity."[3] Thus the

---

[1] Spinoza, *Ethica*, Part I, Propositio XV: Quicquid est, in Deo est, et nihil sine Deo esse, neque concipi potest. p. 56.

[2] *Ibid.*, Part IV, De Servitute Humana, Praefatio: Ostendimus enim in Primae Partis Appendice Naturam propter finem non agere, aeternam namque illud, et infinitum Ens, quod Deum, seu Naturam appellamus, eadem, qua existit, necessitate agit. ... Nihil enim naturae alicuius rei competit, nisi id, quod ex necessitate naturae causae efficientis sequitur, et quicquid ex necessitate naturae causae efficientis sequitur, id necessario fit. (Confer pp. 206-208).

[3] *Ibid.*, Part V, Propositio XXXVI: Mentis Amor intellectualis erga Deum est ipse Dei Amor, quo Deus se ipsum amat, non quatenus infinita est, sed quatenus par essentiam humanae Mentis, sub specie aeternitatis consideratam, explicari potest. (Confer p. 302.).

moral development of man becomes identical with divine life. "There is consubstantial to the God who is from all eternity a God who becomes from all eternity, ... our morality is not only our life in God, it is the Life of God."[1] Spinoza's anthropomorphism was not only a question of introducing characteristics of the subject into the concept of infinite object; this divine subject itself is consequently humanized.

> It was by making morality the principle of total explanation that he (Spinoza) converted morality into metaphysics; it was by projecting the human into God that he succeeded in putting the divine in man. In order to suppress the being of the relative, he put the relative in the absolute. But, in return, to escape from an absolute of becoming, he did not escape the necessity of posing the becoming of the absolute. Thus he was forced to postulate without any other justification the presence of becoming in Being.[2]

Another contributing cause to Spinoza's anthropomorphism was implicit in his project to resolve the problem of being and of human destiny exclusively by the use of reasoning. All human concepts involve a relation between an objective and subjective pole. Spinoza chose to solve his problem by eliminating the subjective pole and by postulating the infinite object as absolute principle. But his mathematical concept of reasoning was derived exclusively from the subjective pole, the subjective relations of concepts in the human mind. Thus it was this purely subjective concept of reasoning which he projected into the absolute object as an explanation of the process of its immanent causality.

> ... In order not to elevate to the absolute the separate being or particular data from our point of view, but rather to eliminate it, he erected as an absolute what is relative to that relation itself (i.e. the internal relation of concepts); and, in order not to fall into the anthropomorphism of the knowing subject, he fell imperceptibly into an anthropomorphism which is much more subtle because it is disguised under the appearances

---

[1] Delbos, *Le Problème Moral dans la Philosophie de Spinoza, pp.* 215-216.

[2] Blondel, "L'Evolution du Spinozisme," I, 267-268. On several occasions in this article Blondel refers to the criticism of Spinoza's doctrine which Schelling made in his work, *Uber das Wesen der Menschlichen Freiheit,* and develops that criticism. In this context he quotes the remark of Schelling: "It is in the autonomous affirmation of the Ego that philosophy has found its ἕν καὶ πᾶν. It is from this affirmation that it has lived, even when it has not been conscious of this fact. So Spinoza, without realizing it, conceived of the non-ego under the form of the ego, when he made it the absolute principle." (Confer Blondel, "L'Evolution du Spinozisme," I, 268-269.)

of its contrary ... the anthropomorphism of the known object, the object posed at the beginning as the absolute principle of everything.[1]

This implicit introduction of becoming into the absolute being will be the point from which all the subsequent evolution of Spinoza's doctrine will be derived.[2] But before the German idealist movement will exploit this aspect of Spinoza's thought, it must first pass through the antithesis of Kantian criticism and the morality of the categorical imperative.

THE REALIST ILLUSION: THE OBJECTIVE IDENTITY OF THOUGHT AND BEING

The introduction of an anthropomorphic subjectivity into the infinite substance led in Blondel's judgment to the basic ambiguity in Spinoza's doctrine, namely, the explicit affirmation and implicit denial of a total identity of objective thought and being. Blondel felt that this ambiguity revealed itself most clearly in the doctrine of divine attributes, each one infinite and eternal in its turn.[3] Man knows only two of these attributes, thought and extension. However, if man is capable of achieving his destiny by thought alone, then our thought must be adequate to the whole of being. What is truth for us must become identical with Truth in Itself. "... If we suppose that we have succeeded in reintegrating into Being everything that we are, we must nevertheless suffer the incomprehensible mystery of all that which we are not, that is, those unknowable attributes of which we do not even have an idea."[4] Consequently, Spinoza must deny and affirm at the same time that, "... man by rendering intelligible all that he is, under-

---

[1] In a footnote Blondel again refers to Schelling's criticism: "It is this which Schelling remarks when he reproaches Spinoza for having ... depended on the realism of the past in the sense that he poses the One as a substance and, consequently, he was not able to explain how that substance arrives at its form, that is to say, its intelligibility."

[2] "It is at this point," Blondel remarks, "that all the movement of thought resulting from Spinozism will insert itself. Elaborate the idea of *becoming* in being; extend the idea of *fieri* to the entire field of history and determine its concrete applications; clarify the principle itself of that becoming, which Spinoza left unclear, but which was the invisible dynamic force of his system; and unite to the doctrine of absolute intelligibility the philosophy of the Spirit or of the Ideas: this was the development of that German idealism which has pretended to resurrect and exhaust the meaning of Spinozism." (Confer Blondel, "L'Evolution du Spinozisme," I, 270).

[3] Spinoza, *Ethica*, Part I, Propositio XI: Deus, sive substantia constans infinitis attributis, quorum unumquodque aeternam, et infinitam essentia exprimit, necessario existit. p. 68, p. 52.

[4] Blondel, "L'Evolution du Spinozisme," I, 269.

stands simultaneously all that is." What began as a pantheism must be transformed into a disguised pan-anthropomorphism.

Blondel returns to this criticism of Spinoza in his article *The Idealist Illusion*.[1] He remarks that there is a sort of metaphysical or realist illusion which is natural and even necessary to spontaneous thought. It is the natural tendency "... to affirm that which is as contained in that which appears".[2] Carried to its logical extreme, this spontaneous realism can be formulated in the thesis that "... thought is the highest and the only form under which absolute being can be possessed."[3] Yet the most radical realism does not escape from the necessity of insinuating a subjective and idealistic sense into every one of its affirmations. "Even in the supposition that one affirms the total and absolute coexistence of our own thought and the subsistent in itself, once again that hypothesis implies that thought is at the same time judge of itself and of being, and that it penetrates there where it itself is not; so that one poses simultaneously the unity and the duality of that which thought is and that which is.[4] This is the problem which, as we have seen, Spinoza experienced in trying to formulate the relation between thought and being. According to Blondel, this is the most fundamental problem of all modern thought. Precisely this problem will govern the evolution of thought consequent to Spinoza, and still remains to be resolved.

> ... The fundamental difficulty remains, to explain how thought and being, interpenetrating without confusing themselves, participate the supremacy without dividing it. All real progress in philosophy will consist in perfecting the formulation, in rendering more intelligible and more accessible the meaning, and bringing closer to us the solution of the problem which Spinoza left open in the imperfect form: How can thought be an attribute among an infinity of divine attributes of Being and, at the same time, become coextensive with Being, as if it were homogeneous with all its attributes?[5]

---

[1] *Ibid.*, "L'Illusion Idéaliste," pp. 97-122. For bibliographical information concerning this article consult below, page 10, footnote 1. In this article Blondel deals with three specific forms of what he calls the generic "intellectualist" illusion: realism, criticism, and idealism. He was quite aware of the ambiguity his double use of the term idealism both as a generic and a specific title involved. However, by so doing he intended to give expression, as we shall see, to his conviction that realism and idealism, considered as contraries, are members of the same idealist or intellectualist genus.

[2] *Ibid.*, p. 91.

[3] *Ibid.*, p. 121.

[4] *Ibid.*, p. 102.

[5] *Ibid.*, pp. 121-122.

The Realist Tradition

For a clear understanding of Blondel's attitude towards the entire realist tradition in philosophy, it is very important to realize that for him Spinoza's doctrine represented the logical development and fulfillment of that tradition. Whenever Blondel speaks of "realism" it is obvious that he considers the word as practically synonymous with Spinozism. Blondel was convinced that Spinoza's doctrine was the end product of the realistic movement which had its roots in the philosophy of Aristotle, especially in his theory of the supremacy of the contemplative act: "... It was the act of rational contemplation which constituted the divine life in man; an act which has its origin and its term in ourselves, and it was metaphysics which was the total science of being and, if one dare say it, the science of salvation itself."[1]

Scholastic philosophy tried to accommodate Aristotle's intellectualism to Christian revelation. But according to Blondel it did not succeed in intrinsically mitigating the exaggerated role which thought had in pagan tradition.

> If one considers the principles and postulates which it derives (from Aristotle), and the very form of the problems which it discusses, Scholastic philosophy is primarily an accomodation of classical thought and, as it were, a handing down of the free spirit of Hellenic speculation. But by its methods, its very aspiration, that previous philosophy tended to envelope the entire order of thought and reality in order to judge absolutely concerning the truth of all objects, in order to propose or substitute theory for practice, and to find in itself the first and last word, a sort of divine sufficiency. Its tacit postulate is the divinity of Reason ..., that our speculative knowledge encloses the supreme virtue, and of itself consummates in us the divine work.[2]

---

[1] *Ibid., Lettre (1896)*, p. 56.

[2] *Ibid.*, p. 55. Blondel's criticism of Scholasticism seems to be based more on what he had been taught at the Ecole Normale and what contacts he had with his Scholastic critics, than on direct contact with Scholastic sources. As such his idea of Scholasticism was more a reflection of the decadent state of Scholastic thought at that period than a true image of the teachings of Saint Thomas. It was this popular image which led him to confuse Scholastic realism with Spinoza's doctrine. For example, in 1896, while answering a friendly, yet critical, letter of the Dean of the department of philosophy at the Catholic University of Lille, Amédée de Margerie, Blondel without hesitation defines his correspondent's Scholastic realism in terms of the exaggerated realism of Spinoza.

> You are realist in the sense that you attribute to the speculative effort of philosophy the ability to attain the real, to make thought adequate to its object, and to permit the integration of the idea into life and being. I am phenomenist in the sense that I consider philosophy as a partial and sub-

What was implicit in Aristotle, the divinity of Reason, was asserted explicitly by Spinoza and made the foundation of his pantheistic system. But the pernicious influence of this idea was mitigated in Scholasticism by the presence of extraneous elements derived from Christian revelation. The trace of this influence can be found in the scholastic concept of the *visio beatifica*, a concept which implies that salvation is a question of seeing or understanding. This is in the spirit of Aristotle's idea that the act of metaphysical contemplation is the most Godlike act of which man is capable. This concept is in sharp contrast with the theological doctrines and ideas which the Scholastics derived from Christian revelation, where salvation is not a *visio* but a *vita*; a life which is a participation in the divine life. Consequently, within the Scholastic synthesis, Blondel finds a matter derived from revelation and a form derived from pagan antiquity which are in conflict with one another: "The Schoolmen admitted a matter which was scarcely assimilable by classical thought, and a form which was not capable of containing its object."[1]

Summary

Blondel, as we have seen, affirmed that his philosophy of action formed a part of an evolution of philosophical thought which had its roots in the moral philosophy of Spinoza. That which Blondel judged particularly valuable in that evolution was the climate of contemporary thought which resulted from it. This climate made possible, perhaps for the first time, the task of establishing an autonomous philosophy of

---

ordinate form of the activity to which it contributes by clarifying and directing it, without substituting for it.

(Confer *Lettres Philosophiques*, p. 105). What is surprising is not the confusion on the part of Blondel of Scholastic realism with Spinoza's doctrine; what is surprising is the fact that his Scholastic correspondents seem to accept Blondel's definition of their position without protesting.

In the years that followed the publication of the *Letter of 1896*, Blondel did come into contact with a more profound Scholastic scholarship, and was led to correct his earlier identification of Scholastic and Spinozan realism. Paradoxically it was, at least in part, Blondel's criticism which led some Thomist scholars, such as Rousselot, to return to Thomistic sources and undertake a reappraisal of Thomistic intellectualism. In 1906, Blondel published an article under the assumed name F. Mallet (in the *Revue de Philosophie*, vol. 6, No. 9 (September, 1906), pp. 227-252) entitled "La Philosophie de l'Action," in which he attempted to show the ultimate compatibility of his philosophy of action with a renewed Scholasticism, despite a divergence in method.

[1] *Ibid.*, *Lettre* (1896), p. 57.

religion appropriate to and compatible with the specifically Christian idea of religion.

After having examined Blondel's comments and criticisms of Spinoza's *Ethics*, we are now in a position to understand why he felt that Spinoza was one of the major sources of that beneficial climate of thought. He saw in Spinoza the first modern to broach the most important and all-embracing philosophical problem of human destiny as the object of an autonomous philosophical enquiry. It was also Spinoza who first established the principle that this problem must be resolved by a method of immanence. That immanence, however, was prejudicially limited to the purely intellectual order; man must find the solution to the problem of his destiny solely by means of the processes of his own thought and reasoning. Nonetheless, by choosing this problem and principle, almost contrary to his own intention, Spinoza opened up the route to that subjectivity which would prove so fruitful in subsequent thought.

It was Spinoza, then, who paradoxically indicated the privileged approach to being from the side of subject. If he unconsciously set philosophy on the route of subjectivity, he also pointed out under what conditions it must follow that route, if it would escape the inherent danger of subjectivism and relativism. The problem of human destiny must never be treated as a special or separated problem but as *the* metaphysical problem par excellence. If Spinoza was wrong to identify absolutely these allied problems of destiny and being, he was right to see in the immanent treatment of the problem of human destiny the best point of departure in order to arrive at a satisfying solution to the problem of being. He was also right in demanding that the route of immanence must lead us to transcendence; that human destiny has no rational solution unless that solution be ultimately founded on the absolute.

Not only did Spinoza appreciate that the problem of human destiny could not be solved apart from metaphysics, in Blondel's opinion he also attributed to that destiny of man a specifically religious and even Christian interpretation. Man's destiny was to achieve eternal beatitude by means of a union in love with God. Here we find that "secret presence of the Christian idea" within the domain of rational philosophy, which Blondel maintained was the unconscious but real dialectical force at work in the evolution consequent on Spinoza's thought. Spinoza tried to conquer a Christian heaven with pagan reason. He failed in that attempt, but his failure itself would eventually lead to a more precise and just concept of both the powers and limits of reason in the task of giving an effective answer to the meaning of life.

Finally, Spinoza sought the solution of his metaphysical-moral problem in the absolute objective identity of thought and being. Yet, as we have seen, this static objective identity could not effectively serve as the immanent solution of man's destiny unless, somehow, the very process by which man achieved his destiny was transformed into a process of becoming and a latent subjectivity in the infinite object itself. Blondel saw Spinoza's failure as leading inevitably to the next step in the dialectical evolution of modern thought. Kant's moral philosophy would appear as a logical antithesis to Spinoza's *Ethics*. Where Spinoza saw an absolute objective identity of thought and being, Kant would argue for a radical dichotomy.

CHAPTER THREE

KANTIAN MORAL PHILOSOPHY AND BLONDEL'S ACTION

Our objective in the present chapter is to establish the nature of the influence of Kant's critical philosophy on Blondel's thought. After a preliminary discussion of Blondel's knowledge of Kant and the role he assigned Kantian criticism in *Action*, we present Blondel's basic concept of Kantian criticism as the antithesis of Spinozan realism and his critique of what he called the "critical illusion". The chapter ends with a short appraisal of Blondel's interpretation of Kant.

The Influence of Kant

From the very first moment when Blondel began to prepare his doctorate thesis, he consciously sought a solution to the problem posed by the conflict between classical realism and Kantian idealism. His starting point was an intuitive conviction that in action he would somehow find a means of resolving that conflict. Thus in 1886, seven years before the publication of his thesis, Blondel, writing to Emile Boutroux, his former professor and director, explained his thesis project in these words: "Between Aristotelianism which depreciates and subordinates practice to thought, and Kantianism which detaches and exalts the practical order to the detriment of the other, there remains something to be defined, and it is in a very determined way, by the analysis of action, that I should like to establish what it is."[1] A year later, when he wrote to the Dean of the Sorbonne to inscribe the subject of his thesis, Blondel explained his choice of subject in almost the same terms:

> ... Between the classical doctrine according to which the will acts in conformity with its object to the point that it is one with it, and the Kantian doctrine which places the will exterior to and above reason, there is something to define; it remains true that to act well, one must think well; it is even more true to say that to think well, one must act well. *In Operibus Lux.*[2]

---

[1] Blondel, *Lettres Philosophiques*, p. 10.
[2] *Ibid.*, pp. 12-13.

Nor did Blondel change this orientation during the subsequent years before he submitted his thesis. When in July, 1892, Boutroux sent Blondel a copy of his letter of approval to the Dean of the faculty of letters for the submission of *Action*, Blondel took exception to a phrase in this letter to the effect that the thesis "can be considered as a refutation of pessimism." Blondel answered:

> Without doubt, I did not have solely nor even principally in view the refutation of pessimism; I had thought to define, otherwise than Kantianism had done, the relation of the speculative and the practical, knowledge and existence. I had thought above all to show the indestructible reality and the radical insufficiency of every natural order in order to expose the vice which I believe I had discovered in every separated philosophy.[1]

Thus Blondel leaves no doubt that his thesis was an attempt to redefine the relationship between the rational and practical orders in such a way as to transcend both the realist and Kantian critical position as he understood it. As he himself put it in a note on the plan of redaction of the last chapter in the manuscript of 1893, "... find for thought an ultra-Kantian attitude."[2]

This desire to, so to speak, use Kant's criticism against Kant himself was profoundly connected with Blondel's objective of establishing a valid philosophy of religion. In his private daily journal, on the 3rd of February, 1887, Blondel wrote: "Is it impossible to destroy the magic spell of Kantian thought, as Kant did for Cartesianism, as Descartes did for peripatetic thought? Can one create a Catholic Kantianism?"[3] In the same letter to Georges Perrot, in which he announced his objective to establish a philosophy of religion compatible with Catholic thought, Blondel represents Kant as the "Luther" of German philosophy; he remarks that the separation of faith and science in Kant's doctrine is, as it were, a philosophical restatement of the Protestant doctrine of the separation of faith and reason. He, in turn, seeks in his philosophy of action a point of contact between faith and reason which would be compatible with the Catholic tradition of a compenetration of faith and reason.[4]

---

[1] *Ibid.*, p. 20, footnote 1.

[2] Blondel, "Le Dernier Chapitre de L'Action," edition critique établie par Henri Bouillard, *Archives de Philosophie*, Tome XXIV (Janvier-Mars, 1961), 65.

[3] *Ibid., Carnets Intimes (1883-1894)*, (Paris: Les Editions du Cerf, 1961), p. 105.

[4] *Ibid., Lettres Philosophiques*, pp. 32-37. In *Action* itself Blondel attempts to show that Kant's dichotomy is by no means an accurate explanation of the Christian tradition as some of his disciples had claimed:

Were one to accept the fact that Blondel sought to "answer" Kant, it would follow that in that very process his *Action* would necessarily reflect in many ways the doctrine which it proposed to refute. But, in fact, Blondel did not consider his thesis as a refutation of Kant but, rather, as a continuation and a fulfillment of that critical philosophy of which Kant was the author. As a matter of policy, Blondel did not believe that any great philosophy could be effectively refuted. In his own words, "... in order to discuss a great philosophy, the most efficacious means is not to react against it from without, but by entering fearlessly into it to push its analysis further along than it had gone before."[1] That this was his tactic in relation to Kant, he testifies in a letter to a philosopher friend from the *Ecole Normale* who charges him with a negative attitude towards Kant:

> I have not remained outside critical idealism; I have accepted it in order to go beyond, ... One does not leave valid grounds for criticism, except by resisting it. By giving way to it, I abandoned beforehand more than it demanded. Don't believe, then, that I acted from a desire to go against Kantianism, or that I adhered to a spontaneous and naive realism.[2]

Nor do we do justice to Blondel's judgment on the intrinsic value of Kantian critical philosophy, if we see in his use of Kant's thought only a sort of philosophical compromise in order to be able to communicate with the spirit of his own age. Blondel saw in Kantian critical philosophy many positive and definitive contributions to perennial philosophy.[3]

> By remarking that the Christian does not live in the world of science but that of faith, one has pretended that Kantianism had definitively substituted the Christian spirit for the Hellenic spirit in metaphysics. This is an error. The Word is no less light than life. And, just as dogma teaches the distinction and the unity of divine operations, so too, in man the knowledge and possession of real truths, although identical in one sense, remain distinct and, in fact, separable.

Confer Blondel, *L'Action*, p. 148, footnote.

[1] *Ibid.*, "L'Evolution du Spinozisme," I, 263.

[2] *Ibid.*, *Lettres Philosophiques*, pp. 40-41.

[3] To a young seminarian who inquired whether or not he thought Kant would pass from the picture as did Aristotle and Plato, Blondel answered:

> ... That which seems certain to me is that Plato and Aristotle are by no means outmoded; and likewise in critical philosophy there are definitive gains ... by means of which, thanks to certain insights which become more and more clear, philosophy tends to lose its literary indetermination in order to become a more scientifically technical discipline, whose latent influence from a Catholic viewpoint has been considerable and ought to be decisive in the ever more precise constitution of that philosophical science.

Confer Blondel, *Lettres Philosophiques*, pp. 117-118.

What these contributions were, will be discussed in some detail during the course of this chapter. It will suffice here to remark that, perhaps above all else, Blondel attributed to Kant the introduction into modern thought of the all-important insight that "... science does not suffice for life; there is something for which thought does not supply."[1]

Granted that Blondel saw Kant's critical philosophy as a positive, if limited, contribution to the evolution of modern thought, it is no less true that he had a strong personal distaste for the Kantian critical spirit. The anti-metaphysical spirit, particularly of the French neo-Kantian school of his time, represented the exact opposite of his own spontaneous philosophical spirit. In June of 1889, he jotted this reflection in his diary:

> ... Kant, by ruining speculative reason in order to enhance practical reason, has killed, without willing or realizing it, the force of life with the daring of thought. Pessimism has resulted from his criticism, because he has broken the highest faculty in man, extinguished all light and, by displaying I don't know what obscure, impenetrable, and illogical reality, has plunged us into a darkness full of nightmares. So true is it that the problem of life is for everyone a question of metaphysics.[2]

He calls Kant "... the persecutor of thought", but hastens to add "... but beneficial for the persecuted."[3] And again he writes: "no thought is more antipathetic to me than that of Kant."[4] This antipathy for the anti-metaphysical spirit of the neo-Kantians explains in part the strong reaction of Blondel when his Catholic critics accused him of being a neo-Kantian. When a clerical critic published an article charging him with Kantian subjectivism, phenomenism and fideism, Blondel retorted: "I am not a 'neo-Kantian', and if it is true that the contraries are species of the same genus, his Thomism is closer to Kantianism than I am: I am neither 'subjectivist', nor 'phenomenist', nor 'fideist'."[5] What was understandably galling to Blondel was that his critic should accuse him of those very failings which he himself disliked so intensely in neo-Kantianism, and which he believed he had effectively corrected by means of an internal criticism:

---

[1] *Ibid.*, *Lettre (1896)*, p. 62.
[2] *Ibid.*, *Carnets Intimes (1883-1894)*, pp. 223-224.
[3] *Ibid.*, p. 84.
[4] *Ibid.*, *Correspondence M. Blondel - Auguste Valensin*, ("Editions Montaigne," Paris: Aubier, 1951), Vol. II, p. 183, footnote.
[5] *Ibid.*, *Lettres Philosophiques*, pp. 108-109.

... that which proves once again how far they are from entering into my point of view, who believe they understand it, is the fact that they pretend that I am Kantian or neo-Kantian precisely when I am trying to throw off the yoke of that system and go beyond it. I conclude that all those who have received a traditional formation, lacking a precise knowledge of the various systems, confuse Kantianism and the philosophies which have followed it or discuss it by entering into its point of view; the most unjust confusion possible![1]

This curious intermixture of respect and antipathy serves as a fore-warning of the difficulties which will beset us in trying to determine the exact nature of Kant's influence on the philosophy of action. It is, in fact, almost impossible to determine by exterior evidence to what extent Blondel studied directly the texts of Kant: what evidence we do have is almost contradictory.[2] However, from internal evidence, it is certain that Blondel did have an extensive and profound knowledge of Kant's moral philosophy at the time he wrote *Action*. There are well over thirty major references to Kant's thought which demonstrate a knowledge of his *Critique of Pure Reason*, his *Fundamental Principles of the Metaphysics of Morals*, and his *Critique of Practical Reason*.[3] In fact, in view of Blondel's professed purpose to define the relation of practice and reason other than Kant had defined it, one would not be far amiss to see in the subtitle of *Action: Critique of Life and a Science of Practice*, a deliberate play on the title of Kant's *Critique of Practical Reason*.

However, even if we cannot determine with accuracy the extent of

---

[1] *Ibid.*, p. 111.

[2] On the ninth of January, 1886, Blondel wrote in his diary: "... I must occupy myself with philosophy ... I shall put myself to studying Kant." And the frequent reflections on Kant's thought in the weeks that follow seem to indicate that he had kept his resolve. (Confer *Carnets Intimes (1883-1894)*, p. 71.) However, in the same letter in which he rejected the charge of Kantianism he wrote: "I had written *Action* before I read Kant." (Confer *Correspondence Blondel-Valensin*, Vol. II, p. 183, footnote). It is important to note that this statement that he had not read Kant is taken from a *brouillon* of a letter in which Blondel prepared his reply to his critic Père Schwalm. The letter which was actually sent can be found in *Lettres Philosophiques*, pp. 95-99. The reader will note that the line about not having read Kant was eliminated. As the letter which was actually sent seems to indicate, what Blondel had in mind was to insist that he did not draw his fundamental inspiration from Kant.

[3] For a rapid view of the extent to which Blondel refers explicitly to Kant's critical philosophy in *Action* consult the following pages: pp. XXI, 27-28, 80 footnote, 84, 88 footnote, 97 footnote, 299, 314, 451-452, 457, 460, 481-484, 490-491. Dumery, in his most recent publication concerning Blondel, *Raison et Religion dans la Philosophie de l'Action*, has undertaken to list all the direct references and quotations in Blondel's *Action* to the various works of Kant. Confer pp. 441-452.

Blondel's direct reading of Kant, we do have certain evidence for a most important indirect contact with that source. Once again, as in the case of Spinoza, it was Victor Delbos. One of the chapters of Delbos' thesis on the moral problem in Spinoza's philosophy was dedicated to the study of the influence of Kant's moral philosophy in the evolution of that tradition.[1] Blondel read and discussed this chapter with his friend, who was destined to become in a few years' time one of the most outstanding Kantian scholars in France. Blondel, in turn, wrote several revealing pages on the role of Kant's moral philosophy in the evolution of modern thought in the article "The Evolution of Spinozism" which he published in 1894.[2] As we noted previously, Blondel considered his book *Action* as absorbing, integrating and carrying forward all that was valuable in that evolution, including, of course, that which was positive in the critical philosophy of Kant.[3]

There is no room, then, for legitimate doubt that Kantian critical philosophy was one of the most important influences on the formation of Blondel's method in *Action*. But that influence takes the form of a subtle mixture of acceptance, rejection and transformation. For a proper understanding of Blondel's method, in its originality as well as its historical continuity, an unraveling of that triple thread of Kant's influence is of primary importance. We shall treat, here, three aspects of that influence: first, the role that Blondel attributed to Kant in the evolution of the Spinozan tradition; second, how Blondel understood his method as being more truly "critical" than that of Kant; third, the key role that Kant's idea of the "synthetic a priori" played in the development of Blondel's philosophy of action.

---

[1] Delbos, *Le Problème Moral dans la Philosophie de Spinoza*, pp. 242-255, 533-565. A few years later Delbos also published his major work on Kant, *La Philosophie Pratique de Kant* (Paris: Félix Alcan, 1905).

[2] Blondel, "L'Evolution du Spinozisme," I, 273-275; II, 337-341.

[3] This influence of Delbos does not exclude many other mediate influences. As we have already seen Blondel himself attributed the primary influence on the form of his thesis to his professor, Emile Boutroux, who was also a proponent of critical philosophy. Blondel followed Boutroux' course on Kant and post-Kantian German philosophy at the Ecole Normale in the years 1882-1883.

There is also evidence of considerable influence by the neo-Kantian, Lachelier. In a reference which is probably to the latter's book, *Du Fondement de l'Induction* (Paris: 1871), Blondel states as one of his objectives in the plan for the redaction of 1893 to "... give a scientific character to the doctrine of Lachelier." (Confer "Le Dernier Chapitre de 'L'Action'," p. 65, footnote).

There is also the problem, to be treated in part II of this study, of the extent to which Blondel interpreted Kant's philosophy in terms of the critique and development of Fichte, Schelling, and Hegel.

THE ANTITHETICAL RELATION OF KANT'S MORAL
PHILOSOPHY AND SPINOZA'S ETHICS

In Spinoza's *Ethics* Blondel saw the problem and the methodological principle which would determine the movement of modern philosophical thought. It was his conviction that the "seed" planted by Spinoza reached its logical flowering and completion in the philosophy of Hegel. Paradoxically, that flowering was made possible by the apparently irreconcilable opposition of the critical spirit.

> Before it could blend together in a rational synthesis all those elements which seemed to resist Spinoza's doctrine rather than to enter into it, German philosophy had to undergo the great test of Kantian criticism. It was necessary that what had remained as the reverse side of Spinoza's doctrine should become the starting point of a new system, and that the hidden postulate of *Ethics* should be accepted as the very principle of an original doctrine in order that, each of the rival doctrines having revealed all their meaning, a conciliation should become possible, and the systematic union of both doctrines could be accomplished.[1]

Blondel traces this divergence between the moral philosophy of Kant and that of Spinoza to their contrary points of departure. Whereas Spinoza's *Ethics* begins with the affirmation of an infinite substance or object, and the corresponding denial of the distinct reality of a moral subject apart from that object; Kant, in the *Critique of Practical Reason*, begins with the consciousness of obligation on the part of a free subject and denies, if not the existence, at least the possibility of a valid theoretical knowledge of the infinite object as such.

These contradictory starting points can be traced back even further to contradictory methodological principles. Blondel understood the whole of Kant's critical philosophy as founded on what he called his "Copernican revolution": "Hitherto it has been assumed that all our knowledge must conform to objects. ... Let us try, then, whether we may not make better progress in the task of metaphysics if we assume that objects must conform to our knowledge."[2] This principle, Blondel held, led Kant to assume an agnostic position concerning objects or things-in-themselves. The result was a direct conflict with Spinoza's

---

[1] Blondel, "L'Evolution du Spinozisme," I, 273.

[2] Emmanuel Kant, *Kritik der reinen Vernunft*, Zweite Auflage, 1787, "Vorrede zur zweiter Auflage," Vol. 6, Sect. XVI:

> Bisher nahm man an, alle unsere Erkenntniss müsse sich nach den Gegenständen richten; ... Man versuche es daher einmal, ob wir nicht in den Aufgaben

parallel principle; "The order and connection of ideas is identical with the order and connection of things." Whereas Spinoza understood our ideas as giving direct access to a knowledge of things in themselves; Kant understood them, on the contrary, as essentially subjective a priori constructions, which by their very nature rendered impossible any direct access to a speculative knowledge of the "order and connection" of things in themselves.

This opposition in starting point and methodological principle led to two systems of moral philosophy which seemingly contradict each other in every essential feature. Spinoza's starting point in moral philosophy is the infinite object; his moral ideal is the total conformity of the mind with its object; there is a total identity of moral philosophy and metaphysics. The object of moral philosophy is being, that which is already fully determined. The moral process is a matter of reintegrating ourselves into total being by the dissipation of the illusion of individual separateness and freedom; and this process is contained within the universal determinism of the absolute object.

For Kant the starting point of moral philosophy is the subject; the moral ideal is the conformity of the mind with itself; that is, with its consciousness of duty or rational law. There is a dichotomy between speculative reason and practical reason, between speculative metaphysics and morality. The object of moral philosophy is not that which is, but that which ought to be. The moral process is a matter of the exercise of liberty by an autonomous will. The essence of moral action as such lies in the fact that it derives its practical ends from itself, free from all determination.

For Spinoza, that which is phenomenal or merely apparent in moral activity is freedom; the synthetic process of human activity is an illusion. For Kant, Blondel maintained, that which is phenomenal or merely apparent in moral activity is determinism; the development of analytic reason and the determinism of science is an illusion when applied uncritically to objective reality.

> In Kant's doctrine, everything is evidently related to reason considered as the law-making, autonomous faculty; nothing is related to Being, and above all to Being such as Spinoza defined it, under the form of

---

der Metaphysik damit besser fortkommen, dass wir annehmen, die Gegenstände müssen sich nach unseren Erkenntniss richten.

All volume and section or page references will be to *Kants gesammelte Schriften*, critical edition sponsored by the Prussian Academy of Science (22 vols. Berlin: Georg Reimer, 1911).

Eternal Thing. In the universe of Spinoza everything takes place under a law of identity, which is at the same time a law of intellect and nature; with the result that there is no such thing as obligation but a development in Being. For Kant, on the contrary, the question is not to know what Being is, but to determine the law of becoming and action. But in science and in life nothing takes place except by synthesis.[1]

Despite this impressive series of contrasts, Blondel judges that even more fundamentally these two doctrines resemble each other more than they truly contradict each other. If the synthesis which transcendental idealism would achieve were possible, it was due to the fact that both doctrines were partial aspects of the total moral philosophy; their opposition is merely a matter of stressing the contrary aspects of a higher synthesis. Both Spinoza and Kant agree in proposing to solve the ethical problem; both have the intention "of explaining, the one by transposition, the other by promotion, the process of *becoming*, which is manifestly our human role and our moral destiny."[2] By considering moral obligation as the moral absolute, affirming the free autonomy of the will, and asserting the subordination of the phenomenal order of pure reason to the synthetic constructions of practical reason, Kant, in effect, took as the fundamental principle of his system the principle of becoming; which, according to Blondel, while explicitly rejected by Spinoza as an illusion, remained nonetheless as an implicit postulate of his system. Spinoza, in turn, based all his morality on the infinite object as such, the thing-in-itself, which, despite all the ingenuity of Kant's criticism, continued to exist as an implicit postulate of his system. "The result is that each of these two systems seems to constitute an inconsistent monism; each system surviving only at the price of secretly borrowing from the other."[3]

Because Kant's subjective moral autonomy and Spinoza's objective moral determinism are at base contrary aspects of the same total moral philosophy, Blondel held that they were both guilty of the same basic error, exclusive rationalism:

> ... If there is one idea which is common to the idealism of Kant and the pantheism of Spinoza; an idea which is the πρῶτον ψεῦδος of every exclusive rationalism, it is the idea that man can succeed by his own powers to reintegrate himself into the absolute, and fulfil perfectly

---

[1] Blondel, "L'Evolution du Spinozisme," I, 274. The citation Blondel employs is taken from Delbos, *Le Problème Moral dans la Philosophie de Spinoza*, pp. 252-254.

[2] Blondel, "L'Evolution du Spinozisme," I, 275.

[3] *Ibid.*

his being or his duty. This is the central idea concerning which modern thought must be disabused.[1]

The specific criticism which Blondel levels against Kant's concept of morality concerns his idea of a formal autonomy of reason and its independence of any given material in its moral action.

> In vain will one try to derive the definition of positive obligation and the very material of precise obligation from formal autonomy as Kant conceived of it. One will never succeed. For it is impossible to isolate oneself in the purity of autonomous reason. One cannot will oneself entirely without willing, by the mediation of the idea of infinite being, the universal order.[2]

In this argument Blondel refers us to Victor Delbos' criticism of Kant's moral philosophy. According to Delbos no intelligible relation is possible between the law of an autonomous practical reason and the material object of the will. What led Kant to hold such a position was a false concept of the nature of human freedom.

> That which is without question, according to Kant, is the given fact which, in itself, is not intelligible; while that which is intelligible does not exist. It is due to this dissociation of the intelligible and the real that Kant uncovers an interval in which the human will is free to move at its ease. ... We have here the basic illusion concerning the human will, namely, that we act more freely in so far as we experience the least possible influence of Truth or Being. ... On the contrary, it is precisely the role of the will to introduce the idea into the fact.[3]

But this interpenetration of idea and fact presupposes a certain correlation between our ideas and reality. Matter itself must, somehow, have a rational structure capable of being actualized by our rational will-acts.

> ... If the law is capable of shaping and penetrating matter, it is because matter, in the last analysis, is of the same nature as the law; that is to say that Reason must find itself not only in that which ought to be, but also in that which is. The objects on which the will acts must include a sort of potential reason which the rational will determines and actualizes. There is a virtual or real unity of the ego and the thing in itself.[4]

Delbos claims that Kant implicitly conceded this presence of reason in the thing-in-itself in the example he gave of immoral actions which,

---

[1] *Ibid.*, II, 338.
[2] *Ibid.*, II, 338-339. Blondel again refers to Delbos, *op. cit.*, p. 540.
[3] Delbos, *op. cit.*, pp. 535-536.
[4] *Ibid.*, p. 538.

although they manifest no purely rational or logical contradiction, yet remain immoral in the sense that they manifest a contradiction in the will itself.[1] "Kant recognizes in the end that there is, as it were, a sanction of reason by the universe; that the world is sufficiently rational in its essence that it cannot somehow tolerate an irrational act."[2]

It is precisely at this point that Kant's moral philosophy rejoins Spinoza's *Ethics*. If it is true that the universal determinism of the objective rational order in Spinoza's system demanded a secret supposition of free human activity and a principle of becoming, it is also true that the autonomous reason of Kant is incapable of establishing a concrete moral philosophy without presupposing a rational order present in the objective order of being; an order which somehow manifests its presence to man and serves as a judicative norm for the morality of his actions.

THE CRITICAL ILLUSION: THE DUALISM OF THOUGHT AND BEING

As we have seen, Blondel held that there is a realist or metaphysical illusion which is natural and even necessary to spontaneous thought. So too, he maintains that there is a second illusion, equally natural and necessary, which is at the base of every reflexive movement of thought. Just as it is natural for our spontaneous thought to identify that which is with that which appears; so it is natural and even necessary for our reflexive thought to fear to mistake appearances for being. "Just as, by a first movement we are inclined to accept our immediate ideas as the final truth; so too, by a second movement, inseparable from the first, we are determined to search incessantly beyond that which seems directly present, under, behind, or in the real, something which is even more real."[3]

Just as Spinoza's pantheistic realism represented a consistent effort to develop the realistic illusion into an exclusive philosophical system; so too, critical philosophy represented a consistent effort to develop this second illusion into a rigorous and exclusive system.[4] We have

---

[1] Confer Chapter V, pp. 88-90, where this intrinsic contradiction in the immoral will is discussed.

[2] Delbos, *op. cit.*, pp. 538-539.

[3] Blondel, "L'Illusion Idéaliste," p. 97.

[4] Blondel formulates the contrasting epistemological norms of realism and criticism as follows:

The two extreme formulas which result from intellectualism, and which

already discussed Spinoza's failure to erect a consistent philosophy on the exclusive realist premises of the objective identity of thought and being. The effort to achieve an exclusively critical philosophy based on the irreducible dualism of thought and being is equally doomed to failure. "If only because idealism does not admit anything in common between the object of thought and reality itself; it maintains a dualism of being and knowledge; and every dualism is a hybrid union of realism and idealism."[1] Whereas Spinoza was compelled to introduce an implicit principle of becoming into the infinite object; Kant, in turn, is equally compelled to place the unknowable X of the object-in-itself outside the domain of knowledge.

> Thus from a sufficient distance Kant does not appear to us to be much further from Spinoza than Aristotle was from Plato. Just as Spinoza could not conceive of being as object without secretly insinuating the essential attribute of a subject, in order to render it intelligible; so Kant, forcing himself never to permit being to be known within the material or the objects of thought, could not escape from the trap of the "thing-in-itself".[2]

Blondel concludes from this double failure that both these illusions are equally legitimate and equally deceiving. They are both deceiving in so far as they both try to create a system based on one of these natural tendencies to the exclusion of the other. For to do so is to "artificially limit the movement of the dialectic in act." They are both legitimate and founded in the sense that they are necessary aspects of consciousness of which "they form a part of the internal determinism, and they are a source of the dynamism of intellectual life."[3] Consequently, Blondel is convinced that as long as philosophy remains within the framework of the realist-idealist controversy, it condemns itself to a sterile and insolvable quarrel.

> ... To pretend to deal either with realism or idealism as an illusion which one must remedy by seeking the secret of the cure either in

---

involve a mutual implication, are the following: "The knowledge of absolute truth, being the unity of science and life, is eminently the science of life: thought is the highest and, seen close up, the only form under which the absolute can be seized." Or, on the contrary: "Being and thought, essence and existence, morality and metaphysics are necessarily irreducible and heterogenous."

Confer "L'Illusion Idéaliste," p. 121.

[1] *Ibid.*, p. 104.
[2] *Ibid.*, pp. 104-105.
[3] *Ibid.*, p. 98.

idealism or realism itself, is *the* illusion itself; the only way to find a
remedy will be to reintegrate these two terms in abstract thought with
the same character of spontaneity, necessity and solidarity which they
possess in living thought; this will necessitate subordinating them both
systematically to a doctrine different from the one and the other; a
doctrine which will eliminate the false appearance of incompatibility
and will show them to be necessarily and intelligibly united in theory
as they are in practice.[1]

Thus Blondel outlines the epistemological ambition which he had
sought to accomplish by means of his philosophy of action—to find
a starting point and a method which would transcend the artificial
opposition of realism and idealism—to find a point of view from
which one could integrate what was necessary and true in both doctrines into a higher synthesis. He finds that point of departure and that
method precisely, we shall see, in what could be called his second
Copernican revolution:

... It is necessary to substitute in place of the problem of the harmony
between thought and reality, or that of the objective value of the subjective, the equivalent but absolutely different problem of an immanent
adequation of ourselves with ourselves.[2]

But before passing on to a study of Blondel's original effort at
synthesis, and the positive transposition he attempted of Kantian
criticism, we should note the point where we have arrived in our
study of the historical sources of his method in the philosophy of
action. As we noted, Blondel stated as his purpose in *Action* to redefine
the relation of reason and practice, thought and being, otherwise than
that had been done by the realist tradition epitomized in Spinoza's
Ethics, or the idealist tradition founded in Kant's critical moral philosophy. This critical search amid the various doctrines which form the
major steps in the historical evolution of modern thought will be
continued through the efforts at synthesis of Fichte, Schelling and
Hegel. But with the conflicting doctrines of Spinoza and Kant,
Blondel felt that the two major, if relatively partial, contributions to
that synthesis had displayed both their fecundity and their relative
sterility. Consequently, as a result of his critical study and evaluation
of these two doctrines, he was now in a position to judge the validity
of past efforts at synthesis and undertake his own positive task of
synthesis. As he stated in the conclusion of *Action* itself:

---

[1] *Ibid.*
[2] *Ibid.*, p. 110.

The conclusion of such a research as this has been to lay bare the chimerical and superstitious character of every effort made to establish directly a morality capable of being self-sufficient, and of forming a science apart. There is no independent idea of obligation which is valid in itself, and which is capable of establishing what is good by means of totally formal precepts (Kant). Nor is there a speculative truth, the adequate knowledge of which engenders the perfect life (Spinoza). Neither the ethical problem nor the metaphysical problem will ever be resolved alone. No morality apart from truth; but truth completely understood is not, by itself alone, morality. The secret of life lies on a higher level than Kant or Spinoza realized.[1]

CONCLUSION: BLONDEL'S UNDERSTANDING OF KANT

There is no reason to doubt that the influence of Kantian criticism on Blondel's philosophy of action was of primary importance in the formation of Blondel's own thought and method. Blondel's own personal attitude towards Kantian philosophy was ambivalent, but the repugnance he felt for the anti-metaphysical tendency of Kantian critical thought was due more to the interpretation of Kant's thought prevalent in French neo-Kantian circles of his day than to the actual doctrine of Kant.

Despite this repugnance Blondel remained true to his own norm that the only way to "refute" a great philosopher is by entering oneself into his method and by pushing its analysis further along than it had gone before. How precisely Blondel understood his "Critique of Life" as both a utilization and transformation of Kantian criticism will form the subject matter of our next chapter.

In terms of modern critical understanding of Kant's philosophy, the antithetical relation which Blondel established between Spinoza and Kant can be interpreted as an exaggeration on Blondel's part of the dichotomy of reason and practice in Kant's thought. This exaggeration can be attributed in part to a lack of familiarity with Kant's *Critique of Judgment*. Jean Lacroix, however, maintains that despite his miscomprehension Blondel shared exactly the same intention as Kant. Both philosophers shared the conviction that philosophy is moral of its very essence. "If metaphysics is necessary, it is because man, a moral being, needs a metaphysics in order not to despair of the sense of life."[2] But in Lacroix' opinion, even if their intention was identical,

---

[1] *Ibid., L'Action,* p. 475.

[2] Jean Lacroix, *Maurice Blondel, Sa Vie, Son Oeuvre* ("Philosophes," Paris: Presses Universitaires de France, 1963), pp. 66-71.

Kant and Blondel follow different routes; and even if one grants that there is no "irrationalism" or "fideism" in Kant's concept of a metaphysics based on practical reason, yet Blondel did succeed better than Kant in rendering precise the exact type of vital knowledge which is proper to metaphysics. "It remains true that the excessive distinction of intellectual life and moral life (in Kant's thought) scarcely permits an understanding of the concrete elaboration of practical belief. Concerning this precise and capital point Blondel's thought is really different from Kant's."[1]

---

[1] *Ibid.*, p. 70.

CHAPTER FOUR

BLONDEL'S ULTRA-KANTIAN CRITIQUE

We have already noted that in *Action* Blondel consciously sought lan "ultra-Kantian attitude". He hoped, by entering into critical philosophy, to push its analysis further along than it had gone before and, by this means, correct what he considered to be the deficiencies of Kantian criticism by means of critical philosophy itself. This intrinsic critical development, as Blondel's subtitle, *Critique of Life and Science of Practice*, suggests, refers primarily to Kant's moral philosophy as it was developed in his *Critique of Practical Reason*. In order to appreciate Blondel's idea of the relation between his own critical moral philosophy and that of Kant, we must attempt to answer these two questions: What precisely did Blondel understand to be the positive contribution and negative limitations of Kantian criticism? By means of what aspects of his own method did Blondel try to transcend and transform the limitations of Kantian criticism, while preserving all that he found valuable in that criticism?

THE ROLE OF CRITICISM IN PHILOSOPHY

In two important articles published after *Action*, "The Idealist Illusion" and "The Point of Departure of Philosophical Research," Blondel himself undertook the task of clarifying and rendering explicit the method and point of departure of his philosophy of action.[1] Just as that philosophy had been created, at least in part, as a response to the challenge presented by neo-Kantian criticism, so too Blondel's reflection on the method implicit in his original doctrine was a conscious effort to clarify the relation between his method and that of the Kantians as he understood it.[2]

---

[1] Confer Chapter 1, p. 4, ftnt. 2 and p. 10, ftnt. 1 for bibliographical information concerning these two articles.

[2] The subsequent investigation of the influence of Fichte and the Idealists will help us to appreciate more accurately Blondel's understanding of Kant and his own point of departure and method.

THE CRITICAL SPIRIT

Blondel, as we have seen, maintained that the critical spirit was a necessary moment within the context of philosophical endeavor. It corresponds to the spontaneous act of reflection, just as the realistic spirit corresponds to the spontaneous moment of direct or prospective knowledge. We have seen that Blondel rejected the effort to base philosophy exclusively on that critical or reflexive moment in human knowledge. The great advantage that philosophy derived from Kantian criticism was to be disabused of a naive realistic illusion. "Critical philosophy ... made clear the artificial or 'constructed' character of the object of intellectual reflection."[1] Thus it saved philosophy from accepting its direct and spontaneous knowledge as an "objective intuition". Criticism, in its turn, brought into philosophical thought the danger of a new illusion. For it did not escape the temptation to confer a sort of ontological value on a privileged part of knowledge. "... It is founded on the reflexive action of judgment as a *moral intuition*."[2] Kant's philosophy of practical reason was the first effort to reconstruct philosophy by means of an intuition of moral consciousness. What was the result?

> It suffices to remark to what point the living intuition is reduced to abstract forms of a theoretical analysis, and how it results in a rationalism which has modified the matter of the ancient systems without changing their spirit, in order that the artificial character of such a rational undertaking and the arbitrary character of such a fideism should appear.[3]

All the doctrinal conclusions of *The Critique of Practical Reason* have validity, Blondel maintains, only in so far as it is possible and legitimate to employ this exclusive reflexive methodology which abstracts and isolates the fact of moral activity. In itself this isolation of the moral fact was a positive accomplishment. For it was necessary in order to better comprehend moral reality in its specific attributes. But where Blondel saw Kantian criticism as wrong was in investing that isolated and abstracted element "with a sort of power of exclusion in regard to anything in the neighboring forms of moral life, such as religion, which could not be strictly reduced to it."[4] By reason of this abstract

---

[1] Blondel, "Le Point de Départ de la Recherche Philosophique," I, 351.
[2] *Ibid.*
[3] *Ibid.*
[4] *Ibid.*, I, 352. The phrase is quoted by Blondel from Delbos' book, *La Philosophie Pratique de Kant* (Paris: Félix Alcan, 1905), p. 751.

treatment of morality, Kant's critical moral philosophy became a moralism and, as such, is, Blondel contends, merely a new form of that rationalism which treats human thought as absolute, and confers ontological value on the artificial abstractions and divisions which thought introduces into being. This exclusive moralism in which one isolates and opposes practical and speculative knowledge is ultimately meaningless. There is no reason to speculate, if speculation has no meaning for one's moral activity and destiny; there is no reason to act, if one's action is necessarily blind and one is incapable in any rational sense of ascribing existence to the object of one's action.

> ... That which has no relation with my destiny does not exist for me; further, I would not exist for myself unless I have the possibility of extracting from the primitive *continuum* of consciousness and sensation those objects concerning which I must be able to affirm *that* they are in order to continue with my analysis, even when I have nothing but a rudimentary knowledge of *what* they are or what it is *to be*.[1]

Thus Blondel concludes that the reflective critical process by which Kant isolated practical reason was an artificial process, but a natural and even indispensable artificial process, which has its legitimate role in so far as one does not try to arbitrarily isolate that role. "That which is artificial and deceiving is not to employ reflection according to the intention of nature in the unified task of thought and action; rather, it is to pretend to use it exclusively or to eliminate totally the results of its analysis in constituting speculatively a philosophy of knowledge and existence."[2]

However, criticism participates in that vice common to all rationalism. It seeks "knowledge for the sake of knowledge and by means of knowledge." With the resulting paradox that, having systematically subordinated theory to practice, the criticist presents his doctrine once again as a theory which is an end in itself and a means for itself. The result is a basic ambiguity concerning the meaning and value of action in philosophy. From the viewpoint of practical reason action is presented as "... the superior form, as the most adequate bearer of reality itself."[3] But from the viewpoint of speculative reason it appears as "... a means of deformation from which thought must free itself, if it wishes to free our intellectual life from practically useful but unintelligible symbols."[4]

---

[1] Blondel, *op. cit.*, I, 357.
[2] *Ibid.*
[3] *Ibid.*, I, 358.
[4] *Ibid.*

Blondel traces this ambiguity back to an arbitrary restriction introduced into Kantian criticism. "... The only way to rescue philosophy from the theory of critical reflection alone will be to restore to speculative thought all and nothing but its place..."[1] Criticism is arbitrarily restricted because it remains within the confines of thought; it does not criticize thought itself, but only ideas. By artificially abstracting the subjective a priori aspects of ideas from their objective references it brings to light the constitutive role of the subject and the unique characteristics of moral action. What remains to be found is a point of departure which would permit a simultaneous criticism of the whole of reason both practical and speculative. "... The spirit of criticism does not consist merely ... in *criticizing our ideas*; it consists in the investigation of what a given science (and all the sciences together) can and can not hope to accomplish, in brief, *in criticizing knowledge itself*."[2] Thus in Blondel's estimation the basic task of Criticism remained to be accomplished, to establish the value and the limits of all knowledge, both speculative and practical.

THE METHOD OF IMMANENCE

As we have seen, Blondel was of the opinion that it was Spinoza who rightly understood the methodological principle of immanence. This principle is valid only in so far as it can legitimately serve as the principle of a total philosophy. Thus the consistent application of the principle must "open an access to the transcendent." Kant, on the contrary, believed that his immanent critical method resulted in an exclusion of all transcendent reality from speculative thought. The logical result of this exclusion, a conclusion Fichte would draw, would be to erect human subjectivity as an absolute. Blondel saw in this conclusion, not a failure of reflexive criticism as such, but a lack of fidelity to the critical method of immanence itself. To derive such a conclusion one must profit from an ambiguity concerning the words

---

[1] *Ibid.*, I, 359.

[2] Blondel, "Histoire et Dogme," *Les Premiers Ecrits de Maurice Blondel* ("Bibliothèque de Philosophie Contemporaine," Presses Universitaires de France, Paris, 1956), p. 164. Republished from *La Quinzaine*, Tome 56 (1904), 145-167, 349-373, 433-458. Blondel insists on this meaning of criticism in his "Notes for the second edition of *Action*": "I must put across the idea that criticism does not consist in restraining thought in relation to its object, but in determining its role and its function in relation to action and to life." *Etudes Blondéliennes*, Fasc. 2, (Paris: Presses Universitaires de France, 1952), p. 20.

immanent and *transcendent*. If one remains within the restricted framework of our static intellectual representations or ideas, one can distinguish, as Kant did, a subjective and objective pole or reference. In this context the subjective reference can be called immanent in contrast to the objective reference. But if one regards the idea as a whole, both its subjective and objective references are equally immanent to our activity of thinking. "... Our idea of truths or of transcendent exigences, real or not, remains immanent in so far as it is our idea."[1]

Consequently, the true critical method of immanence has as its task to determine what we actually think, the integral series of our inevitable ideas, both in their objective and subjective correlatives. In other words, we must undertake a complete phenomenological investigation of consciousness without any realistic or idealistic prejudice. "... In order to *remain consistent with his critical spirit*, he (Kant) ought simply to have *described the totality of the phenomena of thought and action in consciousness.*"[2] From this perspective practical and speculative reason alike represent legitimately different points of view, but in no way involve an ontological opposition of contradiction. "... No science ... can be irreducibly contradictory to another because none of them contribute an ultimate answer; each ought to concur with the others to furnish the evidence of the metaphysical, moral and religious problem."[3]

Blondel accepted Kant's distinction of the phenomenal and noumenal orders as a methodological procedure, but he rejected what he felt were the unwarranted doctrinal conclusions drawn from that method of procedure.[4] In the third part of *Action*, he proposes to develop all the content implicit in the phenomenon of action (le phénomène de l'action). As his subtitle indicates, Blondel accepts Kant's conception of the order of phenomena or appearances, but only as a hypothesis.

---

[1] Blondel, *Lettre (1896)*, p. 39.

[2] *Ibid.*, p. 62.

[3] *Ibid.*, "Histoire et Dogme," *op. cit.*, p. 166.

[4] By phenomenal order Blondel understood Kant as implying a subjective order of appearances as contrasted with a real, noumenal, or objective order of existing beings. By "noumenal" Kant meant in general the intelligible, that is a positive reality which could be the object of an intellectual intuition. The noumenon in its negative sense signifies the thing-in-itself in so far as it is *not* the object of a sense intuition. In its positive sense it signifies the object of an intellectual intuition. (Confer Kant, *Kritik der reinen Vernunft*, Vol. III, Section 307). According to Kant no intellectual intuition is given or even possible. Thus all human knowledge is limited to the immanent or phenomenal order. Further, phenomenal knowledge

> How one attempts to define action by means of science alone and restrain it to the natural order. ... Perhaps without going outside the phenomenal and by considering it as everything that is, I will be able to form a total idea of my action and find a satisfying solution to the problem of life.[1]

This effort to remain exclusively within the phenomenal order and to find a solution for human destiny within that order, is, then, a hypothesis which by no means implies a doctrinal position. By employing a method of immanence, Blondel does not commit himself to a doctrine of immanence as many of his critics claimed.[2] On the contrary, Blondel sought within the boundaries of the method a refutation of the doctrine.

> Let us consider, then, beginning with the first sensible data, how one tries to confer on the phenomenal order all the consistency and all the sufficiency possible and, always failing in this project, how one will perhaps be drawn on endlessly ever further, not further than one wills, but further than one imagines oneself to will.[3]

The ultimate aim of the critical spirit is to find that viewpoint which transcends all thought and all the sciences; a viewpoint from which one can discover both the continuity and unity of all the sciences as well as their ultimate limitation. That viewpoint, according to Blondel lies in *action*.

> By simply seeking to understand that which we truly and invincibly think, we render evident that truth which dominates all the others and which provokes all the research of science as well as the movement of life: even supposing it complete, thought is different from action and cannot substitute for it.[4]

BLONDEL'S COPERNICAN REVOLUTION

Blondel also wished to achieve a Copernican revolution in philosophical thought; a revolution which would be even more radical than

---

has objective or theoretical validity only when it corresponds to an object given in a sense intuition. Metaphysical objects being by definition suprasensible, no theoretically valid knowledge of them can be had.

[1] Blondel, *L'Action*, pp. 43-44.

[2] "(Philosophy) has arrived at the comprehension that a 'method of immanence' excludes a 'doctrine of immanence'; that is to say that one cannot make the negation of the transcendent or the supernatural a transcendent truth." *Lettre (1896)*, p. 62.

[3] *Ibid.*, p. 44.

[4] *Ibid.*, "L'Illusion Idéaliste," p. 113.

that of Kant. Whereas Blondel understood that the Kantian revolution consisted in considering the object as conformed to our knowledge, his revolution will consist in considering the whole of knowledge both in its objective and subjective correlatives as implying a certain necessary conformity, whether positive or negative, to our voluntary activity. In imitation of Kant's formula, we could formulate Blondel's methodological principle as follows: Hitherto it has been assumed that our action must conform to our ideas. Let us try, then, whether we may not make greater progress in the task of metaphysics, if we assume that our ideas must conform to the action from which they derive and to which they lead. "The problem involves the total man. Consequently one must not search for the answer in thought alone. It will be necessary *to transpose the center of philosophy* into action, because there one finds the center of life."[1]

The Criticist limits the quest for the a priori of morality to the a priori structure of practical knowledge. He thereby limits his effort to give a philosophical answer to human destiny to that which is immanent to thought. "The *fact* of thought is taken in itself, separated from the *act* itself of thinking ... and considered ... as a reality in the air, uprooted from its vital origins, cut off from its natural ramifications."[2] Blondel's contention is that even more immanent than the "thought of action" is "the act of thinking" and action which produces thought and accomplishes it has its own proper a priori structure from which the whole of thought, both in its objective and subjective correlatives, derives its meaning.

> We must never forget, in effect, that every thought is, at one and the same time, act and knowledge; and if that knowledge is the extract or the residue of an entire life which is projected and concentrated in the thought, the act itself which operates that synthesis transcends the abstract representation which remains.[3]

Just as every idea is immanent in the action which produces it and finds its meaning in that action; so too all the sciences are immanent in the human activity which produces them and explains their significance. Nor is philosophy, precisely as a speculative science, free from this basic truth. Critical philosophy can succeed in indicating the limits of knowledge and the means of transcending these limits, but it itself is incapable of that act of transcendence.

---

[1] *Ibid., L'Action*, Introduction, p. XXIII.
[2] *Ibid.*, "L'Illusion Idéaliste," p. 120.
[3] *Ibid.*, p. 115.

... Since critical philosophy is restricted to the task of determining the relation of ideas and practical exigencies, it itself cannot effectively procure a solution to the problem of life, although it defines the conditions under which that problem is capable of solution. Philosophy remains *immanent* in the sense that it shows under what conditions we can attain a transcendental reality ... which remains outside our grasp, not in so far as it is an idea, but in so far as it is a reality.[1]

THE POINT OF DEPARTURE

As we have seen, what Blondel was seeking in his philosophy of action was a methodological point of departure for philosophy which transcended both the realist position of Spinoza and the critical position of Kant. His reflection on Kant's critical philosophy led him to the conclusion that "... there is no direct method by which we can first isolate and afterwards reunite "speculative knowledge" and "practical knowledge'.''[2] The result of taking such a distinction as the point of departure of philosophy is to fall back immediately into the abstract dichotomies of rationalism. As a result we substitute a system of artificial oppositions for the living unity of thought and life.

We have also seen that Blondel accepted Spinoza's insight that the problem proper to philosophy is the problem of human destiny, and that this problem cannot be solved apart from the problem of being. However, contrary to Spinoza's method, the problem of being cannot be liminal. One cannot begin to philosophize by speculating on the possibility of affirming the existence of a certain object. To ask concerning this paper, such as a summary reflection reveals it to me, *if it exists*, when one initially poses that question in such an abstract way, is nothing more than a superficial curiosity which can receive only a verbal answer.[3]

Such an initial affirmation of existence can only be a hybrid mixture of "the abstract existence of *ens generalissimum* with a bit of the concrete essence of the *individua ineffabilia*."[4] Thus, in such a premature affirmation, we are tempted to attach ourselves to our own intellectual representations as if they were distinct and integrating parts of reality.

The metaphysical problem of existence cannot be legitimately posited except in function of the total activity of the mind. "The first

---

[1] *Ibid.*, *Lettres Philosophiques*, p. 106.
[2] Blondel, "Le Point de Départ de la Recherche Philosophique," I, 358.
[3] *Ibid.*, II, 231.
[4] *Ibid.*, II, 245.

task of philosophy is to determine exactly what we think in order to arrive at the definition of those conditions on which those realities which thought inevitably affirms are suspended."[1] Thus the solution to the problem of existence must presuppose this critical study, this phenomenological inventory of the conditions of thought and action, which Blondel maintained was the true purpose of critical philosophy. We must suspend our metaphysical judgment until that critical analysis is completed.

> ... To demand *what a thing is*, to arrive bit by bit at filling out that idea with ever more concrete knowledge, to render explicit all the implicit conditions of that perception which, although it appears simple, is nonetheless an immensely complex synthesis, this is the normal method which, without betraying the realist instinct of thought, does not compromise the critical need of the spirit.[2]

Consequently, Blondel's phenomenology is a parenthesis which he places on the objective value of our necessary and spontaneous existential judgments. It is important to comprehend how he understood that parenthesis. Blondel in no way denies the necessary presence in consciousness of objective existential judgments which resist every effort at critical reduction. "There is a natural knowledge of objects, an inevitable affirmation of their reality which, in fact, rests independent of the explicit and total justification which one can provide for it."[3] Thus Blondel acknowledges the necessity to conceive of objects as objectively existing. Nor does his parenthesis represent a denial of the metaphysical value of that necessity; rather, it involves a critical search for the conditions of its validity. "... The problem is to know under what conditions all those objective realities are really thought and legitimately affirmed; they are so inevitably, but it remains to be defined how and at what price."[4]

What Blondel understands by a philosophical affirmation of objective existence is an *absolute* affirmation. That which ultimately constitutes the existential reality of things is "their connection with the total problem of being." Just as the problem of the destiny of man cannot be solved apart from the solution to the total problem of being, so too, the separate existence of every object poses a philosophical problem which remains unsolved until we understand how that

---

[1] *Ibid., Lettres Philosophiques*, p. 134.

[2] *Ibid.*, "Le Point de Départ de la Recherche Philosophique," II, 231.

[3] *Ibid., Lettres Philosophiques*, p. 166.

[4] *Ibid.*, p. 168.

existence is integrated into the whole of being. "Our intellectual assertions are neither strangers nor indifferent to the reality which they express and by which we live; nor do they deal with the absolute and integral reality of being itself which is the object of knowledge."[1] What Blondel is seeking, then, is the absolute ground on which all existential judgments must ultimately be founded, namely, the existence of the absolute. But in order that our existential judgments be absolutely founded on that existence, it does not suffice to justify a purely speculative objective affirmation of the existence of the absolute. Such a speculative affirmation, as we have seen, can be either privative or possessive of the truth which it necessarily and legitimately affirms. The existential norm which Blondel demands for a valid metaphysical judgment is the actual subjective identity or participation in the existence affirmed.

> ... My *realism* does not consist only in affirming speculatively that the object is, but in affirming that that objective certitude put us in a position to choose the alternatives on which it will depend whether we will be deprived of that objective existence or whether we will possess it.[2]

As we have seen, Blondel's basic methodological principle in his philosophy of action can be expressed in the formula: our ideas are determined by the actions from which they derive and to which they lead. Applied to our idea of God, Blondel sees the speculative affirmation of God as a necessary and inevitable idea which gives expression and direction to a basic subjective movement. This idea in turn leads to the action of option which, if properly made, gives us effective possession of, or rather, participation in the reality which we affirm and choose.

> ... It is necessary, in order to possess the real in ourselves in the very knowledge which we have of it, to pass by means of the option which confers on our speculative idea of things the fullness of its meaning and its content. This is the obvious proof that our intellectual vision, even when it is a logically demonstrated vision of God, is by no means vision in God, nor ontological solution.[3]

However, this existence, objectively affirmed and subjectively possessed, is, as we have seen, not the starting point but the conclusion of the philosophical endeavor. Blondel was convinced that the only valid approach to the problem of being was that which began from

---

[1] *Ibid.*, p. 161.
[2] *Ibid.*, p. 166.
[3] *Ibid.*, p. 165.

within human consciousness and subjectivity. He was in full agreement
with modern philosophy in general that the method of immanence
was a *sine qua non* of philosophy. He was inclined to reject the realist
position as a starting point because he felt that the failure of Spinoza
was conclusive. One could never legitimately understand and integrate
the immanent and subjective into a totally objective concept of being.
But, on the contrary, a method of immanence, properly understood
and employed, could lead to a total philosophy which would embrace
both the immanent and the transcendent, the objective and the subjective, essence and existence, in a higher unity of being.

> *Ab exterioribus ad interiora, ab interioribus ad superiora.* But if, of these
> three terms which Saint Augustine indicates, one suppresses the inter-
> mediary, the bridge is broken, and one has only incommunicable entities
> present to each other. From objective knowledge to the reality of the
> subject, there is no direct route by means of theory or abstract logic.
> One cannot attain or define the transcendent except by the route of
> immanence, exteriority except by interiority.[1]

There is a priority of the subjective over the objective as a starting
point for philosophy. Blondel saw the evolution of philosophy as a
"continual striving towards an ever greater interiorization."[2] He
believed that his idea of action was a further step in that direction.
But he felt that in contrast to Kant's critical idealism, his position
could not be legitimately considered as a subjectivism.

> ... In order that one can speak of subjectivism, one must first of all,
> by an artificial dichotomy, separate and oppose the subjective and the
> objective as distinct entities. To maintain that nothing is given to us
> except as states of consciousness implies a reference to an unconscious
> objectivism. On the contrary, one escapes from this deceiving opposi-
> tion from the moment when one places the point of departure of philos-
> ophy anterior to all realism or idealism, when one is concerned first of
> all to make explicit the given, to ascertain that which we cannot help
> but think, and determine that which we cannot help but include in the
> spontaneous affirmation which is produced in us and thought of as be-
> ing.[3]

While it is true that the subjective moral problem of human destiny
considered immanently provides us with a privileged point of de-

---

[1] *Ibid.*, "Le Point de Départ de la Recherche Philosophique," II, 237.

[2] "It is true that, since Socrates, philosophy in many respects is nothing other
than a prolonged effort to become ever more interior; but it is not subjectivism
which is the normal term of that movement." *Ibid.*, II, 231.

[3] *Ibid.*

parture, such a starting point does not restrict philosophy to the moral problem alone. On the contrary, this problem, if it is posed not as a problem of speculative knowledge alone but as a problem of action, is privileged precisely because it necessarily involves in its solution the whole of reality: the subject, the universe, and God.

> In posing the problem of interior self-adequation, philosophy poses, at the same time, the problem of universal reality under the only form in which it can be resolved. From the apparent *ego* to the integral *ego* there is in effect an infinite to be opened up and filled. To accomplish and possess myself, I must include the universe and God in that need for being, eternity and happiness which constitutes the ego.[1]

The solution to the problem of human destiny necessarily involves the solution of the problem of being, because it necessarily involves our participation in the universe and in divine life. "... The plenitude of being resides exactly in that which separates the abstract idea from the act from which it issues, and from the act to which, as its unique mission, the idea should orient us."[2]

Because of this priority of the subjective or immanent over the objective as a starting point for philosophy, Kant was right to seek in the immanent and subjective moral problem the only valid approach to a restoration of metaphysics. But the true point of departure must not be considered as "... a definition in the intellectual order; one must begin with a *concrete fact* of conscious life in every man."[3] The problem of human destiny is by no means artificial or constructed. It has its roots in a conscious subjective fact which is the implicit dynamic force from which all thought and action, all science and practice derive.

> Anterior to any speculative prejudice, that which is given is neither a determined static reality, nor a process of becoming; it is what Malebranche called "anxiety" (l'inquiétude), that state of perpetually unstable equilibrium and intrinsic disproportion, such that every effort undertaken to satisfy previous exigencies, which manifest themselves spontaneously to thought, reveals further exigencies which impose themselves morally on action.[4]

---

[1] *Ibid.*, II, 237.

[2] *Ibid.*, "L'Illusion Idéaliste," p. 116.

[3] Confer also "Notes for the second edition of *Action*": "I need not search for that which *man* is *in se*, in the abstract. One cannot *know* him as such. There is only question of searching for self *in concreto*—in the determinism of lived consciousness." *loc. cit.*, p. 34.

[4] *Ibid.*, "Le Point de Départ de la Recherche Philosophique," II, 234.

Since the philosophical process has its true origin in this existential anxiety which is the source of all human thought and activity, one can understand why the problem of both realism and idealism, the question of the relation of thought to its object, is merely an abstract aspect of this more fundamental problem. The unknown to be discovered by philosophy is not an objective definition of being but the conditions necessary in order to achieve that total fulfillment or equilibrium, that real identity with self, of which our actual thoughts and actions are both the effects and the means. And, Blondel argues, whereas that abstract problem has proven incapable of an ultimate solution, the real living problem of our adequation with ourselves is necessarily solvable.

> As long as we see the X to be discovered in the relation of thought and object, as long as one pretends to penetrate into the subject by means of a dialectical analysis which effectively treats the subject once again as an object, there is no solution and no real progress is conceivable. But it is altogether different once the unknown is within us, is ourselves; once, in a word, the truth to be conquered is not an external abstraction, but an internal concrete reality.[1]

This unknown interior equation of ourselves with ourselves is factually resolved, for better or for worse, at every moment of our life by the action to which we are committed. The role of philosophy is to render explicit and to engender as far as possible the true, most perfect response to that inevitable problem.

> For if the X of objective thought is inaccessible and indeterminable, the X of our own proper equation with ourselves can be obtained and determined step by step... The solution is already within us, already provisionally determined by each of our moments which could be our last; that solution is produced and enriched by the very effort which we make to clarify it.[2]

THE MEANING OF ACTION

It is the totality of this constant movement towards self-fulfillment, the constant searching of self-adequation, which Blondel wished to designate by the terms philosophy of action.

---

[1] *Ibid.*, "L'Illusion Idéaliste," p. 111.
[2] *Ibid.*

> For the sake of designating that melange of obscure potentialities, conscious tendencies, and implicit anticipations, the word *action* seems well chosen. For it comprehends both the latent potentialities, the known actualizations, and the confused presentiments of all that in us which produces, clarifies, and animates the movement of life.[1]

It is very important to note that action, as Blondel understood it, is not the *object* of his philosophical study. This would necessarily involve that objectification, that substitution of the idea of action for the living reality which was precisely the charge Blondel made against exaggerated criticism. Action is not seen as in opposition to thought. Rather, thought is seen as contained within action: "... study, in action, that which precedes and prepares, that which produces and nourishes, that which follows and develops the fact itself of distinct thought."[2] Action, then, is the "center of perspective," in a sense, the instrument itself which the philosopher employs.[3]

> Action ... indicates principally that human composite, that synthesis "of body and soul", that unity half ideal and half real which makes action an incomparable *center of perspective*, a meeting place between the determinism of thought and the determinism of nature, the point of repère and of departure for a double investigation which tends to render thought one with action and action one with thought.[4]

The unique value of action as a center of perspective lies in the fact that human action is the meeting place between liberty and determinism, between thought and being. Action is, so to speak, the incarnation of thought in being. "There is in action an element which, even when entirely penetrated by knowledge, is more than knowledge itself."

Blondel also employs the terms "philosophy of action" to indicate that what he proposes is a *genetic* study, which traces the unfolding of action in our intellectual and moral life.

> ... In place of the reasoning processes concerning our concepts and our perceptions in order to draw metaphysical, critical and relativist

---

[1] *Ibid.*, "Le Point de Départ de la Recherche Philosophique," II, 234-235.

[2] *Ibid.*, "Lettre concernant le rapport A. Lalande: "Constitution d'un Vocabulaire Philosophique," *Bulletin de la Société Française de Philosophie*, Tome 2, (1902) Discussion of 22 May, 1902, p. 182.

[3] This idea of action as the "instrument" of philosophy will be discussed later in the next chapter under the heading "The Science of the Practical." Confer below, pp. 94-98.

[4] Blondel, *Lettres Philosophiques*, p. 82. Confer also the entry "Action" in *Vocabulaire Techniques et Critique de la Philosophie*, 1926, p. 17; 1947, pp. 20-21.

theses from that *logomachie*, one must first of all study *ideogenesis*, seek out the beginning and consequences of our states of consciousness.[1]

As we have seen, Blondel maintained that even more immanent than the "thought of action" is "the act of thinking"; and this action which produces thought has its own proper a priori structure from which the whole of thought derives its meaning. It is the study of ideogenesis which should lead us to a knowledge of that a priori structure in the act of thinking. This genetic study should be extended not only to personal thought but to the whole scientific endeavor of humanity as revelatory of human nature and destiny.

> It is no less important to study the *fieri* than the *esse* of the sciences, ... the object of philosophy is not purely science already constituted; it is the *genesis* of the sciences, the process of the mind which spontaneously produces scientific ideas. ... Consider the effort of science as an infinitely enlarged, enriched and precise expression of the initial activity of the mind.[2]

This genetic study of thought and action will result in an understanding of the structure implicit in the will itself. "... It is the relation of the will-willing and the will-willed which we must determine, and thought is nothing more than the middle term, the fruit of action and the seed of action."[3] Blondel contends that within the unified and total action which constitutes our person there is an internal principle which orients, demands and judges all our fragmentary thoughts and actions. It is this internal principle which spontaneously determines our intellectual and moral ideas. Consequently this a priori structure present in the will ultimately explains the a priori necessity and structure in our thought. Thought is seen as giving an ideal expression to the aspirations hidden in that a priori structure of the will and, thus, arousing that conscious anxiety or sense of disproportion between the actual and the potential within us.

> ... It is in order to achieve a clear consciousness of that primal orientation, to determine and realize those normative exigencies, to discover and anticipate those judgments that philosophy must work, so that it can integrate into consciousness and science all that is spontaneous in life, and in order to integrate into life all those truths which are manifest in consciousness and science.[4]

---

[1] *Ibid.*, *Lettres Philosophiques*, p. 83.
[2] *Ibid.*, p. 185.
[3] *Ibid.*, p. 84.
[4] *Ibid.*, "Le Point de Départ de la Recherche Philosophique," II, 235.

Traditional philosophy, the philosophy of ideas, conceived of its task as a search for abstract truth, an *adequatio speculativa rei et intellectus*. Blondel's philosophy of action is an intellectual search for the meaning of the fulfillment of human life and action. The acquisition of speculative truth is seen as a subordinate part of that enterprise. Thus he proposes to substitute for the search of abstract truth, a search for concrete reality, an *adequatio realis mentis et vitae*.[1]

SUMMARY

Blondel believed that the critical movement, introduced into modern philosophy by Kant, was a legitimate and even necessary movement in philosophical thought. It corresponded in the science of philosophy to the reflexive movement in individual thought. By means of Criticism, philosophy had been freed from that realistic illusion which was the cause of Spinoza's failure in his *Ethics*. Further, the critical isolation of moral activity had served to bring to light and clarify the specific characteristics of moral activity. But the true point of departure for philosophical research is neither the critical act of reflection nor a realistic affirmation of existence. If one accepts either of these starting points, one will inevitably introduce an artificial and arbitrary division into reality or being itself, and end up by giving substantial or ontological value to that abstract aspect of the real to which one's methodological starting point committed oneself.

Consequently, the primary task of Criticism, according to Blondel, still remained to be accomplished; namely, to find that point of departure by means of which it could transcend its own limits. Criticism must forsake its claim to give a final answer to the problem of human destiny and be content to determine the necessary limits of all thought and science. In fact, in order to be logically consistent with itself, Criticism must determine the limits of speculative philosophy itself. It must determine what philosophy can and cannot hope to contribute to the solution of the problem of life; where exactly philosophy must by its very nature abdicate in favor of a superior instrument. This search for the limit of philosophical knowledge involves a phenomenological analysis of the whole of knowledge and science independent of any realist or idealist presupposition. This analysis, Blondel believed, will lead us to the fundamental truth, that action is

---

[1] *Ibid.*

the limit of all knowledge. "... Just as it is useful in mathematics to study the limiting factor, so too it is useful in philosophy to refer philosophy to its limit, action."[1]

All human thought has its source in action. Even more immanent in man than his thought is his activity of thinking. This activity of thinking is a conscious activity. It is precisely in his activity that man has conscious awareness of his subjective identity with himself. Thus Blondel was convinced that the starting point of philosophy lies in this consciousness of self in action. However, there is no question of subjective conscious activity serving as an *object* of reflection. To so objectify this conscious awareness would be to substitute, once again, the idea or theory of action for action itself and, thus, to fall back into that abstract dichotomy which was in Blondel's judgment the primary flaw in Kant's *Critique of Practical Reason*. Rather man's immanent conscious identity with himself in his actions will serve, not as the object, but as the *center of perspective* or methodological point of departure for his philosophical endeavor. The unique value of this starting point is its completeness. For it is only as immanent in our conscious identity with ourselves in our actions that the subjective and the objective, freedom and necessity, essence and existence, coexist in the synthesis of being without those apparent contradictions which they manifest in the abstractions of thought.

The primary characteristic of this conscious identity with self is its dynamism; or, as Blondel called it, "anxiety." In our activity we have conscious awareness of ourselves as a perpetual state of unstable equilibrium, as being intrinsically disproportioned with ourselves. All our activity of thinking and doing is seen as a necessary means which, paradoxically, we freely employ to quiet that anxiety and achieve that stability and that total identity of self with self which is man's destiny. Thus, this conscious experience of anxiety or instability serves as the existential ground which justifies the distinction within the human will as source of that activity of a potential and actual metaphysical principle. By the terms will-willing and will-willed Blondel wished to designate that unlimited potency in man for an ever more perfect living identity with himself in consciousness, which is more or less actualized by every specific thought or action. From this center of perspective all specific thoughts and deeds are considered as symptomatic of that hidden structure within the human will from which they

---

[1] *Ibid., Lettres Philosophiques*, p. 84.

derive their existence and their ultimate value. Thus, the phenomenological investigation of consciousness should lead to a genetic study
of thought and action, an effort to comprehend that principle interior
to the will which is the source of all partial thoughts and acts and the
norm by which we can judge their efficacy. That which is a priori in
thought should serve as a means of understanding that which is the
a priori structure of the human will.

> It is the relation of the will-willing and the will-willed which we must
> determine, rectify and lead back to its identity. And knowledge is
> nothing more than the middle term, the fruit of action and the seed of
> action, which has as its function to lead action to that immediation of
> identity with self.[1]

Philosophy, then, is seen as a critical search, undertaken from the
immanent perspective of action, for the necessary conditions of the
perfect accomplishment of action, a search to know what action or
actions will effectively lead to that perfect identity of will, that perfect
equilibrium of self with self, that *adequatio realis mentis et vitae*, which is
the destiny of man. When it has found those conditions, philosophy
has found its limits. For thought can not effectively substitute itself
for action.

Once again in the light of more recent interpretations of Kantianism
one can question to what extent Blondel's idea of a "Critique of Life"
actually goes beyond at least the intention if not the reality of Kant's
Critiques and especially his *Critique of Judgment*. The interpretation of
Kant's thought which one finds in Nabert's *Avertissement à Kant*, for
example, or more recently in Eric Weil's *Problèmes Kantiens*, present
Kant himself as employing a method remarkably close to that which
we have described here as Blondel's "Ultra-Kantian Critique". Despite
the various dichotomies in Kant's thought, Nabert contends, "it is
quite apparent that the concern to establish a concrete knowledge of
nature and to develop a concrete morality also penetrates his entire
doctrine."[2]

What remains certain is that this idea of criticism, man's laborious
searching out of the value and limits of his knowledge and action

---

[1] *Ibid.*

[2] Jean Nabert, "Avertissement à Kant," *La Philosophie de l'Histoire de Kant*
("Bibliothèque philosophique" Paris: Aubier, 1947). Jean Lacroix, in his recent
work, *Maurice Blondel, Sa Vie, Son Oeuvre*, inaugurates a comparison between
Nabert's interpretation of Kantian ethics in his work *Eléments pour une Ethique*,
(Paris: Presses Universitaires de France, 1943) and Blondel's *Action*. Confer
Lacroix, *op. cit.*, pp. 64-67.

combined, was the central inheritance from Kant which Blondel employed in his critical effort to assimilate all that was of value in subsequent absolute idealism without, however, falling victim to what he considered as its uncritical absolutism.

Delbos once claimed that what preserved him against the temptation of Hegel's absolute knowledge and its pantheistic implications was the critical spirit he inherited from Kant. This led him to realize constantly the limits of the human spirit and, thus, to forsake any metaphysics which sought to be the human manner of approaching a divine knowledge of Being.[1] If it was "the secret presence of the Christian idea" which according to Blondel led Spinoza to seek man's destiny in terms of a union in love with God, it was that same secret Christian idea which led Kant to destroy critically the human pretension to a self-elevation to that union by means of metaphysical knowledge.

---

[1] Delbos' statement concerning the influence of Kantian criticism on his thought is reported by Raissa Maritain in her work, *Les Grandes Amitiés*, (Bruges: Desclée et Brouwer, s.d.) p. 103.

CHAPTER FIVE

ACTION: A GENETIC STUDY OF THE SYNTHETIC A PRIORI

INTRODUCTION

While he was in the process of writing his thesis on the philosophy of action, Blondel composed three preliminary redactions before that of 1892 which was submitted to the Sorbonne.[1] At the end of the third redaction, that of 1890 entitled "Projet de Thèse", he wrote a conclusion in which for the first time he attempted to render explicit the original methodology involved in his effort to create a philosophy of action. He speaks of two keys ideas, the synthesis of which would form the originality of his methodology.

> The unique inspiration of this work of philosophical apologetics has brought together two ideas in order to produce their synthesis. It is now necessary to dissociate these ideas in order to make a rapid résumé of the movement of thought and in order to formulate more clearly the purpose which has been the source of this entire undertaking.[2]

Blondel designates one of these two key ideas as the concept of the synthetic a priori which he had received from Kant. In fact, the whole of the dynamic development of his philosophy of action is described as a genetic study of the synthetic a priori.[3] What exactly was the role of this Kantian idea and how Blondel made use of it will be the central object of a final investigation into the relationship between Blondel's philosophy of action and Kant's philosophy of practical reason.

---

[1] For a history of the various redactions of *Action*, confer the article of Henri Bouillard, "Le Dernier Chapitre de 'L'Action'." (Confer page 43, footnote 2.)

[2] Blondel, *Projet de Thèse*, "Conclusion" p. 185. The unedited manuscript is to be found in the Blondel Archives at Aix-en-Provence. The importance of these two ideas, the synthetic a priori and, as we shall see later in the chapter on logic, the concept of a dialectical logic, for the consequent development of Blondel's systematic philosophical thought is particularly noticeable when one reads the various redactions of his thesis in their temporal order. Until this conclusion of the third redaction, *Action* for the most part took the form of a moralizing tract without particular philosophical originality. But from this point on the original philosophical genius and inspiration became more and more evident.

[3] Confer above pp. 61-72, where we discussed Blondel's idea of *Action* as a genetic study or *ideogenesis*.

Although he accepted the idea of the synthetic a priori from Kantian thought, Blondel believed that he had transformed that idea in terms of his second Copernican revolution. Just as the "action of thinking" is prior to the "thought of action", so also prior to the synthetic a priori structure present in reason as such, he maintained, there is a vital synthetic a priori structure in action. This living synthetic a priori structure can be determined by a "Critique of Life" which would take the form of a genetic study of the a priori in reason. This genetic study would result in a "Science of Action."

Our first objective is to determine what Blondel meant by the synthetic a priori of action. In terms of this synthetic a priori Blondel believed that he could overcome all the dichotomies which he found in Kantian criticism. Thus we will examine briefly how Blondel attempted to overcome the dualisms of speculation and practice, pure and applied science, necessity and freedom, metaphysics and morality, by means of his science of the synthetic a priori function of action. This outline leads us into the question of what Blondel meant by an experimental or a posteriori science of action. The chapter ends with discussion of the relation of Blondel's idea of a second metaphysics with Kant's concept of a restored metaphysics based on practical reason.

THE CONCEPT OF A METAPHYSICAL SYNTHESIS

Blondel speaks of two central ideas, the synthesis of which forms the originality of his method. The second of these ideas, he tells us, has a "metaphysical character and a moral form." This second idea is entitled "The science of moral experimentation and the metaphysical synthesis of action." In the opening paragraph he tells us that this idea has to do with the reality and origin of the composite.

> The dominant idea of all philosophy, in the middle ages as in our own day, has been to know whether or not the composite has its own proper reality; if, up to a certain point, it is distinct from its elements and independent of its conditions of existence. This was the great argument on substantial forms of the Schoolmen; the great debate, with Descartes and Leibnitz, on the reality of corporal multiplicity and on the substantial unity of sensible phenomena; the great difficulty, with Hume and Kant, concerning the value of the unity of consciousness and perception, and the great battle today with the phenomenists and the evolutionists concerning the solidarity of integrated phenomena and organized species.[1]

---

[1] Blondel, *Projet de Thèse*, p. 192.

The problem, as Blondel sees it, is the metaphysical nature of the composite as such. Does a composite being have a substantial unity, a proper existence, which renders it a being apart, irreducible to its elements or conditions of existence? He understands this properly ontological problem to be the real issue underlying the epistemological difficulty of Hume and Kant concerning the unity of consciousness or perception.

It was Hume's psychological and empirical doctrine about the origin and formation of ideas which posed the problem of the nature and value of scientific knowledge for Kant. Hume's method, Blondel contends, was one of exclusively reductive analysis; the complex finds its total explanation in its constitutive elements. The synthesis as such is a psychological phenomenon, an illusion, without objective value. For example, the self is resolved into a series of distinct perceptions. On the contrary, Kant, in his *Critique of Pure Reason*, introduced the concept of a synthetic a priori proposition as an explanation of the nature and universal value of scientific ideas.[1] Kant conceived of metaphysics also as consisting exclusively of synthetic a priori propositions.[2] In other words, each metaphysical proposition represents a unique hypothesis, whose connection cannot be analytically demonstrated without logical inconsistency; nor is it a contingent fact derived from experience.

Blondel also maintained that there are synthetic a priori propositions. In keeping with his perspective, he understands these synthetic a priori ideas or propositions as the fruit of the living existential a priori synthesis present in human action.

> Now I have held, as founded on evidence, that the whole is distinct from the sum of its parts everywhere where there is a synthesis properly speaking; the unity of the whole is something extra, something other than the totality of the elements. There is, then, in opposition to the analytical sciences of positive conditions and subordinated elements, another science to be constituted which deals with the successive syntheses, the ideal realities, the intelligible forms; a science which is equally positive and more real than the others.[3]

---

[1] A synthetic proposition is one in which we affirm or deny of a subject a predicate which is not contained in the concept of the subject. The synthetic proposition is a posteriori if the connection is factual or contingent, that is, given in or through sense experience. It is a priori when the connection cannot be known by the mere analysis of the subject, but is, nonetheless, necessary and strictly universal. The positivists deny the existence of such a proposition, maintaining that all necessary propositions are a priori, and all synthetic propositions are a posteriori and, consequently, not necessary. Confer Kant, *Kritik der reinen Vernunft*, Sections 11-19.

[2] *Ibid.*, Section 19.

[3] Blondel, *Projet de Thèse*, p. 192.

The problem of the influence of a priori forms on sensation was the theme of the first known publication of Blondel entitled "An Inseparable Association: The Growth of Stars at the Horizon."[1]

Blondel examines the evidence for the cause of the phenomenon of the seeming expansion of the stars and planets as they approach the horizon. He excludes any purely physical explanation and derives the conclusion that there is a sort of preconscious logic which regulates the genesis of sensation itself.[2] Thus sensible data enter consciousness only after they have already undergone a logical elaboration.

Blondel concludes that in the subjective preconscious life of man there is a special logic or rationality at play. If we could discover and understand the laws of that logic immanent in life, we could comprehend the meaning of what factually appears as an illusion. "If space is an illusion, it is a normal illusion directed to an end, and we must account for the useful, intelligible and in certain regards truthful "deception"." Thus, he writes of Kant's theory of the a priori forms of sensation in the notes for the second edition of *Action*: "If then he (Kant) was right to declare, for example, the subjective character of those things which involve space and time, he was wrong not to have recognized his own "idealist illusion," and to have failed to determine the conditions, inevitably required by the spirit, for the objectivity of matter and all things which impose themselves on us."[3]

The problem which both Kant and Blondel faced was to explain the genesis or origin of such synthetic a priori propositions. Kant had recourse to what he called the act of constructing. A synthetic a priori proposition cannot be deduced rationally, nor given empirically. Therefore, the existence of such a proposition must be ascribed to an a priori intuition. The intuition is a priori because no object is given to which the intuition corresponds. Therefore, to explain the origin of such an intuition Kant maintains that we are able to construct in our mind ideas or objects which enable us to enunciate synthetic a priori propositions. Kant illustrated this with the geometrical procedure of constructing the idea of circle or triangle.

Blondel poses the same problem, namely, the origin of synthetic a priori phenomena, and he finds the answer in action. "But what is it

---

[1] Blondel, "Une Association Inséparable: L'Agrandissement des Astres à l'Horizon," *Revue Philosophique de la France et de l'Etranger*, Tome 26, (1888), pp. 489-497; Tome 27 (1889), pp. 197-199.

[2] *Ibid.*, Tome 27, p. 199.

[3] Blondel, *Etudes Blondéliennes*, No. 2, p. 15.

which operates and explains this synthesis? It is action. How does this reality manifest itself? In its very self-production by action (en se faisant, par l'action)."[1] In his study of the nature of mathematical phenomena, in *Action* Blondel accepts Kant's analysis of the constructive a priori nature of mathematical syntheses. But he poses a further question. Why does the human intelligence spontaneously tend to construct these synthetic a priori intuitions? He finds the answer, once again, in the internal structure of will-activity.

> These sciences rise up from the very foundation of our activity and are spontaneously organized under the rule of that same interior law which governs all our life. Thus even mathematics will be seen as a form of the development of the will; it will enter into the series of means which we employ to resolve the problem of action; it will become, by means of the enlightened knowledge which we will have of our acts, that which it is in the living reality of our operations, one element of the solution.[2]

But going a step further Blondel finds in the synthetic function of action the only answer to the problem posed by the synthetic nature of experimental sciences. "Neither experience can furnish us with the purely abstract, nor number the true concrete; for mathematics is founded precisely on the premise that a real analysis can be carried on *ad infinitum*; and experimentation on the premise that mathematical construction can never produce a real synthesis."[3] The paradoxes of Zeno retain all their force for speculative thought. But the ancient retort to the paradox of Achilles and the turtle, *solvitur ambulando*, contains within itself the germ of the solution. The dilemma of the contradictory nature of mathematical and physical reality is resolved in fact; and it is by his synthetic activity that man effectively produces that solution. All the antinomies which Kant discovered in the domain of metaphysical speculation are equally present within the domain of the positive sciences themselves.

> It was on the possibility of synthetic a priori judgments that Kant made metaphysics depend. In other words, it is the possible conciliation between the a priori of analytic synthesis and the a posteriori of synthetic analysis which is in question. But it is within the domain of the sciences that the conflict and the reconciliation have taken place without one's being obliged to consider the phenomena other than phenomena, nor to suppose anything else apart from or beyond them.[4]

---

[1] Blondel, *op. cit.*, p. 192.
[2] Blondel, *L'Action*, p. 55. footnote 1.
[3] *Ibid.*, d. 79.
[4] *Ibid.*, p. 80.

Thus, not only the constructions of mathematics but also the application of mathematics to sensible phenomena in the applied sciences can only be explained in terms of our voluntary activity which constructs the synthesis. "The positive sciences do not subsist except by reason of a permanent postulate. They have a continual need to admit that the intelligible or organic systems that they consider are distinct from the elements from which they are formed, and that the synthesis and the analysis are not reciprocal."[1]

Blondel sees in the a priori synthetic function of action a universal law. In every step of the development of human action we have to do with a new and unique level of a priori synthesis. But what exactly is the essential characteristic of this a priori synthetic unity? Blondel finds that characteristic in its subjectivity. "... Each synthesis is something original, irreducible to its components, and it is in its subjective reality that the new excellence of each degree of composition resides."[2] The unity of every synthetic a priori reality resides in "an internal relation of parts, an ideal projection of the whole on a center of perception."[3] But such a unity partakes already of the intelligible and, in a certain way, of the subjective, in the sense that it implies a within, an interiority.

> ... In all scientific truth, as in every human reality, in order that it be known, one must suppose a center of concentration imperceptible to the senses or to the mathematical imagination, an operation immanent to the diversity of its parts, an organic idea, an original action which escapes positive knowledge at the very moment that it renders that knowledge possible. That is — a *subjectivity*.[4]

Now, the subject, or ego itself, in its conscious activity is a synthesis of pre-conscious energies and the source of a new synthesizing power. The diffusion of reflexes cannot result in action except on condition that they are represented in a conscious synthetic idea. In order to become an effective principle of action, these diffused energies must be gathered in a mental synthesis and represented under the form of an end to be realized. "... Consciousness results from a series of elementary pre-conscious acts. ... It constitutes a synthesis and a distinct act; it prepares and inaugurates a series of new acts ... which it proposes to itself as an end."[5] Blondel insists once again in terms of his Copern-

---

[1] *Ibid.*, p. 87.
[2] *Ibid.*, p. 96.
[3] *Ibid.*, p. 89.
[4] *Ibid.*, p. 87.
[5] *Ibid.*, p. 109.

ican revolution that we must pass from the idea of synthesis to the very act of synthesis. It is not enough to posit the fact of consciousness or ego in order to explain the process of synthesis from without. We must place ourselves within the dynamic point of view of that subjective activity itself.

> There is nothing in the properly subjective life which is not act. That which is properly subjective is not only that which is conscious and known from within (every phenomenon, if correctly understood, is that); it is that which causes the fact of consciousness to be; it is the internal and ever singular act of thinking. ... One cannot penetrate that living reality except by placing oneself, not in the static point of view of the understanding, but at the dynamic point of view of the will. One must try not to imagine action, because it is action itself which creates the symbols and the world of the imagination. The true science of the subject is that which, considering from its point of departure the act of consciousness precisely as act, discovers in that act by a continual process its inevitable expansion.[1]

The Synthetic a priori in Moral Activity

There is a sharp distinction between the application Kant made of the synthetic a priori in pure reason and the application which he made of it in practical reason. These two reasons are, according to Kant, "... ultimately one and the same reason which has to be distinguished simply in its applications."[2] The application of practical reason is distinguished from that of pure reason because it is concerned, not with determining the object which has been given from some other source; rather, it is concerned "... with the grounds of the determination of the will, which is a power either of producing objects corresponding to ideas or of determining itself to produce them (whether the physical power to do so is sufficient or not), that is, of determining its causality."[3] Thus practical reason is directed towards choice in

---

[1] *Ibid.*, pp. 99-100.

[2] Kant, *Grundlegung zur Metaphysik der Sitten*, "Vorrede", *loc. cit.* Vol. IV, p. 391: "... weil es doch am Ende nur eine und dieselbe Vernunft sein kann, die Bloss in der Anwendung unterschieden sein muss."

[3] Kant, *Kritik der praktischen Vernunft*, "Einleitung," Vol. V, Sections 29-30: "In diesem beschäftigt sich die Vernunft mit Bestimmungsgründen des Willens, welcher ein Vermögen ist, den Vorstellungen entsprechende Gegenstände entwieder hervorzubringen, oder doch sich selbst zu Bewirkung derselben (das physische Vermögen mag nun hinreichend sein, oder nicht), d.i. seine Causalität, zu bestimmen."

accordance with moral law and, when physically possible, the implementation of choice in action.

In the *Critique of Practical Reason* Kant is exclusively interested in determining the a priori or formal elements of morality. He deliberately excludes the a posteriori or empirical elements of an applied ethics from his consideration. Further he explicitly rejected the idea of founding a metaphysics of morals on human nature or experience. "... The basis of obligation must not be sought in human nature or in the circumstances of the world in which he (man) is placed, but a priori simply in the concepts of pure reason." A pure formal ethics must be worked out which "... when applied to man, does not borrow the least thing from the knowledge of man himself, but gives laws a priori to him as a rational being."[1] Thus Kant is interested in the study of practical reason *as such*, that is, as applicable to all possible rational beings capable of being subject to obligation and not exclusively to man.

The most fundamental a priori factor of morality is, according to Kant, the concept of duty or obligation. This concept is formulated in the categorical imperative, "act only on the maxim through which you can at the same time will that it should become a universal law."[2] Duty, then, is the necessity of acting out of reverence for the law and it is precisely its universality which is the distinguishing characteristic of the law. Thus the "oughtness" of the imperative manifests a certain necessity and strict universality. But as the word "ought" implies, the will remains free to ratify or reject the imperative.

The problem which Kant poses is to prove that such a categorical imperative exists.[3] This proof takes the form of a search for a synthetic a priori connection between the concept of rational will as such and the categorical imperative. That which serves the will as objective ground of its self-determination is the end. We know beforehand that to fulfil its role as the ground of necessary and universal law for all rational beings this end or connecting link must have the absolute value of an end in itself.[4] Kant finds this absolute value of end in itself in the rational will of man regarded precisely as autonomous or capable of freely legislating for itself. Thus the necessary condition for the possibility of obligation is the idea of freedom or the autonomy of the

[1] Kant, *Grundlegung zur Metaphysik der Sitten*, "Vorrede", Vol. IV, p. 389.
[2] *Ibid.*, p. 421.
[3] *Ibid.*, p. 425.
[4] *Ibid.*, pp. 428-429.

rational will. Freedom or the autonomous will is the a priori agent capable of synthesizing universal laws of reason with moral action.

> And thus categorical imperatives are possible because the idea of freedom makes me a member of an intelligible world, in consequence of which, supposing that I were nothing else, all my actions *would* always conform to the autonomy of the will; but as I at the same time intuit myself as a member of the world of sense, my actions *ought* so to conform. And this *categorical* "ought" implies a synthetic *a priori* proposition...[1]

We have already seen that it was the problem of human destiny as such which served Blondel as his starting point in his moral philosophy. In direct contrast with Kant's procedure of first determining the absolutely formal principles of morality for all rational beings and only afterwards seeking their application to man, Blondel searches within man's consciousness of his own moral experiences and activity for the a priori structure of moral philosophy. Corresponding to this reversal of starting points, is a reversal of process in moral philosophy itself. As we have seen, Kant postulates the idea of freedom as the synthetic agent in moral obligation and maintains that "it is the idea of freedom which makes me a member of an intelligible world". From the point of view of action Blondel, on the contrary, sees reason as the source of our necessary idea of liberty. The problem he poses initially is "How is reason constituted in regard to consciousness, and how does (reason) ... result in the necessary idea of liberty?"[2] Blondel's search for the meaning of moral obligation begins with the necessary genesis of the universal or metaphysical idea in consciousness. "One cannot understand the parts except by the whole; one does not know the whole except by distinguishing himself from the *universe* by the perception of the universal." Blondel calls this awareness of the universal the relative infinite; that is "that which transcends all distinct representations and every determined motive."[3] The very presence of this universal idea or relative infinite in consciousness gives us an awareness of ourselves as distinct from the universe. The conscious-

---

[1] *Ibid.*, p. 454:
Und so sind kategorische imperativen möglich, dadurch das die Idee der Freiheit mich zu einem Gliede einer intelligibilen Welt macht, wodurch, wenn ich solches allein wäre, alle meine Handlungen der Autonomie des Willens jederzeit gemäss sein *würden*, da ich mich aber zugleich als Glied der Sinnenwelt anschaue, gemäss sein *söllen*, welches *kategorische* Sollen einen synthetischen Satz a priori vorstellt.
[2] Blondel, *L'Action*, p. 117.
[3] *Ibid.*, p. 118.

ness of that action itself which gives birth to the idea of this relative infinite leads us necessarily to the idea of freedom. We necessarily conceive of ourselves as capable of the infinite, as having a creative power of act which transcends all particular determinations.

> The consciousness of a motive is always accompanied by the presence of other motives; the awareness of a multiplicity of reasons for action implies at least a confused idea of their opposition and the system they form; the consciousness of these contrasts contained within an organized unity is necessarily accompanied by the thought of that which is inaccessible to relativity and limitation, the presence, known and possessed, of an absolute, the regulative idea of the infinite.[1]

Thus our conscious action "cannot be explained nor given its total reason except in terms of a principle irreducible to either the facts of consciousness or to the sensible phenomena."[2]

Consequently, whereas Kant postulates freedom or autonomy as the necessary condition for the existence of obligation, Blondel attempts to trace the genesis of the idea of freedom as a further product of the necessary determinism of human action.

> ... In order to act one must participate in an infinite power; to have consciousness of action it is necessary that one have consciousness of that infinite power. It is, then, in the rational act that there is synthesis of the potency and the idea of the infinite, and that synthesis is what is called liberty.[3]

The rational human act is, then, a synthesis of our necessary idea of ourselves as infinite, transcendent, creative or autonomous with the infinite potential resident in our will. And the necessary idea of such a synthesis is the necessary idea of liberty. In all our free acts we are conscious that "to that which is insufficient to determine it, (the will) adds from its own sufficiency to determine itself."[4]

Kant, Blondel held, understood freedom and necessity, the autonomous action of the will and the determinism of nature and thought, if not as contradictory, at least as exclusive of one another. Blondel himself sees them as continuous and complementary. Liberty springs from one necessity and leads to another. It springs from the determinism of nature and leads to the determinism of thought. "... Liberty consists in creating a new order, distinct from nature ... It is that ac-

---

[1] *Ibid.*, p. 117.
[2] *Ibid.*, p. 119.
[3] *Ibid.*, p. 121.
[4] *Ibid.*, p. 130.

tion, ultimate and essential, by which we substitute for the determinism of inferior desires, the determinism of pure reason and obligation."[1] In fact, Blondel's major criticism of Kant's moral philosophy was, as we have seen, this tendency to establish a dichotomy between theoretical reason, which reflects the absolute determinism of nature, and practical reason, which reflects the absolute autonomy of the will. Because of this dualism Blondel accuses Kant of giving metaphysical value to the phenomenal order and thus transforming what should have been only a methodological procedure into a metaphysical doctrine.[2]

> If at times the determinism of thought and nature has seemed to be in contradiction with liberty, it is only because one has attached an ontological value to both of them and because one deals with these positive facts and states of consciousness as if they were absolute beings which fall under the application of the principle of contradiction.[3]

Strict contradiction can only be had where there is question of substantial realities. Thus, if Kant finds an absolute dichotomy between the phenomenon of determinism and the phenomenon of liberty, it is because he has implicitly attributed the metaphysical value of being or *ens in se* to the very phenomena which by his own definition are only the appearances of being. "There is solidarity between reason and liberty, between the consciousness of the infinite and the power of the infinite."[4]

---

[1] Blondel, *Lettres Philosophiques*, p. 15.

[2] In one sense Kant's concept of the dualism of practical and theoretical reason can be seen as a return to Descartes' position. The basic problem which Kant faced in *The Critique of Pure Reason* was the same as that of Descartes, namely, the necessity to found Newtonian physics. The difference lies in the fact that Kant could not share the confidence of Descartes in the power of traditional metaphysics to perform that task. Kant was convinced that Hume's psychological explanations of knowledge had established the point that we should not expect to derive any necessity or strict universality whatever from objective experience.

But Kant and Descartes were in complete accord in their refusal to extend mechanical causality and determinism to include man in his totality as did Spinoza. They both maintained a sharp dualism in the sense that the laws of determinism and causality hold good in the material world, while teleology and freedom belong exclusively to the spiritual world. Thus for Kant there are two main objects of wonder, the starry heavens above (the symbol of causal determinacy), and the moral law within. Descartes, however, was inclined to assign the source of moral values to the transcendent divine will and to make of faith a sort of fideism. Kant, as Blondel understood him, finds that source immanent in the human will and reduces faith to a sort of pragmatic rationalism. As we shall see, Blondel will search for a source of moral values which is simultaneously immanent and transcendent. For he was convinced that only by means of such a source could a rational faith be justified.

[3] Blondel, *L'Action*, p. 122.

[4] *Ibid.*, p. 120.

THE GENESIS OF THE CONCEPT OF OBLIGATION

It is only after he had already established the genesis of the idea of liberty that Blondel undertook to explain the genesis of the moral idea of obligation. Parallel to the dependence of the idea of liberty on the consciousness of universal ideas, the moral idea finds its foundation and sufficient reason in the consciousness, at least implicit, of a metaphysical system of ideal realities.

> The metaphysical order is certainly not something which is outside the will as an extraneous end to be attained; it is contained within the will as a means to move beyond. It does not represent a truth already constituted in fact, but it places that which one wishes to will as an ideal object before thought. It does not express an absolute and universal reality; rather it expresses the universal aspiration of a particular will.[1]

This presence of an ideal metaphysical order in consciousness moves the will to the effort of incorporating that ideal order, which it conceives as the transcendent end of the natural order, into its voluntary action. Just as the perception of the universal is necessarily transformed by our consciousness into the necessary idea of freedom and an awareness of self as a creative source independent of the determinism of nature or thought, so too the conscious awareness of the possibility of incorporating the metaphysical transcendent ideal into action leads to an awareness of that action as a properly moral action and self as a moral agent. By means of the mediation of metaphysical ideas "... the will is led to place the center of its equilibrium beyond all given factual realities; to live, as it were, on itself, and to search in itself alone the purely formal reasons of its act."[2]

Kant, Blondel believed, understood the moral act as an autonomous will freely legislating its own universal law by a sort of creative *fiat*. Blondel himself finds the creative power of the moral act, not in the creation of a universal law, for this is necessarily given in the implicit metaphysical idea, but in the power of the will to synthesize that ideal into the reality of its activity by a free choice.

> In order that the very notion of morality can be a phenomenon of consciousness, in order that the idea itself of right can be a fact, in order that the sentiment of a practical obligation can arise as an imperative before the will, it is first necessary that we have learned to place the true motive of our behaviour elsewhere than in the factual; it is by the

---

[1] *Ibid.*, p. 293.
[2] *Ibid.*, p. 298.

mediation of an implicit metaphysics that moral duty appears before the consciousness as a reality. Within the phenomenon of a conscious obligation (whether practiced or not), a synthesis of the real and the ideal takes place.[1]

Consequently Blondel held that moral obligation was also a necessary phenomenon in the sense that it has its foundation ultimately in the determinism of the will. By reason of this determinism the will necessarily projects into conscious thought a system of metaphysical ideals as transcendent ends which must be incorporated into our free activity if our will is to achieve its fulfillment.

> Neither the form, nor the matter of moral obligation are to be found in the expression of an imperative without roots in real life, a sort of mystic and arbitrary commandment. Obligation is neither a given fact, nor a command which is imposed blindly on our conscience. It is a necessary postulate of the will. ... That which appeared in the ascending movement of our study as a necessary development of determinism, will appear to the descending view of reflexive thought as a hierarchy of obligatory relations and of duties to be consecrated by a practical acceptance.[2]

Blondel understood Kant to have placed the essence of duty or obligation in the concept of universality, and to have found the genesis of his universal imperative in the free choice of an autonomous will. Blondel also places the essential characteristic of obligation in its universality. It is the universal metaphysical ideal which gives rise to moral consciousness. But Blondel attributes the genesis of that universal ideal to the very structure of the will, to that which is determined in will-action.

> Without even having a clear idea of it, or without willing to regulate decisions on the sentiment which one can have of it, human action factually implies the total solidarity of all men and expresses the unity of the species. ... If then one seems to impose on the will as a law the obligation to make of itself a universal maxim, if one commands each individual to act with the intention of doing that which everyone ought to do ..., this is only the translation, not only of that which ought to be for the deliberate and express will, but also of that which exists already for the will-willing and operating.[3]

Kant seems to have been very much aware of the gulf which he had created between practical and pure reason, between freedom and determinism. He tried to bridge this gulf in his *Critique of Judgment.*

---

[1] *Ibid.*, pp. 298-299.
[2] *Ibid.*, p. 302.
[3] *Ibid.*, pp. 276-277.

But there are certain ideas and expressions already present in the *Critique of Practical Reason* which seem to hint at a continuity of pure and practical reason, freedom and determinism in the sense that Blondel understood it.

Amid other formulations of the categorical imperative, Kant gives us this formulation: "Ask yourself whether you could regard the action which you propose to do as a possible object of your will if it were to take place according to a law of nature in a system of nature of which you were yourself a part."[1] Here Kant employs an analogy between the natural law of mechanical necessity and the moral law. But one can demand if there is not more involved here than a purely hypothetical analogy. Kant finds the form or essence of the moral law in its universality. All concrete principles of conduct must partake of this universality if they are to be moral. But precisely what he meant by "being able" or "not being able" to will the universality of a maxim of conduct is unclear. In some of the examples he gives he seems to imply merely a logical contradiction. In others, as Delbos noted, where no apparent logical contradiction is found, he speaks of an intrinsic contradiction in the will. "... But it is still impossible to *will* that the maxim should be raised to the universality of a law of nature because such a will would contradict itself."[2] What Kant would seem to be implying is that the will, by reason of its subjective constitution, although free to refuse adherence to the law without logical contradiction, cannot do so except at the price of contradicting its own determinism. This interpretation is reinforced by still another means he employed to describe the categorical imperative: namely, the concept of a divine command. We must "... recognize all duties as divine commands, not as sanctions, that is, as arbitrary commands of an alien will which are contingent in themselves, but as essential *laws* of every free will itself...".[3]

---

[1] Kant, *Kritik der praktischen Vernunft*, Vol. V, Section 122:
Die Regel der Urteilskraft unter Gesetzen der reinen praktisches Vernunft ist diese: Frage dich selbst, ob die handlung, die du verhaft, wenn sie nach einen Gesetze der Natur, von der du selbst ein Theil wärest, geschehen sollte, sie du wohl als durch deinen Willen möglich ansehen könntest."

[2] Kant, *Grundlegung zur Metaphysik der Sitten*, Vol. IV, p. 424:
Bei andern ist zwar jene innere Unmöglichkeit nicht anzutreffen, aber es ist doch unmöglich, zu *wollen*, dass ihre Maxime zur Allgemeinheit eines Naturgesetzes erhoben werde, weil ein solcher Wille sich selbst widersprechen würde.

[3] Confer below, p. 99 ftnt.1 , for Kant's text. It is important to note that despite their differences Kant and Blondel end with the same truth. As Kant puts it: "The

Blondel also speaks of the immoral will as a will which contradicts itself in its actions.

> It is always its acts which manifest the agreement or disagreement of the double will, the willing force and the action willed, which is implied in every reflective movement of every deliberate attitude of man. The act results from the one and the other at the same time, even when these two wills are hostile. For the act is a synthesis of these two hostile orientations. ... The action draws its character from the consequent will (volonté voulue) which it realizes, without for all that ceasing to be founded in the primitive will which it perverts.[1]

What Blondel is referring to here is his theory of the metaphysical structure of the will-act as a composite of a relatively infinite, yet determined, potency with a limited operation, which only partially actualizes that potency in any given operation.[2] Despite the terminology which he employs here, for example "two wills", he does not intend to imply that there is a question of two distinct wills in man, nor two distinct operations of the same will. It is one and the same operation which is founded in the power of one and the same will, while frustrating the ultimate determinism of that will. Consequently, Blondel feels that the dilemma between freedom and necessity is a false problem. The necessary law of nature and reason is not found outside the will as an extrinsic imposition, but within the will itself as its intrinsic structure.

---

moral law leads us to religion, that is, to the recognition of all duties as divine commands." This idea of the substitution of the divine will for the human will constitutes the essence of the supreme option for Blondel. But for him there is question of not only making a substitution in thought but also of making an effective substitution in action;

> Man cannot conquer his being except by renouncing it in some way in order to lead it to its foundation and true end. ... It is his way of contributing to his own creation to consent to the invasion of all that which is anterior life and superior will to his own. To will all that which we will with a total heartfelt sincerity, is to place the being and the action of God in ourselves.

Confer *Action*, p. 491. This curious parallel is carried a step further with Kant's final effort to find a more immediate proof for God's existence in his *Opus Postumum*:

> Das Princip des Befolgung aller Pflichten als Göttlicher Gebote ... ist zugleich in Beziehung auf practische reine Vernunftprincipien ein Beweis vom Dasein Gottes als Eines Gottes.

What Kant seems to be seeking in this and similar passages is some form of awareness of God as immanent in moral consciousness.

[1] Blondel, *L'Action*, p. 19.
[2] Confer above, Chapter II, pp. 27-32.

There is no need, then, to talk about the supremacy of action and the sovereign autonomy of the will, as if it were necessary, in order to maintain the primacy of practical reason, to isolate the voluntary action from nature and break the bond which unites speculative thought with moral practice. It is the contrary which is true; there is correlation between these things which are too often opposed. It is by working within nature and by searching for itself in nature that the will is led to place outside the real order a system of metaphysical truths; and because these ideas inclose a further impenetrable virtuality—impenetrable to thought whose movement comes to a halt with these ideas, but accessible to the movement of action—the will is freed without denying its origins, and freely pursues its moral synthetic a priori within this new domain.[1]

But this reconciliation of freedom and necessity which Blondel envisages is only conceivable in terms of his revolutionary philosophical point of departure. "Here, as everywhere, effective action is the great mediator; it is action which succeeds in conciliating what from the static point of view of thought is formally self-excluding for a critical philosophy or an idealism."[2]

We are now in a position to understand the nuances in Blondel's judgment on the Kantian analysis of morality, as he understood it. Kant was wrong to separate morality from metaphysics, to "have done away with knowledge to make room for faith." He was right to assert the superiority of practical reason over pure speculation.

One is wrong then to pretend to destroy metaphysics in order to build up morality; the solidarity of the phenomena remains just as indisputable as their difference. ... One is right to think that the great regulative truths of life are required by morality rather than that morality is demanded by them. One is right to recognize that there is more in the system of practical postulates than in the system of metaphysical hypotheses, because action always carries us further than speculation.[3]

If both Kant and Blondel are in agreement in granting practice priority over speculation, their motive for doing so is quite different. Kant sees the priority of practical reason precisely in the fact that practical reason can "assume and think as given things which speculative reason can not affirm from its own insights."

---

[1] *Ibid.*, p. 300.
[2] *Ibid.*, p. 301.
[3] *Ibid.*, p. 299.

If practical reason could not assume and think as given anything other than that which *speculative* reason can offer from its own insights, then the latter would have the primacy. But if we suppose that practical reason has of itself original a priori principles with which certain theoretical positions are inseparably united, though they are at the same time withdrawn from any possible insight of speculative reason (which they, however, must not contradict), then the question is what interest is the superior (not which must give way, for they do not necessarily conflict).[1]

Kant's answer is that practical reason must prevail. So speculative reason is obliged to accept the propositions offered it by practical reason and try "... to unite them with its own concepts."[2] Thus Blondel understood Kant as holding that practical reason as giving new knowledge or concepts different from and superior to the ideas of speculative knowledge but not necessarily contradictory to these latter ideas. Blondel, on the contrary, does not conceive of practical reason as a source of new ideas or concepts. Moral activity does not create its own metaphysical ideas. Rather, it operates a new and original synthesis; it is an incorporation of the hypothetical metaphysical idea into the living reality of willed action. Just as that synthesis is unique and irreducible to its components, so the consciousness of that synthesizing activity gives a new conscious awareness or intuition which is irreducible to the results of pure metaphysical speculation. It is the same idea which precedes moral choice and remains after choice; but it is only after choice that we can say of that idea with complete certitude, it is!

This priority of practical reason as a synthesizing agent is the key to Blondel's answer to the problem of value judgment. As Cartier remarks, one can comprehend what Blondel means when he holds with Kant that moral obligation is a postulate of the will and like Jeanson that all value is valorization.[3] From what has gone before it is evident

---

[1] Kant, *Kritik der praktischen Vernunft*, Vol. V, Sections 216-217:

Wenn praktische Vernunft nichts weiter annehmen und als gegeben denken darf, als was *speculative* Vernunft für sich ihn aus ihrer Einsicht darreichen konnte, so führt diese das Primat. Gesetzt aber, sie hätte für sich ursprüngliche Principien a priori, mit denen gewisse theoretische Positiones unzertrennlich verbunden wären, die sich gleich wohl aller möglichen Einsicht der speculativen Vernunft entzögen (ob wie zwar derselben auch nicht widersprechen müssten), so ist die Frage, welches Interesse das oberste sei (nicht welches Weichen müsste, denn eines widerstreitet dem andern nicht nothwendig).

[2] *Ibid.*, Section 218.
[3] Albert Cartier, *Existence et Vérité*, p. 98.

that Blondel did not hold a pure autonomy of human liberty. He does not imply that each individual creates his own values. But what he wished to escape was the contrary position, which he found equally untenable and, perhaps, more widespread: namely, a pure heteronomy of obligation. If moral obligation has its source totally exterior to the will and liberty, then all obligation would be a tyranny which could only result in the denial of liberty as an illusion. But the problem is resolved once we understand that moral law is not an imposition exterior to the will, but the reflection in consciousness of the very structure of that will. Thus liberty is not the contradiction of law; it is the product of an interior law and the necessary means for the accomplishment of that law.

The Critique of Judgment

When Kant formally posed the problem of the relation of speculative and practical reason, freedom and necessity, in his *Critique of Judgment*, he did not return to develop the implications of his idea of a self-contradiction in the immoral will or his analogy between the natural and moral law.[1] Rather, he finds that link in the reflexive a priori regulative concept of the purposiveness of nature. This concept enables us to think nature as not being alien to a realization of ends. Thus we can conceive the possibility of an actualization of ends in nature in harmony with nature's laws. Blondel interpreted Kant's thought as an attempt to establish a subjective connection in thought.

> Without doubt, Kant, in his ever increasing concern to achieve a complete system of pure reason, did not resign himself to "simply leave the world of sense experience and the moral world in the presence of each other without seeking a means to bring them together and unite them." But it was those habits of thought contracted in the analysis of perception and in the critique of science to which he made appeal in order to pose and resolve by means of reflection a problem which, by definition, escapes from these conditions. It is as if, advancing by backing away, he keeps his eyes on an ideology, seeing in it the only possible form of metaphysics. Here once again philosophy lacks a distinct and original point of departure. It begins in the midst of derivative forms of reflection and action; it remains dependent on results of an anterior effort of which it itself is the result, in place of beginning with that initial effort itself.[2]

---

[1] Kant, *Kritik der Urteilskraft*, "Einleiting," Vol. V, Section XX.
[2] Blondel, "Le Point de Départ de la Recherche Philosophique," I, 352.

Blondel, as we have seen, true to his perspective, sought a subjective connection between speculative thought and practical reason in the very action itself which gives rise to the necessary idea of freedom and to a system of metaphysical ideals. These ideals will, in turn, be synthesized into consequent actions in order to obtain the realization of the incorporation of our ideals or purposes into the determinism of nature. Thus consciousness of action serves as a pivotal point of a process wherein that immanent necessity which gives rise to the act of consciousness is transformed necessarily by consciousness itself into an idea of transcendent finality. "... The real knowledge is that reflection which projects our interior regard ahead to the ends which solicit our will, because only there can one find the sufficient reason of free determination."[1] As a result of this transformation our action becomes dependent on an efficient finality. "... The will accepts and ratifies not only the appearance of a universal determinism, but that universal reality which is its source. ... It is necessary to become in some way that determinism itself ... in order to conspire fully with the total immensity of the mystery of nature."[2]

Freedom, emerging as it does by a necessary and continuous process out of the determinism of nature, must, in order to achieve its destiny, freely become one with that determinism. The analogy between natural and moral law in Kant is transformed into an effective synthesis by Blondel.

THE SCIENCE OF THE PRACTICAL

A strict science of concrete human actions was doubly inconceivable to Kant. First of all, practical reason by its very definition does not deal with objects given in sense intuition; and Kant had limited science, defined as theoretical knowledge with objective validity, to the task of determining the conditions of possibility for objects to be given in sense experience. Secondly, the actual concrete choices of an autonomous will are necessarily devoid of any necessity or scientific pattern. But Blondel was convinced that a science of the practical was possible. It was possible because, contrary to the Kantian position, as he understood it, liberty is by no means a simple power of choice, a question of permitting or denying the arbitration of an extrinsic reason. Precisely because liberty is necessary, that is to say, because it is the result of

[1] *Ibid.*, *L'Action*, p. 123.
[2] *Ibid.*, p. 288.

a dynamic spontaneous process in human activity, it tends necessarily to the dynamism of reflective action. To refuse to reflect, to refuse to choose rationally is also a choice and of necessity a free choice. But, on the contrary, when we faithfully do that which we sincerely will, "... we obey an obligation which far from depending on our free command, is an imperative end for us."[1] It is the continuity of this determinism, automatic before it gives rise to the necessary idea of freedom, free after it synthesizes the universal concept with its own infinite potency, which makes possible a science of free human actions. In fact, this continuous determinism is the object of that science.

> If this indeterminate power is defined by the fact alone *that* it wills and not by that *which* it wills; further, if in the very activity itself of the will is revealed the end to which it tends and the series of means it uses, then that rigorous continuity (enchainement) contains a scientific determination; there is a necessary logic of liberty.[2]

Blondel was aware of the evident paradox in suggesting a science of free activity. The primary quality of the free act is both its uniqueness and existential singularity which cannot be expressed in any generality, as well as its independence of any determinism which would permit it to be subsumed entirely into any rational pattern of cause and effect.

> Without doubt because of the intimate and always singular nature of the act, a subjective science would at first scarcely seem to possess the abstract and impersonal generality of the sciences. For this science supposes an initiative and experience proper to each person who creates anew this science for himself, and which no artifice of exposition can dispense with. Despite this, however, this science has a universal character and a precision which is superior to the exactitude and generality of all the others. There is no one who, in fact, is not submitted to the necessity of practical experience, and there is no act which does not carry with it a train of secret consequences, a rigorous logic which is superior to the most subtle reasoning.[3]

As this quotation reveals, Blondel did not consider it possible to develop a science of action by speculation alone. This science is possible only to the extent that man effectively commits himself in action. As we have seen, Blondel understood moral activity as creating a synthetic reality, as incorporating the ideal into reality. Like all other synthetic a priori realities, this synthesis which is the product of moral action, by reason of its uniqueness and originality, cannot be deduced

---

[1] *Ibid.*, p. 127.

[2] *Ibid.*

[3] *Ibid.*, p. 101.

from nature or from thought. "Since moral action finds in itself something which is derived neither from nature nor from thought, in so far as it nourishes itself by activity, it becomes more conscious of its own relative autonomy."[1] Thus there is a type of conscious subjective knowledge, essential to a science of action which can only be had at the price of the action completed. The subjective synthesis of the will-willing and will-willed cannot be achieved by thought alone. Thought can indicate the probable path to be pursued; it is only action which operates the synthesis and, thus, creates the conscious adequation or inadequation within the will.

> ... It is the initiative a priori of a free activity which, by its expansion, ought to reconstruct the necessity to which it is submitted, so to speak, a posteriori. Thus, the heteronomity of its law corresponds to its interior autonomy. ... This is the uniqueness of practical experimentation; the voluntary action provokes, as it were, a response and an instruction from without and these instructions which impose themselves on the will are actually enclosed within that will itself.[2]

The moment freedom enters the picture, only action itself gives an absolute answer to the moral value of a given free choice. "... We learn by acting, what we must do; that is to say that our will succeeds bit by bit to understand and fulfil itself."[3]

In the final chapter of his manuscript "Projet d'une Thèse", which we mentioned above, Blondel developed this theme of a "Science of moral experimentation" which he links to the concept of a "metaphysical synthesis of action."

> Consequently, for all that which has to do with substantial life, and not with the phenomena of being or the laws of sensible material, it is by means of the practical that one arrives at the theoretical, and there is a moral experimentation, a method analogous to that of the sciences of observation, which has its proper rules whose character and usage must be determined.
> Thus, far from being impractical or superfluous in the moral sciences, this experimentation is its true territory; it is indispensable, regulative and almost creative or, at least, constitutive. It is by experience that the synthetic a priori is achieved, through the exercise of a will which searches out what it desires and encounters what it loves, without ceasing for all that to conserve its primitive and basic drive.

---

[1] Ibid., p. 301.

[2] Ibid., p. 127. The relation between the concept of an a posteriori science of freedom and Schelling's method in his positive philosophy will be discussed in Part II, Chapter 15.

[3] Ibid., p. 142.

In brief, the synthesis, as a unity of a multiplicity, as an action of a *synergie*, has a substantial reality and a relative excellence. The inferior does not explain the superior; but, also, the superior does not sovereignly dominate the inferior.

For that reason we freely admit the necessity of a verification or of an experimental construction, a reconciliation of the a priori and the a posteriori, a true definition and a justified role for the empirical control of practical hypotheses, a new method, at the same time moral and metaphysical, which, uniting with a continuous relation and a scientific experimentation, the study of phenomena with that of being in the reality of action, confers upon them the character of an original science which is as positive as is becoming to them.[1]

THE DOUBLE METAPHYSICS

Both Kant and Blondel understood their critique as an effort to restore metaphysics on a new basis. In both *Critiques* the nature and value of metaphysics is considered on two occasions from two different viewpoints and receives two quite different evaluations according to the divergent contexts.

In *The Critique of Pure Reason*, metaphysics, it is true, is eliminated from the category of scientific knowledge. But Kant recognizes it as a "natural disposition." The mind naturally and spontaneously tends to unify the conditions of experience as far as the unconditioned. By following out this innate tendency man is obliged to posit the central metaphysical ideas, God, world and the ego, as principles of the unity of categorical thinking. Kant ascribes a heuristic value to these ideas. "... The transcendental ideas will, in all probability, have their proper and consequently *immanent* use."[2] Their use is to serve as stimulants, which, by rendering us discontent with present perceptions, urges us to indefinite further scientific unification. The idea of world, for example, as a concept of the total system of causally related phenomena, continually spurs us on to develop ever wider scientific explanatory hypotheses. Or, again, the idea of God, as supreme intelligence and

---

[1] *Ibid.*, *Projet d'une Thèse*, pp. 192-193.

[2] Kant, *Kritik der reinen Vernunft*, Vol. III, Section 671:

Also werden die transzendentalen Ideen allem Vermuthen noch ihnen guten und folglich *immanenten* Gebraucht haben, obgleich, wenn ihre Bedeutung verkannt und sie für Begriffe von wirklichen Dingen genommen werden, sne transzendent in der Anwendung und eben darim trüglich sein können. Dien nicht die Idee an sich selbst, sondern bloss ihr Gebraucht kann entweder in Ansehung der gesammten möglichen Erfahrung überfliegend (transzendent), oder einheimlich (immanent) sein. ...

cause of the universe, leads us to think of nature as a systematic teleo-logical unity. In the context, then, metaphysical ideas are conceived as ideal limits towards which pure reason must strive in its effort to unify the conditions of experience.

In *The Critique of Practical Reason*, Kant broaches a second time the problem of the value of metaphysics and, once again, he assigns it a utilitarian value. But this usefulness in the context of moral activity is seen as dependent on practical faith in the noumenal reality of these ideas.[1] The metaphysical process in practical reason is an effort to discover and affirm by faith that view of reality which alone gives full meaning and value to the awareness of moral obligation.

Here, for example, God is no longer understood as a sort of imag-inary limit-concept with exclusively speculative value. The idea of the existence of God becomes a necessary postulate in order that the syn-thesis of virtue and happiness can be realized. Again, this idea of God's existence is subjectively necessary as idea. But since God is "thought" as object and not "given" as object, the assent to the objective existence of God remains free or, as Kant prefers to call it, an act of faith of the practical reason.

In the course of his proof of God's existence from practical reason, Kant makes use of a form of the *summum bonum* argument. The highest good is necessarily thought of as the unconditioned totality of the objects of practical reason; that is, as a synthesis of virtue and happi-ness. Virtue is seen as the cause of happiness. However, from experi-ence one realizes that there is no necessary agent of this causal connec-tion in this world. Happiness, which consists in the fact that "every-thing goes according to one's wish and will," demands a perfect harmony of physical nature with our will. Consequently, God, or the supreme cause of nature, must be postulated as the grounds of that harmony.

---

[1] In the *Critique of Pure Reason* Kant speaks of removing thought in order to make room for faith: "Ich musse also die Wissen aufheben, um zum Glauben Platz zu bekommen." (Vol. III, Section XXX.) However, Kant clarifies in the *Critique of Practical Reason* that his intention was not to destroy metaphysics. Rather, it was to reinstate on a new basis the metaphysics which he had exorcised from pure reason. He hoped to place the great truths of metaphysics beyond the reach of destructive criticisms and continual controversy by the very act of removing them from the position of conclusions to "worthless metaphysical arguments," and by linking them to the indisputable evidence of moral consciousness.

It is important to note that the "faith" of which Kant speaks is by no means that which is irrational: "Glaube (als Habitus, nicht als Actus) ist die moralische Denkungsart der Vernunft im Fürwahrhalten desjenigen, was für das theoretische Erkenntnis unzugänglich ist." (Confer, *Kritik der Urteilskraft*, Vol. V, Section 462).

Through the idea of the supreme good as object and final end of the pure practical reason, the moral law leads us to *religion*, that is, to *the recognition of all duties as divine commands, not as sanctions,* that is, *as arbitrary commands of an alien will which are contingent in themselves,* but as essential *laws* of every free will itself, which, however, must be looked on as commands of the supreme Being, because it is only from a morally perfect (holy and good) and at the same time all powerful will that we can hope to obtain the highest good, which the moral law makes it our duty to take as the object of our endeavors.[1]

Kant felt that these arguments for the existence of metaphysical realities were a definite advance over the arguments encountered in *The Critique of Pure Reason*. "... Theoretical reason's knowledge of the suprasensible is increased to this extent, that it is compelled to admit that there are such objects."[2]

Blondel first deals with metaphysical knowledge in his development of the phenomena of action.[3] In this context Blondel prescinds from the problem of the objective value of metaphysical ideas. He recognizes the necessity of thinking such ideas as objectively given, but refuses an ultimate judgment until the absolute ground of that existence can be established. Thus he concedes with Kant that metaphysics is a natural disposition, in the sense that the basic metaphysical ideas are inevitably thought by us as objective ideals. "Our action cannot be organized except by means of a total idea, and by projecting that total explanation of its own production under the form of a final end to be

---

[1] Kant, *Kritik der Praktische Vernunft*, Vol. V, Section 233:

Auf solche Weise fuhrt das moralische Gesetz durch den Begriff des hochsten Guts, als das Object und den Endzweck der reinen praktischen Vernunft, zur *Religion*, d.i. *zur Erkenntniss aller Pflichten als Göttlicher Gebote, nicht als Sanctionen,* d.i. *willkürliche, für sich selbst zufällige Verordnungen eines fremden Willens,* sondern als wesenlicher *Gesetze* eines jeden freien Willens für sich selbst, die aber dennoch als Gebote des hochsten Wesens angesehen werden müssen, weil wir nur von einen moralisch vollkommenen (heiligen und gütigen), zugleich auch allgewaltigen Willen das höchste Gut, welches zum Gegenstände unserer Bestrebung zu setzen und das moralische Gesetz zur Pflicht macht, und also durch Uebereinstimmung mit diesem Willen dazu zu gelangen hoffen können.

[2] *Ibid.*, Section 244:

Also war es keine Erweiterung der Erkenntniss *von gegebenenüber sinnlichen Gegenständen,* aber doch eine Erweiterung der theoretischen Vernunft und der Erkenntniss derselben in ansehung des Uebersinnlichen Uberhaupt, sofern als sie genöthigt wurde, *das es solche Gegenstände gebe.* ...

[3] Confer Blondel, *L'Action*, pp. 290-297.

achieved."[1] Consequently, he also considers this first metaphysics as primarily having utilitarian value, not exclusively for reason, whether speculative or practical, but for the orientation of voluntary action. "In the meaning which it had for traditional ontology *metaphysics must enter into the ranks* (*Action* 291-7), that is to say, it must be considered as a moment contained in the general development of our life and simply as a reflexive principle of action."[2] The spontaneous function of metaphysical ideas is, as we have seen, to give rise to moral consciousness and moral activity as such. "It is that necessary action of the necessary idea of God which must be determined."[3] The necessary result of the necessary idea of God is to place man before the supreme alternative, to make himself the final end of his will effort, or to attempt to substitute the divine will for his own. "Man aspires to be God; to be God without God and against God, to be God by God and with God, this is the dilemma."[4] Thus the dialectic of the will under the influence of the metaphysical idea of God places God as the *unique nécessaire*, the only possible foundation of a harmony between the will-willing and the will-willed. But Blondel insists, "the demonstration here does not result from a logical construction of the mind. ... The problem is not to know if this "uniquely necessary" is the abstract term of a rational process, but if it can also enter as a living reality into the development of willed action."[5] Thus the effect of option is not to give speculative knowledge of the existence of an object but actual possession within the context of subjective consciousness of that object.

Since Blondel sees all reason as practical reason in the sense that all ideas and reasonings are seen as means which the will necessarily employs in its development, both the metaphysics of pure and practical reason as they were understood by Kant seem to be included in this first metaphysics of Blondel, whose function it is to place the will before the supreme option. It is only after the option is made, only after man effectively possesses, as it were, the absolute, no longer as a hypothesis but as a living reality, that a second metaphysics becomes

---

[1] *Ibid.*, p. 292. Blondel's utilitarian attitude, however, did not involve a denial of the objective validity of our speculative metaphysical ideas. Rather, he acknowledges the necessity of this inevitable and spontaneous belief, while reserving judgment on its absolute validity.

[2] Blondel, *Lettres Philosophiques*, pp. 125-126.

[3] *Ibid.*, *L'Action*, p. 351.

[4] *Ibid.*, p. 356.

[5] *Ibid.*, pp. 339-340.

possible. It is this second metaphysics to which Blondel refers at the very end of the last chapter of his book.

> To justify that exterior subsistence of a truth interior to man, there is a need of a sort of metaphysics to the second power (métaphysique à la seconde puissance), which establishes not only that which the first metaphysics, as yet entirely subjective, presented to us wrongly (à tort) as the very reality itself of being, while it was only a simple view of the mind or a speculative phenomenon, but the entire determinism of nature, life and thought. ... Once the circle is closed, this total determinism, which has appeared as a phenomenon of the human will in reason, will appear from then on at the same time as an absolute reality which imposes that reason on the will.[1]

Consequently, to affirm the existence of God can have one of two meanings depending on the context in which it is made, namely, before or after the supreme option.

> What does it mean *to affirm the reality of God*? Does it mean that we must pretend that the knowledge we have of God is God himself? That there is an ontological intuition or an immediate adequation? Certainly not. To affirm the reality of God is to establish, in effect, that we cannot legitimately refuse to conceive of Him as real. ... From this example you will understand the meaning and the relation of an immanent metaphysics (which limits itself to determining the normal and necessary connections of our transcendental ideas, in the measure that they serve to order the relations of thought and practice), and that metaphysics to the second power which, following the study of the total determinism of our thoughts, and establishing that we invincibly affirm the objective reality of *what we have invincibly conceived and thought*, searches out the conditions under which these truths, which *we cannot, neither by right, nor in fact, consider as purely subjective, can be real, independent of our thoughts*, absolutely real... From the point of view of a metaphysics to the second power, *the pure intellectual and speculative knowledge of pure reason, that knowledge which is not directed to action and love, is privative* of that being which it has proposed to us, (it is the condition of the damned). Whereas the real possession of the living truth supposes the *cooperation* of the *pure and practical reason*, considered as concurrent powers, and serving each other mutually as means and end.[2]

It is evident, therefore, that Blondel himself believed that his metaphysics to the second power differed from the restored metaphysics in Kantian thought. For a clearer idea of what Blondel understood, however, by his second metaphysics, we must wait until we discuss the influence on his thought of Schelling's final philosophy.

---

[1] *Ibid.*, pp. 464-465.
[2] *Ibid.*, *Lettres Philosophiques*, pp. 126-127.

However there are two further ideas of Kant contained in his *Opus Postumum*, both of which he outlined but did not develop, which manifest an even closer resemblance of his final thought to that of Blondel. The first is the concept of man as mediator. "God, the world, and the Ego, the thinking being in the world, who links them together. God and the World are two objects of transcendent philosophy and ... there is the thinking man, the subject which links them together in one proposition."[1] The synthesis between the idea of God and the World is effected by man, the thinking subject. Man is himself the mediating being who belongs to both the suprasensible and the sensible world, the phenomenal and the noumenal spheres. In his teleological judgments man incarnates idea into reality; he inserts freedom into determinism.

If in place of teleological judgment one were to insert moral action, the thesis of Blondel would emerge. The concept of man as mediator by his action led Blondel to speculate on the hypothesis of a sort oe metaphysical necessity of a God-Man as the absolute mediator of thf entire universe.

> Perhaps because he is destined to receive divine life in himself, man is capable of playing the role of the universal bond and suffices for this creative mediation, because this immanence of God in us will serve as a magnetic center which will reunite all things. ... But, also, in order that, despite everything, the mediation could be total, permanent, voluntary, such in a word that it would assure the reality of all that which without doubt does not necessarily exist (pourrait ne pas être), but which granting that it is, needs a divine witness, perhaps there is needed one mediator who renders himself passive to that integral reality and who becomes as the *Amen* to the universe.[2]

The second idea, also in the *Opus Postumum*, is what Kant refers to as the construction of experience. Here we have an application to the practical order of the theory of construction of intuition which Kant employed to explain the origin of mathematical ideas. Kant describes this process as a "self-positing, self-making, or self-constituting" of the noumenal subject. In terms of this process the thing-in-itself becomes "... the mere representation of its (the subject's) own activity."[3]

---

[1] Kant, *Opus Postumum*, Vol. XXI, pp. 36-37.

[2] Blondel, *L'Action*, p. 461.

[3] Kant, *Opus Postumum*, Vol. XXII, p. 37:

Das Ding an sich ist nicht etwas das gegeben wird (dabile) sondern was blos als correspondirend zur Eintheilung gehörend uneracht dass es wegbleibt gedacht wird (cogatibile).

The subject necessarily projects its own unity or activity of unification in the negative idea of the thing-in-itself. Thus the necessity of the affirmation of objective reality is reduced to the necessity of the subject to achieve actively its own unification. This theory, as we shall see, was developed by Fichte into a subjective transcendental idealism. It bears a striking resemblance to Blondel's concept of the necessary production of our ideas and the whole phenomenal order, as also the subjective necessity of affirming the objective validity of these ideas, as means which the subject is determined to employ to achieve the unity of adequation of the structural principles of his will. This resemblance will be discussed in the subsequent chapters.

SUMMARY

Human action, according to Blondel, is a synthetic a priori reality. It is synthetic, that is to say, a composite reality, and it is a priori in the sense that this composite has its own proper substantial unity or existential reality which is irreducible to its conditions of existence. Consequently a philosophical study of human action cannot be exclusively analytical. Any effort to understand that synthesis by reducing it to its component elements necessarily involves the dissipation of that synthesis and the loss thereby of that very reality which one wishes to comprehend.

The philosophy of action must, as a consequence, be a sort of experimental science. For the very datum of this science is that unique synthetic reality, that fusion of thought and being, which only human action itself can create. *Qui facit veritatem, venit ad lucem.* The problem of human destiny is not posed originally by thought, but by the necessity man experiences to act and to choose; nor is that problem resolved ultimately by thought but by our actions, which successfully synthesize in reality what our speculation cannot unite by means of its categories. Thus action itself must be the starting point and the center of perspective for a philosophy of action. It is from within action, from within our consciousness of ourselves in our actions, from within that synthesis of the real and the ideal which we have consciously achieved by our living actions, that we must attempt to seek the answer to the problem of human life.

From this vantage point our study can proceed in two directions. The synthesis we have factually accomplished by our present actions having been accepted as a given fact, we can analyze the necessary

conditions of that synthesis and seek out the vital laws which determine its formation. Every step in the development of human action
presupposes a series of previous synthetic steps. There is a rigorous
continuity in the development of human action. While it is true that
each new synthesis transcends in its reality its component elements
yet, for all that, it does not destroy in any way their validity nor deny
their necessity. Freedom, for example, being an original power of
action resulting from the synthesis of the idea of the infinite or unlimited with the power of the infinite, transcends in its reality all
determinism. Still that liberty in act is a necessary result of those
automatic and deterministic synthetic processes which necessarily gave
rise to the universal idea and to conscious reflection.

Just as Kant conceived of a science of reason which would study
that which is necessarily and universally present in the immanent a
priori structure of all reason independent of its empirical content, so
Blondel conceived of a science of action which would study that which
is necessarily and universally present in the immanent a priori structure
of all human action regardless of its specific end. By means of this
science of action he hoped to uncover the basic synthetic laws which
govern the evolution of human action from its preconscious origins
to its final fulfillment in the total adequation of self with self.

That instable equilibrium or synthesis which we have factually
accomplished within ourselves by our present commitments in act can
also serve as the starting point for a prospective search for that synthesis which has yet to be accomplished. Once we have grasped that
secret logic which governs the synthetic evolution of human life, we
are in a position to search out speculatively those possible actions
which, true at the same time to our factual existential situation, the
degree of self-adequation we have actually accomplished, and also to
the universal determinism of life, offer a new goal and promise a new
fulfillment. "In reality the rhythm of knowledge and practice constitutes an infinitesimal progression. ... We act continually in order to
know, and we know continually in order to act."[1]

Finally, once human action has touched its goal, once it has not
only posed speculatively, but begun to achieve synthetically in act that
total adequation of self with self, once the absolute has become not
only a privative concept before the mind, but a living reality in which
we immanently participate by our actions, then, and only then, can a

---

[1] Blondel, *Lettres Philosophiques*, p. 222.

true metaphysics of being, simultaneously essential and existential or, as Blondel calls it "a metaphysics to the second power" be erected.

In the course of this final chapter concerning Kantian influence on Blondel's thought the new philosophical synthesis which Blondel sought in terms of action begins to take shape. But before we can fully understand the originality of Blondel's synthesis in relation to his primary sources, we must study the previous efforts to achieve that same synthesis which served as the stimulants of Blondel's thought and greatly influenced it, namely, the efforts of Fichte, Schelling and Hegel.

PART TWO

THE INFLUENCE OF IDEALISM ON BLONDEL'S PHILOSOPHY OF ACTION

INTRODUCTION

SPINOZA AND THE IDEALISTS

Blondel understood his basic objective in *Action* to be an attempt to achieve a new reconciliation between the realism of Spinoza and the critical idealism of Kant. He was, however, quite conscious that, even if his specific approach was new, the idea of reconciling the thought of these two philosophers into a higher synthesis was by no means original; rather, three of the greatest German idealist philosophers, Fichte, Schelling and Hegel, had preceded him in that attempt. As Blondel remarks himself: "It was after having encountered an apparent contradiction in transcendental idealism that that same idealism, by a powerful effort to which Fichte, Schelling, and Hegel have attached their names, would attempt to reconstruct a renewed Spinozism."[1]

As we have seen, Blondel understood the hidden flaw in Spinoza's doctrine to be his failure to explain the process of becoming in being. He understood Kant to have isolated this same process of becoming and exploited it in his doctrine of practical reason. The history of subsequent German idealism was, in his opinion, a prolonged effort to develop fully that idea of becoming and reconcile it with Spinoza's doctrine of the absolute intelligibility of being.

> Elaborate the idea of *becoming* in being; expand that concept of *fieri* to the entire field of history and determine its concrete applications; bring to light the principle itself of becoming which Spinoza had left in the shadows, but which had been the invisible agent of his system, and join to the doctrine of the absolute Intelligibility the philosophy of the Spirit or of the Idea: this was the development of that German idealism which has pretended to resurrect and exhaust the meaning of Spinoza.[2]

The result of this movement, according to Blondel, was in fact a restoration of Spinoza's doctrine joined to a new and more perfect

---

[1] "L'Evolution du Spinozisme," 1, 271.
[2] *Ibid.*, I, 270.

form. The spirit of Spinoza continued to act in German thought by a sort of immanent operation. It was this spirit which led Fichte to apply the monist idea to the very concept of becoming and moral liberty. It led Schelling to return once again to the notion of absolute being as the generating principle; and, finally, it led to the renewed Spinozism represented by Hegel's philosophy of the spirit which, Blondel maintained, "... had succeeded in so far as that was possible in adjusting perfectly its form with its matter and in constituting an exact rational system."[1]

What we propose, then, is to try to uncover the influence these pre-Blondelian efforts at synthesis had on Blondel's thought at the time he wrote *Action*. There is no room for doubt that Blondel did know a great deal about the doctrine of these philosophers and that their doctrine did have considerable influence on his own philosophy of action. In fact, Blondel himself seems to have had a certain pride in the knowledge he acquired of post-Kantian German idealist thought. He was inclined to believe that the lack of accurate knowledge of the development in this area of thought was a serious flaw in the French philosophical thinking of his day. "If in France, too many thinkers have arrested their investigations with the doctrine of Kant, it is time now, perhaps, to show that since the *Critique of Practical Reason* thought has moved on."[2]

It was this same lacuna in the knowledge of post-Kantian German thought which, Blondel held, explained much of the misunderstanding and lack of appreciation regarding his own initial work, *Action*. As we have seen, he found many elements in his thought labeled Kantian or neo-Kantian, which he had derived from post-Kantian idealist sources, and which were originally proposed by their authors precisely as efforts to remedy the deficiencies they found in Kant's system. "I conclude," Blondel tells us, "that all those who have received a traditional formation, lacking a precise knowledge of the various systems, confuse Kantianism and the philosophies which have followed it or discuss it by entering into its point of view."[3] Where Blondel was grappling with the insights and problems posed by the philosophical systems of a Fichte, Schelling, or Hegel, his critics were discovering the suspicious suggestions of Kantian or neo-Kantian influence.

In yet another context Blondel is quite explicit in acknowledging the

---

[1] *Ibid.*, I, 271.
[2] *Ibid.*, I, 275.
[3] Blondel, *Lettres Philosophiques*, p. 111.

influence of the German idealists on his thought. As we noted previously, Blondel understood his philosophy of action as the most
recent step in a long evolution beginning with Spinoza.[1] It was,
according to Blondel, Spinoza who, by implicitly introducing the
Christian idea of human destiny into modern philosophy, had launched
that long process of evolution which resulted in the transformation of
modern philosophy into an apt instrument for the rational study of
religion—an instrument fully conscious of its resources and limitations. But, as Blondel insisted in his *Letter of* 1896, one must study the
successive steps of that evolution; otherwise one remains incapable
of an exact understanding of the meaning and impact of that transformation of philosophy, Both in his article "The Evolution of
Spinozism" and in his *Letter of* 1896 Blondel calls attention to the three
great German Idealists, Fichte, Schelling, and Hegel, as contributing
an important step in that evolution.

The Subjectivist Illusion

In his article entitled "The Idealist Illusion," Blondel develops three
specific forms of what he calls the generic intellectualist illusion,
namely, the capacity of man to understand totally and possess completely absolute being by the exclusive means of a philosophical system.
The first of these illusions, as we have already seen in connection with
Spinoza's objective realism, was the belief in the absolute objective
identity of thought with being.[2] The second, the critical illusion, tended to establish an absolute dichotomy between thought and being.[3]
With absolute idealism we come into contact with the third and final
species of the evolution of this intellectualism, the subjectivist illusion,
or the subjective identity of thought with being.

Here again, from an epistemological viewpoint Blondel sees an
evolution of philosophical thought which leads inevitably to a philosophy of action as the only means to escape from the impasse of intellectualism.

> The purpose of this study is to show that ... if from the point of view
> of action all the traditional problems seem to be transposed, that change
> is neither arbitrary nor optional; nor is it detached from the evolution
> of human thought. The philosophy of action is not another doctrine

---

[1] Confer above, pp. 10-15.
[2] Confer above, pp. 36-39.
[3] Confer above, pp. 52-55.

simply juxtaposed or substituted for the others, but an extension and utilization of the philosophical tradition. From this viewpoint of action the oppositions of the majority of the previous systems are reduced to the common note of "intellectualism."[1]

Idealism in general represents, according to Blondel, not a solution to the problem of the relation of thought and being but, rather, a transposition of that conflict of subject and object into the heart of the subject, where it becomes a conflict between the actual and the virtual, the apparent and the fundamental.

> Unless one is willing to grant that ... all distinct consciousness has been abolished (which is impossible), one is forced to admit a distinction between that which is actually thought under a definite form and that which is within us as grounds of truth (comme vérité enveloppée), practicable experience, virtual science or tendency. Thus there is no longer question of realizing a conformity between concept and being; rather it is in consciousness itself, between that which is present and that which is represented in consciousness, that conformity must be achieved.[2]

Blondel maintains that just as in the absolute realism of Spinoza there is an explicit affirmation and an implicit denial of a total objective identity of thought with being, so, conversely, in absolute subjective idealism there is an explicit affirmation and an implicit denial of the total subjective identity of being with consciousness. This is especially true of the doctrine of Fichte. Although his initial monist premise leads him to maintain that consciousness and being are one, yet in his reconstruction of consciousness he is obliged to deny actual consciousness to that infinite spontaneous activity which constitutes the absolute ego and to conceive of it as an infinite potentiality for progress in the acquisition of conscious existence.

This transposed conflict between actuality and virtuality in the subjective sphere of consciousness, according to Blondel, determined the evolution of idealist thought both in the subsequent forms of Fichte's doctrine, as well as in the evolution of the doctrine of Schelling and Hegel. However, if Blondel rejects the dogmatic character of idealist subjectivism, as well as its abstract intellectualism, he did see in idealism in many respects a forward step in the evolution of modern thought. What these contributions were in Blondel's opinion and how they influenced his philosophy of action will be the object of our research.

---

[1] Blondel, "L'Illusion Idéaliste," p. 99.
[2] *Ibid.*, p. 106.

CHAPTER SIX

THE INFLUENCE OF FICHTE

Sources of Blondel's Knowledge of Fichte

The question arises once again as to the extent and nature of Blondel's knowledge of these philosophers and, specifically, of Fichte. The problem of determining the influence of Fichte's *Theory of Science* (Wissenschaftslehre) on Blondel's thought is even more difficult than was the case with Kant or Spinoza, because, in contrast to these other two philosophers, there is not one explicit reference to Fichte in the text of *Action*. However, as early as April, 1889, Blondel jotted down in his private diary a reflection on the relation between his concept of action and Fichte's concept of action in *The Theory of Science*. This reflection leaves us in no doubt that before Blondel began to write the 1890 redaction of his thesis, which contained for the first time an explicit statement of the central ideas of his own original philosophical synthesis, he already grasped the central point of agreement and disagreement between his philosophy of action and Fichte's philosophy of the Ego as pure activity.[1]

As far as direct contact with Fichte's writings is concerned, Blondel, always a voracious reader, had read those works of Fichte which were available in French translations. Apart from the popular works, these translations were limited to the first *Theory of Science* of 1794 (Grundlage der gesammten Wissenschaftslehre) in the particularly bad translation of Grimblot (1843), and *The Way to the Blessed Life* (Die Anweisung zu einem seligen Leben) translated by Bouillier in 1845.[2]

However, as was the case with Kant so here also, it would seem that the indirect contacts with Fichte's thought exercised a much more

---

[1] Blondel, *Carnets Intimes (1883-1884)*, pp. 194-195. Confer below, pp. 113-114 for an important discussion of this text.

[2] Among the French translations of Fichte's works which can be found in Blondel's library at Aix, and dating from the period before the publication of *Action*, are the Grimblot translation of the *Theory of Science* and two popular works, *The Vocation of Man* and *Considerations to Correct the Judgment of the Public on the French Revolution*. Also a notebook of Blondel, containing his reflections on Fichte's thought, can be found.

important influence on Blondel than did the direct contacts. The manuscript copy of Victor Delbos' book, *The Moral Problem in the Philosophy of Spinoza*, which Blondel had read before writing *Action*, devoted a chapter to the place of Fichte's doctrine in the evolution of Spinozism.[1] Xavier Léon, the founder of the *Revue de Métaphysique et de Morale*, who would later become one of Blondel's intimate friends, was already at work on his book, *The Philosophy of Fichte*; but it would seem that Blondel's contact with Léon began only after the publication of *Action*.[2]

However, if Blondel, Delbos, and Léon, all three, manifest an interest in and a knowledge of Fichte's work at the same period, there is a common source of that interest and knowledge, Emile Boutroux. As we have noted, Blondel and Delbos both followed Boutroux' course on Kant and post-Kantian idealist philosophy at the Ecole Normale in the years 1882-1883; and subsequently it was Boutroux who directed their work. Blondel acknowledges that the primary exterior influence on the "form" of his thought was the teaching of Boutroux.[3] In the preface to his work *The Philosophy of Fichte*, Léon also acknowledges that the original inspiration for his life-long research and study of the life and writings of Fichte was derived from a course of Boutroux on modern philosophy which he had audited at the Sorbonne.[4]

There is one other indirect source from which Blondel derived his knowledge of Fichte and which had, apparently, considerable influence on his understanding of Fichte's doctrine. This source was Schelling. In the year 1889-1890 Blondel, with the assistance of Delbos, undertook a rather intensive study of Schelling's work, *System of Transcendental Idealism*, in which the influence of Fichte's *Theory of Science* is evident.[5] This approach to Fichte through the writings of Schelling had an important bearing on the understanding that both Delbos and Blondel manifest of Fichte's doctrine, especially in its later forms.[6]

---

[1] Delbos, *Le Problème Moral dans la Philosophie de Spinoza*, pp. 255-272.

[2] Blondel's first correspondence with Xavier Léon can be found in his *Lettres Philosophiques*, p. 38, and dates from the 22nd of October, 1883.

[3] Confer above, pp. 6-9.

[4] Xavier Léon, *La Philosophie de Fichte*, pp. III-IV.

[5] For evidence of Blondel's study of Schelling confer *Lettres Philosophiques*, pp. 20 and 23. Xavier Léon discusses the influence of Fichte's thought on Schelling's *System of Transcendental Idealism* in his work *Fichte et son Temps*, (Paris: Librarie Armand Colin, 1924) Tome II, Col. I, pp. 342-371.

[6] This influence is treated below, pp. 114-117.

BLONDEL'S UNDERSTANDING OF FICHTE'S PHILOSOPHY

In his article of 1894, "The Evolution of Spinozism," Blondel, following Delbos' lead, was inclined to see in the first *Theory of Science* what Jacobi had termed a "turned-about Spinozism." The center of that revolution was the Kantian concept of practical reason. However, Fichte's interpretation of that concept was by no means a simple restatement. What Fichte found unacceptable in Kant's critical philosophy was his concept of the thing-in-itself as something both real and unknowable. This to Fichte's mind was an unwarranted compromise with realism or, as he called it, "dogmatism." If idealism as a philosophical system was to be fully consequent with itself, it must reduce this Kantian dualism to an absolute unity. It must find the unique principle of all that exists and is known in the subject or ego which becomes and produces itself by means of its moral activity.

Blondel employs this formula of Delbos in which he relates Fichte's idealist program to Spinoza's *Ethics*: "Transform the being of substance into action; the unlimited reality into idea; consider the *Ego* not as a derived expression but as the primary form of the absolute."[1] Here, according to Blondel, we find once again the monist idea of Spinoza; but now the infinite subject replaced the infinite object. Further, this infinite subject is understood not as a static reality but as a pure activity, a moral process of becoming. "In place of an ontological pantheism where God is the one and all, we have an ethical pantheism where the moral law is one and all."[2]

In this brief summary which he gives of Delbos' much more complete description of Fichte's *Theory of Science*, Blondel tends to retain those elements of Delbos' description which emphasize the systematic, idealist features of Fichte's doctrine. However, he refrains from mentioning those other aspects of Fichte's doctrine which Delbos also develops, and which resemble closely certain features of Blondel's own position. For example, the quotation which Blondel employed above from Delbos' book, summarizing Fichte's doctrine in contrast with Spinoza's *Ethics*, continues as follows:

> Make the universe, not the static product of a universal law but the indefinitely perfectable instrument of the human will; eliminate the metaphysics of nature and intellectual contemplation in order to substitute

---

[1] Blondel, "L'Evolution du Spinozisme," II, 324. Blondel's quotation is from Delbos, *Le Problème Moral dans la Philosophie de Spinoza*, p. 265.

[2] Blondel, *op. cit.*, p. 324.

a metaphysics of liberty and practical action. Maintain that moral action contains an intuition of truth infinitely superior to scientific knowledge. ... Maintain that philosophical and moral truths cannot be imposed on man from without, ... that they become light only if first they are action, living personal action.[1]

All these features of Fichte's philosophy find their analogy in Blondel's own philosophy. Nor are these similarities surprising when we recall that for Fichte in the first *Theory of Science*, as for Blondel in *Action*, the ego or subject is understood as an active striving for a total identity of self with self. And this ego unfolds and realizes its infinite potential in the progressive accomplishment of free moral activity. Fichte's *Theory of Science* can be considered as a philosophy of action in a sense analogous to that of Blondel's and, as such, inevitably prefigures many of the essential features of Blondel's philosophy of action. Blondel, himself, was quite aware of this basic similarity between his position and that of Fichte. As early as 1889 he wrote in his private journal:

> There is only one truth worthy of man ... it is that moral world which he fashions and deploys little by little in so far as he acts. There lies the solution to the major metaphysical problem. ... We construct in our wills and by our acts that reality itself, not by a mysterious deduction as in the subjective idealism of Fichte, but by reflection on and by possession of self, by freedom and voluntary commitment.[2]

This text gives us a very important clue to Blondel's idea of the exact relation between his philosophy and Fichte's. Although there is a basic similarity in the starting point, an intuition into the importance and meaning of moral action as the center of philosophy, Blondel rejects the systematic scientific apparatus, that "mysterious deduction," which he felt was commanded by Fichte's initial commitment to an absolute, subjective idealism. As Copleston points out, there are two levels of meaning present at nearly every stage of Fichte's *Wissenschafts-lehre*. The first is a rather original and profound phenomenology of consciousness; the second is an idealist metaphysics in which the elements of that phenomenological analysis are absolutized as metaphysical principles. "To a certain extent at any rate," Copleston remarks, "the two aspects can be separated. Hence it is possible to attach some value to a good deal of what Fichte has to say without committing oneself to his metaphysical idealism."[3] It would seem that this

---

[1] Delbos, *op. cit.*, p. 265.
[2] Blondel, *Carnets Intimes*, pp. 194-195.
[3] Frederick Copleston, *A History of Philosophy*, (London: Burns and Oats, 1963), Vol. VII, p. 44.

was the program that Blondel followed in regard to Fichte. Blondel continually insisted that his phenomenal study of action was a purely methodological procedure. His initial effort was to undertake a thorough analysis of human action as this action reveals itself in consciousness without introducing any undue metaphysical conclusions. In fact, this tendency to absolutize the elements of the analysis was the principal charge which Blondel brought to bear against Kantian criticism in general.[1] This charge more properly applies to the much more explicit metaphysical idealism of Fichte.

FICHTE'S FINAL PHILOSOPHY

Both Delbos and Blondel after him were inclined to understand what they called "the second or final stage" of Fichte's philosophy as a return to Spinoza's original position of an affirmation of absolute Being which transcends consciousness and, consequently, as more or less in contradiction with his own original idealist premise of the identity of being with consciousness. They were aware, however, that there was a controversy as to whether the consequent development of Fichte's original position represented an organic evolution of his thought or a basic change of position. "As a matter of fact," Delbos writes, "whether there was a process of evolution or an about-face in the thought of Fichte, that which is unquestionable is that his final philosophy openly inclines towards Spinozan ontologism."[2] Fichte, according to Blondel, came to realize that the Infinite is such only if, after suppressing all limits and negations, it is.

> Consequently, Fichte finds once again in the certitude and love of Being, defined otherwise, it is true, than in Spinoza, the source of the blessed life, which the *Ethics* had also placed in the adequate knowledge and intellectual love of God. Thus beyond the metaphysics of moral duty we find restored in this manner a metaphysics of being and of life.[3]

There are several factors in both Delbos' and Blondel's interpretation of Fichte's thought, which seem to indicate that one of the primary sources of their interpretation of Fichte, and especially of his later philosophy, was the writings of Schelling. Both seem to be aware primarily of the first *Theory of Science* with its two *Introductions*. Both seem to be relatively unaware of the gradual development of Fichte's

---

[1] Confer above, pp. 55-60.
[2] Delbos, *op. cit.*, p. 267.
[3] Blondel, "L'Evolution du Spinozisme," II, 325.

thought in the subsequent *Theories of Science* of 1801 and 1804. What they call the final philosophy of Fichte seems to derive primarily from *The Way to a Blessed Life*, a series of lectures delivered in 1805-1806. But both seem to be unaware, once again, of the defense Fichte made against Schelling's charges of plagiarism and inconsistency in the final writings of 1812-1813.[1]

The essential elements of Fichte's first *Theory of Science* were incorporated and developed by Schelling, especially in two of his earlier works, *On the Ego as Principle in Philosophy* (Vom Ich als Prinzip der Philosophie) published in 1795, and System of Transcendental Idealism (System der transzendentalen Idealismus) published in 1800. Further, it was Schelling, in his later work *Exposition of the True Relation between the Philosophy of Nature and Fichte's improved Doctrine* (Darlegung des wahren Verhältnisses der Naturphilosophie zu der verbesserten Fichteschen Lehre) published in 1806, who first maintained that Fichte had contradicted the basic premise of his first *Theory of Science* in his work *The Way to a Blessed Life*.[2]

A careful study of Delbos' book, *The Moral Problem in the Philosophy of Spinoza*, would seem to confirm the point that Schelling was the primary source for his understanding and critique of Fichte. Delbos' chapter on Fichte does not contain a single exact reference to any of Fichte's own writings. In sharp contrast, the chapter in the same book dealing with Schelling's philosophy is a work by work analysis of the development of Schelling's thought with abundant, detailed reference to the original works.[3]

These facts, plus the intrinsic evidence of the understanding Blondel himself manifests in *Action* concerning the idealist movement, lead us to believe that Blondel, again following Delbos' lead, was greatly influenced in his understanding of Fichte by Schelling's early development and later critique of that doctrine. This influence would also help to explain why Blondel's knowledge of Fichte was seemingly limited to the two major works translated into French, the first *Theory of*

---

[1] An excellent summary of this controversy between Schelling and Fichte can be found in Léon, *op. cit.*, Tome II, vol. 1, pp. 342-371, 498-519.

[2] Léon, *op. cit.*, pp. 502-504.

[3] There are only two reference footnotes in this chapter concerning Fichte in Delbos' work. Both notes refer the reader to commentaries on the recent history of German philosophical thought: Windelband, *Geschichte der neueren Philosophie* (Leipzig: 1880), and Jodl, *Geschichte der Ethik in der neueren Philosophie* (Stuttgart: 1889). Confer Delbos, *op. cit.*, pp. 266-267. It is interesting to note also that Delbos' latin thesis published in 1902 was entitled *De posteriore Schellingii philosophia quatenus Hegelianae doctrinae adversatur* (Paris: félix Alcan, 1902).

Science of 1794 and *The Way to a Blessed Life* of 1806. The first was incorporated into the one work of Schelling which we know Blondel studied intensively in the years 1889-1890, *System of Transcendental Idealism*; the second was the object of Schelling's criticism as contradicting the essential postulate of the first *Theory of Science*. Consequently, Blondel was inclined to accept the prevalent opinion that the only real contribution of Fichte to the evolution of modern thought was his first *Theory of Science*; and, with the appearance of Schelling on the scene, all that was important in Fichte's thought was assimilated and surpassed in a superior synthesis.

These precisions concerning the various indirect sources of Blondel's understanding of Fichte's philosophy are important from the perspective of this study. We are not concerned here primarily with an effort to achieve an objective understanding of the system of Fichte in itself and the justice of Blondel's interpretation of that system; nor are we concerned with a totally objective comparison of Fichte's theories with the corresponding positions of Blondel. Rather, what we must try to capture and appreciate, in so far as that is possible, is the understanding Blondel himself had of Fichte's philosophy and of the position of that philosophy within the context of the evolution of modern thought. For it is that understanding which actually entered into and helped to determine Blondel's own concept and methodology in his philosophy of action, and our ultimate objective is to try to arrive at as clear an understanding as possible, in the light of his sources, of the originality of Blondel's own philosophical synthesis.

Blondel's attitude towards Fichte's philosophy did not differ from his attitude towards any of the other sources which influenced his thought. He was never interested in an accurate reconstitution of an historical system but, rather, he saw all the previous systems as only means by which he could "pull out what was still vital" and "gather up the seeds of his own personal thought."[1] From this perspective what interested Blondel was not the historical problem of an objective reconstitution of Fichte's teaching. Rather, he was interested in understanding what his own contemporaries saw as the primary vital contribution Fichte had made to the evolution of modern thought. Blondel's

---

[1] In his own use of idealist sources it is evident that Blondel himself followed the advice that he sent to his friend Delbos in 1889, when he was composing his work on Spinoza: "In dealing with the successive forms of dialectical pantheism you ought to consider these various doctrines ... in so far as they form the various levels of your own intellectual evolution and the sources of your own synthesis." (*Lettres Philosophiques*, p. 16).

comprehension of that contribution was determined by the prevalent interpretation of his contemporaries and, in particular, by the teaching of his professor. Emile Boutroux, and the writings of his friends, Victor Delbos and Xavier Léon.

Our point of departure, in our attempt to grasp Fichte's influence on Blondel, then, is the various comments and allusions Blondel himself makes either to Fichte's ideas or to the position of the Idealists in general. Where it proves useful, we will consult the works of Blondel's contemporaries, and especially Delbos and Léon, in order to place Blondel's comments in their context of contemporary interpretation. Once we have explored the basic agreement and disagreement of Blondel's philosophy of action with Fichte's system as Blondel himself understood that relation, we can undertake an exploration of the consequences of that similarity and divergence in the actual working out of the two systems.

In chapter seven of this comparative study we deal with what Blondel saw as the most basic point of disagreement with Fichte in particular and Idealism in general, namely their intellectualism or confusion of theory and reality, which had its foundation in their concept of philosophy as a strict science based on a mathematical model. In chapter eight, we attempt to trace the positive influence of Fichte's theory on Blondel, especially as concerns their analogous concept of action as the point of departure for philosophy. We trace, also, the progressive breakdown of that initial agreement due to the rejection by Blondel of Fichte's idealistic postulate and of his mathematicism. This study of the progressive divergence in these two theories leads us, in chapters nine and ten, to a comparison of the two systems as concerns the nature of the absolute and the problem of man's union with the absolute. Chapter eleven deals with the consequence of this divergence in the concept of the absolute as it is revealed in Blondel's and Fichte's respective theory of interpersonality. In chapters twelve and thirteen we will attempt to compare the logic or dialectic of action contained in these two philosophies.

The analysis we undertake in chapter thirteen of Blondel's concept of the living dialectic present in life and the resulting dialectical logic of action is of utmost importance in determining the originality of Blondel's effort at synthesis in relation to his sources. For in this chapter we attempt to present the central insight which at least implicitly controlled the entire process of assimilation and rejection which Blondel employed in relation to his sources.

Chapter thirteen serves also as a pivotal point for our transition from a consideration of Fichte's influence to the question of the influence of Schelling and Hegel. For it presents the primary means Blondel employed in his effort to assimilate and complete the phenomenological element present in Fichte's thought within the context of a dialectic such as Schelling and Hegel developed. Consequently, Blondel's insight, presented in chapter thirteen, permits us in chapter fourteen to sketch rapidly the further evolution of moral philosophy within Schelling's and Hegel's doctrine as Blondel understood it in the light of his own concept of the logic and dialectic contained in action. Finally, in chapter fifteen we consider the influence on Blondel's thought of the effort of Schelling in his final, positive philosophy to transcend the position of Hegel and arrive at an existential philosophy capable of assimilating real religious experience.

CHAPTER SEVEN

PHILOSOPHY AS SCIENCE

FICHTE'S PROBLEM

It would seem, as the previous quotation from Blondel's diary indicates, that, although from the very beginning Blondel found himself inclined to agree with Fichte concerning the role of the moral activity of the subject as the ideal center of perspective of philosophy, he also sharply disagreed from the start on the precise systematic or scientific nature of that philosophy of will-action.[1] Thus one of the first and most fundamental influences of Fichte's *Theory of Science* on Blondel's philosophy of action has to do with Blondel's rejection of Fichte's concept of the systematic or scientific character of philosophy as he understood it. A study of this predominantly negative relation can help us to appreciate more fully why Blondel in his early notes spoke of philosophy as a sort of "science of moral experimentation," and how he intended that experience itself should enter as an integral factor into the very scientific and systematic development of philosophy.

The problem of the scientific nature of philosophy posed itself for Fichte as a result of his early study of Spinoza. In order to understand the nature of the synthesis Fichte sought in his first *Theory of Science* between Spinoza's *Ethics* and Kant's *Critique of Practical Reason*, it is important to keep in mind that in his youth Fichte himself, despite his own religious convictions and personal preferences to the contrary, became convinced of the rational validity of Spinoza's determinism. What impressed Fichte most of all in Spinoza's doctrine was its strict rational and scientific development.[2] But despite what he considered to be the intellectual superiority of determinism as a rational system,

---

[1] Above, pp. 112-113.

[2] Xavier Léon lists four principle characteristics of Fichte's philosophy which were derived from his study of Spinoza: his moralism—the moral and religious sense of the philosophical problem, his monism— the necessity of the absolute unity of the first principle, his rationalism—the perfect intelligibility and universal necessity of all that exists, and finally his pantheism—the absolute reality of all existence when it is referred back to its eternal, immanent essence. (Léon, *op. cit.*, p. 56).

Fichte could not bring himself to relinquish his belief in human freedom. While engaged in this conflict between his determinist philosophy and personal convictions, he read for the first time *The Critique of
Pure Reason* of Kant. He immediately saw in the limits which Kant
posed for theoretical reason a scientific justification for religious belief
based in sentiment, a sort of scientific confirmation of the Protestant
concept of the separation of faith and reason.[1]

But Fichte found himself incapable of accepting such a total division
between "heart and head," belief and thought, as the final word for the
human intelligence. "The only manner of solution for such a person
would be to forbid himself those speculations which pass beyond this
established limit. But can he do this when he so wishes? ... Can he do
so when that attitude (of speculation) is already natural for him; when
it is inseparable from the entire cast of his mind?"[2] Thus Fichte found
himself faced with the dilemma of either following out the metaphysical and speculative bent of his nature and as a result falling inevitably,
as he thought, into a sort of determinism, which conflicted with his
religious and moral convictions concerning personal liberty, or of
refusing speculation any rights in such matters and thus producing
within himself a constant insoluble conflict between faith and reason.
Here we have a concrete example of what Blondel describes as the
presence of the Christian idea of human destiny—in this case, specifically, the idea of a destiny based on the use of freedom—implicitly at
work determining the evolution of modern philosophy.

While in the process of debating how to resolve this dilemma,
Fichte began to read Kant's *Critique of Practical Reason*. This study of
Kant's second Critique would prove to be the decisive factor in determining the shape of his own philosophy. By limiting the field of determinism to the phenomenal order and by disclosing in the very existence of moral consciousness the causal efficacy of liberty, Kant had,
in Fichte's estimation, given the key to the solution of the conflict
between faith and reason. "I owe him (Kant) my present belief with
all my heart in the liberty of man, and I understand very well that it is
only under this hypothesis that obligation, virtue, and morality in
general are possible."[3]

---

[1] *Ibid.*, pp. 81-82.

[2] Fichte, "Aphorismen über Religion und Deismus," Vol. V, pp. 7-8. (All
volume and page references hereafter will be to *Fichte's sammtliche Werke*, edited
by J. H. Fichte (Berlin: Verlag von Veit und Comp., 1845).

[3] Léon, *op. cit.*, p. 88.

As we have seen, Blondel accredited Spinoza with being the first of the moderns to have posed human destiny as the central problem of philosophy. Fichte inherited this problem from Spinoza but, unlike Spinoza, he was unwilling to sacrifice human liberty to the needs of a rationally consistent system. Whereas Spinoza sought to justify the universal determinism of the infinite substance despite the appearance of human liberty, Fichte on the contrary, tried to justify freedom despite the appearance of universal determinism. The initial problem he poses is: "Can man be free in the midst of the causal determinacy of all things?"[1] Or as Maurice Gueroult rephrases it: "How can one reconcile liberty in its most extreme form, as creativity or absolute contingent choice, with a speculation which is totally evident and, consequently, necessary?"[2] Thus it can be said that Fichte was the first of the moderns to identify the problem of human destiny with the problem of human liberty. He was quite aware that any philosopher who attempts to answer the problem of human destiny must succeed in justifying man's liberty or admit his impotency to give any satisfactory answer to the problem of the destiny of man. Thus Fichte brings us one step nearer to the precise problem which Blondel poses at the beginning of *Action*: "I shall know if at present or in the future I shall have sufficient knowledge and force of will never to experience any tyranny whatever it may be."[3] Blondel also calls attention to the apparent determinism and necessity which seems to render illusory the pretension of man to be truly free. Yet, despite these appearnaces, freedom must have the last word, or the very existence of man as a free rational being must be put in question. "That necessity which appears to me as a tyrannical constraint, that obligation which at first appears despotic, it is necessary that in the last analysis I see that it manifests itself and is put into motion by the deepest activity of my own will; if not, it will be my destruction."[4]

However, as we shall see, Fichte understood the choice between liberty or determinism as itself a free initial option, which could be justified consequently only in terms of its superiority in providing the basic principle for a scientific idealist system. Blondel, on the contrary, refused any a priori option for or against freedom or determinism,

---

[1] Fichte, *Leben und Briefwechsel*, ed. I. H. Fichte (Leipzig: F. - A. Brockhaus, 1862), Zweite Auflage, Vol. I, p. 21.

[2] Maurice Gueroult, *L'Evolution et la Structure de la Doctrine de la Science chez Fichte* (Pairs: Société d'Editeurs: Les Belles Lettres, 1930), Vol. I, p. 1.

[3] Blondel, *L'Action*, p. VII.

[4] *Ibid.*, p. XXIII.

but sought only to analyze and reveal the continuity of both phenomena in the total reality of being.

The Role of Free Option in Philosophy

No sooner had Fichte accepted Kant's concept of practical reason than the influence of his previous study of Spinoza began to show itself. He began to find Kant's philosophy unsystematic. He felt obliged to reduce the whole of Kant's philosophy to an absolute first principle from which the entire system could be derived *more geometrico*, just as Spinoza in his *Ethics* had deduced the whole of his system from one absolute principle. Thus he wrote to a friend:

> I've discovered a new foundation from which the whole of philosophy can be deduced quite easily. Kant in a general way possessed the true doctrine but in its end products only and not in its principles. ... In brief, I believe that in one or two years we shall possess a philosophy which will be equal in its evidence with geometry.[1]

In fact, it was this systematic rational development of an idealistic system based on a mathematical model which Fichte considered as his most important original achievement. He prided himself as being the Euclid of philosophy. And it is this mathematicism, this desire to erect a deductive philosophical system based on the ideal model of a geometric system, which will most radically distinguish Fichte's philosophy of action from Blondel's.

If philosophy was to be a true science equal in its evidence to geometry, then Fichte saw as his first task the discovery of the absolute first principle from which the entire system of philosophy could be deduced rationally. He maintained, however, that the first principle itself could not be deduced rationally nor proven in any way, because it was itself the absolute first principle on which any such deduction or proof would depend. "All other propositions will possess only a mediate certainty derived from it, whereas it must be immediately certain."[2] Thus Fichte concludes that the starting point of philosophy, that is, the principle from which our philosophical theory will be derived, is necessarily a question of a free option. But for Fichte that initial choice is reduced to an either-or proposition. Either one can begin with an objective realist first principle and develop a systematic objective determinism as Spinoza did; or one can choose a subjective

---

[1] Fichte, *Leben und Briefwechsel*, Vol. II, pp. 511-512.

[2] Fichte, "Ueber den Begriff der Wissenschaftslehre," Vol. I, p. 48.

principle and develop a systematic idealism based on creative thought. Thus both a systematic realism and a systematic idealism are both ultimately irrefutable, once one has accepted their basic first principle.[1] Any attempt at compromise between these two possibilities would necessarily lead to inconsistencies and would, as a result, be rationally unacceptable. Fichte was inclined to see in the Kantian concept of the thing-in-itself just such an attempt at compromise, a hybrid of formal idealism and material realism.

The rational inconsistency which results is proven, Fichte claimed, by the insoluble difficulties one has in determining the role the thing-in-itself would play in an idealist system. If it had a function, that function could only be understood in terms of a transcendent causality.[2] But Kant himself proved that such a transcendent application of the concept of causality was illegitimate. Consequently, no such compromise is logically possible. If one chooses a subjective idealistic starting point, as Kant did, one is obliged to deduce not only the formal but also the material elements of all knowledge from the subject alone. Thus Fichte maintained that a pure systematic idealism was the only means of defending Kant's primacy of practical reason or moral will. The thing-in-itself must be totally eliminated, if we are to escape the danger of ultimately falling back into dogmatic determinism.

Since no rational grounds exist for the choice between these two alternatives, Fichte held that the basis of choice between the two ultimate possibilities is factually determined by "inclination or interest"; that is to say, the choice which a given philosopher makes depends on the kind of man he is. If the philosopher is naturally conscious of his freedom as revealed to him in his moral experience, he will naturally tend to find the first principle of his philosophy in the free moral subject and develop an idealist system. If, however, he is naturally

---

[1] An excellent discussion of Fichte's concept of the problem posed by Kant's thing-in-itself and his idea of the necessity of an initial option can be found in Delbos' *De Kant aux Post-Kantiens* (Paris: Aubier, Editions Montaigne, 1940), pp. 89-96. This book was published after Delbos' death by Maurice Blondel himself from the notes of a course Delbos gave at the Sorbonne in 1909. Blondel also contributed an interesting preface on the relation between German and French philosophy in his friend's thought.

[2] Fichte was inclined to accept the criticism of Kant's thing-in-itself presented by Jacobi as valid. If the thing-in-itself was understood by Kant as expressing a real transcendental causality, it would involve a contradiction within his system. However, Fichte held that, despite appearances to the contrary, Kant himself could not have held such a position in flagrant contradiction with the entire spirit of his own system. (Delbos, *op. cit.*, pp. 40-58.).

predominantly conscious of being determined by exterior objects, he will seek his first principle in the object and develop a dogmatic realist system. Even if one could demonstrate objectively to a dogmatist the insufficiency of his principle, it would be wasted effort; for it would be necessary that that insufficiency should become evident to him from within his own consciousness by a personal action which he is incapable of placing.[1]

In his *First Introduction to the Theory of Science* Fichte attempts an analysis of the process by means of which this natural tendency leads to the choice of a first principle. Philosophy has as its purpose to make clear the grounds of experience. But experience, as we have seen, can be reduced to two basic kinds, those accompanied by feelings of freedom and those accompanied by feelings of necessity. When the feeling of freedom predominates, the subject appears actively to cause its objects to be what they are. Where necessity predominates, the object appears to be imposed on the subject. Actual consciousness is always consciousness of an object by a subject. By a process which Fichte calls abstraction, the philosopher can isolate conceptually two factors which in actual conscious experience are always joined, that is, the concepts of intellect-in-itself and thing-in-itself. Thus, the philosopher can either attempt to explain experience as the product of intellect-in-itself or as the product of the thing-in-itself. As a result two paths, idealism or realism, are open to him.[2]

It is important to note that Fichte understood his initial option as necessarily involving an abstractive process, whereby one deliberately isolates a factor of conscious experience and erects this isolated factor as the explanatory principle of the whole of reality. Further, this process of abstraction is, in Fichte's opinion, the essential characteristic of philosophy as such, and distinguishes it as a science from experimental knowledge. It is precisely by separating by means of an abstraction one of these two factors inseparably joined in consciousness and by constituting this factor as the first principle, that the philosopher elevates himself above experience and fulfills his task. Fichte attempts to justify his seemingly arbitrary initial option for one of the aspects of lived experience in terms of the abstract nature which philosophy as a distinct discipline must necessarily possess. Philosophy as such is not life, nor should it attempt to reduplicate the processes

---

[1] Delbos, *op. cit.*, p. 92.
[2] Fichte, "Erste Einleitung ...," Vol, I, pp. 422-423. Confer also Delbos, *op. cit.*, pp. 89-90.

of life. Philosophy, as a technical discipline, can not proceed except by abstraction. Just as the mathematician, for example, is obliged to abstract a certain aspect of corporeal reality, so the philosopher by means of his freedom of thought must isolate a certain aspect of that which is factually united in experience.[1]

This abstractive concept of philosophy is one of the principal errors concerning the nature of philosophy which Blondel seeks to refute in his article "The Point of Departure of Philosophical Research." Blondel concedes that, in the past, a majority of philosophers seem habitually to have adapted their universal object to a particular method which, "under the guise of the impersonal form of a technical discipline, expresses in reality the singularities of their intellectual preferences and moral experiences." But Blondel denies that this is a necessity for philosophy; and he resolutely refuses to grant Fichte's dissociation of life and philosophy:

> Cannot one realize a doctrine in which the human, or even universal, subject matter and the specific form of philosophy harmonize in such a way that ... philosophical research would be in perfect continuity with the natural movement of life or, even better, would be that life itself, in so far as it perfects itself by the acquisition of understanding and reality?[2]

Philosophy, for Blondel, "is life itself is so far as that life assumes consciousness and undertakes the direction of itself."[3] However, Blondel does not deny that philosophy must also be a technical discipline, clearly distinguished in its form from every other species of scientific knowledge. But the essential characteristic which distinguishes philosophy from all other sciences is, in Blondel's opinion, the exact opposite to that which Fichte proposes. All other sciences are specified by the particular aspect of being which they abstract and deal with apart from the totality of being. The specific characteristic of philosophy is its refusal to abstract any aspect of being or life from the total context which gives it its meaning and value.

> From its point of departure, specifically philosophical research ought to be distinguished from common experience and from the exact sciences which deal with particular objects. For it is not with a particular object that philosophy begins, but with the *total manner* (facon totale) of posing the problem of destiny or the problem of being, and

---

[1] Fichte, *op. cit.*, Vol. I, pp. 524-426.
[2] Blondel, "Le Point de Départ de la Recherche Philosophique," I, 339.
[3] *Ibid.*, II, 227.

the permanent difficulty which it must overcome is precisely to carry out its investigation without the support of imaginary ontological entities.[1]

Consequently, Blondel calls nonsensical any effort to resolve the philosophical problem of being and destiny by artificially abstracting one aspect of conscious experience and attempting to construct a solution to the total problem of life based on this artificially constructed aspect. Everything which is given in consciousness ought to be considered equally as real and true and as forming an homogeneous series, without considering any element as privileged or excluded. "All the data of consciousness are equally an aspect of reality (du réel), without being *the* real (le réel)."[2]

Nothing could be more basically contradictory to Blondel's point of departure than the Fichtean idea of an initial option between a realist or idealist starting point, which Blondel thus formulates: "Conceding that there are two apparent terms, act as if there is only one."[3] A philosophy based on such a starting point is doomed to failure, Blondel claims, since "it is impossible to define, much less to choose effectively, one of these two attitudes to the exclusion of the other."[4] Fichte, Blondel argues, was no more capable of constructing a consistent system based on the dynamic principle of intelligence as a pure principle of active becoming, than Spinoza had been on the pure principle of static absolute substance. "Just as in the system of Spinoza the *fieri* of human morality was necessary in order that God could manifest himself, so in the system of Fichte the *esse* of the world was necessary in order that the moral law could be realized."[5] Pure becoming does not offer an explanation of anything, because it does not explain itself. Blondel sees in Fichte's famous theory of the imagination as an unconscious process by which the ego creates its own objects not so much an ingenious deduction of the matter of consciousness, as an effort to conceal the fundamental inadequacy of his starting point. He maintains that Fichte was constrained to introduce into his system a means whereby the ego could transform itself into nature or object and thus manifest itself by means of its infinite power in the accomplishment of a determined end.

---

[1] *Ibid.*, II, 248. *Underlining* added.
[2] Blondel, "L'Illusion Idéaliste," p. 108.
[3] *Ibid.*, p. 105.
[4] *Ibid.*, p. 98.
[5] Blondel, "L'Evolution du Spinozisme," II, 324.

For Blondel both the realist and idealist principles are complementary aspects of our conscious experience, both equally deceiving and equally justified. They are deceiving in so far as one tries, as Fichte did, to artificially reduce the dialectic of consciousness in act to one of its elements. They are justified since both constitute a moment of internal determinism and a dynamic source of our conscious life. Instead of isolating these aspects of conscious experience, Blondel saw as the primary task of philosophy the undertaking of an analytic description of consciousness which would attempt to reveal the real connection in experience of these apparently contradictory but really complementary aspects of consciousness. "Reintegrate in thought these two terms with the same characteristics of spontaneity, necessity, and solidarity which they possess in living consciousness."[1] Thus, the first task which imposes itself on the philosopher is to analyze the total content of consciousness as it unfolds itself in action without any realist or idealist prejudice of any sort.

The Role of Experience

If Blondel differs from Fichte concerning the question of an initial option and the abstract nature of philosophy, these differences spring from an even more fundamental opposition concerning the nature of philosophy as science and the role of experience in philosophy. Fichte's model for the scientific development of his philosophy was, as we have seen, geometry. Fichte begins with an intuition of the conscious self as pure activity; he then proceeds to reconstruct the essential characteristics of that consciousness of self. "The *Theory of Science* reconstructs the form of consciousness common to all rational beings entirely a priori in its essential traits, in exactly the same way as in geometry one constructs a priori the universal modes of the limitation of space."[2] Once this reconstruction of consciousness has been accomplished, the deduction properly speaking of the *Theory of Science* begins. Fichte makes an initial appeal to the living experiential intuition of the ego or self as the original source of a special sort of material certitude which differs from the purely formal certitude of mathematics. It is this

---

[1] Blondel, "L'Evolution Idéaliste," p. 98.
[2] "Die Wissenschaftslehre construit das gesammte gemeinsame Bewusstseyn aller vernünftigen Wesen schlechthin *a priori*, seinen Grundzügen nach, ebenso wie die Geometrie die Allgemeinen Begrenzungswesen des Raumes... schlechthin *a priori* construirt." (Fichte, "Somnenklarer Bericht...," Vol. II, p. 379.)

material certitude which will justify the application of the conclusions of his deductions to reality. However, once he has abstracted the pure form of that initial intuition of self as activity, no further appeal to the facts of experience is necessary or possible within the system.

> In the course of this construction any effort to return to experience would be an effort to falsify the deduction. Those who advise that in philosophy one should always have an eye open on experience are, in effect, counseling you to modify a bit the factors and to falsify a bit the calculation in order to obtain the desired numbers, a process which is as dishonest as it is superficial.[1]

Blondel was quite aware that this refusal to admit any continuing role to experience in the deductive process of philosophy was the central point in method which, in his opinion, rendered Fichte's "mysterious process of deduction" invalid. According to Blondel, even if Fichte did understand the moral intuition of self consciousness or free activity to be the true point of departure for philosophy, his mathematical concept of philosophy as an abstract science led him to falsify that initial perspective.

> It suffices to remark to what extent that vital intuition of moral consciousness and of pure practical reason is subjected to the abstract form of an idealized analysis, and how it finishes by establishing a rationalism which has modified the nature without changing the spirit of previous philosophies, in order that one can grasp the artificial character of such an undertaking.[2]

As we have seen, Blondel understood, as the proper model of a philosophy of action, the experimental sciences. The true object of philosophy is precisely that unique synthesis of the real and the ideal which cannot be reproduced by a pure deductive process but only by living concrete action. Thus, moral experience, far from being a distortion of philosophical truth, is the indispensable organ of that truth. "Philosophy does not begin until, refusing to attach itself to the idea of action as its proper object, it subordinates itself to effective action and becomes practicing."[3] By refusing a continuing role to moral experience in the theoretical development of a philosophy of action, Fichte, in Blondel's opinion, had effectively substituted a theory of action for the reality of action. But such a substitution is based on the false premise that the philosopher can effectively place himself outside

---

[1] *Ibid.*, "Erste Einleitung...," Vol. I, pp. 446-447.
[2] Blondel, "Le Point de Départ...," I, 351.
[3] *Ibid.*, II, 239.

the movement of consciousness in order to deal with it abstractly by
a sort of formal absolutism.

SUMMARY

From the very first moments of his philosophical endeavor Fichte
posed the basic problem of philosophy in almost identical terms as did
Blondel after him. The primary task of the philosopher was to uncover
the meaning of human destiny. But human destiny has meaning and
reality only on condition that one can establish the ultimate validity of
human freedom. Simultaneously with the need to defend liberty,
Fichte experienced a necessity, equally if not more imperious, to create
a strict philosophical science in imitation of Spinoza's geometrical
development of determinism. Hidden behind this second ambition
was the assumption that, if a philosophy of liberty could not be
developed with the same rational clarity and purity as Spinoza's *Ethics*,
it must be rejected as invalid and liberty must be dismissed as an
illusion.

The only means Fichte saw that could guarantee the success of his
ambition to create a strict science of freedom was to postulate an
initial option for freedom and against determinism. If freedom is real,
then that subjective active striving of the rational will *exists*; and all
else, all objects which apparently exist independently of that will-
activity and impose themselves on it, *do not exist* but receive their
ultimately illusory being from the will-act itself.

Paradoxically, Blondel, who rejects totally any idea of an initial
option as the point of departure for philosophy, does agree with
Fichte that it is by means of a fundamental option that man wins
access to a true metaphysics of absolute being—his "metaphysics to
the second power." And it is also by means of this final option that
human liberty receives its ultimate justification. But Blondel's option
has nothing to do with a choice between liberty or determinism, idealism or realism. A true option, according to Blondel, can only be made
where the law of contradiction can be applied in all its vigor, and liberty
can be exercised in all its force.[1] But the law of contradiction applies
in all its vigor when, and only when, we find ourselves in the presence
of absolute Being itself. Liberty and determinism, the intellect-in-itself
and thing-in-itself are not Being; they are only partial aspects of being.

---

[1] Blondel, *L'Action*, p. 356.

If one mistakenly begins philosophy with an arbitrary choice of one of these aspects of being and the elimination of the other, one is doomed from the very beginning to mistake the part for the whole and an artificially constructed ontological entity for the absolute reality of Being itself.

Nor can one justify this arbitrary option in terms of the necessarily abstract nature of philosophy as a technical discipline. For the specific character of philosophy as a science is precisely its effort to understand human destiny in its relation to the whole of being, to the entire universe, which includes all of nature, other egos, and the absolute itself. The surest way to fail to arrive at the true absolute is to create a false one by a *fiat* of the will. Consequently, what must distinguish philosophy as a science is not the type of abstraction which it employs but, on the contrary, its refusal to abstract. The true movement of philosophy is to plunge every individual being and every aspect of being into the whole from which it derives its meaning and ultimate justification.

This relation to the whole cannot be had without a constant reference to experience as such. For it is precisely the role of living action, Blondel insists, to create, as it were, the synthetic whole, that living, concrete interrelation to all of reality. This synthesis of its very nature escapes any purely abstract formulation or rational production. Thus, Fichte was right to place the vital, conscious intuition of the ego as moral activity as the true center of perspective of philosophy. But his univocal concept of science based on the model of an abstract and purely rational mathematicism led him to falsify that perspective from the very start. It is not by prescinding from experience but by a total fidelity to experience that philosophy can best achieve a truly scientific and universal character.

CHAPTER EIGHT

THE EGO AS ACTION

As the reference in his private diary indicates, Blondel was aware of a fundamental agreement between his philosophy of action and Fichte's theory of science and an equally fundamental diaagreement.[1] We have already analyzed the nature of that disagreement, the basic disaccord concerning the nature of philosophy as a technical or scientific discipline. However this divergence, important as it is, should not hide the fact that there was a basic intuition in Fichte's philosophy with which Blondel was in accord and which had an important influence on his own idea of a philosophy of action. Blondel himself insisted on several occasions that each of the major steps in the evolution of modern thought had brought an important contribution to the synthesis which he attempted in *Action*. He maintained, further, that it was impossible to fully appreciate what was the exact meaning and originality of that synthesis without some knowledge of the contributions which these previous philosophers had made.

What was the major positive influence of Fichte's thought on Blondel's synthesis? We have already had a hint as to the direction our investigation must take in Copleston's suggestion that at every step in Fichte's deduction of consciousness there are, as it were, two levels. The first is a remarkably profound phenomenological analysis of consciousness; the second is a systematic development of an idealist philosophy. It is this phenomenology of consciousness then, that we ought to investigate in order to try to grasp Fichte's positive influence on Blondel's philosophy of action. "The essence of the *Theory of Science*," Fichte tells us, "consists in a search for that root which was inaccessible to Kant, from which as from a common source spring the two worlds of the sensible and the intellectual; it consists, further, in the deduction, at the same time real and intellectual, of these two worlds from this unique principle."[2] If, as we have seen, Blondel was

---

[1] Above, pp. 112-114.

[2] "... in der Erforschung der für Kant Unerforschlichen Wurzel, in welcher die sinnliche und die übersinnliche Welt zusammenhängt, dann in der wirklichen und begreiflichen Ableitung beider Welten aus einem Prinzip, besteht ihr (die Wissenschaftslehre) Wesen." (Fichte, "Wissenschaftslehre (1804)," Vol. X, p. 104).

inclined to reject the idealist, rationalistic implications of the second objective, he was in complete accord with the first objective. In fact, there is a remarkable similarity between Fichte's and Blondel's philosophy from the viewpoint of this first objective. Both arrive at an almost identical concept of the point of departure of philosophy as being a conscious intuition which the subject has of itself as a genetic synthetic activity.

THE SEARCH FOR A FIRST PRINCIPLE

K. L. Reinhold, Fichte's predecessor in the chair of philosophy at Jena, had already demanded that the Kantian system should be systematized, that is to say, that it should be derived systematically from one fundamental principle.[1] According to Reinhold the first principle must take the form of a unique proposition which will determine the form of all other propositions without, however, determining the subject or predicate itself. Since it is the formulation of the first principle, this proposition cannot be proven; therefore, it must be the expression of a fact capable of being known by every man merely by reflection. This fact, however, cannot be a determined experience, a particular empirical fact, but must accompany and make possible every experience. Reinhold finds that first principle in the fact of consciousness, considered as the faculty of representation, which necessarily and universally accompanies every experience and thought. By reflection on this fact of consciousness the philosopher can formulate the principle of consciousness which constitutes the basic proposition of all philosophy; "The representation in consciousness is distinct from both the one representing and the thing represented, while, at the same time, it is in relation to both."

Fichte, in his article "Recension des Aenesidemus" (1795), agrees with Reinhold on the need of a unique, fundamental proposition from which the whole of philosophy could be derived. But he disagrees with Reinhold that this first principle, which the proposition formulates, determines philosophy only in its form. If the first principle is certain in itself, this is only possible because the content of the principle determines its form and, reciprocally, the form determines its content. This concept of both the material and formal validity of the first principle was essential to Fichte's effort to erect an absolute idealism. For, in terms of his initial option, he is committed to explain

---

[1] Léon, *op. cit.*, Vol. I, pp. 219-223.

the genesis of all experience, both in its formal and material aspects, from the side of intellect-in-itself.[1]

Reinhold's mistake, according to Fichte, was to identify consciousness with the representation. The representation, such as Reinhold understood it, in which one distinguishes subject and object and their relation, cannot serve as the first principle, because it is already something derived from consciousness. It presupposes the synthesis of the manifold of intuition into a unity, the accomplishment of an operation of which consciousness itself is the principle. Every representation is a synthesis which presupposes a connecting, that is, a thesis and an antithesis subordinated to something above them which is itself not a fact (Thatsache), but an action (Thathandlung).[2] Thus from the earliest moment of his philosophical career Fichte, like Blondel after him, envisaged the first principle and starting point of his philosophy in terms of that action which constitutes the essence of consciousness or subjectivity, and which is itself the genetic source of all the a priori syntheses of our conscious life.[3]

As D. Julia points out, by taking the synthetic reality of action as his first principle, Fichte was the first to direct modern philosophy into a search for that ultimate synthesis of thought and reality which in German idealism is called absolute knowledge. Fichte conceived of absolute knowledge as a unity of pure reflection and real experience, as simultaneously a logic and a phenomenology. According to Julia's interpretation, it was this concept of absolute knowledge which led Fichte to inaugurate a philosophy of action; for Fichte realized that "only a philosophy of action is capable of seizing the *real* unity of the spirit and of being, because such a unity is realized only in an effective commitment, in a real will-act by means of which the spirit truly descends into the world to carry out an effective action."[4]

---

[1] Delbos, *De Kant aux Post-Kantiens*, pp. 60-69.

[2] Fichte, "Recension des Aenesidemus," Vol. I, pp. 4-9.

[3] Delbos calls attention to the fact that at the same time as Fichte but independent of him Sigismund Beck turned to action as a solution to the problem of unifying philosophy. Beck proposed that one substitute the *act* of representation for the *fact* of representation, This action is the original reality. Consequently, just as geometry begins with the postulate: make a representation of space, so the first principle of philosophy formulates the act of representation in the postulate; make an original representation of an object. This postulate expresses that act by which our reason produces the unified manifold of the representation. Therefore, the first principle is indissoluably an act and a postulate. It is not, however, a representation by concepts. (Delbos, *op. cit.*, pp. 84-86).

[4] D. Julia, "Le Savoir Absolu chez Fichte," *Archives de Philosophie*, Tome XXV, Cahier III-IV (Juillet-Décembre, 1962), 356.

The Intuition of the Ego as Action

Once he established that the first principle of philosophy could not be the representation as a given empirical fact but must be the synthetic action which gives rise to the representation, Fichte maintained that this activity of the subject was not merely a hypothesis presented as an explanation of the synthesis contained in conscious representation; he insisted, rather, that there is an intellectual intuition of this act. In his "Second Introduction to the Theory of Science" Fichte undertook a phenomenological analysis of this intuition. In order to discover this act, which Fichte calls the ego principle, one must go behind the objectifiable self, the ego as object of introspection or of empirical psychology, to the pure ego (Ichheit). However hard we try to completely objectify the self, that is, to turn it into an object of consciousness, there always remains an I or ego which transcends objectification and is itself the condition of objectification; this is the pure ego which is the first principle of philosophy. We are not necessarily reflectively and explicitly aware of this intuition. That transcendental reflection by which attention is reflected onto the pure ego is a philosophical act. If the philosopher wishes to convince anyone of the reality of this intuition, he can only draw that person's attention to the data of consciousness and invite him to reflect for himself." Everyone must find it immediately in himself or he will never be able to know it."[1]

The problem arises that Fichte, who accepts Kant's view that theoretical knowledge cannot legitimately extend beyond conscious experience, seems to have transgressed that limit. Fichte answers, however, that the intellectual intuition of the pure ego is not an intuition of an entity behind or beyond conciousness, but the awareness of the pure ego or I-principle as an activity within consciousness, a component element of all self consciousness. "I cannot take a step; I cannot move hand or foot without the intellectual intuition of my self-consciousness in these actions. Everyone who attributes activity to himself appeals to this intuition."[2] Fichte argues that in this intellectual intuition an activity is intuited, but no entity behind consciousness is affirmed. Consequently we must not conceive of the pure ego as something which acts but simply as an activity or doing. "For idealism

---

[1] Fichte, "Zweite Einleitung...," Vol. I, p. 463. Copleston gives an excellent summary of this analysis. (Copleston, *op. cit.*, Vol. VII, pp. 40-44).

[2] Fichte, *loc. cit.*

the intellect is a doing and absolutely nothing else; one should not even call it an active thing."[1]

Fichte was also aware that his claim that man has an intellectual intuition of self would seem to contradict Kant's position that the human mind has no faculty of intellectual intuition. But he maintains that, due to his understanding of the ego as pure activity, there is no direct contradiction with Kant. Kant maintained that we have no intellectual intuition of suprasensible entities which transcend experience. Fichte affirmed that we intuit the pure ego, not as a spiritual substance or entity transcending consciousness, but simply as an activity within consciousness. Rather than contradict Kant's position, Fichte maintained that his doctrine of intellectual intuition of the pure ego as activity was implicitly contained in Kant's doctrine of the unity of apperception and, especially, in his assertion of a conscious awareness of the categorical imperative.

By the "unity of apperception" Kant understood that unity which is founded in the relation to one thinking and perceiving subject. Objects are thought by means of the categories, but without this unity of the thinking subject they would not be thinkable. Thus, for Kant, the synthesis produced by the act of understanding is not possible except within a unity of consciousness. Self-consciousness must be capable of accompanying all representation. An explicit reflexive awareness of my thinking as mine is not necessary, but the possibility of such an awareness is necessary. "The *I-think* must be capable of accompanying all my representations. For otherwise something could be represented in me which could not be thought at all. ... Therefore, every manifold of intuition has a necessary relation to the *I-think* in the same subject in which the manifold is found."[2] Kant distinguishes this I-think or unity of apperception from the empirical or contingent apperception of a given psychical state. The empirical apperception is fragmentary and disunited. But the possibility of an identical I-think accompanying all representations is a permanent condition of experience. It presupposes a transcendent unity of self-consciousness which is not given to me as object but which is the fundamental necessary condition for there being any objects for me. It is, according to Kant, by means of its judgments, which apply the various categories to the manifold of intuition, that the understanding brings the manifold

---

[1] Fichte, "Erste Einleitung...," Vol. I, p. 440.

[2] Kant, *Kritik der reinen Vernunft*, Vol. III, Section 132. Confer also Copleston, *op. cit.*, pp. 42-43.

of representation into the unity of apperception. "A manifold which is contained in an intuition that I call mine is represented by means of the synthesis of the understanding as belonging to the *necessary* unity of self-consciousness, and this takes place by means of the categories."[1] This synthetic unity (Verbindung, Conjunctio) of a manifold is "an act of the spontaneity of the power of representation."[2] Fichte understood this intuition of the pure ego as activity as an intuition of this "act of the spontaneity of the understanding," namely, that activity by means of which the manifold of intuition is synthesized.

The transcendental ego, according to Kant, is a logical maxim of pure reason. Reason tends to complete the synthesis present in the unity of apperception by assuming an unconditional, permanent ego or thinking subject conceived as substance. This transcendental idea arises as a result of pure reason's drive towards completing the synthesis achieved by the understanding and represents an object which lies beyond experience. Because we do not possess any faculty of intellectual intuition, no object is given to us according to these transcendental ideas. The empirical ego is the self as studied in psychology; it is an object in time and is reducible to successive states. The substantial or transcendental ego, which is not reducible to successive states and which cannot be thought except as subject, is not given in an intuition. Therefore, its existence as subject is not a question of direct intuitional evidence.[3]

Fichte maintains that there is no contradiction between his position and that of Kant, because the pure ego, which he claims is given in intellectual intuition, is neither the transcendental ego nor the empirical ego of which Kant speaks. It is not the transcendental ego, as we have seen, because it is intuited as pure activity. Nor is it the empirical ego. It is true, Fichte admits, that the act which is intuited is factually not isolated from its empirical context prior to the intuition itself. However, in order to achieve the intellectual intuition of that act, one must, by a process of philosophical analysis, abstract the pure activity of the ego from its empirical context. "The principle must express an *action* which is abstracted, in fact as in right, from all empirical determinations of our consciousness, because this action is the foundation as well as the necessary condition of the possibility of all consciousness."[4]

---

[1] Kant, *op. cit.*, Section 144.
[2] *Ibid.*, Section 130.
[3] *Ibid.*, Section 288-294.
[4] Fichte, "Grundlage der gesammten Wissenschaftslehre," Vol. I, p. 91. Confer

Every time Kant rejects explicitly the possibility of a faculty of intellectual intuition, Fichte claims, he has in mind a faculty which would have the intuitive power of directly knowing the thing-in-itself, in this case specifically, of knowing a substantial subject. Fichte claimed complete agreement with Kant on this point. By suppressing the thing-in-itself, he claimed to suppress by the same blow, and in a manner more radical than Kant's, any faculty corresponding to it. But by maintaining that there is an intellectual intuition of the act itself by which the judgment synthetizes the manifold in intuition into the unity of apperception, Fichte believed that he was merely explicitating a conclusion implicit in Kant's premises and never formally denied by him.[1]

Fichte claimed, further, that the primary manifestation of the activity of the ego is not contained in every judgment whatsoever but specifically in the moral judgment. Thus the central locus where his doctrine on the intellectual intuition rejoins that of Kant is in Kant's assertion that man is consciously aware of a categorical imperative. "In the consciousness of this law ... is grounded the intuition of self-activity and freedom. ... It is only through the medium of the moral law that I apprehend *myself*. And if I apprehend myself in that way, I necessarily apprehend myself as self-active."[2] Copleston maintains that there are several passages in the *Opus Postumum* which lend weight to Fichte's claim that this theory of an intellectual intuition of self-activity and freedom have a true foundation in Kant's concept of the consciousness of the categorical imperative.[3] On one occasion Kant himself seems to imply that there is such an intuition when he speaks of man's consciousness of himself in his moral acts as being "not phenomenon but noumenon." "Man in the world belongs to the knowledge of the world; but man as conscious of his duty in the world is not phenomenon but noumenon; and he is not a thing but a person."[4] In yet another passage Kant speaks of the reality manifest in moral consciousness as being "an active suprasensible principle which, indepen-

---

also Léon, *La Philosophie de Fichte*, pp. 18-19, for a discussion of Fichte's theory concerning the relation of the intellectual and sensible intuition.

[1] Maréchal claims that Fichte's critique of Kant's position was in large part justified: "Kant did separate too radically the formal and static viewpoint from the dynamic viewpoint..." (Joseph Maréchal, *Le Point de Départ de la Métaphysique* (Bruxelles: "L'Edition Universelle", Desclée et Brouwer, 1947), pp. 351-352.

[2] Fichte, "Zweite Einleitung...," Vol. I, p. 466.

[3] Copleston, *op. cit.*, Vol. VI, pp. 391-392.

[4] Kant, *Opus Postumum*, Vol. XXI, p. 61.

dent of nature and of natural causality, determines phenomena and is called freedom."[1] The consideration of these and similar passages leads Copleston to conclude that if Kant had developed his theory of moral reason as constitutive of experience, he might, indeed, have derived the empirical ego and man as phenomenal being from the self-positing of the noumenal ego with a view to moral self-realization.

Fichte's appeal to Kant's doctrine on the categorical imperative adds an important note to his description of the intuition of the ego as activity. That activity is intuited as a self-positing, that is to say, as an autonomous or free action. In fact, it would seem that Fichte held that it was by means of that very act of abstraction by which the philosopher freed the activity of the ego from its determined empirical context that the pure ego as an autonomous moral activity was both constituted and revealed. "It is through the act of the philosopher through an activity directed towards an activity ... that the ego comes to be originally (ursprünglich) for itself."[2] Consequently the intellectual intuition of self as a free moral agent is identical with the initial option of which Fichte spoke, whereby man seizes the fundamental principle of a philosophy of freedom. It is by an act of free production that the pure ego possesses itself, and it is by an intellectual intuition that it knows itself. It is only by means of this initial exercise of freedom that man both constitutes and knows himself as free.

THE RESEMBLANCE TO BLONDEL'S POINT OF DEPARTURE

As we have seen, Fichte announced that the first objective of his *Theory of Science* "consists in a search for that root, inaccessible to Kant, from which as from a common source spring the two worlds of the sensible and the intellectual." Both Blondel and Fichte understood their philosophy as an attempt to overcome the dichotomy between the sensible and the intelligible world and between the determinism and liberty which characterized these two worlds, a dichotomy which they believed remained unresolved in Kantian philosophy. Both also endeavor to satisfy, each in his own way, the demand of Kant's doctrine for the primacy of practical reason and the sovereignty of liberty.

In their search for the starting point of a philosophy which would vanquish this dichotomy, both try to pass beyond representations and

[1] *Ibid.*, p. 50.
[2] Fichte, *op. cit.*, p. 459.

ideas to the act itself which is the genetic source of all our ideas. Both see in this activity the synthesizing power of the spirit, the unifying principle of the real and the ideal. Both maintain that this unifying action is capable of being intuited subjectively by a reflection on our own conscious experience. Consequently, in both analyses there is a parallel progress of reflexive consciousness from the objective synthesis through the subjective act of synthesizing to a subjective awareness of the acting self or ego as the a priori active source of synthesis. Both agree that this subjective consciousness of self as action constitutes the privileged starting point of philosophy, since it is the only viewpoint from which a unified and total explanation of the subjective and objective, the real and ideal, can be given.

From the beginning Fichte affirms with Kant the primacy of the practical, but he searches, precisely against Kant's position, to suppress by a superior unity the dichotomy which he saw as separating pure and practical reason. He found the answer in action, or rather, in the ego which is essentially active. The ego is not only the principle of free moral action; but, in so far as liberty includes or presupposes necessity, that is to say, the ontological substructure and the laws within which action is accomplished, it is also a principle of knowledge. Thus it is the principle from which all experience can be deduced a priori with certitude.[1]

In their philosophy of action both Blondel and Fichte attempt to respect Kant's critical norms. Fichte does so by his insistence on the fact that what is intuited is a pure activity and not a substantial entity; Blondel does so by refusing any metaphysical judgment, even concerning that activity itself, until the whole of the dialectic of that activity has been both actually deployed and reflectively analyzed.

In both systems there is an intuition of the ego as a free source of initiative. This intuition is based in the reflexive awareness of the subject as capable of synthesizing the universal law into a specific act. It is because of this freedom of the ego as a moral agent that Fichte is led to insist that action itself is a source of understanding and knowledge which cannot be obtained apart from action. It is to this element of Fichte's thought that Delbos refers when he asserts that Fichte maintained that moral action contained an intuition of truth infinitely superior to scientific knowledge, "...that philosophical and moral truths cannot be imposed on man from without, that they become

---

[1] Fichte, "Erste Einleitung...," Vol. I, pp. 440-441.

light only if first they are action, living personal action."[1] This role of action in philosophy as the subjective originating source of a knowledge which it is impossible to acquire apart from effective action represents, perhaps, the most fundamental agreement between Blondel's and Fichte's doctrines at their point of departure: "Effective action is an integral condition of philosophical knowledge ... if reflection, in some respects, clarifies and controls practice, on the other hand it is practice which provides reflection with a teaching which cannot be obtained by any other method."[2]

THE PRACTICAL DEDUCTION OF CONSCIOUSNESS

Once Fichte arrives at the intuition of the subject as free activity, his scientific drive takes over. Instead of remaining within the perspective of subjective action, Fichte proceeds to abstract the pure form of that activity. He then attempts an objective deduction of consciousness from a series of fundamental propositions which are derived from that form. If this "theoretical deduction of consciousness" constituted the totality of Fichte's doctrine, then the resemblance with Blondel's doctrine would be limited to Fichte's initial analysis of the intuition of self as free action. But Fichte did not remain content with a purely theoretical deduction of consciousness from his first principle. He was convinced that his initial intuituon of action as a synthesis of the real and the ideal permitted him to undertake the development of a complementary "practical deduction of consciousness."

In this practical deduction, Fichte considers that action which is the vital essence of the ego as an "organic living intention or effort"; and he traces the series of stages by which this organic effort passes from an inert force through its identity with the mechanism of nature to the point where it arrives at a consciousness of its infinite potential and its consequent liberty. Although there are significant differences in the details of their respective developments, yet all the essential steps of Fichte's pragmatic deduction of consciousness can be found in Blondel's subjective analysis of the unfolding of action in consciousness in the section of *Action* entitled "The Phenomenon of Action."

There is a striking parallel, for example, with Fichte's study of the transformation of infra-conscious impulse or drive (Trieb) into the sensible form of feeling (Gefühl) which is, according to Fichte, the

---

[1] Delbos, *Le Problème Moral dans la Philosophie de Spinoza*, p. 265.
[2] Blondel, "Le Point de Départ de la Recherche Philosophique," II, 239.

beginning of consciousness. The ego feels impulse or drive as an unlimited power or force (Kraft) which is hindered in its fulfillment.
This feeling of constraint, of not-being-able, compels the ego to posit
the non-ego as a felt obstacle or check. Thus, this impulse is transformed into "impulse towards the object." "Here," Fichte tells us,
"lies the ground of reality. Only through the relation of feeling to the
ego ... is reality possible for the ego."[1] Fichte concludes from this
analysis that objective intelligence is nothing more than a reflection
on our vital action and, as it were, a mirror in which the diverse forms
of the limitation of our essential activity are projected under the form
of various objects. Consequently, objective knowledge as such is not
primary. Rather, it is a function of our practical life which is incapable
of realizing itself without this elevation of its spontaneous effort to the
level of thought by means of reflexive self-consciousness. The production of the presentation (Vorstellung) in objective thought is the work
of the theoretical power. But this product presupposes the drive-to-
presentation (Vorstellungstrieb), which drive is the object of the practical study. Thus these two deductions are complementary, although
the theoretical deduction finds its ultimate explanation in the practical.
This subordination of knowledge as means to the realization of practical action as end is, in Xavier Léon's judgment, the master idea of
the whole ensemble of the *Theory of Science*.[2] On this point there is a
perfect accord with Blondel's central idea. "It is the relation of the
will-willing and the will-willed which must be determined. Knowledge is nothing more than the middle term, the fruit of action and the
seed of action."[3]

By thus establishing the primacy of the practical over the theoretical,
Fichte believed that he had successfully destroyed the very basis of
determinism, which in his judgment rests entirely on the hypothesis
that the action of the will is determined by the intellectual representation; that is, that there are data anterior and exterior to will-action
which necessitate that action. On the contrary, it is the will-action
which is primary, and the representation is nothing more than its

---

[1] Fichte, "Grundlage...," Vol. I, p. 30.
[2] Léon, *La Philosophie de Fichte*, p. 184.
[3] Blondel, *Lettres Philosophiques*, p. 84. Blondel, however, did not agree with
Fichte that the positing of the obstacle or check of the non-ego to the ego was an
unconscious process. In note 919 of the notes for the preparation of *Action* he
observes: "Fichte submits liberty to the necessity of a development by shock.
One must go even further and show that that apparent necessity is intelligibly free
and voluntary."

symbol.[1] In almost identical fashion as Blondel, Fichte traces the development of that vital will-action from its initial spontaneity through consciousness of its infinite power, which it projects as idea of the infinite, to, finally, its self-possession as free moral activity whose essence lies, for Fichte as for Blondel, in the conscious synthesis of this idea of the infinite with the power of the infinite.[2]

As we have noted, Fichte stated that his objective in the *Theory of Science* was to find the common source and synthetic origin of the sensible and intellectual worlds, in other words, to establish the continuity between the world of determinism and the world of liberty by tracing them back to that vital action which is their integrating source. In his description of the evolution of modern philosophy prior to his *Action*, Blondel acknowledges that, stripped of its idealistic pretentions, this was the essential contribution of the idealist philosophers to his own philosophy of action. The idealist philosophers by taking the subject as their point of departure "uncovered that there is a unity and integral continuity in the philosophical problem"; yet they were mistaken in understanding their method of immanence as a doctrine of immanence and in concluding that "their subjective and immanent solution had an objective or absolute value."[3]

ORDO ORDINANS AND ORDO ORDINATUS

This solution to the problem of unity and continuity in Fichte's *Theory of Science* is based on his intuition of the ego as, so to speak, a metaphysical composite of the pure ego, which reveals itself to consciousness as an infinite potentiality for self-identity by means of moral striving, and the finite ego, which reveals itself as a limited realization of that potential. Thus it is likely that Blondel's concept of the will as a composite had, as one of it sources, Fichte's distinction of the two component factors of the ego. For Blondel understood the composite nature of our will-act as a similar composition of the will-willing, conceived as an infinite potential for self-identity in consciousness, and the will-willed conceived as a limited realization of that potential in any given act. Blondel himself on one occasion uses the word ego to designate this will-activity, but he substituted for Fichte's terms: absolute and finite ego, the purer phenomenal terminology: apparent

---

[1] Fichte, "Grundlage ...," Vol. I, pp. 294-295.
[2] Fichte, "Grundlage ...," Vol. I, pp. 327-328.
[3] Blondel, *Lettre* (1896), p. 62.

and integral ego. "In posing the problem of interior self-adequation, philosophy poses at the same time the problem of universal reality under the only form in which it can be resolved. From the apparent ego to the integral ego there is, in effect, an infinite to be opened up and filled."[1]

If on this occasion Blondel employs a terminology which is close to that of Fichte, Fichte also employs another terminology which brings us closer to Blondel's concept of will, the concept of *ordo*. In his use of the concept of *ordo*, Fichte takes his inspiration from Spinoza's couplet, *natura naturans* and *natura naturata*. He desired, however, to suppress the substantialist and objective implications in the word nature, and to emphasize the substitution of action for the static concept of substance. Thus he substitutes the couplet *ordo ordinans* and *ordo ordinatus*.[2] The reason for this new terminology lies in Fichte's understanding of the intuited ego as an activity guided by an immanent moral law or order. "In the consciousness of the law is grounded the intuition of self-activity and freedom."[3] In the intuition of the ego, the pure or absolute ego is revealed as the moral ideal, the infinite potentiality for self-realization and self-possession which, at the same time, determines the series of means necessary for the finite ego in order to achieve this fulfillment. This moral order is not intuited as an order of things objectively presented to action, an *ordo ordinatus*, but as the living order immanently present in the action of the will itself, an *ordo ordinans*. Again, in his essay *The Vocation of the Scholar* (Bestimmung des Gelehrten) of 1794, Fichte changes the wording of the categorical imperative of Kant in order to bring out the active voluntary aspect of that imperative: "Act as if you could consider the maxim of your will as an eternal law for you." Thus, he concludes, the imperative imposed on man is "an accord *of the will* with the idea of an eternally valid will."[4] As Copleston points out, if this moral order is really an *ordo ordinans*, it must obviously possess an ontological status. Thus, in his later work *The Vocation of Man* (Bestimmung des Menschen) of 1800, the moral order appears as identical with the eternal, infinite will.[5] Consequently, in Fichte's religious philosophy, this living and operative moral order becomes one with

---

[1] Blondel, "Le Point de Départ de la Recherche Philosophique," II, 237.
[2] Fichte, "Aus einem Privatschreiben," Vol. V, p. 382.
[3] Confer above, pp. 188-189.
[4] Fichte, "Ueber die Bestimmung des Gelehrten an sich," Vol. VI, p. 299.
[5] Copleston, *op. cit.*, Vol. VII, p. 83.

God, just as Spinoza's *natura naturans* was identical with the divine essence. "This is the true faith, this moral order is the divine."[1]

Needless to say, Blondel rejects this effort to absolutize an element of what was for him a purely phenomenal analysis of will-activity. However, Blondel also understood his will-willing as an *ordo ordinans*. This a priori structure present in action ultimately gives rise to the a priori structure in thought; there is a sort of determinism present within the free act itself. In a word, there is a living, concrete logic of action.

The Necessary but Impossible

The final similarity between Fichte's pragmatic deduction of consciousness and Blondel's development of the phenomenon of action, which we shall deal with here, lies in the idea of the final goal of action as simultaneously necessary and impossible.

> The idea of an infinite task to be accomplished ... derives from the most profound roots of our being. We must—it is the necessity of our essence—resolve the contradiction which is in us; we must resolve that conflict even when that very solution is actually and forever unthinkable, for it is the very march of our destiny, our eternity.[2]

This is the same conclusion Fichte reaches at the end of his pragmatic deduction of consciousness. The perfect identity of self with self, which is the necessary and spontaneous goal of our moral striving, reveals itself as impossible of ever being actually achieved. This is also the analogous conclusion of Blondel. After tracing the development of the phenomenon of action through every possible human action designed to resolve the contradiction within man's will, Blondel concludes that a perfect harmony of will is both necessary and impracticable. "Behold in all its brutality the conclusion of the determinism of human action."[3] But despite the similarity of these conclusions,

---

[1] "Das ist der wahre Glaube; diese moralische Ordnung ist das Gottliche ..." Fichte, "Ueber der Grund unseres Glaubens an eine göttliche Weltregierung," Vol. V, p. 185.

[2] "... die Idea einer solchen zu vollendenden Unendlichkeit ... ist im Innersten unseres Wesen entholten. Wir sollen, laut der Anforderung desselben an uns, den Wiederspruch lösen; ob wir seine Lösung gleich nicht als möglich denken können, und voraussehen, dass wir sie in keinem Momente unseres in alle Ewigkeiten hinaus verlängerten Daseyns werden als möglich denken können. Aber eben dies ist das Gepräge unserer Bestimmung für die Ewigkeit." (Fichte, "Grundlage ...," Vol. I, p. 270).

[3] Blondel, *L'Action*, p. 319.

there remains an important difference between them. For Blondel substitutes the word "impracticable" in place of Fichte's word "unthinkable."

The reason for this difference in terminology lies in the fundamental divergence between Fichte and Blondel concerning the true nature of a philosophy of action. As we have seen, in the *Theory of Science* Fichte undertook a twofold deduction of consciousness; the first, theoretical, in which consciousness was deduced objectively from the first principle which expressed the pure form of the absolute ego; the second, a practical deduction which began with consciousness and ascended from condition to condition until it arrived once again at the absolute ego as an infinite potentiality for perfect self-identity in consciousness, but a potentiality incapable of ever being fully act. Since, in Fichte's opinion, these two deductions of consciousness are perfectly complementary, everything which can be proven in the first can be proven in the second. But that which is "unthinkable" in a theory of action is necessarily equally "impracticable" in a practical deduction of consciousness.

This juxtaposition of the theoretical and the practical is, in Blondel's estimation, one of the fundamental errors of idealism. "If one limits oneself to juxtaposing the dialectical and the practical, one leaves outside of metaphysics an irreducible and irrational element."[1] That element, in Blondel's opinion, is precisely the synthesis between theory and practice, the ideal and the real, which is the original synthetic reality of action itself. Fichte, in his initial intuition of the subject as moral act, understood this synthetic role of action. But, because of his insistence on a separation of the theoretical and practical development of philosophy, this synthetic reality of concrete action necessarily escapes the grasp of Fichte's system. For, despite his theoretical subordination of theory to practice, Fichte did insist, in terms of his idea of the scientific nature of philosophy, that the theoretical and practical developments of philosophy must be rigorously distinguished and separately developed. Let us investigate, then, how this separation of the theoretical and practical works out in practice in Fichte's system, in order to understand why Blondel saw in that separation a loss of the synthetic reality of action and a consequent failure to understand how the final goal of that action, the perfect synthesis of the real and ideal, could be achieved.

---

[1] Blondel, *Lettres Philosophiques*, pp. 68-69.

THE ROLE OF EMPIRICAL REALITY

We have already noted that, in the theoretical deduction of consciousness, Fichte attempted by a process of construction and deduction, using geometry as his model, to arrive at a total deduction of the object both in matter and form. In the first *Theory of Science*, Fichte maintains that the objective material world, the world of the finite non-ego, is posited by the ego as a necessary means in order that the ego can acquire self-consciousness. Material reality, because it is a preconscious projection of the ego, appears to us under the illusory, but inevitable and necessary, appearance of an existence independent of the ego. In one of his expositions of 1801 (Darstellung der Wissenschaftslehre), Fichte proposes to prove that this sensible world, both in its form and in its content, is essentially nothing other than "the form, in itself empty and without content, of consciousness at its origin, and the foundation (Hintergrund) which determines and supports it is the absolute being."[1] This form serves as the principle of division, multiplication and change—all synonymous terms. At this point in the development of his doctrine Fichte conceived of material reality as being the principle of quantification and as expressing the purely formal relation which forms the basis of mathematics. However, Fichte's deduction did not stop here. This matter-in-general provides us with a form which serves as a principle of multiplication. But Fichte was aware that it could not serve as the basis for real empirical self-consciousness. For this real foundation Fichte made appeal, in his practical deduction of consciousness, to "feeling". Feeling, as we have seen, represented in Fichte's system the experience of a determination or limitation of the potentially infinite activity of the ego. As such it represents a conscious experience of the synthesis of the universal and the singular. It is this potential infinite contained in felt-experience which renders possible that reflection which frees the intellectual intuition from its empirical context, and thus raises the universal to the level of clear consciousness.[2]

One could conclude that Fichte has assigned the same function to the potential infinite in action as did Blondel. But his idealistic interpretation of the evidence is totally other. For Fichte hastens to add that there is ultimately only one and the same universal; there is only one and the same reason conscious of itself. The individual as such

---

[1] Fichte, "Darstelling der Wissenschaftslehre," Vol. II, p. 86.
[2] *Ibid.*, p. 112.

represents, then, an illusory but necessary difference in the empirical point of view in relation to that universal reason.[1] Just as the geometrician constructs a triangle in his imagination in order to obtain conscious awareness of the essential relations which govern that act of construction, so universal reason must employ the phenomenal individual in order to arrive at a conscious awareness of its own universal law. After the individual has served its function, then it must disappear, even as the geometrician, once he has obtained consciousness of the essential relations, forgets his imaginary figure and retains only that form which is its essential reality.

Therefore, even if Fichte reaches at one moment of his dialectic the actual synthetic reality of action, the synthesis as such contained in that intuition has no organic function in his philosophy. We have already seen how insistent Fichte was that experience in its existential concreteness had no role to play in his deduction apart from supplying it with a consciousness of the universal, that pure ideal form which serves as the starting point and term of the *Theory of Science*. Concrete action, it is true, represents for Fichte, as for Blondel, a synthesis of the universal with the indivudial, the ideal and the real. But once one has arrived at a consciousness of the universal, it is precisely the task of the philosopher to dissolve that synthesis, and attempt a total explanation of the real in terms of the ideal or universal.

We have also seen how insistent Blondel is that a philosophy of action must be modeled on an experimental and not a geometric science. For it is only in the lived experience of human action that there is an intuition of that synthetic reality, that fusion of the real and the ideal, which is the specific property of living action. The task of the philosopher, far from being accomplished by the dissolution of the synthesis, can only be accomplished by seeking to comprehend and carry to its completion this synthetic function of action. However, once one accepts a mathematical model for one's methodology, one has effectively renounced fidelity to the real synthesis found in human action.

> Neither experience can furnish us with the purely abstract, nor number the true concrete; for mathematics is founded precisely on the premise that a real analysis can be carried on *ad infinitum*, and experimentation on the premise that mathematical construction can never produce a real synthesis.[2]

---

[1] *Ibid.*, p. 115.
[2] Confer above, pp. 77-82, for a discussion of this text from Blondel, *L'Action* p. 79.

Consequently, when both Blondel and Fichte reach, at a given point in their dialectic, the same conclusion, namely, that a real synthesis between the infinite potential contained in the pure ego or will-willing and the active realization of that potential in the finite ego or will-willed is necessary but impossible, it should not come as a surprise that this is the final word of Fichte's dialectic, whereas Blondel's dialectic continues. At every stage in Blondel's dialectic it was living concrete action which successfully synthesised form and matter, the ideal and the real. "Here as everywhere, it is effective action which is the great mediator; it succeeds in conciliating those things which, for a critical or idealist philosophy, formally exclude one another from the static viewpoint of knowledge."[1]

In his analysis of the phenomenon of action Blondel traced the entire range of all the concrete synthesis which human action, precisely as human, is capable of achieving. The final stage of that analysis was the superstitious effort on man's part to subordinate divine power itself to his own individual will. It is only after exhausting all these possibilities that he acknowledges the impossibility for man to achieve his destiny by his own powers alone. As we noted, the impossibility in question is not a question of finding a theoretical or thinkable solution; but, in an even more radical sense, it is a question of placing a concrete action which can successfully synthesize that infinite ideal which is the very law and essence of man's will with the concrete reality in his determined action. This impossibility does not necessarily represent for Blondel an absolute contradiction within the dialectic of his system, as it does for Fichte. From the very start of his deduction, Fichte understands that subjective activity which reveals itself in our consciousness to be the form of the absolute. The pure ego is the absolute ego; the *ordo ordinans* of the will is the dynamic essence of the divinity itself, the very law of its creative action. Man's search for his own self-identity is identical with God's search for his self-identity in consciousness. In Fichte's philosophy, Xavier Léon tells us, the absolute ceases to be a superior and mysterious God: "The absolute, having become immanent in the Spirit, is nothing more than the interior stimulus of Reason which compels it to search out an ever more profound comprehension of the relative being to which it is immediately united."[2] Here we find the fundamental reason within Fichte's system why, once he has examined all the possible means by which the

---

[1] *Ibid.*, p. 301.
[2] Léon, *La Philosophie de Fichte*, pp. 182-183.

pure ego can achieve conscious fulfillment through the development of human consciousness, he is constrained to find the very idea of such a fulfillment a contradiction. He is forced to conclude that the absolute is a process of becoming, an eternal striving after an impossible goal. Just like mathematical analysis, philosophy is a process *ad infinitum*. What in Blondel's philosophy is an impossibility for man by his own powers alone, is in Fichte's idealist system an intrinsic impossibility within the absolute itself to achieve its ideal conscious fulfillment.

Blondel's dialectic escapes such an impasse because from the very start Blondel understood that he was undertaking a pure phenomenal analysis of human action. As a result he refused at any stage of that analysis to assign a metaphysical value to any of the elements or successive syntheses which his analysis uncovered. Consequently, the impossibility which Blondel uncovers at the end of this analysis remains phenomenal, that is, in the order of the relative. It is a purely human impossibility. "Man can never succeed, *by his own powers alone*, to place in his willed action all that which is at the origin of his voluntary activity."[1] What Blondel understood as impracticable is precisely what is impossible for man to accomplish by his own personal forces alone. But another solution is not absolutely excluded as unthinkable. For it is possible, and as Blondel will argue, necessarily thinkable that what man cannot do by his own power is still capable of being achieved by a power which is not that of man alone.

SUMMARY

We have seen that both Blondel and Fichte began their respective philosophies from what appears to be an identical point of departure, namely, an intuitive awareness which the subject as such has of itself as a synthesizing process of moral activity. At least, this resemblance seems to be true in so far as one is justified in abstracting a purely phenomenological analysis from the idealist context of Fichte's writings. This resemblance continues with Fichte's pragmatic deduction of consciousness, considered once again as a phenomenological analysis, where the progressive development of that synthetic action is analysed as a progressive search for self-adequation between the will-willing and the will-willed.

However, within this resemblance at every point is concealed an

---

[1] Blondel, *op. cit.*, p. 321. *Underlining* added.

even greater divergence, once we take into consideration the idealist implications which Fichte reads into his analysis. We have already examined that divergence in so far as it concerns the nature of philosophy as science. Fichte's concept of philosophical science as a strict mathematical procedure of rational deduction led him to separate radically theory and practice as two distinct procedures which coalesce only in their final result. But that final harmony of theory and practice, the ideal and the real, proves to be impossible of achievement within Fichte's system. For the very concept of an absolute identity of consciousness and being is unthinkable. One ultimate reason within Fichte's system for this failure of action to achieve its goal has to do with the role of concrete material reality in his system. The concrete material individual in Fichte's idealist system has only a pragmatic and ultimately illusory, if necessary, function. The concrete as such, the non-ego, serves as a necessary means for the ego to achieve consciousness of itself. But the material in human consciousness is at the same time precisely the ego's experience of its determination or limitation in its drive towards total self-identity. Consciousness, if it is to reach its ideal state of perfect identity with self, must necessarily suppress and eliminate that finite reality of the individual. However, if consciousness succeeds in totally eliminating the finite real, paradoxically it destroys itself by destroying a necessary condition of its own existence. For the ego, to be reflexively aware of itself, has an absolute need of the non-ego, of concrete reality, as a necessary means of reflecting back its spontaneous activity on itself.

From the viewpoint of method, Blondel was convinced that this failure of Fichte's idealist system to arrive at absolute knowledge, the perfect harmony of thought and practice, being and consciousness, was due directly to his failure to remain faithful to the synthetic reality of concrete action. Once one has separated the theoretical and the practical, the real synthesis between the universal and individual facets of being, between the ideal and the real, necessarily escapes one's system. The inevitable result is that one identifies one of these facets with the absolute and suppresses the other.

Consequently, despite the similar appearance of their conclusions concerning human destiny, namely, that the total harmony of self with self is necessarily man's goal but impossible to achieve, there is a radical divergence in the import of that conclusion. For Fichte, this is not a relative defeat, a question of purely human limitation and impotence; it is an absolute defeat, a problem which involves a limitation within the absolute itself. Thus, behind the divergence in method lies an even more fundamental divergence concerning the idea of the absolute and concerning the manifestation or trace of that absolute in human consciousness. At every step in Fichte's phenomenology of consciousness this concept of the absolute, which derives from his systematic idealism, changes radically the metaphysical implication of his phenomenological analysis. What we must investigate, then, is this concept of the absolute and the role it plays in Fichte's system in order to better understand the originality and value of Blondel's solution to the problem of human destiny, precisely as a question of the relation between man and the absolute.

CHAPTER NINE

THE PROBLEM OF THE ABSOLUTE

Introduction

At this point we touch the most fundamental difference between the philosophy of Fichte and Blondel; namely, their respective ideas of the absolute. Both Blondel and Fichte began their philosophy with a search for a solution to the problem of human destiny and human freedom. Both envisage the solution of that problem as contained somehow in a communication of man with the absolute. Both agree from the start that the absolute does not reveal itself to man by imposing itself exclusively from without with a consequent destruction of our liberty. On the contrary, it manifests itself to us from within consciousness in the very use we make of our liberty. It was Fichte's conviction, Xavier Léon remarks, that "we cannot touch the absolute except from within ourselves as the most profound condition of our personal activity, as the originating source of our ego, and itself eminently an Ego." However, if Blondel and Fichte agree that the absolute is itself a subject and that it reveals itself to man from within his consciousness, they disagree radically in their interpretation of the nature of the absolute, the place and meaning of the trace of the absolute in man's consciousness, and the consequent method and means by which man comes to know and communicate with that absolute.

The Meaning of Fichte's "Ego"

We have already analysed the relation between Fichte's concept of the ego as action and Blondel's concept of the subject as synthetic activity. But, as we have noted, Fichte's phenomenological analysis of subjective consciousness takes place in an a priori context of idealist metaphysics which colors the meaning he attaches to the results of his analysis. What did Fichte understand by this ego which he claimed was the foundation and first principle of philosophy? If Fichte had remained exclusively within the realm of a descriptive analysis of consciousness, one would be justified, perhaps, in interpreting the ego as the individual self, as Fichte's early critics did. But Fichte proposed to develop a system of idealist metaphysics based on the ego as the fundamental principle. He proposed to derive the whole sphere of the objective both materially as well as formally from the pure ego. "Everything without exception must be posed in the ego."[1] Consequently, if he wished to escape the charge of solipsism, he was obliged to interpret the pure ego as a supra-individual productive activity which manifests itself in all finite consciousness.

As we have already seen, Fichte claimed that this ego is not identical with Kant's empirical ego, because the action which is its essence is abstracted from all empirical determination. In Kantian philosophy the constitutive activity by which a priori forms are applied to phenomenal reality is an unconscious activity of the human mind as such; it is not specifically the activity of any one individual mind, whether that mind be human or divine. One would be tempted to assume that what Fichte understood as the abstracted form of the ego would be the form of this human activity as such. But Fichte leaves us in no doubt that this is not the case. For he was aware that, if he granted this, he could not go beyond Kant's formal determinism and attribute the material production of nature to the abstracted form of the human mind as such.

In order to understand what Fichte meant by the ego, we must keep in mind the distinction he made between the spontaneous activity of the pure ego and the philosopher's consciousness of that activity. The ego as spontaneous activity is the ground of consciousness which is not itself conscious. Thus this ego is said to exist in itself (in sich) but not for itself (für sich). Fichte distinguishes here between the initial state of pure being (sein) of the ego and its state of conscious being (dasein).[2] By means of the abstractive reflection of the philosopher the pure ego as conscious being comes to be originally (ursprünglich) for itself.[3] In this intellectual intuition the pure ego is said to posit itself

---

[1] Fichte, "Grundlage ...." Vol, I, p. 260.
[2] In the *Wissenschaftslehre* of 1804 Fichte distinguishes between "inner" and "outer" being. Absolute Being cannot sort outside of itself but it can "project itself" (proiectio per hiatum) towards the exterior (Vol. X, pp. 217-218). Consequently inner absolute being is called "light", and ordinary consciousness is described as "the projection or apparition of this light," or, again, *"Daseyn of the light"*: "Das Seyn ist eine schlechthin in sich geschossene lebendige Einheit. Seyn and Licht Eins. Da in dem Daseyn des Lichten dem gewöhnlichen Bewusstsein, ein Mannigfaltiges angetroffen wird... so muss in dem Licht selber, als absoluter Einheit, und seiner Erscheinung, ein Grund dieser Mannigfaltigkeit sich aufzeigen lassen..." (Vol. X, pp. 245-246. *Underlining* added).
[3] Fichte, "Zweite Einleitung ...," Vol. I, p. 459.

(sich setzen). Consequently, the fundamental proposition of a philosophy of ego states: "The ego simply posits in an original way its own being."[1] Not unnaturally Fichte's early critics assumed that, by using the word "ego" to describe this initial spontaneous activity which is intuited as a component factor of our individual consciousness, Fichte understood by it the spontaneity of the individual human ego. In his winter lectures of 1810-1811, Fichte explicitly denied this interpretation:

> People have generally understood the theory of science as attributing effects to the individual which can certainly not be ascribed to it, such as the production of the whole material world. ... They have been completely mistaken; it is not the individual but the one immediate spiritual life which is the creator of all phenomena, including the phenomenal individuals.[2]

It is obvious, as Maréchal points out, that what Fichte understood as the spontaneous activity of the pure ego, is in reality the creative activity of the absolute ego intuited not in its substantial source but in its progressive unfolding in time within our consciousness of self.[3] In the citation above Fichte has substituted the word "life" for the word "ego". As Copleston notes, Fichte in the course of time saw that it was inappropriate to describe that spontaneous activity which grounds all consciousness, including the finite self, as itself an ego, because this term implies a conscious subject.[4]

Ego and Non-Ego

In order to appreciate fully what Fichte means by this concept of the pure ego, we must understand the relation of this ego to the non-ego and to the finite conscious self. In Fichte's idealist system all activity must be referred ultimately to the pure or absolute ego. The entire world of non-ego must exist only for consciousness; for to admit a world of non-ego which exists independently of consciousness would be equivalent to admitting the idea of the thing-in-itself and abandoning idealism. Thus Fichte is obliged to show, in a manner consistent with his idealist premise, how ordinary consciousness can arise, in which the finite ego is distinguished from the finite non-ego with which

---

[1] *Ibid.*, "Grundlage ...," Vol. I, p. 98.
[2] *Ibid.*, "Die Tatsachen des Bewusstseyns," Vol. II, p. 607.
[3] Maréchal, *op. cit.*, p. 409.
[4] Copleston, *op. cit.*, p. 44.

it is in conscious relation. In his theoretical deduction of consciousness, Fichte postulates as the third proposition of consciousness that the absolute ego, considered as unlimited activity, must "posit in itself a divisible non-ego as opposed to a divisible ego."[1] This positing of the limited non-ego and limited ego is seen as a spontaneous preconscious activity of the absolute ego which Fichte terms the "productive power of the imagination."

Because it takes place below the level of consciousness and is itself the ultimate necessary condition of all consciousness, this process explains our belief in a nature existing independently of our finite ego. Fichte saw in this theory of the productive power of the imagination a refutation of any accusation of solipsism. The absolute ego is not understood as positing the world by means of the infra-conscious levels of the human being. Rather, this absolute ego determines *immediately* the non-ego which enters into representation (das vorzustellende Nicht-Ich), and *mediately*, that is, by means of the non-ego, the ego as representing (das vorstellende Ich). "It is not the individual as such but the one Life which intuits the objects of the material world."[2]

This unconscious process of the imagination has its explanation in the nature of the absolute ego. As we have seen, Fichte understands the absolute ego as a spontaneous activity possessing no consciousness of itself. The entire process by which the absolute ego limits and incarnates its infinite activity in the world of nature, the world of the non-ego and the finite ego, is dictated precisely by a necessary striving of the absolute ego to achieve perfect self-consciousness. For by its nature the absolute ego is an infinite striving (ein unendliches Streben) towards perfect self-consciousness. The fundamental condition, however, for this self-consciousness is the reciprocal activity of a finite non-ego on a finite ego. There can only be consciousness where the spontaneous activity of the ego can be turned back on itself by the "shock" of the resistance of the non-ego. Consequently, Fichte understands the ultimate rational necessity of the finite world as a necessary means which the absolute ego must employ in order to be conscious, that is, in order to exist for itself.

But what exactly did Fichte understand by the state of perfect self-consciousness which he postulates as the goal of the absolute? We have already traced the process which Fichte developed in his pragmatic

---

[1] Fichte, "Grundlage ...," Vol. I, p. 110.
[2] *Ibid.*, "Die Thatsachen ...," Vol. II, p. 614.

development of consciousness, whereby the absolute ego strives to achieve this perfect self-consciousness. Beginning with the empirical individual consciousness Fichte traces the development from initial effort through sensation, understanding, and judgment to self-consciousness properly speaking. Self-consciousness, according to Fichte, differs from understanding and judgment because it requires more than the power to abstract from the particular object in favor of the universal; it presupposes the power to abstract from the object-in-general in order to achieve a pure reflection on the subject. This power of absolute abstraction Fichte calls reason (Vernunft). The pure ego of which Fichte speaks is precisely this reason, that is, the potentiality of the absolute ego or infinite spontaneous activity to arrive by means of the development of consciousness at the total elimination of the ego-object and the total conscious identity with itself as ego-subject.

If we are to understand the consequent evolution of Fichte's doctrine, it is important to note that, in the initial intuition of the ego in which the philosopher abstracts and intuits the first principle of consciousness, what is given, according to Fichte, is not the actual identity with self in consciousness of the absolute ego; rather, what is given in this intuition is only the abstract form of that total identity or, in other words, the ideal possibility for such a total identity. This form is obtained by abstracting the pure form of the absolute ego from its empirical content; "The more a determined individual can think him self away, the closer does his empirical self-consciousness approximate to pure self-consciousness."[1] Fichte not only insists that this pure self-consciousness, in which the absolute I-subject would be completely transparent to itself, is not initially intuited as actual but only as potential; he also insists that this pure self-consciousness represents an ideal which can never be actually achieved. In as much as the ego is an infinite striving for perfect self-identity, it cannot rest in any particular achievement but must seek to absorb the whole world of the non-ego and its own infinite potential into that perfect identity of self with self. But such an ideal is, according to Fichte, necessarily contradictory. A state of actual pure self-consciousness on the part of the absolute ego presupposes the total elimination of the non-ego. Yet the non-ego is a necessary condition for self-consciounesss. Consciousness is of its very essence a *Dasein*, a being-there, an actual relating of the ego to the non-ego in a specific empirical context. If the absolute ego were

---

[1] *Ibid.*, "Grundlage ...," Vol. I, p. 244.

to succeed in eliminating totally all non-ego, it would no longer have the necessary obstacle which could reflect its activity back on itself. Thus it would revert back once again into that state of pure spontaneous activity which was its initial condition. For this reason Fichte envisages the ideal goal of the absolute ego as always receding, and the absolute ego itself as infinite striving after an impossible goal. This striving is fulfilled in so far as possible through the convergence of the determined moral action of finite subjects towards the ideal goal. Thus beyond the endless moral striving of each individual lies the fulfillment which is derived from the common moral effort of the human community. But this communal moral evolution is also an endless process, always nearing its goal but never capable of actually achieving it, since that actual achievement would be its own negation and destruction.[1]

Consequently, in Fichte's position concerning the absolute there is a certain ambiguity due to the fact that this concept is derived from a reflection on human consciousness. Fichte leaves no doubt that he considered the pure ego as spontaneous activity to be the supra-human creative activity of the absolute ego. In his later philosophy, particularly in *The Facts of Conciousness* (Tatsachen des Bewusstseins) of 1813, this pure ego is transformed into absolute being. However, if Fichte liberates his absolute ego from an identity with the individual ego, yet the conscious existence of this absolute ego remains identified with the sum total of human consciousness. As Copleston notes, although consciousness is said to be the absolute's consciousness, the absolute is also said to be conscious through man, and not in itself in so far as it is considered apart from man. This ambiguity seems to result from an arbitrary elevation of the conditions of human consciousness to the level of absolutely necessary conditions of all consciousness, even the divine consciousness. The end-result, in Fichte's theory, is that the absolute ego is understood as necessarily independent of man in its spontaneous activity and necessarily dependent on man for its conscious existence.[2] It is this very ambiguity in Fichte's concept of the ego, and especially of the absolute ego, which will provide the source and motivation for the subsequent evolution of his system.

The first *Theory of Science*, as we have seen, seemed to its critics to imply an implicit destruction of the absolute by an identification of

---

[1] Fichte, *op. cit.*, Vol. I, p. 268.
[2] Copleston, *op. cit.*, Vol. VII, p. 58. Confer page 143, footnote 3 where Blondel explicitly rejects the unconscious absolute role of Fichte's "productive imagination."

the absolute with the human ego. However, Fichte insists in his later works that the true conclusion of his philosophy is just the contrary. In his idealist system there is only one real being and that being is the absolute. The impossibility which the individual man encounters of reconciling the infinite striving which is the essence of his consciousness with his individual effort leads Fichte to the same conclusion as that reached by Spinoza, only the absolute is and all else is illusion. As Léon remarks, for Fichte the sovereign good for man consists precisely in the triumph of universal reason over that which one still possesses of the individual and the sensible. The individual as such is only a means, an instrument of universal reason. "The individual ought morally speaking to disappear and be absorbed with all other individuals in universal Reason."[1] Fichte could see no reason whatever to grant the individual as such a sort of absolute and eternal value as an immortal being. For the individual has no existence outside of the eternal and absolute life of the Spirit.

> The problem is to conciliate, to unify two things: the infinite and the finite. However, such a unification is in itself an impossible task. ... When one has recognized the absolute impossibility of such a conciliation, it is necessary to arrive at the universal suppression of the finite; it is necessary that all limitations be eliminated so that only the infinite Ego, at the same time one and all, remains.[2]

One can understand, in terms of the postulates of Fichte's system, why he was obliged to end up with the suppression of the individual ego as such. If material reality, which is the foundation of all individuality is a being of the imagination, as Fichte believed, one can effectively suppress the finite individual by that intellectual process which robs material reality of its pseudo-independence of the mind. But what factually remains after one has suppressed the individual?

UNION WITH THE ABSOLUTE

As far as Blondel is concerned, the absolute ego of Fichte is neither one nor all. For it is neither a real singular nor a true universal. Fichte was guilty in his methodology of a double error which led him ultimately to confuse a generalized concept of totality with the true absolute. By abstracting the intuition of the subject from its empirical context, he imprisoned himself in a subjective phenomenology, where

---

[1] Léon, *op. cit.*, p. 383.
[2] Fichte, "Grundlage ...," p. 144.

he was obliged to explain the whole of being exclusively in terms of the subject. By abstracting what he considered to be the pure form of the subject, the purely rational element of that subject, he effectively eliminated any possibility of rejoining the concrete.[1] It is this product of a double abstraction, this generalization of the form of human consciousness, that Fichte identified with the absolute. Consequently, having, as he believed, uncovered this absolute as immanent in human consciousness, Fichte confused the relative infinite potential present in our consciousness with the infinite in itself.

Blondel is convinced that this confusion concerning the true nature of the absolute in Fichte's system can be traced back to his point of departure, his search for a first principle from which the whole of philosophy could be deduced. "By a sort of passage to the limit ... one imagines oneself to have attained the principles, the elements, the unities, the concrete facts, the intelligible natures; then one proceeds as if that generality gives simultaneously the essence of the singular and the equivalent of the universal."[2] The absolute for Blondel is the concrete as against the abstract; it is the perfect identity of the true universal with the real singular, of essence with existence. Consequently, that science which alone can possibly give access to the true absolute and avoid all confusion between generality and true universality, is a science of the concrete. "That which we ought to dare, and to attain, is a science of the concrete in which the singular and the universal participate in thought and in action."[3] If by means of this "science of the concrete" we intend to search out in man's consciousness that trace of the absolute, we must seek it, not in some abstract aspect of man's consciousness, but in the concrete composite reality which constitutes his uniqueness and true individuality. "The truly infinite is not to be found in the abstract universal but in the concrete singular."[4] Thus it is not by abstraction from man's material concreteness that one can arrive at an understanding of man's destiny. If man has a divine vocation, a call to communicate with the absolute, he has it only on condition of remaining a distinct, individual person. "The individual determinations of man are both the condition and the means of his access to the absolute."[5]

[1] Blondel, L'Action, p. 449.
[2] Ibid., L'Itinéraire Philosophique (Paris: Collections "La NEF," ed. by Frédéric Lefèvre, Editions Spes, 1928), p. 132.
[3] Ibid., p. 76.
[4] Ibid., L'Action, p. 449.
[5] Ibid., p. 448.

This, then, is the ultimate and decisive reason why Blondel insists that philosophy must take the form of a philosophy of action and be modeled on experimental science. For philosophy, if it is to arrive at the absolute, must have as its center of perspective the concrete reality of action. It is incarnated human action which prefigures by means of its partial synthesis of the universal and the singular, the ideal and the real, the intelligible and the sensible, that perfect identity of essence and existence which is the distinguishing characteristic of the absolute. Consequently, it is the concrete, material context, the whole natural order into which man must incarnate his action, which serves both as a bond and obstacle, as a necessary means of union and an equally necessary means of distinction between the absolute and man. "It is by means of that very matter that the truth of the overwhelming infinite communicates itself to man, and it is by it that each one is protected against being overwhelmed by the infinite."[1] If Blondel insists on the need of introducing the total incarnate reality of living action into the philosophical dialectic, his reason is to preserve the distinct individual as such and to find the true access to the concrete reality of the absolute. For Blondel was convinced that man could never truly reach the absolute by means of a purely abstract thought but only by a living synthesis of thought with action.

The absolute of consciousness at the point of departure of Fichte's system is understood as an ideal potentiality for a total identity of the ego with itself. The means by which the subject can arrive at this ideal and activate this potentiality is a process of elimination of all non-ego and empirical content from consciousness in order to become one with the pure reflection of reason on itself. In other words the absolute which is achieved at the end of this process is the absolute of consciousness itself, the absolute as idea; it is not the absolute as being, that spontaneous activity which is in itself but does not exist for itself. Consequently, Léon informs us, Fichte did not pretend to affirm that the very being of the absolute is immanent in our consciousness, but simply the existence (Dasein) of the idea or form of the absolute. It is this dichotomy between the absolute as form of consciousness and the absolute as being which provides Fichte with the final development of his theory. Pure self-consciousness, which is the organic, active principle in the development of reflexive consciousness and which we objectify in our idea of the absolute, does not contain within itself the being of the Absolute.

---

[1] *Ibid.*, p. 449.

In his later work of religious philosophy: *The Way to the Blessed Life or the Doctrine of Religion* (Die Anweisung zum seligen Leben oder auch die Religionslehre), Fichte explains the differences between these two absolutes in terms of the three fundamental principles of consciousness. The first principle, expressed in the proposition: "The ego simply posits in an original way its own being," now represents the original action which is the unconscious identity of the absolute act with itself. The second fundamental principle is expressed in the formula: "A non-ego is simply opposed to the ego." In this second principle, Fichte maintains, the non-ego is unlimited in the sense that it represents objectivity in general. Thus we have two unlimited or infinite realities which tend to cancel each other out. Consequently, we are obliged to posit the third fundamental principle of finite consciousness: "I posit in the ego a divisible ego as opposed to a divisible non-ego." This third principle, Fichte tells us, represents the world of actual empirical consciousness, the starting point of the practical deduction of consciousness. The synthesis represented in the third principle is absolute neither in its form nor in its content, since both, being finite, are dependent on the positing activity of the pure ego. The whole of the theory of science represents the process by which one resolved that illusory synthesis by suppressing the finite. As late as in the *Theory of Science* of 1804, as D. Julia points out, Fichte was convinced that by means of this process one arrived at absolute knowledge which was a perfect synthesis of the real and the ideal, a perfect synthesis of a pure philosophical act with itself in the pure becoming of moral reason.[1] In *The Way to the Blessed Life*, however, Fichte maintains that this pure ego or active self-consciousness corresponds to the ego of the second principle and not of the first. The unity expressed by this principle is the unity of the pure idea or concept, a purely formal unity without content. This pure ego of reflection is absolute in form only; in its content it is entirely relative to the first principle, the absolute being, of which it is the reflection. The first principle alone expresses a material as well as a formal unity and is, consequently, absolute both in its form and in its content.

Since the absolute of pure consciousness is the absolute of the second principle alone, there is another step to be taken in Fichte's dialectic. Absolute knowledge or reflection, instead of attributing to itself a false status as absolute being, should become aware of itself as pure

---

[1] D. Julia, *op. cit.*, pp. 366-370.

reflection and acknowledge the purely formal character of the unity which is its essence.[1] It is this same relativity of pure consciousness which Fichte expressed in his earlier work, *The Destiny of Man* (Bestimmung des Menschen), in 1800.

> Nowhere is anything lasting, neither outside of me nor in me, nothing but an unceasing change. Nowhere do I know a being, not even my own. Being is not. *I myself*, I know nothing and I am not. There are only *images*. They are all that exists and they do not know themselves except as images, and I am only a confused image of those images. ... The *intuition* is a dream; *thought* ... is a dream of that dream.[2]

Maréchal sees in this passage Fichte's concept of the culminating point of all knowledge and all consciousness.[3] For at this point the pure ego of reflection becomes conscious of its own non-being, of its purely formal unity. Up to this point, Fichte maintains, reason or consciousness was necessitated to place existence in itself and identify being with the absolute form immanent in consciousness. From the point of view of consciousness, which is necessarily man's point of view, the infinite ego is, and the infinite non-ego or object-in-general is not. But at this point reflexive consciousness becomes aware of its own relativity. Man becomes aware that the state of pure consciousness is not absolute being but merely the absolute principle of consciousness of that being. Although absolute itself in form, it is entirely relative in content to the non-ego.[4]

Consequently, man must, so to speak, reverse the signs. It is the non-ego which is, and the ego represents only the reflection or image of that being.

> You have now penetrated the illusion (of knowledge) ... and this is the true usefulness of the system; it overturns and destroys the error. It cannot give you truth, for it is in itself completely empty. However,

---

[1] Fichte, "Die Anweisung zum seligen Leben, oder auch die Religionslehre," Vol. V, pp. 439-440.

[2] *Ibid.*, "Die Bestimmung des Menschen," Vol. II, p. 245.

[3] Maréchal, *op. cit.*, pp. 415-416.

[4] E. Coreth finds the transition from absolute ego to absolute being formally enunciated for the first time in the *Wissenschaftslehre* of 1801: "Here and in all his subsequent works Fichte speaks of an "absolute being" which must be presupposed in all thought and which preconditions all thought; thus he manifestly overturns the fundamental principle of the first *Wissenschaftslehre*. Absolute being is no longer enclosed within the consciousness of the finite spirit but is postulated as a condition of that consciousness." (E. Coreth, "Le Développement de la Théologie de Fichte," *Archives de Philosophie*, Tome XXV, Cahiers III-IV, (Juillet-Décembre, 1962, 510).

I know you continue to search beyond the pure representation something real, a real whose reality is different from that which you have
succeeded in reducing to nothing .... Your effort will be vain if you
pretend to draw out that reality from your knowledge and by means of
your knowledge. If you do not possess any other faculty capable of
grasping reality, you will never find it.[1]

We do possess such a faculty, according to Fichte, and that faculty is
belief (Glaube). In the third section of the trilogy contained in *The
Destiny of Man* (Doubt, Knowledge and Faith) Fichte attempts to show
how we can escape this deception of knowledge and seize the reality
of the absolute by means of faith. As E. Coreth points out, what Fichte
has in mind by faith is not the Christian concept of supernatural faith,
but the faith of practical reason in the sense of Kant.[2] Fichte attempts
to show that the being of the absolute imposes itself on us as an object
of belief, that is to say, as a postulate of our moral activity. Thus at
this point in the development of Fichte's doctrine we are faced with the
paradox that, having set out to reunite Kant's pure and practical reason
in a higher synthesis, Fichte in face of the problem of the absolute re-
affirms perhaps an even greater separation. All the subsequent works
of Fichte are dedicated to the effort to try to bring this belief and knowledge back together into a true unity; a program which, from Blondel's
viewpoint, will be doomed to failure, since Fichte's philosophical
method necessarily excludes the only true means of establishing that
unity, the concrete reality of synthetic action.[3]

Xavier Léon sees in Fichte's theory of religion an attempt to explain
how faith, which postulates the existence of the absolute, is transformed into an effective possession of, or unity with, the absolute.[4] In this
context Fichte makes use of a trinitatian image derived from the fourth
gospel, referred to by commentators as his johannine theory. In this
theory the first principle is considered as God, the father; the second,
the Word (Verbum) is the perfect reflection of the Father. The Word
is identical in Fichte's system with absolute reason or the *ordo ordinans*
which reveals itself as immanent in our reflexive consciousness. The
Word, since it is identical to the second principle, is absolute in form
only; it is the infinite of reflection. The process described above,

[1] Fichte, "Die Bestimmung ...," Vol. II, pp. 246-247.
[2] E. Coreth, *op. cit.*, pp. 538-539.
[3] For example in the *Way to a Blessed Life* (1806) Fichte writes "... die Wissen-
schaft hebt allen Glauben auf und verwandelt ihn in Schauen." (Fichte "Die Anweisung ...," Vol. V, p. 472.)
[4] Léon, *op. cit.*, p. 400.

whereby pure reason becomes conscious of its essential relativity, becomes, in the philosophy of religion, the process whereby the Word or *Dasein* realizes itself as the image of the father. "The *Dasein* must seize itself, recognize itself, and constitute itself as pure *Dasein*; and it must, in opposition with itself, pose and constitute an Absolute Being in relation to which it is itself none other than the simple image, representation, or consciousness of Being."[1]

It is in this context that Fichte develops his theory of love. The dualism between the Word or *Dasein*, as form of the absolute, and God, as the being of the absolute, is the extreme limit which human consciousness can achieve. For human consciousness in its essence is identical with the Word or *Dasein*. "Nothing exists outside of God but Thought and that Thought is absolutely and immediately the divine *Dasein* itself; and in so far as we are Thought, we are ourselves in our most profound roots the divine *Dasein*."[2] But the doctrine of love necessitates that we transcend in some way the point of view of our own consciousness to become one with the point of view of God himself. "Between the absolute or God and thought, at the very root of its (the Word's) existence, this separation does not exist; rather there is a complete compenetration."[3] This compenetration necessarily escapes the power of our reason and is unintelligible for reflection. It is, none the less, the postulate of faith and the ideal term of all moral activity. This compenetration is ultimately that which for Fichte is necessary but unthinkable. It is only when God and the Word become one that humanity by realizing the Word realizes God and becomes one with God. But the act which achieves this ultimate unity is not an act within reason or consciousness; rather, it is that act by which reason recognizes its relativity and annihilates its own false semblance of being. This act of self-annihilation Fichte calls love.[4] Coreth sees in this concept the origin of the Hegelian concept of the "negation of the negation," in which is expressed a pure affirmation of the absolute

---

[1] "Das Daseyn muss sich selber als blosses Daseyn fassen, erkennen, und bilden, und muss, sich selber gegenüber ein absolutes Seyn setzen und bilden, dessen blossen Daseyn eben es selbst sey ... was eben der Charakter des blossen Bildes, der Vorstellung oder der Bewusstseyns des Seyns gebt." (Fichte, "Die Anweisung ...," Vol. V, p. 441).

[2] "Er ist, ausser Gott, gar nichts ... da, denn — das *Wissen*: und dieses Wissen ist das göttliches Daseyn selber schlechthin und unmittelbar, und inwiefern wir das Wissen sind, sind wir selben in unserer tiefsten Wurzel das göttliche Daseyn." (*Ibid.*, "Die Anweisung ...," Vol. V, p. 448).

[3] *Ibid.*

[4] *Ibid.*, Vol. V, pp. 539-542.

Being, but an affirmation which can never be immediately seized.[1] This love first manifested itself in Fichte's system in the vital tendency (Lebenstrieb) towards that object which is totally fulfilling. It was this same life-drive which gave rise to consciousness and to the entire process by which one achieves one's identity with the Word as pure reflection. This same drive now leads the Word to the realization of its own relativity and, consequently, to place that supreme act of love by which it annihilates itself and thus effectively unites man to the divine being by its mediation.[2]

Summary

The brief development given above of Fichte's later religious philosophy can help us considerably to understand Blondel's criticism of Idealism, as well as what he meant by the role of action as a means of arriving at the true absolute. Fichte did begin his search for the absolute, as we have seen, with an understanding of the synthesis contained in human action between the infinite and the finite, the ideal and the real. But, in Blondel's opinion, he lost that clue to a true solution to the problem of human destiny because of a double error in his method. By reason of his idealist premise he arbitrarily dissolved within the knowing and conscious subject the synthesis between subject and object and thus imprisoned himself within a dogmatic subjectivism. Thus the only route left open to him in his effort to reach the absolute was a process of elimination of the reality of the objective finite world as illusory. By reason of his rationalist premise he was ultimately obliged to make a division between the theoretical and the practical and, consequently, to distinguish within the subject a purely rational and a purely pragmatic activity. This distinction involved in turn a further distinction within the absolute itself between an absolute of reason and an absolute of love.

In the theoretical approach to the absolute, the philosopher is obliged to undertake a progressive suppression of the real contained in the dynamic synthesis of human action and consciousness in order to arrive at a pure act of consciousness without content, the pure reflection of reason on itself. The end result of this process, Fichte finds,

---

[1] Coreth, *op. cit.*, pp. 513-514.
[2] Coreth maintains that Fichte's theory of love does not arrive at a true union with God. Rather, according to the logic of Fichte's theory love must remain outside of God even as thought remains outside. (Coreth, *op. cit.*, pp. 539-540).

is the possession of a purely formal idea of the absolute the very existence of which contradicts the being itself of the absolute. Consequently, in a second purely practical approach, Fichte appeals to the existential life-force which by a process of suppression, this time of the
essential or rational, postulates the being of the absolute by an act of
faith and achieves unity with that being by an ultimate act of love,
which represents effectively an annihilation of reason and consciousness, a sort of rational suicide. Thus by dissolving the synthesis of
theory and practice, the ideal and real, in action Fichte concludes to a
necessary contradiction or, at least, opposition between essence and
existence in the absolute. Paradoxically, having begun with the postulate that being and consciousness are identical, once he suppressed the
real being of the finite, he is obliged to suppress, as it were, self-
consciousness in the absolute. In the following chapter we will develop
Blondel's solution to the problem of the absolute and his attempt to
correct what he considered to be the methodological failures of Fichte
precisely by remaining faithful to the total synthetic reality of action.

CHAPTER TEN

BLONDEL'S SOLUTION TO THE PROBLEM OF THE ABSOLUTE

INTRODUCTION

As we have noted previously, Blondel's dialectic of action does not stop with the conclusion that the total identity of self with self, the goal of human action, is both necessary and impossible, and that the means of achieving this goal, a union with the absolute, remains necessary for man as an ideal but inaccessible to him by his own proper forces. Blondel also proceeds to an affirmation of the absolute as idea, and a consequent possession of or, better, participation in the absolute as being. The study we have already undertaken of Fichte's philosophy in relation to the problem of union with the absolute will be of considerable help in clarifying the exact meaning and nature of Blondel's development of the same problem. For, as will become clear in the course of our analysis of Blondel's position, that position seems undoubtedly to have been thought out and proposed precisely as an effort to respond to Kantian criticism and Fichtean subjective idealism as he understood them.

We have already seen that the basic difference between Fichte's method and the method by which Blondel arrives at the affirmation of, and participation in, the absolute lies in the use Blondel made at his point of departure of the total synthetic reality of human action as it reveals itself in consciousness and in his continual refusal to concede any valid methodological distinction between a theoretical and practical approach to the absolute as necessarily destructive of that synthesis which was his point of departure. Let us trace, then, how this difference in starting point and method works itself out in practice and why Blondel arrives necessarily at a totally different concept than did Fichte of the absolute itself and of man's relation to that absolute.

The most important thing to establish at the very beginning concerning Blondel's proof for the existence of the absolute or *Unique Nécessaire*, as he calls it, is the context in which that proof occurs. That context is a search for the meaning of human destiny. Blondel assumes that it has already been conclusively established that man is necessitated from within himself to search continually by means of his voluntary action a total fulfillment of himself; and that fulfillment necessarily involves a perfect identity within himself of the will-willing and the will-willed. Once the human will has exhausted the entire relative or phenomenal order in its search for perfect identity with itself, it finds itself still unsatisfied. This apparent failure would not be a conscious fact except in contrast with a previous desire. By his voluntary actions man necessarily goes beyond the phenomenal order; he can not by his own will satisfy his own exigencies. Consequently, man necessarily comes to the realization in and by his own conscious experience that there is a greater potentiality in his will than he can possibly put into exercise by his efforts alone. "Man cannot succeed by his own forces alone in employing in his willed action all that which is at the origin of his voluntary activity."[1]

At every stage of his dialectic Blondel holds that our ideas are determined and necessitated by the action from which they derive and to which they lead; at every stage of action man is determined to conceive of some further object, which is, as it were, a projection of a possible means by which the will can achieve a more perfect identity with itself. This is equally true, in Blondel's opinion, of the idea of the absolute; it is also a necessary and inevitable idea which gives expression and direction to that basic subjective movement of the will. Thus what Blondel proposes to undertake is a study of that genetic process whereby the idea of the absolute arises from subjective action. He maintains that this idea has its source precisely in man's subjective experience of apparent failure in the drive of his will for self-identity. Consequently, by the proof of the existence of the absolute, Blondel understands a reflexive phenomenological analysis of one's willed-action with the objective of grasping or intuiting that which is already present in the will-willing. For the absolute reveals itself most clearly at the very moment of apparent failure and necessarily arises as a goal before consciousness. "How does this contradiction (in our will) present itself to our knowledge; where it would seem nothing can rise up which is not the expression of a hidden will, and an extract of our interior initiative or of our spontaneous action?"[2]

In Blondel's opinion, only this genetic study of the necessary formation of the idea of the absolute has the value of a constraining proof of the existence of the absolute, because this genetic study is based on

---

[1] Blondel, *L'Action*, p. 321.
[2] *Ibid.*, p. 326.

the total synthetic reality of action. Any proof, Blondel tells us, which is nothing more than a purely logical argument always remains abstract and partial. "Such a proof does not lead to being and does not succeed in uniting thought with the necessarily real."[1] We have already seen how this criticism proved true in Fichte's theory. By abstracting the purely ideal or rational aspect of action, one can arrive at the idea of the absolute as pure form, the term of a purely abstract philosophical process. Or, again, by abstracting the purely real and voluntary aspect of action, one can postulate by a basically a-rational act of faith and love an identity with the absolute as being. In both arguments the absolute which one affirms is arrived at by an abstraction of one aspect of the synthesis between thought and reality in human action and by the erection of that partial aspect as an absolute.

The privilege of action as such, Blondel argues, is to be total, to be the synthesis of the real and the ideal. "Here as everywhere, effective action is the great mediator; action succeeds in conciliating what, for a critical or idealist philosophy, is formally self-excluding from the static viewpoint of thought."[2] If one can establish a proof which results from the total movement of life itself, Blondel is convinced that it will necessarily lead to such a synthesis of the real and the ideal. Consequently, in the dialectical exposition of the proof one must try, in so far as possible, to recapture that spontaneous synthetic movement of life itself. "It is the privilege proper to action to form a whole; thus it is by action that all the partial arguments will unite among themselves to form a demonstrative synthesis."[3]

In imitation, then, of the dialectical movement of action itself, there are three steps or moments in Blondel's attempt to prove the existence of the absolute. The first, corresponding to the traditional cosmological argument, argues from all that has already been willed and that manifests itself as necessary but insufficient. In this argument Blondel seeks the foundation of the affirmation of the *reality* of the absolute in our consciousness of the synthesis already achieved. The second argument corresponds to the traditional teleological argument. Here Blondel argues from the evidence provided by the subjective act of the will reflecting on itself. In this argument he seeks in the subjective will-act itself the basis for the affirmation of the absolute as *ideal*. The third and final argument corresponds to the traditional ontological

---

[1] *Ibid.*, p. 341.
[2] *Ibid.*, p. 301.
[3] *Ibid.*, p. 341.

argument. Here the argument is based on the synthetic act of the will precisely as a synthesis of the real and the ideal. In this proof, which itself represents the synthesis of the previous two arguments, Blondel attempts to analyse the basis in our will-activity for the necessary affirmation of the absolute as the *perfection* of being, "the existential ideal and the ideal existence."

MEANING OF THE COSMOLOGICAL ARGUMENT

In his development of each argument Blondel presupposes a knowledge of the traditional argument and limits himself to a search for the foundation of that argument in our living conscious experience of the synthetic power of our will-action. The cosmological or *a contingentia* argument has, according to Blondel, a different meaning from that normally ascribed to it. There is a sort of negative proof, in which one argues to the impossibility of absolute non-being, based exclusively on the insufficiency of relative being.[1] The true cosmological argument however, is not based solely on the fact of contingency experienced in our conscious will-action exclusively as need and dissatisfaction. On the contrary, the contingent reveals itself to consciousness as both necessary and insufficient, as that which "one can neither renounce nor be content with."

Therefore, in contradiction with Fichte's judgment, the reality of the finite reveals itself to our consciousness as that which cannot be suppressed or eliminated in order to leave us with a purely formal ideal. "Instead of placing its force in the fiction of a necessary ideal, the argument is based on the very necessity of the real."[2] The finite is that which need not have been but, once it has been, necessarily is. Thus the true character of the contingent is "to participate in the necessity of the real without participating in its privilege." This relative necessity of the contingent reveals the absolute necessity of the absolute. Instead of searching for a necessity which is completely exterior to the reality of the finite as an ulterior term, the argument shows that necessity as present in the finite itself, as immanent in all that which is and has already been willed. It proves not only the impossibility of affirming the contingent alone; it proves also the impossibility of denying the necessity which founds it. "At the

---

[1] *Ibid.*, pp. 341-342.
[2] *Ibid.*, p. 343.

moment when anything has been, the uniquely necessary eternally is."[1]

According to Fichte's third principle, the world of finite being, as it reveals itself to us in consciousness, is absolute neither in its form nor in its content. Consequently, it has only the appearance of being. The only means of arriving at the absolute is to suppress that finite synthesis of form and matter in order to arrive at an absolute of pure form or, conversely, at an absolute of formless being. According to Blondel, the world of phenomena is not absolute in form; it is not of its essence to exist. Nor is it absolute in its content which is limited. But there is a trace of the absolute precisely in the synthesis which binds together thought and action, form and content. For the finite, once it exists, necessarily exists and necessarily is that which it is. Even if its reality has been synthesized into our subjective life by an act of our will, it cannot consequently be suppressed by an act of our will.

This relative necessity of these finite syntheses reveals itself in the living conscious experience of relative fulfillment of the will at each step of the development of the dialectic of action. Consequently, this proof for the necessity of the absolute takes its force and value from the entire order of phenomena: nature, science, consciousness itself, society, metaphysics, morality. All these phenomena, once they have been, necessarily exist for our will in its search for the absolute without being sufficient for it. The progress of the will towards the absolute has manifested itself not in a process of suppression and annihilation of these syntheses but, rather, in a process of assimilation and transcendence, where all that was of value in the previous synthetic step is preserved and continued in the next. Thus one is forced to conclude that there is something "which is neither nothing nor phenomena, which sustains the phenomena in being and makes them participate, but only participate, in its absolute necessity."

As D.-C. Dhotel remarks, what we have here is not so much a proof of the existence of the absolute as an indication of the necessity we are under to continue our search and of the direction that search must take.[2] Whatever the absolute might be, it does not yet exist for us in itself, nor is it to be found in the order of extension, that is, in the phenomena. Therefore, I cannot continue my search either with the phenomena or with the uniquely necessary itself; rather, I must continue my search with myself, and with that power of synthesis which

---

[1] *Ibid.*

[2] D. - C. Dhotel "Action et Dialectique. Les Preuves de Dieu dans "L'Action" de 1893," *Archives de Philosophie*, Tome XXVI, Cahier I (Janvier-Mars, 1963), 12.

I find in myself. "In order to find it we cannot begin with it where we are not, but from ourselves where it is."[1]

MEANING OF THE TELEOLOGICAL ARGUMENT

In keeping with the dialectical concept of the proof for the existence of the absolute, Blondel calls our attention to the fact that this second argument necessarily presupposes and includes the first. It includes that relative necessity of the world of phenomena and adds to it the subjective history of its discovery. "One should keep in mind the extension of this proof. It reassembles all that we have discovered outside ourselves and in ourselves of intelligibility and intelligence, movement and force, truth and thought, in order to reveal their common origin."[2] Each of these couplets represents a synthesis of the effect or content of our action with the action itself. Thus we find the same totality of the exterior world contained in our ideas and sensations, but considered here in so far as it is interiorized in the subjective experience of our thought and action.

When we reflect on our past actions, what we find is a continuous process taking its origin in the spontaneous preconscious life-force within us and necessitating us to think and act continually in such a way as to acquire a true adequation within ourselves. "Continually the ideal conceived is overtaken by the reality of the action, and continually the reality obtained is overtaken by an ever renewed ideal."[3] For the purpose of the argument what is important in that process is the experiential fact that in the dialectic there is always an indefinable moment when thought and action, the ideal and the real, coincide in a momentary harmony, only to be immediately separated. Blondel compares this spiritual process within us to the process of balancing in walking, where a moment of equilibrium is achieved but immediately broken again in order to carry us forward in our march. "It would seem that all our efforts oscillate about that point of coincidence where they can never rest, yet through which they must continually pass."[4]

Just as in the first argument one proves that it is necessary that the absolute be real because the phenomena are real, so here it is necessary that the perfect coincidence of thought and action, "the pure act of the

---

[1] Blondel, *op. cit.*, p. 344.
[2] *Ibid.*, p. 345.
[3] *Ibid.*, pp. 344-345.
[4] *Ibid.*, p. 345.

perfect thought," must exist, and not merely be postulated, because a
fleeting glimpse of that harmonious synthesis is given us in fact. However, even if it is by means of our free will-acts that we experience a
fleeting and partial harmony, this experience, Blondel argues, also
testifies that it is not by us that the union is effected. It is not from ourselves that we draw either the light of our thoughts nor the efficacy of
our acts; nor can we succeed by our thought and action to produce a
durable harmony. Even if one grants that all the rest, all phenomena,
are resumed and founded in our thought and action, yet it remains
true that at the beginning we did not will to act or think. "We wish to
suffice for ourselves and we cannot .... We are forced to recognize a
determinism in our will preceding, enclosing, and outreaching our
personal action; a determinism which is within us as the principle of
our will."[1]

Blondel insists on the reflexive character of the proof. The objections
which Kant brought to bear against the traditional proof from finality
or universal harmony do not apply here. It is not by abstraction nor
by contrast that we discover the absolute, as if it were an ideal exterior
to us and without roots in our own life. Far from being a projection
or an imaginary prolongation of our thought or action it is at the very
center of all that we think and do. "I find in the imperfect wisdom of
things and my thought the presence and necessary action of a perfect
thought and power."[2]

But if Blondel insists on the reflexive character of the proof, he
leaves no doubt that what is uncovered in this reflection on action is
not that pure ego or pure form of the absolute on which Fichte bases
his deduction. Precisely what is intuited here is the ideal nature of that
necessary source of the real syntheses of the first argument.

Blondel, in agreement with Fichte, does conclude from this argument that the absolute reveals itself as subject, as an ego. "There is at
the root of my consciousness an *ego* (moi) which is no longer *my ego*."[3]
Blondel feels justified at this point in identifying this source of our
partial synthesis of thought and action as a subject or ego, because the
primary trait which characterizes a subject as such is precisely the
power to synthesize thought and action.[4] And the absolute reveals
itself to consciousness in this argument as necessarily "the pure act of

---

[1] *Ibid.*, pp. 326-327.
[2] *Ibid.*, p. 347.
[3] *Ibid.*
[4] *Ibid.*, pp. 97-100.

the perfect thought." Blondel, however, is careful to preclude Fichte's conclusion that, since the activity of the absolute ego reveals itself as immanent in our reflexive consciousness of self, there is somehow an identity between the absolute ego and all finite egos. Although we find in ourselves that presence and that action, we cannot claim them as our own. "It (the absolute) is not the obscure side of my thought, the invisible side of my consciousness and my action, as if I could not see it except in myself and as if all its reality consisted only in the idea I have of it."[1] The absolute has no reason to be except in so far as we are incapable of achieving our own fulfillment, the perfect synthesis of self with self. We have no reason to affirm its existence except in so far as it is both necessary and inaccessible to us. Fichte arrived at the affirmation of the identity of our ego with the form of the absolute by a process of suppression of the reality of the finite synthesis present in that consciousness. Blondel proved that such a suppression is effectively impossible. Any denial of that finite real synthesis which is the reality of our action is purely imaginary and contradicted by experience. The necessary reality of the synthesis, achieved by our own personal actions and established in the reflection of the first proof, prevents us from confusing ourselves with the absolute. The failure of our free actions to arrive at their ideal goal prevents us from confusing the absolute with ourselves. "In order to find that perfect identity of our voluntary action, we must look within ourselves, until we reach the point where that which is of ourselves ceases."[2] Thus the absolute, which revealed itself as necessarily real, reveals itself in the second proof as the ideal source of all our syntheses and, itself, the perfect synthesis of thought and action. In a word, it is the absolute subject, the *intimior intimo meo* of Saint Augustine. Yet, although it reveals itself as within me at the source of all my thoughts and actions, this absolute subject also reveals itself as necessarily distinct from me. We have seen that the first argument, on the level of phenomenological analysis, was not so much a proof as an indication of the direction our search for the absolute must take, leading us to search for it within ourselves. So too the second argument is not so much a proof as a further indication of the direction our search must take.

This reflection within ourselves on our synthetic activity forces us to become conscious of the limits of the human spirit by reason of our awareness of the continual disproportion between thought and action.

---

[1] *Ibid.*, p. 347.
[2] *Ibid.*

Although we find that the ideal, the perfect adequation of thought and action, is an organic ideal operative within our will, it is impossible for us to call it our own. We must continue to search for that absolute in that which is within us but also in something which transcends us and, so to speak, reduces us to our limits. But this ideal absolute, which our limited spirit cannot appropriate nor entirely absorb in itself and to which, as a result, it must oppose itself, becomes, by reason of that necessary opposition, the reality of the ideal: Being itself. This is the experience of the immanence of the transcendent which will determine "the inevitable transcendence of human action." This is what Blondel attempts to expose in the third and final argument.

MEANING OF THE ONTOLOGICAL ARGUMENT

Once again it is important to keep in mind the context of Blondel's development of the proofs for the absolute. Blondel would have us "look within ourselves until we reach the point where that which is from ourselves ceases." There is no question here of concluding coldly that the absolute exists; rather, in face of the impossibility of absolute non-being, there is question of accepting or refusing without any evasion possible that which founds our action, of willing or refusing to will that very source and being of our own will.

> My realism does not only consist in the speculative affirmation that the object exists but in the affirmation that this objective certitude puts us in a position to choose the alternatives on which it will depend whether we will be deprived of that objective existence or possess it.[1]

This option, however, is not blind; it is not an act of metaphysical suicide, a sort of "leap in the dark." Blondel contends that there is no question of there being no light; rather, the problem is that there is too much light. Yet man has the right and the duty to prove that that light is not an illusion. Blondel's exposition of this proof has three parts: first, a justification of the ontological argument against the criticism of Kant; second, a description of what is found; third, a justification of the action or option which follows.

Justification of the Proof:

Blondel begins by insisting on the necessity of the order of the proofs in a dialectical exposition. The proofs, if they are to have

---

[1] Confer above, Chapter IV, pp. 64-69.

phenomenological validity as a description of experience, must follow the movement of life itself. Consequently, the ontological argument necessarily presupposes the cosmological argument as thesis and the teleological argument as antithesis. Just as action itself is the synthesis of the reality of its own being with the ideal of thought, so the ontological argument simulates and guides the supreme synthesis of the option.

Blondel seems to have accepted the opinion of Kant that there are ultimately only three arguments and all others can be reduced to one of these three. His justification of the use he makes of these proofs seems to be primarily directed against Kant's refutation of the validity of these arguments. Kant maintained that the first two arguments apparently begin within a general or a particular experience, while the ontological proof represents an a priori argument which concludes from the concept of the absolute to its existence. But in reality, he claims, "it is the transcendental concept which guides reason in its efforts and determines the end which is sought out in all investigations of this kind." Kant denies that there is any valid a posteriori argument for the existence of the absolute, that is, an argument based in practical experience; in every such proof the concept of the absolute, explicit only in the ontological argument, is factually posed as an implicit a priori.[1]

Blondel insists that the dialectic and synthetic nature of his deduction, based as it is in the movement of living action as it reveals itself in consciousness, eliminates effectively the grounds of Kant's objection that the probative power of the argument rests on an illegitimate use of the pure a priori transcendental concept of the absolute:

> It is not a matter of indifference which order we follow in the dialectical exposition of the arguments. If it were, one would be exposed to the belief that the idea of perfection is a fabrication, artificially constructed without any real foundation; while the fact is that it is a living reality in our consciousness which borrows from our total action all that there is of positive certitude in us.[2]

What we arrive at in the ontological argument is less an abstract vision than a consciousness of life. This consciousness does not result from a process of pure speculation but is joined to all the movement of thought and action in us. Thus what we arrive at is not an abstraction from which one can draw an abstract idea of existence but a prin-

---

[1] Kant, *Kritik der reinen Vernunft*, Vol. III, Sections 618-619.
[2] Blondel, *op. cit.*, p. 348.

ciple of action leading to action. Fichte attempted to concretize Kant's abstract ontological argument in a conscious intuition of the process of the spirit. In Fichte's exposition, however, all finite reality having been eliminated from human consciousness, one ends up with an experience of the pure form of the absolute devoid of real content. It is only by opposition or contrast with that form that the true being of the absolute manifests itself. Blondel's method of demonstration is exactly the opposite.

> It (the absolute) is not an ideal from which one pretends to extract the real, but a reality in which one finds the ideal. One must not, then, seek in that ideal that which permits us to base an objection against it, namely, a reality which is distinct from the ideal itself.[1]

The movement of Blondel's argument is actually a complete reversal of the movement Kant ascribes to the defenders of the ontological argument and factually retained in Fichte's philosophy. Consequently, it escapes the objection Kant brings against that argument. Assuming that the ontological argument begins in the purely speculative order where the idea of perfection is only an abstraction, Kant objects that to assert that the absolute exists implies either that one identifies one's idea with the absolute or that one has a priori introduced existence into one's concept. As Fichte argues, human consciousness arrives at an intuition of the ego as pure form or idea to which it necessarily but falsely attributes existence; it is only by rectifying that error through an act of faith and love that one can eliminate the illusion of being in the experience of the pure form and arrive at the reality of absolute being. While he was working on the redaction of his chapter on the *Unique Nécessaire* Blondel noted this reflection on Kant's objection:

> The weakness of the Kantian criticisms of the theological proofs: He demonstrates quite well that the idea of God cannot be an extraction from experience, because that idea is its source and its rule. But what is that force which carries the spirit forward? Is it not true that Kant did not pretend to impose the ordinary conditions of the real on the ideal, precisely because, unconsciously, he seems to have started from the idea that the real can never be ideal.[2]

---

[1] *Ibid.*

[2] *Ibid.*, *Carnets Intimes*, p. 160. Jean Lacroix in his recent work gives an excellent explanation of the fundamental importance of this ontological argument in the whole context of Blondel's work. It is here, he claims, that the basic idea which Blondel derived from the *Ethics* of Spinoza, the idea that it is only by means of a total philosophy or a metaphysics that morality can be founded, receives its justification. Lacroix also brings out the relation to Descartes' use of the ontological argument. He concludes: "One seizes here in this argument the very condition

We can translate that preconceived idea of Kant into Fichte's terminology as the assumption that absolute being (sein), the real, can never be identical with conscious being (Dasein), the ideal. Blondel believed that his dialectical approach based in living action itself proves that the real is necessarily ideal, that absolute being is necessarily conscious being, and that ultimate being is precisely the perfect synthesis of the real and the ideal, being and consciousness.

Description of What is Found:

What precisely does the ontological proof add, in Blondel's opinion, to our knowledge of the absolute? It is at this point and only here in the dialectical unfolding of the proof, Blondel tells us, that we are justified in identifying the concept which we have of the absolute with being. Thus, for the first time in the text of *Action* the word phenomenon is replaced by the word being. "In that which concerns the total complexity of life, only action is necessarily complete and total also. It deals with the all, and that is why from it alone comes forth the indisputable presence and constraining proof of *Being*."[1] This conceptual identity of the absolute with being, in Blondel's judgment, is justified at this point because we have placed within it beforehand the real identity of thought and action. The ideal is real because we have discovered the ideal synthesis of thought and action as the source from which the partial synthesis in our actions springs; and we have previously discovered that this partial synthesis of thought and action is necessarily real. Thus, the dialectical movement of thought, in imitation of the movement of living action, is obliged to affirm the absolute as being, that is, as the perfect substantial unity of the real and the ideal. But if the absolute is being, then it follows that the ego or subject, which we have discovered at the source of our action as immanent in us but distinct from us, is not a pure idea, a notional subject, but a subject in a hypostatic sense, a substantial subject endowed with intelligence and will.

Justification of the Option:

Blondel adds immediately that what we have achieved by means of

---

of philosophy in its difficult progress and in the exercise of its most technical function; a philosophy which vivifies knowledge by action, and clarifies action by knowledge, which uncovers within the dialectical progress of knowledge the call of Being ..." (*Maurice Blondel, Sa Vie, Son Oeuvre*, pp. 72-83).

[1] *Ibid., L'Action*, p. 350.

the ontological argument is a description of that movement of life and of vital action in us which necessarily leads us to conceive and affirm the existence of the absolute as substantial being. However, this affirmation of the absolute is by no means possession of the absolute; our idea of the absolute is by no means that idea in itself and for itself. "Without doubt the ontological proof never has all the value for us that it has in itself. For it (the idea of the absolute) is never absolute except there where there is a perfect idea of perfection itself, there where the essence is real and the existence ideal."[1] Blondel's statement, as Dhotel notes, seeks to avoid that misconception of the ontological proof which Saint Thomas refutes:

> Dico quod haec propositio: Deus est, quantum in se est, per se nota est quia praedicatum est idem cum subjecto; Deus enim est suum esse. ... Sed quia nos non scimus de Deo quid est, non est nobis per se nota.[2]

Precisely this difference which Saint Thomas notes between the idea of the absolute which is in us and the idea that the absolute has of itself, in Blondel's opinion, provides the stimulus for that further action which is the function and value of the idea.

> It is necessary, in order to possess the real in ourselves in the very knowledge that we have of it, to pass by means of the option which confers on our speculative idea of things the fullness of its meaning and content. This is the obvious proof that our intellectual vision, even when it is a logically demonstrated vision of God, is by no means vision in God, nor ontological solution.[3]

It is true then, Blondel remarks, that in order to attain the absolute we do not seize it in itself where we are not; but we part from it in us where it is, in order to understand it better by understanding somewhat what it is. We are obliged to affirm the absolute in the measure that we have an idea of it, because that idea is itself a reality.

The affirmation of the existence of the absolute represents, then, only the beginning of a new dialectic of thought and action which has as its purpose "to penetrate the very mystery of perfection." That mystery is not absolutely unknowable. We are certain that the absolute knows us even as it knows itself. Blondel insists that the absolute is a mystery which always escapes us not because it is exterior or strange to us but because it is more interior to us than our own interior cons-

---

[1] *Ibid.*, p. 348.
[2] Saint Thomas, *Summa Theologica*, I, 2, 1 c.
[3] Blondel, *Lettres Philosophiques*, p. 165.

cious self. "That which disconcerts us in ourselves is the fact that we cannot be one with ourselves; that which disconcerts us in it (the absolute) is the absolute unity of *being, knowing,* and *acting.* It is a subject in which everything is subject."[1]

Blondel returns once again to a final refutation of both Kant's and Fichte's position. "To speak of this mysterious perfection as if the existence differs in it from knowledge and knowledge from action is to lower it to the imperfections which we recognized in ourselves and arbitrarily apply to it."[2] In Blondel's opinion this position ends up in a final and more subtle form of superstition which pretends itself to be a refutation of superstition.[3] The more obvious forms of superstition, which direct man towards an object exterior or superior to himself, are replaced by the superstition of pantheism or panentheism. One suppresses a transcendent object of cult in order to place man in the presence of a mystery which he contains totally within his own consciousness or thought. Blondel quotes Kant's famous moral dictum with which Fichte was in complete accord: "Anything which man believes he is capable of doing in order to make himself pleasing to God, if that is not merely to conduct himself well, is pure superstition."[4] What does this mean, Blondel demands, if not "that human action by its own powers pretends to absorb to the point where it completely exhausts that which our knowledge cannot succeed in understanding nor our will succeed to embrace completely." Blondel sees in Kant's and Fichte's moralism, then, another and more subtle surrender to the superstitious pretention to possess and employ the absolute by human forces alone. It consists in willing that the absolute be simultaneously outside of action in order to become its conclusion and in action in order that it suffice for itself.[5]

This superstitious conclusion, Blondel contends, is the necessary result of a separate, fragmentary use of the proofs. In so far as a proof is an elaboration of reason alone, its conclusion appears as dependent on the reason which forms it. Consequently, any proof of the existence of God, objectifying that existence which it pretends to found, ends

---

[1] *Ibid., L'Action,* p. 349.

[2] *Ibid.*

[3] *Ibid.,* pp. 313-316.

[4] *Ibid.,* p. 314. The corresponding statement in Fichte's doctrine can be found in "Aus einem Privatschreiben": "Jeder Glaube an einem Göttliches, *der mehr enthält,* als diesen Begriff der moralischen Ordnung ist insofern Erdichtung und Aberglaube." (Fichte, Vol. V, pp. 394-395).

[5] Blondel, *op. cit.,* p. 314.

up with an idol of reason, even if that reason is practical reason. For Blondel, the only truly ultimate a priori is existence itself. It is impossible to give an account of any existence apart from the absolute existence itself. Consequently, the real basis for a "proof" of the existence of God is a reflexive awareness that the very activity itself of our mind, which necessarily elaborates a proof and arrives at an affirmation of the existence of God, was put into motion a priori by the absolute subject and not originally by an idea which one freely proposes to thought. By means of this reflection on the combined dialectic of thought and action embracing the totality of our being, we are led into the presence of a person and not, as would be the case at the term of a pure speculation, to the possession of an abstract idea. Just as, on the level of thought, Blondel first substitutes here the word *being* for the word *phenomenon*, so too on the level of phenomenological description of experience, he substitutes for the first time the word *God* for the word *absolute*. For the ontological argument, in his opinion, represents that living movement of our spirit which leads us into the presence of a person who is immanent in our action but not identical with it: a person who is the absolute identity of existence, knowledge, and act: in a word, God.[1]

The Necessary Action of the Necessary Idea

As we have noted, Blondel continually insists that the idea of the absolute is a necessary idea. He does not contend, however, that this idea must always reach that degree of clarity and precision which it has at the end of his dialectical demonstration; on the contrary, the idea seldom reaches such a clear formulation. No matter under what form it presents itself to consciousness, the thought of the absolute or God is produced in us by a determinism which imposes that idea from within as a necessary result of the dynamism of our interior life; and this idea, in turn, produces a necessary effect and has a necessary influence on the organization of our conduct.

What necessarily rises up in every consciousness, what has, in practice, an inevitable efficacy, is not the concept of a speculative truth to be defined; rather, it is the conviction, perhaps vague but certain and imperious, of a destiny and an ulterior end to be attained. "There is no need to have resolved any metaphysical question in order

---

[1] *Ibid.*, p. 350.

to live, so to speak, metaphysically."[1] The vital source of this sense of destiny is, in fact, the presence within us of the absolute person. No matter under what form that presence reveals itself to consciousness, whether it be clear or confused, accepted or hidden, admitted or unnamed, the living truth of that presence has a certain efficacy. The fact remains that human action is a sort of *théergie*, as Blondel calls it; we cannot place a free human action without cooperating with the absolute subject in us and, at the same time, without causing him to cooperate with us. In order to insert the character of transcendence into our lives, it is not necessary that we must always perceive the presence or distinctly recognize the action of the absolute in us and on us. Even if we deny that presence and that action, we displace only the object of affirmation; but the reality of human action is not affected in its source by this superficial play of ideas and words. "That which escapes knowledge is the abstract formula but not the concrete reality of the choice."[2]

This idea of the absolute, then, no matter what form it takes, is necessarily projected as our destiny, that is, as the ultimate term of our thought and action combined. Therefore, it is equally necessary that we sense the need actually to achieve that destiny with the combined force of our thought and action. Human action has the inevitable ambition to realize in itself that idea of perfection. "What we know of God is the surplus of interior life which demands its employment; we cannot, then, know God without willing in some way to become God."[3] Just as the idea of the absolute represents a paradoxical reality which is both immanent in us and transcendent to us, so too the choice and the action which inevitably follows on this idea takes on a paradoxical nature. The grounds on which our affirmation of God as absolute subject rests in the fact that he represents exactly that which we can not be by ourselves nor accomplish by our forces alone. Yet the fact remains that we have neither being, will, nor action except on condition of willing and somehow becoming him who is the very source and being of our own will and action. Blondel insists that the very intellectual and experiential grasp of this paradox carries with it an understanding of the means of resolving it. The ultimate means of becoming one with ourself is by admitting another being within us, by the substitution of another will for ours. But this admission does

---

[1] *Ibid.*, p. 353.
[2] *Ibid.*, p. 362.
[3] *Ibid.*, p. 354.

not represent an intrusion from without. Rather, it is a free consent or recognition of that which is already within.

It would be false to understand the supreme option as necessarily a final, clear choice distinct in time and reality from all other choices. Perhaps it is that occasionally. However, just as the idea of the absolute can be relatively confused or clear, so too the reality and import- ance of that fundamental option itself in the presence of the absolute can be implicit or explicit. Whenever man places a fully human action, the option is always present at least implicitly. Every free will-act, since it is potentially our last, implies an eternal response to that in- evitable implicit presence of the absolute. Blondel understood the true usefulness of all the preceding analysis of the determinism of human action to be precisely its power to lead us to a clear realization of the nature and importance of this supreme option of the will. He wished to lead us to the realization that man's destiny is ultimately a question of consenting voluntarily to the presence within himself of the abso- lute subject which transcends him or of refusing that consent. "Yes or no, does he wish to live enough to die, if one can so speak, by con- senting to be supplanted by God? Or indeed will he pretend to suffice for himself without God?"[1] This is the fundamental limiting choice which is granted to human freedom. For it is always possible for man to refuse his destiny. Man can profit from God's necessary presence without rendering that presence voluntary. Man can, so to speak, borrow from God himself the force to do without him; he can "will infinitely without willing the infinite." Man can choose whether that presence shall be a fulfillment or a privation; he cannot choose to suppress that presence, any more than Fichte could effectively choose to suppress the reality of the finite synthesis within our consciousness.

Blondel also felt that the final victory of liberty over determinism is assured by this option. According to Coreth, because Fichte placed absolute being completely outside of man's consciousness of self, he effectively arrived at a necessary suppression of that liberty which it was his intention at the beginning to defend. For the liberty which Fichte ascribes to man has its foundation, not in the liberty of absolute being, but in the necessity of divine essence. For Fichte, God is not a person; there is no free act of creation; in fact, there is no action of God which has a real effect outside of himself. There is only a necessary consequence which is posed simultaneously with the Word or essence

---

[1] *Ibid.*, pp. 354-355.

of God. "The liberty and autonomy of a being outside of God seems once again to be suppressed and assumed into the absolute necessity of the unique absolute Being itself."[1] Within Blondel's theory, the option, it is true, is imposed on us; but it is by it that we become that which we will. In the last analysis it is not liberty which is absorbed by determinism; it is the total determinism of human life which is suspended on this supreme free decision.

It is important to note what Blondel considered to be, so to speak, the metaphysical function contained within the psychological experience of the option. The alternatives which present themselves before our will, "To be God with God and by God or to be God without God and against God," give rise to what Blondel calls an *antibolie* as distinguished from an *antinomie*. An antinomy, according to Blondel, exists only from the static point of view of the intellect; it is always resolved in fact because it represents phenomena which are incompatible in appearance, but which are correlative and simultaneous in reality. An *antibolie* on the contrary, represents two opposing actions, two alternatives which, although simultaneously intelligible, factually exclude one another.[2] Fichte's "necessary but unthinkable" represented, then, an antinomy of the intellect. Blondel's "necessary but impracticable" represents an *antibolie* of the will, because an *antibolie* expresses a problem which concerns not appearance only but that which exists. In the proofs of the absolute we are necessarily led to an affirmation of being, of that which is. That affirmation leads necessarily to a choice between two decisions or commitments, each of which radically excludes the other. "In the presence of being, and of being alone, does the law of contradiction in all its vigor apply, and can our liberty in all its force be exercised."[3]

SUMMARY

The contrast which we have developed between Fichte's and Blondel's approaches to the problem of the absolute brings out quite clearly the difference between their respective methodologies. Both agree that the starting point is human action. Both agree, also, on an immanent subjective approach to the problem. However, as we have noted, Blondel's principle of immanence represented for him a methodo-

---

[1] Coreth, *op. cit.*, p. 540.
[2] Blondel, *op. cit.*, p. 323, footnote.
[3] *Ibid.*, p. 356.

logical and not a dogmatic principle. Thus he could justifiably conclude to the existence of the absolute as simultaneously immanent in and transcendent to human subjective consciousness. Such a conclusion was excluded a priori from Fichte's theory by reason of his principle of identity between consciousness and being. Because of this dogmatic principle of immanence Fichte eventually was led to create a sharp distinction between the absolute immanent in consciousness as form and the absolute transcendent to consciousness as being. Blondel, however, finds in the simultaneously transcendent and immanent absolute the unifying principle between his subjective phenomenology and his "metaphysics to the second power" or objective realism.

Blondel's proof can also help us to understand more clearly what he considered to be the originality of his method in contrast with the method employed by the Idealists. Throughout his proof Blondel continually insists on the necessity of remaining faithful to the synthetic reality of human action. This fidelity implies that one can never legitimately separate the practical from the theoretical; rather, one must continually combine these two facets of the problem in a synthetic, dialectical movement which reproduces as closely as possible the synthetic, dialectical movement between thought and act in life itself. The distinctive feature of Blondel's method is, as a consequence, a continual effort to coordinate a rational analysis of the movement of thought with a phenomenological analysis of the real or practical movement of living action. For, as Blondel maintains, it is this practical movement of living action which is both the source and ultimate criterion of the rational movement of thought. Thus, we continually find a conjunction of rational and phenomenological evidence in Blondel's proof. "From action," Blondel tells us, "comes forth the *indisputable presence* and *constraining proof* of Being."[1]

The originality of his method necessarily implied, in Blondel's judgment, an equally original concept of the logic of action. A hint of that logic is already contained in the distinction Blondel made between an "antinomie" of thought and an "antibolie" of will. This distinction will lead Blondel to develop a "logic of action" based on a dialectic between the real and abstract functions of the principle of contradiction.

However, before we undertake an investigation of Blondel's logic of action, we will investigate the relation between his and Fichte's

---

[1] *Ibid.*, p. 350. Italics added.

theory of interpersonality. For this theory best illustrates the consequent effect in both systems of the difference in their respective approaches to the problem of the absolute. The obvious difficulty for any philosophical system which admits a principle of immanence is to justify rationally the affirmation of the existence of the other as a distinct person or ego. We have already had a hint of Blondel's solution to that problem. As we have seen, in his proof for the existence of the absolute he arrives simultaneously at the affirmation of the absolute as being and as subject. Although this absolute subject manifests its activity from within our consciousness, yet it is apprehended as distinct from our conscious self and as transcendent to it. This manifestation of the absolute as "an ego distinct from my ego" will serve as the foundation of Blondel's final theory of interpersonality. Blondel's theory represents practically a complete reversal of Fichte's argument. For, as we shall see, Fichte begins with the moral necessity of recognizing the other as a distinct person, and argues from this given to the necessity of affirming the absolute as a transcendent being. The contrast between these two approaches to the theory of interpersonality will help us to establish more clearly the divergent spirit and method of these two philosophers.

CHAPTER ELEVEN

THE PROBLEM OF INTERPERSONALITY

FICHTE'S THEORY OF INTERPERSONALITY

Fichte was one of the first of the modern philosophers to undertake a specific study of interpersonal relations as such both from a rational and a phenomenological viewpoint. In Lauth's judgment, a careful study of these forgotten texts of Fichte reveal a theory which is doubly remarkable because not only is it the first of its kind, but it already contains most of the essential insights developed consequently in similar studies by the more recent philosophers of personalism.[1]

Fichte's theory, however, like all the rest of his philosophy, suffers from a certain ambiguity which results from the juxtaposition of his theoretical and practical developments of consciousness. The theory to which Lauth refers occurs within the context of the development of Fichte's pragmatic development of consciousness and serves as the basis for his theories of morality and law. Until he arrives at the consideration of these phenomena, however, Fichte maintains that from the viewpoint of theory and pure knowledge other spiritual beings appear as simply "products of our own power of representation" without being in themselves independent and autonomous. The moral law, however, obliges us to treat them as beings like ourselves.

> Speculation carried to its last conclusions has indeed taught me, or will teach me, that the pretended beings endowed with reason outside of me are only the products of my faculty of representation. ... Nonetheless the voice of conscience cries out to me: whatever these beings are in and for themselves, you must treat them as beings existing for themselves, free, autonomous, independent of you.[2]

Precisely at this point in Fichte's system Coreth finds the first breakdown of his initial principle of immanence—the total subjective identity of consciousness with being.[3] It is true, Coreth grants, that from the very beginning, despite his search for a principle of unity between

---

[1] R. Lauth, "Le problème de l'Interpersonalité chez J. - G. Fichte," *Archives de Philosophie*, Tome XXV, Cahiers III-IV (Juilliet-Décembre, 1962), 344.

[2] Fichte, "Die Bestimmung des Menschen," Vol. II, p. 259.

[3] Coreth, *op. cit.*, pp. 500-501.

pure and practical reason in the ego as genetic activity, Fichte did maintain that: "*Reality in general*, that of the *ego* as well as that of the *non-ego*, is uniquely an object of *belief*."[1] Nevertheless, it is within the context of his theory of interpersonality that this idea of practical faith is expressly developed for the first time. In the first *Theory of Science* Fichte rigorously defended the principle of total immanence. It follows logically from that principle that one cannot reach nor even think a being-in-itself outside of one's consciousness but only a being-for-oneself, that is, a non-ego within the ego and for the ego.

However, in the *Basis of Natural Right* of 1796 (Grundlage des Naturrechts) and in *The System of Ethics* of 1798 (Das System des Sittenlehre), both of which represent the development of Fichte's practical philosophy, Fichte recognizes the I-Thou relation, the reciprocal relation of beings endowed with reason and liberty, as a fundamental given of practical philosophy. Consequently, he admits without hesitation the postulate that other men whom we encounter in a personal relationship are noumenal realities, beings-in-themselves, independent of us. Coreth sees here a reversal of Fichte's proper principles under the pressure of phenomena; a reversal which, when Fichte later became conscious of it, led to the breakdown of his entire system of knowledge.[2] This admission of a community of beings endowed with freedom, in Coreth's opinion, forced Fichte to postulate still another foundation for morality outside the moral order within our consciousness despite his frequent earlier denials of any need for such a foundation apart from that immanent *ordo ordinans* itself. He found that foundation in the infinite, eternal will of God which serves as "the universal mediator between us all."[3] This infinite will became, as a consequence, the foundation of Fichte's final theory of love.

The same problem and the same evidence receive a quite different interpretation in R. Lauth's study "The Problem of Interpersonality in Fichte."[4] According to Lauth from the very beginning Fichte accepted the intuition of the other ego as person as a basic datum, an essential, constitutive principle of his total theory of science. In fact this intuition was accepted as equally if not more original than the intuition of self as ego. It is true that this principle was developed independently in the subsequent pragmatic development of conscious-

---

[1] Fichte, "Grundlage ...," Vol. I, p. 301.
[2] Coreth, *op. cit.*, p. 501.
[3] Fichte, "Die Bestimmung des Menschen," Vol. II, p. 301.
[4] Lauth, *op. cit.*, pp. 325-344.

ness. However, one must keep in mind that there are two equally fundamental points of view in the first *Theory of Science*. From the first viewpoint—that of a formal genetic study within consciousness—interpersonality is seen as a moment in the development of absolute knowledge and is deduced from the unity of knowledge. From the second viewpoint—that of content or material development—the interpersonal relation is regarded as something which is accomplished morally in action and is considered as the basis for a theory of love. Lauth also maintains that Fichte did not just juxtapose these two developments. Rather, he tried to subordinate the formal to the material, since he always maintained that real causality is only to be found on the pragmatic or material level, and the formal study was dealt with only in function of the material development.[1]

From the material or pragmatic viewpoint this experiential intuition of the other as an independent ego is also a genetic and constitutive moment in the pragmatic development of consciousness. It is of equal originality and validity with the intuition of self as ego in the theoretical development. In fact, in conformity with his theory of the subordination of the theoretical to the practical, Fichte argues that it is impossible for the ego to intuit itself as a true ego, a process of autonomous moral activity, without simultaneously becoming conscious of the other ego as that which "makes an appeal to its liberty and, thus, evokes consciousness of liberty in itself."[2] Consequently, Lauth contends that the doctrine of interpersonality is not only postulated as a necessary belief from a moral viewpoint; it is also an original point of departure of equal value as the original position of self by the ego. Fichte argues, in fact, that the intuition of the other as ego is a necessary condition in the very act of self-position. The ego cannot pose itself except as interpersonal ego. Otherwise, Fichte maintains, it could not pose its limits; and this delimitation of itself is a necessary condition in order that it become conscious of its freedom. In order for the ego to have seized its own liberty in its own acts it must first seize and delimit "liberty in the object" in opposition to "determinism in the object."[3] In order to recognize oneself as a free ego, it is necessary to have already recognized the liberty of another ego distinct from oneself.

The intuition of self as free activity demands, then, a community of free beings. Fichte finds in this interpersonal community the schema

---

[1] *Ibid.*, p. 344.
[2] Fichte, "Grundlage des Naturrechts," Vol. III, pp. 38-44.
[3] *Ibid.*, p. 43.

or appearance, as it were, of the noumenal unity of God as being. "In the love of God, being (sein) and existence (Dasein), God and man are one."[1] Within the framework of his theory of love Fichte also undertook the proof of a necessary incarnation of a divine person. This image of the absolute being is not accomplished totally except in an individual who "as absolute reason having immediate consciousness of itself" appears "in its existence and its integrity" and unites itself to the ego of appearances.[2] God must ultimately speak to us as a Person and finally appear to us as a "human person."[3] All history ought to be understood as starting with this central personalization of the absolute and the union of rational finite being with the divine person.

BLONDEL'S CRITICISM OF FICHTE'S THEORY

The basic ambiguity in Fichte's system concerning the relation between his theoretical and practical development of consciousness is put into sharp focus by these two interpretations of his theory of interpersonality. As we have noted, Blondel was aware of that ambiguity. He was aware that Fichte's later philosophy could be interpreted either as an "about-face" or as "a process of evolution."[4] Consequently, no matter which of these two judgments we accept concerning the position of Fichte's theory of interpersonality in the context of his total theory of science, whether we see in that theory a reversal of his principles as Coreth does, or an organic development of those same principles as Lauth does, Blondel's basic criticism would seem to remain valid. There is—both interpretors acknowledge it—a breakdown of method into two formally distinct approaches, the theoretical and the practical. There is a consequent conscious breakdown of the synthesis contained in human action between form and matter, the ideal and the real. There is, finally, a double approach to the absolute, the first from the side of form or idea, the second from the side of the matter or being. Consequently, one can question if Fichte ever really succeeded logically to put together again at the term of his philosophy what his method committed him to disunite.

However, apart from this criticism it is important to note the

---

[1] Fichte, "Die Anweisung ...," Vol. V, p. 540.
[2] *Ibid.*, p. 549.
[3] *Ibid.*, p. 567.
[4] Confer above, Chapter VI, pp. 114-118.

respective roles the theory of interpersonality as such plays in these two philosophies of action in order to establish the originality of Blondel's method and theory. First of all there is a striking similarity once again with the phenomenological analysis of the interpersonal experience in Blondel's *Action*. As Cartier notes:

> Well before Buber, Scheler or G. Marcel but in different terms Blondel affirmed that the subject exists only through other subjects, that consciousness is multipersonal, that man is social. Each person is given to himself by the other and, since he does not exist except by means of the other, he cannot will himself except by willing the other precisely as other, that is, as subject.[1]

This similarity between Blondel's and Fichte's analysis is not surprising since Schelling took up and developed Fichte's analysis in his *System of Transcendental Idealism*, the work which Blondel was studying at the time he was composing *Action*.[2]

However, in his analysis of interpersonal relations within the context of the "Phenomenon of Action" Blondel does not give the same fundamental importance to these phenomena as did Fichte. At this point in the development of his overall work Blondel was content to describe the apparent uniqueness of this phenomenon as "an active union of subjects precisely as subjects." Rather than develop all the implications of this phenomenological evidence he presses on quickly to the need of transcending this *égoisme à deux* to the level of a more universal community life in the family, the fatherland, and within the community of humanity as such.[3] We would be mistaken, however, if we were to judge Blondel's final theory of interpersonal relations by this section of his work alone. The true development of a theory of interpersonality occurs in Blondel's thought only after his development of the proofs for the existence of the absolute. At that point, as we have seen, Blondel reaches a simultaneous awareness and affirmation of the absolute as being and person. The process by which he arrives at this affirmation, conceding the differences in method which we have already explored, resembles closely certain features of Fichte's analysis of the phenomenon of interpersonality. By becoming aware of that which reduces me to my limits, by "regarding within myself

---

[1] Albert Cartier, "Condition de la Présence à Soi et aux autres d'après L'Action (1893) de Maurice Blondel," *L'Homme et son Prochain*, (Actes du VIIIè Congrès des Sociétés de Philosophie de Langue Française; Toulouse 6-9, Septembre, 1956), (Paris: Presses Universitaires de France, 1956), p. 267.

[2] Confer above, Chapter VI, pp. 115-118.

[3] Blondel, *L'Action*, pp. 253-255.

until that which is from myself ceases," I become aware of the absolute
as a person who evokes my freedom and calls me to choose my destiny.
However, when Blondel proceeds to the affirmation of the noumenal
reality or existence of that absolute person, this affirmation was not,
in his opinion, a postulate of practical reason independent of or contrary to the principles of pure reason. Rather, it was a truly rational act
based in the combined force of both theory and practice.

There is a methodological reason why Blondel leaves the question
of the ontological value of the phenomenon of interpersonality in
abeyance until after he reached this point in his dialectic. As we have
seen, Blondel choose to follow a method of immanence in order to
remain faithful to the synthesis in action of the real and the ideal. He
maintained this was the only methodological procedure which would
avoid the necessity of splitting his philosophical investigation of human destiny into a separate theoretical and pragmatic development.
Blondel's immanence, then, was a methodological premise which
committed him to develop his dialectic from within consciousness.
Because of this method, Blondel placed within parentheses the question of the ontological value or objective existence of the other as
person until that assertion could be founded both rationally and practically in the perfect synthetic reality of the absolute person itself.
Consequently, to have affirmed the objective existence of the other as
person, that is, as a true noumenal reality, before arriving at the absolute existence would have meant that Blondel must set aside his basic
methodological premise. He would have been guilty of a failure in
method parallel to the failure Coreth attributes to Fichte in doctrine,
when he sees in Fichte's affirmation by faith of the noumenal reality of
the other ego a reversal of his doctrinal principle of immanence. Once
Blondel does reach the absolute the parentheses are reopened; he does
envisage a "metaphysics to the second power" in which one can found
both theoretically and pragmatically the "exterior subsistence of the
truth interior to man," which, of course, includes the affirmation of
the objective existential reality of the other as person.[1]

However, we would also be wrong in judging Blondel's technique
as the result of a purely arbitrary methodological procedure. There is,
in Blondel's judgment, a metaphysical priority of the absolute person
which founds the need of an immanent approach to the question of
interpersonality. From an epistemological viewpoint, in Blondel's

---

[1] *Ibid.*, pp. 424-425.

concept of realism the philosophical assertion of anything as existing implies not only an objective affirmation of the fact of that existence but a conscious subjective possession or participation in that existence. From a metaphysical viewpoint, a true metaphysical judgment on the existence of anything implies both an awareness of and participation in the absolute grounds of that existence. When the object of that affirmation is a person that objective existence must reveal itself, then, as endowed with an independent, subjective life of reason and will. There is actually and there can be a priori only one person, in Blondel's judgment, who can reveal himself from within our consciousness as being other, as both immanent and transcendent; and there is only one being whose personal existence is simultaneously the absolute grounds of all existence; that is the absolute being, the divine person. Consequently, for Blondel the discovery of myself and others as person depends on the discovery of the absolute person within myself, who founds and defines my liberty.

BLONDEL'S THEORY OF INTERPERSONALITY

The definitive theory of interpersonality in the complete context of Blondel's philosophy of action belongs, as we have noted, to what he calls "metaphysics to the second power." That theory could not be developed fully before the question of the option in the presence of the absolute had been resolved because, as we have seen, the phenomenal study of the development of human action up to and including the supreme option systematically brackets the question of the ontological truth and metaphysical value of objective existence; and, for Blondel, the problem of interpersonal relation is of its very nature an existential question, because it is the problem of the possibility of communion in being of two apparently distinct and independent personal acts of existence. Consequently, a definitive analysis of this relation could not be made within the context of a phenomenal study which brackets the problem of existence, but only after these brackets have been opened. At that point the possibility of an interpersonal relation with the objective existential reality of another can be recognized not only as a necessary subjective phenomenon, but also as an objective truth.

Until this point in Blondel's philosophy is reached, however, all other selves, even God, are systematically considered as various phenomena which enter into the sphere of our subjective knowledge only as necessary means subordinated to action. "If one believes that one can arrive at being and legitimately affirm any reality whatever it may be without having arrived at the term of the series ... one will remain in an illusion."[1] We necessarily have an idea of things and others as objectively real, Blondel contends, and we do affirm the reality of these objects, but to do so legitimately in the context of a philosophical system, it is necessary that we have previously posed the problem of our destiny and that we have subordinated all that we are and all that which exists for us to an option. "*The knowledge of being* implies a necessity of option; *the being which is within our knowledge* is not before, but after the liberty of choice."[2] Consequently, Blondel's final theory of interpersonality occurs in *Action* only after he had dealt with the affirmation of the absolute and the option which that affirmation poses. This theory occurs in the final chapter entitled "The Bond between Knowledge and Action in Being," in the third section of that chapter headed "The Real Presence of Being in Thought."[3]

In this final theory Blondel underlines first of all the necessity of a living presence of the absolute person within consciousness, if any real intersubjective communion is to be considered possible among men. "It is impossible to enter really into contact with another being, in fact, it is impossible to enter into contact with oneself, without passing through the Uniquely Necessary, who must become our unique will."[4] Just as two basic alternatives were possible in the presence of the absolute, so two totally different relationships are possible with the other. In a terminology curiously prophetic of his existential successors Blondel analyses the influence of a refusal of the absolute on interpersonal relations. The refusal of the absolute can only result in an isolation of the existent and shut him up in a false subjectivity and interiority which is in reality an avaricious possession of self. The result is that modern world of solitude and hostility, a world without meeting or true presence, a world of refusal and discontinuity. "The Egoist is disconcerted by the very thought of so many hostile egos, and despite all the clarity of our knowledge, we remain enclosed in solitude and obscurity."[5] The only means of escaping this prison of self is by communication with the transcendent who is both immanent

---

[1] *Ibid.*, p. 428.
[2] *Ibid.*, p. 436.
[3] *Ibid.*, pp. 440-447.
[4] *Ibid.*, p. 442.
[5] *Ibid.*, p. 443.

in self and a bridge to the other. "One cannot be for oneself or for another without being for him first of all."[1] We cannot communicate really with anyone unless it be with and by God.

Blondel sees in this act, whereby I achieve communication with the absolute, a sort of living dialectic and an active living metaphysical resolution of the problem of the one and the many. He calls this act the act of dying; it is this death or sacrifice of self which existentially resolves the metaphysical problem. "Sacrifice is the solution of the metaphysical problem by an experimental method."[2] The act by which I choose to supplant my will by the will of the absolute is a negation of my ego and the false appearance of being on me; "it is the destruction of that self-will which holds me in isolation from all the rest." This "death" to self, which is the most perfect act of sacrifice, contains the most perfect revelation of being, because one no longer sees the absolute which is the source of being from without, one begins to possess it within oneself. "In order to be *one*, in order to exist, it is necessary that I do not rest *alone*. I have need of all the others. That which is necessary ,then, is to capture within myself the source and to transmit ... the truth of its intimate action."[3] Therefore, the act by which the divine will express itself in and through me is a negation of that negation; that is, a positive affirmation, in which the total unity as well as the existential individuality of myself, the other, and the absolute is achieved. By means of this communion with the absolute one becomes truly individual and, at the same time, truly universal.

However, it is important to note that, if Blondel insists on a metaphysical priority of communion with absolute being, he is by no means implying a necessity of priority in time, nor a psychological priority of divine love over human love. Blondel has repeatedly insisted that the true nature of the option need not be explicit. It is, however, necessarily implicit in the living reality of every free human action. It is not necessary, he tells us, to have resolved any metaphysical problem conceptually in order to live metaphysically. The true resolution of the problem of unity by love from any one of the three points of view possible, love of self, of God, or of the other, necessarily involves a vital solution of that problem from all three viewpoints.

But undoubtedly the ordinary level on which the problem and its resolution is posed psychologically is within the context of love of the

---

[1] *Ibid.*, p. 441.
[2] *Ibid.*, p. 442.
[3] *Ibid.*

other. "Without that love which is active within the members of humanity, there is no God for man; he who does not love his neighbor has no life in him."[1] In any human encounter, therefore, if a genuine interpersonal bond is factually established, then it necessarily implies an implicit resolution of the option in favor of the absolute will. This is also the case even when there is no explicit psychological awareness of this option. Where, however, there is only the appearance of true charity without that implicit choice of the absolute, that love is ultimately unfounded and deceiving. "At the very root of being, in the common practice of life, in the secret logic of consciousness, without God there is no fellow man for man."[2] A true act of charity necessarily involves that same negation or "death" to self which is factually a positive opening up of the spirit to the action of the absolute. As a result this act goes well beyond an attitude of strict justice in which one considers only the impersonal character of the other and his abstract dignity as man. A true act of charity must contain the will to become oneself, so to speak, an impersonal means at the service of the other. This is the price one must pay in order to become in reality an instrument of the action of divine, unifying love.

A charitable act of self-giving in order to be real must incarnate itself in a material gesture. Blondel explicitly rejects the concept of a purely spiritual union between man and the absolute. In his opinion one cannot deny the objective reality of the sensible and the material without undermining the whole of reality. Nothing can be real or everything must be real. If one denies the reality of the individual and sensible in human action, one has effectively denied the reality of all human activity. That sensible bond itself, as we have seen, forms the universal bond of solidarity.".... Charity is always universal and always, attached to what is unique."[3] This restoration of the role of the sensible, Blondel maintained in a later work, had been one of the central motivations of *Action* from the very beginning. What he found unacceptable in the "hardy virtuosity of radical German idealism" was what seemed to him to be "the triumph of the notional, the formal, that is, the unreal (irréel)." The efforts of the Idealists, in Blondel's judgment, ended with a symbolism which failed to reach a rehabilitation of the concretet the singular, the incarnated. "However, action seemed to me to be that

---

[1] *Ibid.*, p. 446.
[2] *Ibid.*
[3] *Ibid.*, p. 445.

"substantial bond" which constitutes the concrete unity of each being and assures its communion with everyone. ... It is that geometric point where the natural, the human, and the divine meet together."[1]

The application of Blondel's criticism to the Idealists in general as having failed to rehabilitate the concrete can be debated. Certainly the criticism is perfectly justified in relation to Fichte's early theory where, we have seen, he did end up with an explicit denial of the reality of the individual.[2] However, in his later philosophy and especially in his theory of love Fichte also defended the need of an incarnation of act in a material gesture. In fact he even sought to prove the necessity of an incarnation of the divine person himself as the unique mediator between man and God.[3] Blondel also posed the theory of an hypothetical necessity of a divine incarnation. However, Blondel's hypothesis occurs in a different context from that of Fichte. The immanence of the activity of the absolute person within human consciousness had, in Blondel's judgment, already resolved the problem of the mediation between man and God and between man and his fellow man. What Blondel sought by means of this hypothesis was a cosmological principle, a single universal and permanent mediator between the absolute and the material universe. Existence for Blondel implied that the existent must have a real action on a real being. Consequently, as concerns the material universe independent of man, the purely passive relation to the creative act would not suffice to establish its existential reality but it must somehow "receive from the absolute the gift to be a causal agent in relation to the absolute itself."[4] "Perhaps," Blondel surmises, "since he is destined to receive in himself divine life, man alone suffices to play this role of universal bond and creative mediator." However, if man's mediation does not suffice "perhaps there is needed one mediator who renders himself passive to that integral reality and who becomes as the *Amen* to the universe. ..."[5]

SUMMARY

Blondel's complete theory of interpersonality within the context of *Action* comprises three distinct stages of development. The first occurs

---

[1] Blondel, "L'Itinéraire Philosophique," pp. 66-67.
[2] Confer above, Chapter IX, pp. 158-164.
[3] Confer above, p. 272.
[4] Blondel, *L'Action*, p. 466.
[5] *Ibid.*, p. 461.

within the development of "the phenomenon of action," and takes the form of an analysis or description of the phenomena of coactivity and intersubjectivity. This analysis provides the foundation for a study of the function of the various human societies within which man seeks to fulfill his destiny. The second stage occurs, as we have seen, in the proof of the existence of the absolute as person. The third and final theory, which presupposes the first two stages, occurs in the context of the final chapter of *Action*, and represents a central theme of that "metaphysics to the second power" which Blondel merely outlines in this chapter.

The key to the basic difference between Blondel's and Fichte's theories is to be sought in the fundamental role Blondel grants in his theory to the previous proof of the presence of the absolute as both immanent in our subjective consciousness and transcendent to it. This second stage in his theory, in Blondel's opinion, permitted him to escape the difficulty of solipsism implicit in the principle of immanence, while, at the same time, it permitted him to avoid the dichotomy and ambiguity which resulted from Fichte's separate theoretical and practical treatments of this problem. Fichte introduces the postulate of the real existence of the other as the first principle of his practical moral philosophy. This principle serves as the foundation for a proof of the existence of the absolute as being, and the need of material reality as a means of mediation between the absolute and man. However, Fichte seems to consider these practical exigencies as somehow contradicting the exigencies of pure, theoretical reason. Blondel's conclusion, on the other hand, remains a simultaneous result of the integrated forces of both reason and practice.

Once he had completed his study of action Blondel became aware that underneath the various differences in both method and theory which distinguished him from his predecessors was an even more fundamental difference. That difference lay in the respective understanding of the fundamental logical laws which govern both theory and practice and their interrelation. Blondel's attempt to create a new method which would remain faithful to the dialectical synthesis of thought and action had led him to introduce implicitly into his methodology a new logic. This new logic involved an integration of the various traditional formal and material logics into a "total logic" which represented a synthesis of these formal and material logics, just as action itself represented a synthetic integration of the ideal and the real. Consequently, in the conclusion of *Action* Blondel attempted to render explicit the essential features of that new "logic of action" which underlay his solution to the problem of human destiny. This logic will serve as the final point of comparison between Blondel's and Fichte's philosophies and as a transition to a consideration of Hegel's influence.

CHAPTER TWELVE

THE PROBLEM OF THE "LOGIC OF ACTION"

INTRODUCTION

In dealing with the influence of Kantian criticism on Blondel's philosophy of action, we called attention to the third redaction of *Action*, the redaction of 1890. In the conclusion of that redaction Blondel remarked that the unique inspiration of his philosophical work was an effort to bring together two ideas and produce a synthesis between them. We have already developed at some length the second of these two ideas, the genetic study of the synthetic a priori, in our discussion of the influence Kantian criticism had on Blondel's thought.[1] We shall proceed now to a consideration of the first of these two ideas, the idea of a dialectical logic of action.

Blondel insists that, although here in the conclusion of the manuscript of 1890 he develops the idea of a logic of action first of all before dealing with the synthetic character of human action, this logic of action was not the first idea in time; "... it was not by this scientific and logical approach that we arrived at the moral order; if these two ideas which have sustained this work are interdependent, yet each one had its independent evolution."[2] That idea which came first, Blondel tells us, was the moral and metaphysical idea: the idea of "the metaphysical synthesis of action and the science of moral experimentation." Consequently, Blondel leaves us in no doubt that he did not begin with a formal theory of logic which afterwards was applied to reality; on the contrary, he began with a phenomenological analysis of human action precisely as an original synthesis which progressively unfolds itself in time.

> That which first developed, which came before the other (the logic of action) and both protected and sustained it, was the moral and metaphysical idea (the idea of real synthesis); to the point where one could say that the other was only a secondary idea, drawn out from the substance of the first and constructed in order to answer to the exigencies

---

[1] Above, pp. 76-82.
[2] Blondel, *Projet de Thèse*, p. 190.

and needs of the first, which was always first in time, in importance, and in preference.[1]

Blondel thus underlines what, as we shall see, was the major difference in procedure between his system and that of both Fichte and Hegel. This secondary role of logic was not an arbitrary conception of a method or procedure but a necessity: "... it is by practice that one arrives at theory."[2] This necessary precedence of practice over theory is, in Blondel's opinion, the result of the metaphysical nature of the synthesis which he proposed to study. If, as he maintains, the composite as such has a metaphysical reality precisely as synthesis, then one cannot hope by means of a purely logical and formal analysis to arrive at that reality. Action alone both produces and reveals that synthetic reality. Consequently, it is action which leads us to conceive of a new logic capable of giving expression to the synthetic law immanent in itself.

Our entire previous study of the relation between Blondel's philosophy of action and Fichte's theory of science has been a study of Blondel's fidelity to his initial insight: it is by practice that one arrives at theory. The basic agreement which we found between the philosophies of Blondel and Fichte was, in fact, their mutual original concept of action as the true organic, living source of real synthesis. At the same time the basic disagreement with Fichte was Blondel's refusal to accept his methodological principle of a priority of theory over practice; a principle which, in Blondel's opinion, led to a substitution of a purely formal logical approach for a true phenomenological analysis. As D. Julia points out, if there is an initial confusion between an existential phenomenology and an idealist ontology in the first *Theory of Science* of 1794, it is resolved in the theory of 1801 in terms of an identity of Fichte's philosophy with a pure logical system.[3] The form and content of the ego achieve absolute identity precisely as the systematic identity of the form and content of a logical system. Thus, according to Julia's interpretation, Fichte began and ended his theory of science as a pure logical system under the guiding thesis that "philosophy is not life but an explanation of life."[4] Blondel was convinced, on the

---

[1] *Ibid.*, p. 191. Parentheses added.

[2] *Ibid.*, p. 192.

[3] D. Julia, "Phénoménologie, Ontologie ou Logique? A propos de la Théorie de la Science de Fichte," *Revue Philosophique de Louvain*, Tome 57 (Troisième série, No. 54, Mai 1959), pp. 190-195.

[4] *Ibid.*, p. 194 and p. 196.

contrary, that there is a real synthetic identity of thought and practice, the ideal and the real, in human action. The profound error of all idealist, rationalist systems was to confuse the formal logical identity of form and content with that real metaphysical identity. It was this idea of a real synthesis which guided him in his choice of the priority of a phenomenological method over Fichte's logical method.

THE DEVELOPMENT OF BLONDEL'S LOGIC

In the year 1889, Blondel read the final chapter of Delbos' book on the evolution of Spinoza's thought in German idealism. The greater part of that chapter deals with Hegel's concept of a dialectical logic and retraces the development of that logic beginning with the transcendental logic of Kant.[1] Blondel wrote to his friend acknowledging that the chapter dealt with a problem which he himself held very much at heart and intended to treat at the end of his projected work on *Action*.

> Your subject appears to me to be actual, vital and essential. ... We are being overrun by pantheism and monism. Apart from Christianity which, for anyone who understands philosophy, will always dominate the progress of the spirit, they (the new forms of logic) are, I believe, the most "adequate" forms of contemporary thought. The former framework of traditional logic has been shattered. It is a worthwhile task to enlarge that framework of traditional logic, but only on condition that it be restored. It is good to realize that traditional logic is only a particular case of a general dialectic which already has gone beyond, and will continue to go beyond, the territory of clear ideas no matter how much that territory is enlarged.[2]

This passage from Blondel's letter contains in germ all the essential features of his logic of action developed consequently. The most adequate form of logic already existing, in his opinion, was the Hegelian dialectic. This logic of the dialectic had surpassed and outmoded in a sense the traditional forms of logic. But Blondel believed that this logical revolution represented not a negation or refutation of the traditional forms of logic; on the contrary, these traditional forms must be restored within the context of a dialectical logic as particular forms which have an essential role to play within that broader context. Elsewhere he drew a comparison with the role Euclidean geometry plays within the more universal context of a non-Euclidean geometrical system.

---

[1] Delbos, *Le Problème Moral dans la Philosophie de Spinoza*, pp. 446-447.

[2] Blondel, *Lettres Philosophiques*, p. 17.

Finally, Blondel hints at the fact that the Hegelian dialectic itself, since it also has been reduced to the status of a clear idea or theory, is already in the process of being surpassed and reduced to the status of a subordinate form of an even more inclusive dialectic. The cause of this further evolution is the same which had been at work at the heart of the evolution of all contemporary thought beginning with Spinoza's *Ethics*, that is, the Christian idea of human destiny as a participation in the life of the absolute. "I like very much the trinitarian rhythm of Hegel but, whatever may be the height of the thesis and the antithesis, the Christian idea, better understood and more fully developed, will always furnish a superior synthesis."[1]

This idea of a "general logic" was already a part of Blondel's plan as early as 1889. However, as we have seen, Blondel tried first of all to develop fully the synthetic evolution of human action and only afterwards to disengage the dialectical logic implicit in that evolution. The first effort to deal explicitly with this problem is contained in the conclusion of the manuscript of 1890, entitled *Project of a Thesis*.[2] One can find two reworkings of this idea of a logic of action in the fourth and fifth redactions of *Action*.[3] In the published version of *Action* the problem is dealt with in the concluding chapter.[4] After publishing *Action* Blondel returned twice again in published articles to the development of this logic. The first was entitled "Outline of a General Logic," dated the tenth of February, 1894.[5] The final publication was originally a communication to the International Congress of Philosophy of 1900, and was entitled, "The Elementary Principle of a Logic of Moral Life."[6]

Unfortunately Blondel never completed his general logic; a series of more pressing problems occupied his time and poor health impeded his work. In fact, at the time of his death in 1949 this was the one work he most regretted not having been able to complete. Nonetheless, we

---

[1] *Ibid.*, p. 18.

[2] Confer above, Part I, Chapter V, pp. 76-77 and footnotes 1 and 2, for information concerning this as yet unpublished manuscript.

[3] These two further redactions are to be found in the manuscript of 1892. The first is the text sent to Emile Boutroux, and later submitted to the Sorbonne (pp. 403-411), the second is entitled "Pour la *Conclusion* de l'*Action*" and is the closest to the actual text.

[4] Blondel, *L'Action*, pp. 470-474.

[5] *Ibid.*, "Ebauche de Logique Générale," Reprinted in the *Revue de Métaphysique et de Morale*, Tome 65, No. 1 (Janvier-Mars, 1960), 7-18.

[6] *Ibid.*, "Principe Elémentaire d'une Logique de la Vie Morale," *Les Premiers Ecrits de Maurice Blondel*, pp. 123-128.

do have sufficient material in the various essays mentioned above to understand the essential features of that proposed "logic of action" and to judge its relation to the preceeding logics and, especially, to the dialectical logic proposed by Fichte and completed by Hegel.

As we have indicated, in proposing to construct a new logic of action Blondel was very much aware at the time he wrote *Action* of the development in German idealist thought of a dialectical logic. As his letters to Delbos indicate he had reflected deeply on the implications of that logic and, despite serious reservations, he found it to be a significant advance in the understanding of the logical laws which govern action. Fichte was the first to introduce the dialectic into idealist thought in order to formulate the laws which govern the dynamic movement of the ego towards self-fulfillment. Because of the phenomenological element implicit in Fichte's thought, his understanding of the dialectic was, as we shall see, closer to Blondel's thought than that of Hegel. In practice, however, it is impossible to mark off a strict division between the influence of Fichte's and Hegel's concept of the dialectic on Blondel's thought. For Blondel had a tendency to see these two dialectics as forming one system which had its beginning in Fichte and its systematic completion in Hegel. Thus in the notes Blondel jotted down for the preparation of *Action* we find the following entry: "Take up once again the logic of Hegel, not materially, but beginning with a completely different idea of the ensemble. ... It is important to base (this study) on the metaphysical idea of the mediator, to rediscover the point of departure of Fichte and Hegel."[1] As this note indicates Blondel understood his dialectic as a return to the concept of a mediator, which he believed was the point of departure of both Fichte and Hegel. However, Blondel intended to reconstruct a dialectic "within a completely different idea of the ensemble." We have already seen what that new ensemble will be; Blondel's dialectic will be understood not as the law of the absolute spirit but as the law of man's conscious free actions. For in Blondel's judgment by means of his free actions man constitutes himself mediator between the absolute and the finite, God and the world. Because Blondel saw Hegel's logic as a completion of Fichte's, we will be obliged to consider simultane-

---

[1] *Ibid.*, "Notes pour l'*Action*," Carnet V, Section V, note 957. These notes are to be found together with the other unpublished manuscripts in the Blondel archives at Aix-en-Provence.

ously the influence of both Fichte's and Hegel's dialectic on Blondel's thought.

It is difficult to ascertain with certitude to what extent Blondel had contact with the direct sources of Hegelian thought at the time he wrote *Action*. The evidence seems to indicate that in all probability Blondel had studied the French translation by A. Vera of Hegel's *Logic*.[1] In his review of Delbos' book published in 1894 Blondel cites two passages from this work to which there is no direct reference in Delbos' work. Consequently, he must have studied this work independently of his study of Delbos' manuscript in 1889. After the publication of *Action* Blondel constantly refers in his notes to a series of articles on Hegel's logic by George Noèl, published in the *Revue de Métaphysique et de Morale* from 1894 through 1896.[2] However, whatever Blondel's direct sources were, as his letters to Delbos and his published review of Delbos' book indicate, he was in complete agreement with Delbos' understanding of the import of the dialectical logic developed in German idealist thought from Kant through to Hegel. Consequently, the best means to arrive at an understanding of what Blondel himself thought to be the contribution of the idealist dialectical logic to his own philosophy of action is by a study of Delbos' interpretation of that development and Blondel's comments on that interpretation. For, as Blondel himself asserted in a reference to his review of Delbos' book: "... two centuries of history were called as witness to establish that the method and the conclusions of the thesis published a few months ago on *Action*, far from being an isolated effort against the tides, had been prepared and even demanded by a speculative effort which was thoroughly in accord with the exigencies of reason."[3]

---

[1] Delbos himself called Blondel's attention to the parallel between *Action* and Hegel's *Phenomenology of the Spirit*, after reading Blondel's manuscript. But Blondel explicitly denied having read that particular work of Hegel before composing *Action*. Henrici's work, *Hegel und Blondel*, is a thorough analysis of the parallels and differences between *Action* and the *Phenomenology of the Spirit*. Since we have limited ourselves in this study to those ideas of his predecessors which had a formative influence on Blondel's thought, our treatment of his relation to Hegel is limited to the logical question and its consequences in their respective ethics and philosophy of religion.

[2] G. Noel, "La Logique de Hegel," *Revue de Métaphysique et de Morale*, Tome II (1894), 36-57, 270-298, 644-675; Tome III (1895), 184-210, 503-526; Tome IV (1896), 62-85, 585-614.

[3] Blondel, "L'Evolution du Spinozisme et l'Accès qu'elle ouvre à la Transcendence," *L'Archivo de Filosofia*, Anno XI, Fasc. IV (Décembre, 1932), 1-2.

THE EVOLUTION OF A DIALECTICAL LOGIC

Delbos assigned the first major step towards the development of a
dialectical logic to Kant.[1] Kant, Delbos maintained, in his transcendental logic first established that the progress of the spirit is not an
analytical process. Thought itself has a concrete reality and a proper
content; and it expresses itself in synthetic judgments. As a result of
this discovery Kant was led to superimpose a transcendental logic over
traditional formal logic. This transcendental logic was capable, in
Kant's opinion, of comprehending the real, whereas formal logic was
not valid except for the order of the possibles.

This new logic of Kant contained implicitly the idea of a dialectic
of the spirit. This implicit dialectic was to be found especially in the
triadic listing of the categories of the understanding. As Copleston
notes, according to Kant the third category in each triad arises out of
the combination of the second with the first. Thus, under the generic
heading of quantity the third category, totality, is plurality regarded
as unity. Or, again under the heading of quality, limitation is reality
combined with negation. Under relation, community (reciprocity between agent and patient) is the causality of a substance reciprocally
determining and determined by another substance. And finally, under
the heading of modality, necessity is considered as existence given
through the possibility of existence.[2]

Delbos was of the opinion that Kant himself might well have had a
presentiment of the speculative import of his logic .For in his study
of the antinomies he seems to indicate a dialectical movement of the
spirit as the means of resolving the apparent contradiction. Or, again,
at the end of the *Critique of Judgment*, he attempts to show that synthetic
unity requires a condition, a conditioned, and a conciliatory idea.
Finally, by making a distinction between reason and understanding,
he uncovered the inevitable finite character of all the determinations
of the understanding and freed the idea of reason from these determinations.[3]

However, Delbos continues, despite these hints at a dialectic Kant's
method prevented him from developing a true dialectic of the spirit.
As Hegel himself observes, the major failure of Kant's transcendental
logic was the fact that he was content with an empirical classification

---

[1] Delbos, *op. cit.*, pp. 444-445.
[2] Copleston, *op. cit.*, Vol. VII, p. 251.
[3] Delbos, *op. cit.*, p. 445.

of the categories. He was content to transpose these categories, such as he found them in the tables of traditional logic, from experience to the understanding without seeking to discover that internal bond which attached them one to another. He saw the necessity of a dialectical reason, but he did not demonstrate its legitimacy; he did not realize that the thesis and antithesis were not only formal conditions but real elements of the synthesis. Delbos saw in this failure of Kant the ultimate explanation for the dichotomy he established between the laws of thought and reality. "After he had established that the categories inevitably give rise to a contradiction, he humiliated thought before things by rendering it responsible for an absurdity to which, in his opinion, things are not submitted; and thus he arrived at the idea of thought as an empty form of the understanding."[1] The result of this failure in turn, in Delbos' judgment, was that Kant, who was the first to proclaim that liberty is the essence of the spirit from which human morality must be derived, did not succeed in completing a true system of practical reason. "Morality remained, in his system, at the level of an indetermined form."[2]

Delbos understood Fichte's major contribution to the development of a dialectical logic as precisely an effort to correct this failure of Kant. Fichte first attempted to deduce the categories by means of a dialectical logic from one and the same principle. He found that principle, as we have seen, in the affirmation of the ego. It is this self-affirmation or self-positing of the ego which Fichte saw as the true original synthetic a priori judgment which contained within itself the synthesis of thought and reality. Starting with this affirmation Fichte developed the first dialectic of action by demonstrating how the ego by reason of its own essence poses a series of contradictions in order to constitute an object for itself; and which, in turn, it must resolve in a renewed unity with itself in order to assure its own progress in self-realization.[3] Fichte understood the three moments of the dialectic as an analytic description of three aspects of the necessary movement of the spirit towards fulfillment in self-consciousness. Thus self-consciousness is constituted by a sort of rhythm or triple act. The first is the act of affirmation or absolute production, which poses the condition of all intelligibility and is the initial unity or identity of that which thinks and that which is thought. The second act is the act of reflection, which separates being

---

[1] *Ibid.*, p. 446.
[2] *Ibid.*
[3] *Ibid.*, pp. 445-446.

from thought and creates an opposition between them. This second act is the act of negation or exclusion, and is the basic condition of all relation. Finally, the third act is the act of determination, which conciliates the elements in opposition by establishing a community of reciprocity, a mutual limitation of one by the other, between these opposing elements. These three acts, which Fichte called thesis, antithesis and synthesis, form an organic and inseparable whole. "The synthesis and the antithesis naturally imply each other; for conciliation and opposition are inseparable acts; and the thesis is the necessary condition for there being an opposition and a conciliation."[1]

These three moments of the activity of spirit in its effort to achieve conscious self-possession and fulfillment form, according to Fichte, the real or material foundation for each one of the sets of Kant's categories. By abstracting the content of these acts and considering only their form, they give us the basic principles of logic, which are nothing other than the formal expression of the essential acts of the spirit. For example, the first act of the spirit can be logically formulated as the principle of identity: $A = A$. "If the proposition $A = A$ is certain, then the proposition *I am* must also be certain."[2] Fichte understood that within the formal affirmation of the principle of identity, the ego necessarily affirms or posits itself as a material self-identity. There is, then, in this affirmation a perfect synthesis of thought with action. In this sense the principle of identity can be considered as the first principle of philosophy with variables substituted for definite values or contents.

The second moment of the activity of the spirit, the moment of opposition, is formally identical with the principle of contradiction which Fichte expressed as the formal axiom of opposition: *not* $— A = A$. The positing of *not* $— A$ presupposes the positing of A, and is, therefore, an opposing to A which takes place in and through the ego.[3] The third principle, the principle of relation, is expressed in the logical proposition which Fichte calls the axiom of the ground or of sufficient reason: A in part $= — A$, and conversely. This axiom is the logical expression of the third basic proposition of Fichte's philosophy, in the sense, once again, that the axiom is derived by abstracting definite content from the intuition of finite consciousness and substitu-

---

[1] Fichte, "Grundlage ...," Vol. I, pp. 111-122.
[2] *Ibid.*, p. 95.
[3] *Ibid.*, p. 101.

ting variables instead.[1] By means of this derivation of the three fundamental principles of formal logic from the three basic propositions of
his *Theory of Science* Fichte believed that he had fulfilled his promise to
derive formal logic from the activity of the spirit.

Fichte then proceeds to a deduction of Kant's categories. For
example, the first basic proposition gives us the category of reality.
"That which is posited through the mere positing of a thing ... is its
reality, its essence (Wesen)."[2] The second proposition obviously gives
us the category of negation, and the third that of limitation and determination. And so on for all four sets of the categories.

From one viewpoint Fichte's dialectic would seem to be a pure
logical or rational process, a progressive determination of the meaning
of the initial proposition or, in other words, an explicit effort to identify totally the rational and the real as in Hegel's logic. If this were the
case, then the contradiction which arises in the second moment could
be understood as resolved in the sense that it is shown to be merely
apparent. "All contradictions are reconciled by determining more
clearly the contradictory propositions."[3] For example, Fichte remarks
that when he states that the ego posits itself as infinite and as finite "were
it posited as infinite and finite in one and the same sense, the contradiction could not be resolved. ..."[4] But the contradiction is resolved
by so defining the two statements that their mutual compatibility
becomes evident. In this case the resolution involves the awareness
that there is question of one infinite activity expressing itself in and
through finite selves.

However, as Copleston points out, Fichte never truly eliminated
totally the phenomenological and experiential element from the development of his logical system.[5] Thus it would not be accurate to understand Fichte's dialectic as consisting simply in the progressive clarification or determination of meaning. Fichte introduces, in fact, ideas
which cannot be obtained through the strict analysis of the initial
propositions. For instance, in order to proceed from the second proposition to the third in the example given above, Fichte postulates a
limiting activity on the part of the ego; yet this idea of limitation can-

---

[1] *Ibid.*, p. 111.
[2] *Ibid.*, p. 99.
[3] *Ibid.*, p. 255.
[4] *Ibid.*
[5] Copleston, *op. cit.*, p. 48.

not be obtained simply through logical analysis of either the first or the second proposition.

Delbos understood Fichte, in his turn, to have failed in his objective. Despite his ambition to discover the absolute form of science, he did not finally succeed in overcoming Kantian dualism. He never succeeded really in deriving exterior reality from the ego which he made his first principle. As a result he ended up seeking only an ideal or logical unity in consciousness, a unity which itself remained inaccessible. Delbos repeats Hegel's judgment. "This is why Fichte substitutes a purely subjective certitude for the total truth; this is why he considered the absolute, not as an identity of subject and object but simply as the moral order of the universe."[1] The movement of idealism after Fichte expressed a tendency to progressively eliminate the phenomenal and experiential element and to identify the dialectic more and more closely with the interior activity of the absolute itself. Hegel's primary criticism of Fichte's dialectic was directed precisely against the element of a phenomenological analysis of experience as not being sufficiently speculative and philosophical. In Hegel's opinion it was unworthy of a philosopher to introduce a principle which admitted no strict theoretical deduction, and to introduce individual activities of the ego into the system to make possible the transition from one principle to another.[2]

Blondel's criticism was exactly the contrary. What he found faulty with Fichte's dialectic was not the presence of elements derived from experience but a failure to carry out fully a complete analysis of experience before trying to derive the absolute law of action. Consequently, the ambiguity in Fichte's logic between the idea of a purely formal and speculative process and the element of phenomenological analysis corresponds to the previous ambiguity which we have discussed between his concept of the ego in consciousness as an absolute ego or as a human ego. This ambiguity provides the pivotal point for understanding the greater divergence between the consequent absolute idealism of Schelling and Hegel and the philosophy of action of Blondel. Whereas they understood idealism as tending towards a progressive elimination of the experiential and the human and as seeking a rigorously pure speculative and absolute theory, Blondel himself, on the contrary, tended to develop the experiential and human and to

---

[1] Delbos, *op. cit.*, p. 447.

[2] Confer Copleston, *op. cit.*, Vol. VII, p. 48, for a discussion of Hegel's criticism of the dialectic in Fichte.

refuse absolute value to the dialectic until it had achieved at its term a practical union with the absolute, which alone justified a speculative identity of man's dialectical development with the absolute's manifestation in time. In place of the superiority of speculation over practice, Blondel insists that only practice can ultimately justify theory. Instead of beginning with the absolute and trying to deduce concrete finite reality, he begins with the finite concrete reality of human action, and finds in its development towards its end the justification of the affirmation of the absolute.

THE PHENOMENOLOGICAL GENETIC STUDY OF LOGIC

Just as they agreed on action as the point of departure for philosophy, so too Blondel and Fichte were in complete agreement on the point of departure for a study of logic. Both philosophers were convinced that the only fruitful approach to a renewal of logic was to be found in a phenomenological study of the genesis of logical ideas from their source in action. In his article of 1785, "Recension of the Aenesidemus," Fichte undertook to refute the position of Schulze that the first principle of philosophy was to be found in the purely logical and formal principle of non-contradiction.[1] Fichte rejected this idea of a logical first principle because such a purely formal law of thought could not account for the material content of consciousness. It is not in the power of a purely formal law, Fichte argues, to confer real value on the activity of the intellect but, conversely, it must be this act which gives real value to the logical principles of identity and non-contradiction.[2] The mind acts, but it cannot act according to its essence except in a certain way; if we represent by abstraction this necessary manner of acting detached from the action itself, we can thus formulate the laws which govern the activity of the mind. We can also find here an explanation of that feeling of necessity which accompanies determined representations; it is not at base an impression which comes from without; rather, one senses in that activity the limits of one's proper essence. Consequently, Fichte announces, it will be his task in the theory of science to deduce from the activity of the mind the system of its necessary ways of acting and, at the same time, to deduce the

---

[1] "... Der *logische* Grund eines Gedankes sey zugleich der *Real* — der *Existential* — Grund dieses Gedanken." (Fichte, "Recension des Aenesidemus," Vol. I, p. 13).
[2] *Ibid.*, p. 6.

objective representations which result from that intrinsic necessity.[1]

In this passage, as R. Lauth comments, Fichte establishes the fact that his *Wissenschaftslehre* "does not begin with pure thought as the object of logic but with the real activity of knowing which is anterior to pure thought in the order of consciousness. Ordinary consciousness renders evident the fact that knowledge is ... first of all an ontological activity before becoming an object of logic."[2] This plan of Fichte to derive logical laws from their foundation in action corresponds perfectly with the plan of Blondel as he outlined it in the conclusion of his "Project of a Thesis."[3] However, beyond the hasty phenomenological derivation of the three basic principles of consciousness which we outlined above, Fichte never fully carried out this proposed genetic phenomenological study of logic. As we have seen, his idealistic and mathematical prejudices led him to undertake a purely theoretical reconstruction of the dialectic of absolute creative activity. Consequently, although one finds the beginnings of such a study, one will search in vain in Fichte's writings for a clear and complete derivation of the logic of action from a genetic, phenomenological study of conscious human activity.

Blondel, however, believed that his previous development of the phenomenon of human action provided him with the basis and evidence for such a genetic study of logic. In the course of that development he continually returns to the theme that all our thoughts derive from action and find their ultimate meaning and value in the organic relation they have to the action from which they derive and to which they lead. This is not only true of spontaneous ideas but of the whole field of scientific knowledge. Every science that man developes has its final explanation in that human activity from which it derives and which it serves, for all knowledge is a means which man employs to fulfill his destiny. In his study of the logic of action Blondel extends this insight to the logical laws which govern thought. Just as any science must be understood as derived from and ultimately subordinated to action, so too the logical laws which govern the development of the various sciences must be seen as derived from and subordinated to the basic all-embracing dialectical law which governs human action.

As we have seen, Blondel also saw the necessity of restoring tradi-

---

[1] *Ibid.*, "Grundlage ...," p. 441.
[2] D. Julia, "Le Savoir Absolu chez Fichte," *op. cit.*, p. 356.
[3] Confer above, pp. 200-201.

tional logic within the framework of the dialectical logic of action.[1] This restoration will consist in determining the value of that spontaneous logic which necessarily governs our thought, by means of a phenomenological demonstration of the process whereby this law of thought is dervied from the law of action and, consequently, by demonstrating what function this derived logic of thought necessarily plays in the development of that action from which it derives.

Blondel considered this restoration of traditional logic within the dialectic of action as his primary task. He was aware of two opposing tendencies in the logical theories of his time. "One is content either to subordinate as completely as possible the real to the rational, and life or history itself to an idealist dialectic, or to oppose the practical and moral with its own type of certitude and its autonomous laws to the speculative or scientific orders and the laws of thought."[2] The result is that in the first idealist tendency the logic of thought is sacrificed to the logic of action, as if the dialectic must necessarily imply a sacrifice of traditional logic. Whereas, in the second critical tendency one maintains an irreducible dualism of these two forms of logic, as if they had no intrinsic relation.

> What we must do, then, is place ourselves at that point of intersection (because for us, finally, to live is to realize the unity of thought and action) and derive that elementary principle which presides over the development of idea and action within the integral unity of a dialectic which dominates these two aspects of the moral life without sacrificing the one to the other.[3]

This idea of integrating these two dialectics was already present in Blondel's thought in 1889. In a letter to Delbos in that year he speaks of the conflict between the peripatetic logic of non-contradiction and the pantheistic logic of contradiction. Both, in Blondel's opinion, are true but neither is *the* truth. On the contrary, in his reading of St. Paul's epistles, he finds an implicit dialectic which admits and unites both: "... the logic of the bible, the dialectic of St. Paul admitted the one and the other, and by admitting both it surpasses them."[4]

Blondel was convinced that as long as we accept logic as a determined fact, as a sort of static, fixed reality before thought, no systema-

---

[1] Confer above, pp. 202-203.
[2] Blondel, "Principe Elémentaire d'une Logique de la Vie Morale," *op. cit.*, p. 124,
[3] *Ibid.*
[4] *Ibid., Lettres Philosophiques*, p. 18.

tic solution to the conflict is possible. The only means of escaping the conflict between these two positions is by undertaking that genetic study of logic which Fichte proposed but did not accomplish. "Are we not consequently led to investigate just how we become conscious of logical truths, and what is their real genesis; how and why we isolate them from their vital origins; how, finally, according to this genesis itself they are related to action and contribute to moral life?"[1]

Summary

Blondel's search for a logic of action began only after he had developed fully the phenomenological evidence for that logic by a complete analysis of the evolution of human action towards its goal of self-fulfillment. Logic of its very nature is an analytical discipline. If one begins the study of action with an a priori logical system, one necessarily obscures and even falsifies the evidence, because one is obliged to disintegrate the real synthesis contained in action in order to render it apt for a logical analysis. The only way to go about constructing a true philosophy of action is to derive the logical theory, which would be valid in such a philosophy, *post facto* from the evidence contained in practice.

This priority of practice over theory also holds true for a dialectical logic. The synthesis contained in a purely theoretical dialectic is a purely rational synthesis of form and matter. The basic error of the Idealists was to confuse this formal synthesis in thought with the real synthesis in action. In relation to this real synthesis the logical synthesis presupposes an analytic separation of pure form from its real, existential ground and the erection of that abstract form as the artificial material object of a logical study.

Despite this criticism the Idealists and, in particular, Fichte made a substantial contribution to the development of a logic of action. If the true center of perspective in philosophy is dynamic, synthetic action, then the only logic which is adequate for that philosophical discipline must be understood as a dialectical logic. One cannot, however, assume a priori that the laws of this dialectic contradict the traditional laws which govern abstract thought. On the contrary, since the laws of thought are spontaneously derived from the laws of the real dialectic in action and contribute in turn to the understanding and fulfillment

---

[1] *Ibid.*, "Principe Elémentaire ...," *op. cit.*, p. 128.

of that dialectic, there must be a compatibility and synthetic compenetration of these laws even as thought and reality are synthetically one in action.

There is, then, only one way to arrive at a clear understanding of the relation between the law of the real and the law of thought; that is to undertake an analysis of the genesis of the law of thought from the real dialectical law of action. The insight into the need of such a phenomenological analysis of the genesis of logic was Fichte's major contribution to the study of logic. However, the same ambiguity which we have noted constantly in Fichte's philosophy between phenomenological analysis and idealist metaphysics prevented him from developing fully this insight. In Hegel's opinion it was the idealist premise in Fichte's dialectic which was its true foundation, and the element of phenomenological analysis was unjustified; the dialectical law of reason is identical with the creative activity of the absolute spirit; the real is rational and the rational is real; philosophy and logic are one. In Blondel's opinion the idealist premise was unjustified; the real dialectical movement contained in the activity of the human spirit is not necessarily identical with the activity of the absolute spirit. The human spirit can participate in the activity of the absolute spirit, or it can be in contradiction with that activity; but it is never absolutely identified with it. What ultimately determines whether the relation between the activity of the human spirit and of the absolute spirit will be one of harmony or contradiction is precisely the free, conscious option for harmony or contradiction between the will-willing and the will-willed, the law of the real and the law of reason. Therefore, we must return once again to Fichte's point of departure and complete that phenomenological study which he inaugurated; we must uncover and clarify the genetic relation between the logic of thought and the logic of life in order to understand the total dialectic which governs human action and the supreme synthesis which is our human destiny.

CHAPTER THIRTEEN

BLONDEL'S LOGIC OF ACTION

THE NECESSITY OF A REAL EQUIVALENT OF THE LAW OF CONTRADICTION

At every step in his development of the phenomenon of action Blondel found that it was possible to eliminate the variables in order to consider those characteristics which were common and those traits which were essential to the progressive development of all human action. In his opinion this accomplishment necessarily implied that between the contingent and arbitrary forms of living action there is a necessary sequence and, as it were, a rigid framework on which the most supple and varied movements are founded. This discovery led Blondel to the conclusion that the real value and force of a "critique of life," such as he had undertaken in *Action*, was to uncover this secret logic of action. All the various laws of thought and all particular forms of logic would enter into this concrete determinism of life itself as particular, detached aspects of that determinism. The discovery, then, of this logic of action would be, in fact, the establishment at the same time of a "general logic," that theory of science which Fichte had sought before him and in which all other scientific disciplines would find their foundation and coordination.[1]

Blondel, as we have seen, was convinced that this general logic did not exist; a true total logic of living action, which accounted systematically for all the evidence of the phenomena of human activity, was yet to be constructed. This failure was traceable to the synthetic nature of action as a synthesis between the ideal and the real, the formal and the material, thought and act. The various logics which have been developed to clarify particular aspects of this synthesis seem to contradict one another in their essential postulates; and a valid means of reconciling these postulates had yet to be found.

The key problem, in Blondel's opinion, had to do with the role that the principle of contradiction must play in a universal logic. Whereas the abstract sciences of thought, utilizing the traditional formal logic

---

[1] Blondel, *L'Action*, pp. 470-471.

of analysis, isolate ideas and proceed by a process of total inclusion or exclusion; the concrete reality of life perpetually conciliates the contraries. All the possible forms of action have been revealed as compatible in fact; the science of the practicable includes all of them. "In the order of the real there are no contradictions; there are only contraries and the same determinism encloses and orders their development by opposition."[1]

Once we realize as Hegel did —and, Blondel contends, as we must do but from a different viewpoint—that the notion of real existence and of objective being is a synthetic a priori idea, we reach necessarily the realization "that this *objective existence* is not in the absolute affirmation of an apparent reality but in the *relation* which its divers, heterogeneous, and even contrary or contradictory aspects maintain among themselves."[2] Being, then, is relation; when we say that a thing exists, we necessarily affirm implicitly that there is an organic interrelating of heterogeneous elements. Consequently, to establish the reality of that synthetic bond is at the same time to establish the existential reality of the being in question. This is the same insight, essentially, which Blondel claimed to have found in the theory of Leibnitz concerning the *vinculum substantiale*, which formed the subject matter of the latin thesis which accompanied *Action*. According to Leibnitz, in any organic composite the synthesis as such has its own proper and superior existence independent of its component elements.[3] This insight of Leibnitz, Blondel tells us, furnishes the "Key" for understanding *Action*.[4] If this insight is true and the ultimate substantial and existential reality of being is to be found in relation as such, then it follows that in so far as one wishes to consider things *in concreto*, one is necessarily led to conceive of them as submitted to a law other than that of the principle of contradiction. A being whose substantial reality is a real relation must be understood as composed of elements which are simultaneously opposed and complementary, as a unity of opposites.

---

[1] *Ibid.*, p. 470.

[2] *Ibid.*, "Ebauche de Logique Générale," *op. cit.*, pp. 15-16. *Underlining* added.

[3] "... ita ut quod intellectus analytico modo percipit tamquam multorum in uno expressionem, vinculum illum reapse synthetica praeditum sit existentia, tamquam unius in multis praesentia et actus." Blondel, *De Vinculo Substantiali et de Substantia Composita apud Leibnitium* (Paris: Félix Alcon, 1903), pp. 64-65.

[4] "... my long thesis on *Action* became, as it were, the prolongation of my short latin thesis ... Action seemed to me to be the *Vinculum* in act." Blondel, *Une Enigme Historique: Le "Vinculum Substantiale" d'après Leibnitz et l'Ebauche d'un Réalisme Supérieur* (Paris: Bibliothèque des Archives de Philosophie, Gabriel Beauchesne, Ed., 1930), pp. 131-132.

"Hegel was right when he brought to our attention that, the moment when reality is a question of relativity and *liaison* and not a question of things considered in isolation, the affirmation of one of the terms demands as its complement the contrasting term."[1] From a purely static and speculative point of view what is incompatible and formally contradictory is associated factually in such a manner as to constitute a new synthesis distinct from its elements. Within the context of moral action motives which are contradictory in thought remain unified in action. "Nothing is more important in the study of human action than this solidarity of that which one has done with that which one has not done."[2] Whereas from a purely abstract and formal viewpoint conciliation seems to be impossible, from the viewpoint of the real it is contradiction which is impossible and conciliation which is necessary.

If this were the only aspect of the problem, the dialectic introduced by Kant and Fichte and developed by Hegel, considered as the logical form of the real synthetic movement of life, could be accepted as the definitive logic of action. However, in Blondel's judgment the Hegelian dialectic, while it did achieve a formalization of the dynamic movement of life in its material aspect, did so only at the expense of losing an equally important truth concerning that dialectic and overlooking an important phenomenological aspect of human action.

> Without doubt various efforts, since Kant notably and above all by Hegel, have been attempted to constitute a logic of the real. However, if I can be permitted to generalize in so delicate a matter, it seems to me that *they have pretended to formalize what is necessarily material without materializing at the same time what is necessarily formal in that concrete dialectic.*[3]

What is this aspect of the total logic of action which Blondel believed escaped the Hegelian dialectic? It is the possibility that a formal contradiction in abstract thought can become a real contradiction in action. Once human action is considered from the viewpoint of real moral choice, there is a complete inversion of the role of contradiction. From

---

[1] *Ibid.*, "Ebauche de Logique Générale," *op. cit.*, p. 16.

[2] *Ibid.*, *L'Action*, p. 472.

[3] Blondel hastens to make his characteristic reservations concerning this criticism of the Hegelian dialectic: "I do not wish this introduction to take on the form of a properly historical character. I do not speak of Hegel, or Aristotle ... in themselves. Rather I am trying to render an account from my own actual viewpoint of the manner in which I understand each of these types of logic ..." Blondel, "Ebauche de Logique Générale," *op. cit.*, pp. 10-11. *Underlining* added.

this viewpoint future contingents are all compatible in thought as possibles; whereas contradictory past actions are incompatible in reality. What I have done really contradicts and excludes what I have not done. From this viewpoint, Blondel notes, contrary to the common assumption it is thought which deals with the contingent and action which determines the necessary. "We can never put into action anything but the contraries, yet the law of contradiction governs our accomplished actions. The contradictories are never given in fact, yet in acting we insert the contradictory into our actions, which seemed to have to do simply with contraries."[1] Thus we find ourselves faced with the paradox: whereas from a formal logical viewpoint contradictories are thinkable as possibles, they are unthinkable as simultaneously real; but from a real, moral viewpoint nothing can be thought of as formally contradictory to action; yet a contradiction between action and being can be real.

> Underneath the diversely compatible forms of action, there is revealed a principle of contradiction which maintains its rule and decides absolutely the value of being in the real fact itself. *This simultaneous compatibility and exclusion is the ultimate sense of the principle of contradiction which must be clarified.* It establishes the reign of truth amid error without abolishing error; it introduces the absolute of being into the phenomena without suppressing the relativity of the phenomena.[2]

In his final article on logic, "The Elementary Principle of a Logic of Moral Life," Blondel clarifies the moral significance of this problem. If a true moral science of right and wrong, good and bad, is possible, it is necessary that real concrete facts be capable of receiving an absolute qualification. One must be able to establish an absolute difference between the true and the false, the good and the bad. However, if we grant this, then a true science or logic of morality would seem a priori to be impossible. One would be forced to admit that the real facts of moral life are capable of containing a radical opposition to being; whereas the *sine qua non* condition of any formal logic seems to be the denial of the possibility for any such real contradiction to exist. The meaning of the principle of contradiction, which is the foundation of logic, seems to be the affirmation

---

[1] Blondel, *L'Action*, p. 472.
[2] *Ibid.*, p. 470. Since Blondel speaks of the "principle of contradiction" and the "law of contradiction," we have retained that designation rather than the more proper term of non-contradiction for the sake of clarity and consistency.

that the real does not and cannot suffer any such contradiction.[1]

However, if in order to save logic we maintain that the real facts as such are indifferent to the law of contradiction and, consequently, impervious to the formal norm of logical thinking, then we must be ready to accept a purely formal moral doctrine which professes complete indifference to the material element, as did the moralism of Kant.[2] At the extreme we must be ready to accept a solution to the moral problem of human destiny which finishes with the suppression of all individual life and of particular act, a tendency which, as we have seen, was present in Fichte.[3]

Hegel, in Blondel's opinion, attempted to correct this shortcoming of Kant's and Fichte's dialectic by striving to include the material element of becoming within his formal system. Because he attempted to formalize what is necessarily material in the dialectic of action, Hegel fell into a further difficulty; he eliminated by abstraction the true synthetic role of action in the dialectic. As a result he eliminated at the same time the real source of an existing contradiction in action. The antithetical term in the Hegelian dialectic, Blondel argues, is in reality nothing more than the different or the other; it cannot be truly contrary or *a fortiori* contradictory. "In order that these ideas of the contrary or of contradiction appear one must suppose a synthetic initiative of thought, an antecedent affirmation of being, as previously introduced."[4] However, it was precisely this inclusion of the real activity of the spirit within his dialectic which Hegel saw as Fichte's error and which, consequently, he sought to eliminate.

This elimination of the real activity of the spirit was in Blondel's opinion, the source of a basic ambiguity in the Hegelian dialectic between the synthetic and analytical processes in action; "Although it (the Hegelian dialectic) gives the impression that it is an inventive synthesis, in reality it is only an analysis, regressive from the viewpoint of reality, progressive from the viewpoint of knowledge."[5] There is a problem here of a mistaken identity between the progressive, abstract

---

[1] *Ibid.*, "Principe Elémentaire d'une Logique de la Vie Morale," *op. cit.*, pp. 126-127.

[2] On the margin of the first manuscript of 1892 Blondel inserted this note: "Strange error on Kant's part to have believed that the logic of the real is a logic of contraries. That is the logic of phenomena. It is being itself which is the law of contradiction." (Blondel, "First Redaction of 1892," p. 409).

[3] Blondel, "Principe Elémentaire ...," *op. cit.*, p. 127.

[4] *Ibid.*, "Ebauche de Logique Générale," *op. cit.*, p. 16.

[5] *Ibid.*

synthesis in thought of rational relations—even when these relations are thought as expressing the dialectic of the material or real relations of being—and the real progressive synthesis effected by action in its concrete reality. "... This logic of phenomena is a conciliation of two ideas—the idea of the total heterogeneity of the elements to be united, and the idea of the progressive synthesis or functional continuity constituting the process of mathematics."[1]

Hegel mistook a rational for a real synthesis; traditional logic, on the other hand, was wrongly considered as a purely analytical process. Nothing in the activity of the spirit, Blondel argues, can be purely analytical. Formal logic does not only deal with abstractions; it itself exists only by means of an abstracting activity. The data with which it deals are offered to it only by means of a mental act and an intellectual synthesis. This synthetic activity of the spirit, from which the logician prescinds at the very moment that he makes use of it, explains how the law of contradiction can and does enter into the material reality of our actions.

There was, Blondel maintains, an implicit awareness of the synthetic activity of the spirit in Aristotle's transformation of Parmenides' earlier principle: Being is; non-being is not. "Why was it that in order to be able to apply this law of contradiction to reality, Aristotle found it necessary to introduce the double corrective: one cannot affirm and deny something of another at the same time and under the same conditions?"[2] This necessity to specify time and particular viewpoint of judgment, Blondel answers, corresponds precisely to the implicit synthetic act of the spirit. "... only the action of thinking and the initiative of the spirit by means of an original synthesis produce the idea of a possible contradiction."[3] Consequently, we are obliged continually to take into consideration what there is of the necessarily synthetical even in the purest analytical logic. If we totally isolate the analytical function of logic, like Parmenides' principle it becomes an artificial abstraction without meaning or application. Therefore, the source and meaning of formal logic itself must be sought in the synthetic, dynamic process of life itself.

The logical problem, Blondel contends, at its source is identical with the all-important metaphysical problem of the relation of thought to reality: To what extent are facts penetrable to the laws of the under-

---

[1] *Ibid.*, p. 17.
[2] Blondel, "First Redaction of 1892," p. 404.
[3] *Ibid.*, pp. 404-405.

standing? Until this point the problem would have been premature; for there was danger of committing the same error as those in the past "who have confused metaphysical and speculative pretensions with an analysis of phenomena."[1] One must begin by describing empirically all the evidence without taking part in any way. Only on this condition will one possess at the end a logic properly speaking and not an a priori metaphysics, "Logic has no need to be idealist, realist, or criticist."[2]

BLONDEL'S GENETIC STUDY OF LOGIC

According to Blondel, the conflict outlined above between the real and formal roles of the principle of contradiction can be resolved. This resolution is no more impossible than was the successful effort permitting the empirical sciences to receive the intrinsic cooperation of the exact sciences by the implicit mediation of action. However, an implicit resolution, although it suffices in real life, cannot be satisfactory for philosophy as such. "In the more abstract order of logic and of method it is necessary to renew by philosophical reflection what has been accomplished by instinct and by scientific reflection."[3] Just as the scientific problem was resolved, as we have seen, by the implicit synthetic function of action, so too this properly philosophical problem will receive its solution by explicitating the function of human action.

> Action, serving as the source of unity between these opposed forms of thought and life, insinuates the law of contradiction into the heart of the fact, while at the same time perpetually operating an experimental synthesis of the contraries ... if, then, the law of contradiction applies to the past, it does so because the *act*, which is contained within the apparent *fact*, has introduced into the phenomena something other than the phenomena, something other than the possible itself: all the movement of life ends up with the necessary affirmation of being, because that movement is founded on that necessity of being itself.[4]

In his proof for the existence of the absolute Blondel maintained that the dialectic of real action led us necessarily into the presence of being; and only in the presence of being does the law of contradiction apply in all its force.[5] Here from a logical viewpoint that option in the

---

[1] *Ibid.*, "Ebauche de Logique Générale," p. 17.
[2] *Ibid.*
[3] *Ibid.*, p. 18.
[4] Blondel, *L'Action*, p. 472.
[5] Confer above, Chapter X, pp. 183-184.

presence of the absolute represents the foundation and ultimate meaning of the principle of contradiction in thought.

How does the law of thought arise from the law of action and, in turn, influence it? In order to understand how action resolves the problem of the dual role of the principle of contradiction, we must place ourselves in reflection at the point where our logical thought emerges from action and undertake a genetic study of that formation. "Are we not obliged to seek out how we become conscious of logical truths and what is their real genesis; how and why we isolate them from their vital origins; how, finally, according to their genesis itself they influence action and serve our moral life?"[1]

It is important to understand the relation of this genetic study of logic to the phenomenological analysis of action which has preceded it. In the method which Blondel employs the material evidence for this logical study has already been fully developed in his analysis of the dialectic of action up to and including the proof for the existence of the absolute and his analysis of the option in the presence of being. This genetic study of logic represents, as it were, a second degree of abstraction in which one takes the pure form of that dynamic dialectic as object, and one tries to abstract the common logical pattern which characterizes the *aufhebung* or *dépassement* contained implicitly in the passage of that dialectic from each step to the next. A truly complete genetic study would have involved a reapplication of that abstract form of this logical process, abstracted from the real dialectic, to each of the steps in that dialectic in order to clarify the analogous nature of its application. For example, a logical study should be undertaken concerning the similarity and difference of the passage effected by human action between pure and applied science contrasted with the parallel passage between pure metaphysics and morality. Unfortunately, Blondel never completed his logic in this respect. Nonetheless, he did give us an outline of the initial genetic derivation of this logical form.

The problem of the origin of the logical laws of thought is posed, Blondel maintains, by two considerations. The first is the fact that, "since contradictories as such never exist, the principle of contradiction cannot be found in the facts as such."[2] The facts of consciousness cannot produce, suggest, nor even be the direct or indirect occasion of the origin of this principle in consciousness. Thus the very idea itself

---

[1] Blondel, "Principe Elémentaire ...," *op. cit.*, p. 128.
[2] Blondel, "Principe Elémentaire ...," *op. cit.*, p. 129.

of a contradiction already represents an independence of thought over facts. The second consideration is that "the principle of identity is an acosmic principle; it is never realized in the world; it cannot exist *a posteriori* or *a priori* by reason of the lack of identity between that which is thought and that which is the law of thought."[1] However, consciousness itself is a fact; and consciousness, in order to exist, depends on the validity of these principles. From where, then, do the ideas of contradictory, contrary, relativity, and otherness or difference arise? These ideas form the system of logical determinations and, at the same time, represent the necessary condition for all distinct consciousness. "Consciousness is always, at least implicitly, consciousness of a distinction, of a relation, and of an opposition."[2]

Blondel traces the origin of the most primitive of these ideas, the idea of *otherness*, to our spontaneous effort to modify reality by our actions. By means of an automatic psychological process we necessarily tend to insert our proper dynamism into the system of facts. The interreaction of our successive desires or of empirical resistance causes us to become aware of our relative power to change phenomena and adapt them more or less to our activity. It is scarcely by an a priori revelation, nor by an abstract anticipation, that we affirm retrospectively that a possible other than the real was possible and remains conceivable. Rather, it is a consequence of our practical initiative and of our action. "If we did not possess spontaneous tendencies or practical postulates, everything would be indifferent to us, and we would never notice that something did not exist, that an action was not placed or did not succeed."[3] Consequently, the very dawn of our logical life arises from our actions. This is equally true of the more sophisticated idea of the contrary; if we oppose things or acts and evaluate them, we do so in so far as they support or impede the development of our activity. "The *contrary* solutions are contrary among themselves not indeed first of all by reason of an intellectual abstraction but according to their harmony or disharmony with the orientations of our tendencies."[4] The source of the idea of contrary is to be found, then, not originally and immediately in speculative knowledge but in the subjective determination of our activity.

By the time we arrive at the idea of *opposition*, Blondel remarks, we

---

[1] *Ibid.*
[2] *Ibid.*
[3] *Ibid.*, pp. 129-130.
[4] *Ibid.*, p. 130.

are already dealing with a completely abstract and generic idea. Nonetheless, the idea also has a practical origin in action and, more specifically, in the process of choice. The diverse phenomena can only enter
reflex consciousness by attaching themselves to various motives or
mobiles. Further, these phenomena considered as principles of action
are spontaneously organized before consciousness into systematic,
antagonistic groupings. Consequently, when one of the contrary solutions is realized by choice, it is chosen precisely as opposed to the
other possible solution, and also as implicating the intrinsic force of
all the phenomena to the advantage of the solution chosen.[1] In this
manner the reflexive act of choice confers on the empirical relativity
of facts a fixity, an αὐτάρκεια which forms the foundation of all opposition. "The effect of choice is to establish a principle of impenetrability
and exclusivity; because we put ourselves into that which we have
chosen, willed, and accomplished."[2] It is here also that we find the
origin of the principle of identity; we are capable of specifying something as one and the same only by means of "the subjective precision
of the individual motive or intention."[3]

None of these ideas, however, are capable of being conscious ideas
without at least the implicit presence of the idea of *contradiction*. Blondel finds the origin of this idea in "the sentiment of the irreparability
of the past."[4] The law of contradiction does not apply to the future;
logic does not possess any direct means of introducing assertions
concerning the future into its reasonings. Nor, Blondel contends, does
this law apply to the concrete actual, as is frequently asserted. The
"actually true" is once again a simple abstraction. In the concrete
reality of life the law of contradiction is applicable only to the past,
but not to the past as merely thought or known; it is applicable to the
past only in so far as it is "acted" (agi), that is, as constituted in the real.
The fact is that we would be absolutely incapable of conceiving that
something done could have been done otherwise, that there is a
contradictory at the same time conceivable and irrealizable, if we were
not capable of deliberate volition. Consequently, we ourselves insert
absolute contradiction into the relativity of the phenomena.

---

[1] This process outlined here is analysed in detail in the second stage of Blondel's
"Phenomenon of Action," entitled "From the Threshold of Consciousness to
Voluntary Action." (Confer *L'Action*, pp. 103-149).

[2] Blondel, "Principe Elémentaire ...," *op. cit.*, pp. 130-131.

[3] *Ibid.*, p. 131.

[4] *Ibid.*

To have consciousness that a thing could have been otherwise, it is necessary that we have consciousness of our action. ... To know our action, it is necessary that, implicitly conscious at least of our tendencies and of the exigencies of our destiny, we find ourselves obliged to make an option which involves our entire being. In a word, we possess the idea of being and of contradiction only because we find ourselves faced with the problem of resolving the alternatives on which the orientation of our life and our entrance into being depend.[1]

This principle of contradiction, which is born out of option, is the foundation of all speculative use of reason. Consequently, speculative reason is intrinsically united to and dependent on the real, actual exercise of practical reason, which determines its true meaning and legitimate value.

The original and real meaning of the principle of contradiction, Blondel concludes, is to establish that "that which could have been, and could have been incorporated into that which we do and are is forever excluded (στέρησις)."[2]

Yet what has been excluded does not cease to serve as a means of knowing distinctly what has been chosen and done; nor does it cease to serve as an aid for further knowledge and action, and as a means of morally determining the action and the agent himself. However, if we detach the resulting principle from the action which constituted it, we end up with a purely formal logic of facts and a moral science without content. If the principle of contradiction is so closely tied to the option, how did it, and all the logical ideas with it, become isolated from their vital origins in the laws of action?

If we consider the apparent results of our actions, or the facts which seem to exist independent of our actions, everything seems to be reducible to a question of yes or no, affirmation or negation. Thus, losing sight of the complex internal elaboration of results and the complexity of the relations which subsist within the idea of an excluded contradiction, we substitute for them simple artificial verbal relations. Blondel finds this process already accurately described by Aristotle. Aristotle points out that of the ten categories only the category of substance has a real existence in itself. Consequently, only within this category can the opposition of simple affirmation or negation be properly applied. Further, Aristotle notes that "for those things opposed as negation and affirmation, *and only for those things*, is it nec-

---

[1] *Ibid.*, p. 132.
[2] *Ibid.*, pp. 132-133.

essary that one of them be true and the other false."[1] Only substance can receive the contraries without being contrary to itself. But, Aristotle concedes, all the various forms of opposition in all the categories are in ordinary language reduced to the form of contradiction. The other categories, which rigorously cannot receive the contraries, are treated in propositions and reasoning ἐν οὐσίας ἔίδαι and submitted to the law of contradiction.

However, Blondel notes, nature does nothing in vain; there is a profound reason why this verbal denaturing and apparent falsification of the concrete dialectic in favor of an abstract formalism takes place. This spontaneous extension of the principle of contradiction to all the categories and the consequent constitution of an abstract logic based on this principle has its function. This manner of representing all things under the species of substance as submitted to the law of contradiction provides a swift and economic means for man to arrive at a distinct consciousness of himself apart from the world, as well as to provide himself with separate objects and generic types; even if he does so by means of a frequently temerarious denial of the continuity of the phenomena. "There would be no clear, quick, precise, and communicable knowledge without this spontaneous artifice which breaks up the unity of the given, establishes opposition, and constitutes distinct entities which permit the application of logical procedures."[2] This artifice, which at first sight seems to hide and denature the real, actually serves to hasten the development of psychological consciousness.

At the same time this artifice aids in the development of moral consciousness. The logical entities resulting from this process, no matter how arbitrary they may be, serve as the point of reference or even as the object of decision in our immediate choices; and by confering the character of an absolute to the relative they prepare us for the radical option of our will. They do so by presenting us with an occasion for the exercise of our critical powers, which frees us from the given and enables us to undertake those resolutions which effectively engage our destiny. Because of its acosmic nature the principle of contradiction stimulates us invincibly to transcend this empirical world in which our thought and action cannot be entirely circumscribed. But at the same time by confering an absolute character on the diverse objects and opposite alternatives which offer themselves to our

---

[1] *Ibid.*, pp. 134-135.
[2] *Ibid.*, p. 136.

choice, this logical reflection renders us capable of a decisive option which, even under the appearances of the relative, can take on the value of an ontological solution to our destiny. "By expressing symbolically the final necessity of an absolute option the principle of contradiction in its artificial applications leads us to suppose that in some way the passage to the absolute is perpetually effected, and that the supreme option can be decided at every moment and on every occasion *hic et nunc*."[1] No matter where we find ourselves on the ladder of the development of intellect and will, each of us has his problem to resolve; and by reason of his absolutist logic each of us finds within himself the necessary movement to break through the empirical and intellectual orders in order to pose the total problem and in order to determine his place in the moral order by constituting himself within being, which judges him according to his will.

By thus reattaching formal logic to its vital origins, Blondel maintains, we rediscover its relative truth, its natural role, and subalternate legitimacy. But we do so only on condition that we do not isolate it; there is no purely formal logic because there is no idea which is not an act, no thought which is not thinking, no analysis which is not founded on a mental synthesis. "Formal logic is the objective and inadequate phenomenon of a real dialectic."[2]

THE REAL DIALECTIC

At this point in his analysis Blondel seeks to pass beyond the logic of thought to that logic of action which was its source. "Let us consider, not the relation of concepts and abstract terms without vital support and without a subjective content, but the relations of acts, states, or facts assimilated or eliminated by a vital organism which combines, compensates and directs."[3] What is this real dialectic?

In the previous analysis of the genesis of logical ideas what appeared as the source and norm of all logical determinations has been the conscious voluntary choice. This free will-act has the power to cut through the indefinite possibilities of the future and solidify them in the being of a past act which subsists in us and with which we are one. Every voluntary choice, which is carried out in act, is at the same time possession and privation. Both these factors unite in us and help define

---

[1] *Ibid.*, p. 137.
[2] *Ibid.*, p. 138.
[3] *Ibid.*

us. "For this reason there is a determinism which includes all the possible uses of thought and liberty and establishes both an intelligible and real connection between all our states of being, and makes the whole of our life one problem requiring one integral solution."[1] This determinism in action itself, although it is the source of the logical determinism in thought, differs in many respects from that determinism. If we can establish the principle and laws of that vital determinism, Blondel maintains, then we can establish the logic of action, the real dialectic which governs our life.

Blondel finds the elementary principle of that real dialectic in the idea of *privation* (στέρησις). As Aristotle remarks, the idea of privation implies the absence of something which is due or natural; and which had been, can be, or ought to be possessed. The moment that an exigency is rooted in the nature of an agent, no matter whether he satisfies that exigency, or whether he represses it or fails to recognize it, it always produces a series of consequences correlative to the contrary usages made of action. Consequently, it always serves as a fixed point of comparison and as an absolute term of judgment. Whereas a contradiction as such suppresses totally the idea which is negated, privation implies that there is a trace of that negation left in that power which was capable of realizing that of which it is deprived. Privation, then, can be defined as the real presence of that which is absent.

All real relations have their foundation in one of these two component factors of being, actuality (κτῆσις) or privation (στέρησις). Since the potential in man for action is infinite, nothing ultimately escapes either his actuality or his privations. Whereas purely logical relations do not imply organic interrelations, real relations necessarily form an organic whole. Consequently, everything that man does as well as everything that he does not do contribute to define and constitute him; everything enters into his organic dialectic.

As we have seen, the determinations of abstract logic are nothing more than an extraction of that potentially infinite activity spontaneously orientated in us by nature, or an expression of our original intentions projected into the mirror of reflexive thought. Undoubtedly this abstract logic confers a character of necessity on these uprooted ideas. But this necessity is merely extrinsic and does not adequately express that immanent determinism which rules life. "We have need, then, of a logic of the real which includes that which formal logic

---

[1] *Ibid.*, p. 139.

excludes as if it did not exist."[1] This new science has as its object to discover by reflection the *nexus* of all our states of being, that immanent law which renders intelligible all the opposite developments of life and judges them absolutely.

We have established, Blondel remarks, the object or matter of a logic of action; what remains to be established is its scientific form, that is, its basic laws. The basic laws which govern the real dialectic of action can be reduced to five.

The Law of Initial A-Logicism and of Spontaneous Poly-Logicism

Human sensibility and reason are initially universal instruments; and human liberty is "the power of the infinite." Consequently, the initial state of man appears to be an anarchy, an a-logical reality. However, once man acts, this initial a-logical state tends spontaneously to become an order, but a singular and individual order which combines the generic and the individual. "The initial chaos tends, then, to an order and to a certain singular order which is due to a *mélange* of instinct, which determines personal vocation, and of reflection, which becomes the principle of decision and of merit."[2]

The Law of Solidarity of Discordant Forces

This crystallization, both spontaneous and voluntary, of order in each individual determines the features of each one's personality according to a law of logical growth and internal specification. This process does not suppress or neglect any of the elements provided or imposed by nature. We cannot separate ourselves from ourselves; nothing can be inhibited or excluded from our infinite potential without being at the same time included and employed. Of two or more contraries none survives alone after our choice and our action; there is a new reality; for an idea which has been realized is no longer the same as before it was opposed or preferred to the others. Consequently, the result of human activity does not develop along a line marked out by a clear and simple idea which, perhaps, we be-

---

[1] *Ibid.*, p. 140.
[2] *Ibid.*, p. 141.

lieve we follow. "The logic of life deploys its force on the diagonal of a parallelogram of all the concurrent and unified forces of life."[1]

THE LAW OF COMPENSATIONS

What is important is to take into account all the resistances and compensations which determine the orientation of that diagonal. However, this involves a knowledge of our own individual composition at each moment. The difficulty of ethics is precisely that no generic science can ultimately decide one's individual actions; no one has exactly the same obligations, understanding, forces and excuses. On the contrary, each one of us is obliged to develop unceasingly an awareness of his original destiny and incomparable responsibility. A true logic of life must avoid any shadow of legalistic moralism.

THE DETERMINATION OF A LOGICO-ETHICAL CRITERIUM

The previous law would seem to imply the absence of any absolute norm of ethical judgment and, as a result, a moral relativism. This conclusion would be false. Undoubtedly every decision put into execution gives and takes something away from the agent. Nonetheless, the contrary solutions do not possess the same meaning nor, as it were, the same sign. Some are positive in so far as they constitute a positive realization of the essential idea of our being and subordinate the diverse elements to that directive unity; the others are privative in the sense that they upset our virtual and obligatory order.

> It is not the function of a logic as such to follow in concrete detail the application of the rules which govern the actual development of our destiny; but it is its function to discuss, so to speak, algebraically the diverse possibilities of negative or positive solutions and to describe the rigid framework which supports and within which is deployed the free play of human action. It does so by rendering account of the + or − sign which each $\kappa\theta\tilde{\eta}\sigma\iota\varsigma$ or $\sigma\tau\acute{\epsilon}\varrho\eta\sigma\iota\varsigma$ carries in relation to the primitive $\tilde{\epsilon}\xi\iota\varsigma$, abstraction having been made of the variable value of the unknown factors.[2]

There is, then, a necessary pattern or logic of free human action; our liberty of action is necessarily brought into play by this dialectic of action, and necessarily produces its consequences without being

---

[2] *Ibid.*, p. 142.
[2] *Ibid.*, p. 144.

necessitated itself. It is this necessary dynamism, antecedent, concomitant, and consequent to the employment of our liberty, which the logic of action must clarify. Logical truth must be redefined as the accord of thought and life with themselves in a concrete sense; for the task of an integral logic is to lead us into possession of ourselves, to explicitly equivalate that which we are in the implicit concrete. This harmony of the total content is the *genus* of which formal accord is only a species. "Logic is that science which expresses the formula of the solution, which one has only to calculate, once the unknown has been replaced by concrete data, in order to measure the degree of self adequation."[1]

THE LAW OF FINAL INTEGRATION OR TOTAL LOSS

Every action we choose is *de facto* a limitation of our infinite potentiality. However, this limitation from the viewpoint of actual fulfillment can have one of two opposing senses; it can be an enriching mortification or a real loss and impoverishment. Ultimately, our acts are moral only if we search by their means, not relative goods or evils, but *the* good or *the* evil: the divine order or human egoism. In order for our contingent and relative moral acts to enter into this sphere of the absolute, they must be submitted, as we have seen, to the acosmic principle of contradiction. "This intellectual appearance by its very exclusivity provides ... the material for that absolute sacrifice without which morality does not exist."[2] The various objects which present themselves for our choice can only be objects of an apparent and relative sacrifice. Solely by the intervention of the principle of contradiction are we permitted and obliged at the same time to enter into possession of a supersensitive and super-rational life. If the ideal exclusion in spontaneous logical thought seems absolute, it is because the real solution to the logic of life, is, in effect, radically decisive; if human action necessarily finishes in an absolute state of possession or privation, it does so because of the mediation of the formal principle of contradiction. "Only sacrifice gives reality to the contradictory non-being, and by a sort of metaphysical experimentation unites our relative being to absolute being."[3] What was before choice the pure negative non-being of formal logic becomes after choice the positive non-

---

[1] *Ibid.*
[2] *Ibid.*, p. 145.
[3] *Ibid.*, pp. 145-146.

being of privation. Whereas the logic of thought limits itself to the affirmation of an abstract equality and formal incompatibility of the opposite solutions in the order of the possibles; the logic of action, while it justifies that exclusivity whose utility it manifests, transcends it. One and the same subject of inherence remains at the base of every possible solution; and in regard to this subject of inherence the opposing solutions are of unequal value. Thus Aristotle's idea of substance is verified; substance, which alone is true being, admits the contraries but cannot be contrary to itself. The contrary qualities are both present in the moral agent; but only one is present by act; the other is present as a privation.

> In this sense metaphysical reality escapes the logical determinations of the intellect. Thus one must restore the original formula of Parmenides to the principle of contradiction but with a totally different interpretation: non-being is not, neither in itself nor for us; moral being never ceases to be. From the viewpoint of the real it is not pure negation (ἀντίφασις) but positive privation (στέρησις) which is the extreme opposite of being.[1]

The true role of the logical principle of contradiction is less a question of helping us to understand as of helping us to act and realize our destiny. At the moment when the idea of contradiction intervenes as a principle of discernment which clarifies consciousness, a problem is posed and an absolute is in question not speculatively but practically. "The ἀντίφασις (or pure negation of the principle of contradiction) is only an inadequate symbol of στέρησις (or privation)."[2]

SUMMARY

The problem which Blondel attempted to resolve by means of his logic of action was the problem of the role of traditional logic based on the principle of contradiction within the context of a dialectical logic, which is apparently based on a denial of that principle. Although at first sight we seem to be dealing with a purely abstract logical question, Blondel understood that on the solution to this problem depended the all-important question of the basis and value of absolute moral judgment. Whereas the proponents of a purely formal logic tended to limit morality to an abstract, formal sphere divorced from the material reality of life, the proponents of a dialectical logic tended

---

[1] *Ibid.*, p. 146.
[2] *Ibid.*, p. 147. Parentheses added.

to deny any absolute basis in the relative itself for a distinction between good and evil.

As Hegel's criticism had apparently established, although the law of contradiction is the spontaneous law of human thought, that law has no immediate application to the dynamic, synthetic process of becoming, which characterizes the organic interrelations of that living process by which the infinite potentiality of the spirit passes into act. Blondel's study of the logic of action is based on the premise that whatever is spontaneously and necessarily present in human thought must have an organic function in human action. For everything which is found spontaneously in thought has its foundation in the action which produces it and its ultimate justification in the action which follows from it. The simultaneous compatibility and exclusion of the principle of contradiction within a logic of action is, Blondel tells us, its ultimate meaning which must be clarified.

One of the keys to the solution of this problem can be found in an understanding of the inverse function of synthesis and analysis in thought and action. What constitutes a progressive dialectical synthesis for abstract thought represents a regressive analysis in relation to reality; whereas the real progressive dialectical synthesis of action represents from the point of view of thought a regressive analysis. Hegel's mistake, in Blondel's judgment, was to identify that abstract rational synthesis of thought with the living synthesis effected by action — a progressive, living synthesis with the absolute achieved paradoxically in the order of phenomena only by means of the vital analysis, so to speak, of sacrifice. Hegel was led to deny any real function to the principle of contradiction, because his methodological and metaphysical premises had obliged him to deny any real synthetic initiative of human action. Traditional logic, on the other hand, was thought to be a purely formal and analytical process. Consequently, it ignored both the real synthetic function of action as well as the formal synthesis of thought. There is no purely formal logic of analysis, because there is no idea which is not an act, and no analysis which is not founded on a mental synthesis. This synthetic act of spirit, from which both forms of logic prescind at the very moment they depend on it, is the foundation on which Blondel based his explanation of how the law of contradiction can and does enter into the material reality of our action.

In order to clarify the function of this synthetic act of the human spirit Blondel had recourse to a phenomenological genetic study of the spontaneous origin of the law of contradiction in thought. This genetic study represented an effort to place oneself at that point of intersection of thought and action, and to derive that elementary principle which presides over the development of idea and action within the integral unity of a dialectic which dominates these two aspects of the moral life without sacrificing the one to the other. As a result of the genetic study Blondel found the source of the law of contradiction in man's power of free choice. By his choices man has the power to insert the absolute of being into the relativity of the phenomena. Thus man's free will-activity serves as the foundation both for the logic of the dialectic and the logic of contradiction. In so far as universal ideas are a spontaneous projection of the infinite potential of the will into thought, the logic of the dialectic, considered as the logic of that process whereby that potentially infinite passes into act, is justified. In so far as the law of contradiction is a spontaneous projection of the positive power of the will to freely unite itself with being, the logic of contradiction is justified. Action, then, serves as the source of unity between these opposed forms of thought and life; it "insinuates the law of contradiction into the phenomena, while at the same time operating an experimental synthesis of the contraries." The ultimate meaning of the principle of contradiction is to grant man the power to make an absolute judgment within the order of the relative and, thereby, consciously and freely choose his destiny.

This genetic study of the origin of the principle of contradiction led Blondel to envisage a new idea of the real dialectic of the human spirit, which would correct the inadequacies of the Hegelian dialectic. The total structure of this real dialectic would include within an integrated system the combined functions of both thought and action. The human spirit must be understood as an infinite potentiality which passes from potency to act by means of free choices guided by reason. At any given moment the spirit's infinite potentiality represents a synthesis of act or existence and positive privation. Since the potential within the human spirit is infinite, nothing escapes either that actuality or that privation. Thus the real dialectic which rules human life and action is the law which governs that process whereby man evolves towards his self-adequation. There is a necessary logic which governs each individual's evolution towards his own self-adequation. But this necessary logic represents a synthesis of the generic with the individual. Since that logic in its material detail depends on the unique existential situation of the individual which is the result of his past free choices, it is not the function of logic as such to establish concrete rules which apply univocally to each individual. However, Blondel maintains, it is possible for the philosopher-logician to determine the general framework within which the human spirit acts and to establish in general the diverse possibilities of negative and positive solutions to the problem of human destiny. Further, it is possible and obligatory for each individual to determine clearly how these generic rules apply in the context of the concrete reality of his own conscious lived-experience.

These chapters concerning Blondel's logic have, as we foresaw, carried us well beyond the question of Fichte's proper contribution to Blondel's thought into a discussion of the influence of the idealist movement in general. We will return, then, in the next chapter to a more specific treatment of the influence of Schelling's and Hegel's thought on Blondel's philosophy of action. The analysis we have made of the idea of the dialectic in Blondel's philosophy will help us considerably in understanding his reactions to these new stages in the evolution of idealist moral thought; and these reactions, in turn, will help to clarify the origin and import of Blondel's position.

CHAPTER FOURTEEN

THE INFLUENCE OF SCHELLING AND HEGEL

INTRODUCTION

In the course of the previous exposition of the influence of Fichte's thought on Blondel, we were obliged to deal with the influence of idealism in general. This was especially true in our treatment of the logic of action and Blondel's dialectic; for here Blondel himself was inclined to consider the teachings of the three great idealists,—Fichte, Schelling and Hegel—as forming one doctrine with various stages of evolution. Consequently, we can limit our treatment of the early Schelling and of Hegel to certain key issues in which their specific influence is more evident. We shall reserve the question of the influence of Schelling's final "positive philosophy" until the next chapter.

The first point we will treat is an exposition of Blondel's criticism of the doctrine of Schelling and Hegel in so far as it represents a continuation of the "evolution" of Spinoza's moral doctrine beyond the position of Kant and Fichte. Here we will attempt to clarify what Blondel saw as the necessary final transformation of this evolution into a philosophy of action. The second point is an analysis of the moral philosophy of both Schelling and Hegel, especially as that is developed in Schelling's philosophy of art and the concept of a "necessary progress" in history, and in Hegel's concept of the "world-historical individual," in order to understand more clearly how Blondel understood his logic of action as a correction of the deficiencies of these systems. The final point is a comparative examination of the relation of philosophy and religion in Hegel's and Blondel's thought.

BLONDEL'S CRITICISM OF SCHELLING'S AND HEGEL'S PHILOSOPHY

Just as Fichte had understood his theory of science as a return to Spinoza's *Ethics*, while maintaining the valid critical insights of Kant; so too, Blondel maintains, Schelling understood his early philosophy as a renewed effort to restore Spinoza's *Ethics*, while retaining the valid idealist insights of Fichte.[1] The systematic monism of Spinoza's doc-

---

[1] Blondel, "L'Evolution du Spinozisme," II, 325.

trine remained, in Schelling's estimation, the necessary model of all valid philosophy. However, there had been a contradiction between the form and the matter of that system; a non-ego as such cannot possibly be the absolute. Fichte's major and decisive contribution to the evolution of philosophical thought was his proof that the absolute cannot be understood simply as object; one must understand the absolute as affirming itself in an act of intellectual intuition as an ego or subject.

Despite Fichte's accomplishment Schelling felt that he had also failed to achieve a definitive synthesis between the infinite and the finite, being and becoming, in terms of his absolute subject. Schelling's avowed objective, Blondel tells us, "was to reconcile in a new synthesis the indefinite becoming of moral obligation and the living reality of determined Being, which Fichte had considered at two successive moments of his thought."[1] This new synthesis would consist in an effort to rehabilitate within idealism itself the ontologism of Spinoza. This rehabilitation would be accomplished by "characterizing the Ego of Fichte according to the schema of the substance of Spinoza."[2] Thus Schelling understood his new synthesis as "an exact counterpart (pendant)" of Spinoza's *Ethics*. The absolute which serves as the first principle in philosophy must be understood, according to Schelling, as neither pure object nor pure subject but as an identity of subject and object, real and ideal, being and becoming. "Thus from the start in Schelling's opinion both idealism and realism are equally founded in an absolute which is pure identity."[3]

Blondel, then, understood Schelling's early philosophy, expressed in his transcendental idealism, to be a conscious return to the point of departure of Spinoza, namely, to absolute being, but now understood as pure identity. The ambiguity in Fichte's doctrine between phenomenological analysis and idealist metaphysics had been resolved in favor of a pure metaphysical idealism. Consequently, Schelling's return to Spinoza's point of departure represented, in Blondel's opinion, a return to the same basic difficulty which had been the generating force of all the ulterior evolution of Spinozism.[4] "Despite the successive efforts of monist thought, the same problem, continually renewed but as yet unresolved, remained: How can the finite be de-

---

[1] *Ibid.*
[2] *Ibid.*
[3] *Ibid.*, II, 326.
[4] Confer above, Part I, Chapter II, pp. 32-39.

duced from the infinite ...? How justify the necessity of becoming in Being?"[1] Both Fichte and Schelling, Blondel remarks, tried to deduce its finite manifestations from the absolute itself; both relegated in some way the temporal process of finite becoming outside that absolute in what Spinoza called *natura naturata* by opposition to *natura naturans*. The result is that both considered the necessity of becoming in Being as somehow derived or subordinated.

In the evolution of Schelling's thought, however, Blondel finds a progressive tendency to introduce the relative and the process of becoming into the very heart of the absolute. There was a tendency to create so close a union between the infinite and the finite, being and becoming, "that the Perfect had need of becoming in order to be."[2] This process led Schelling to subordinate his metaphysics of the absolute to a sort of "*théogonie transcendentale*: a history of a necessary process in which God as principle is not yet that which he is as end."[3] Spinoza had assigned becoming the last place in his theory, as the domain of pure appearances, with the design to make it disappear by absorbing it totally into the unity and immobility of being. With Schelling's doctrine the idea of becoming within the absolute became the most fundamental truth. Hegel's doctrine, in turn, represents the final stage in that evolution.

> With Hegel it (the identity of becoming and being) becomes not only the primary truth but the only truth. For him the unity of the infinite and the finite is not only the most fundamental affirmation among others; this idea is the productive source of all truth. One need only develop its dialectical meaning for it to become the truth itself.[4]

Thus Hegel's doctrine, in Blondel's judgment, represented the logical fulfillment of Spinoza's *Ethics*. Spinoza had implicitly introduced the anthropomorphic idea of becoming into his objective pantheism in order to resolve the human ethical problem within the context of the total metaphysical problem of the absolute. In Hegel's philosophy we

---

[1] Blondel, *op. cit.*, II, 326.

[2] *Ibid.*, II, 327.

[3] Blondel's reference is to Delbos' work *Le Problème Moral dans la Philosophie de Spinoza*, pp. 433-435. The text Delbos refers to is taken from Schelling's work, *Denkmal der Schrift von den göttlichen Dingen des Herrn Jacobi* (1812). "Ich setze Gott als Erstes und als Letztes, als Alpha und als Omega, aber als das Alpha ist er nicht, was er als Omega ist..." Confer *Schelling's Werke* (München: Beck und Oldenburg) 1927), edited by Manfred Schröter, Vol. IV, p. 81. All future references to Schelling's works will be to this edition of his collected works. Six supplementary volumes were published in 1956.

[4] Blondel, *op. cit.*, II, 327.

find Spinoza's two principles, being and becoming, equally developed and entirely adjusted as matter and form. The idea of becoming, the concept of the spirit which is not but which produces itself, had produced all its consequences; it is becoming itself which is being. Spinoza's idea that the order and connection of ideas is identical to the order and connection of things reaches its fulfillment in Hegel's idea that the real is rational and the rational is real.

This was the logical outcome, Blondel argues, because in effect one cannot suppress or reduce the being of the relative except by implicitly postulating the becoming of the absolute, as Spinoza did. But at the very instant that one has placed the relativity of becoming within absolute being, it becomes necessary to conclude to Hegel's position and place absolute being within the relativity of becoming:

> Spinoza attempted to absorb our relative being and all being within absolute Being itself. The definite result was to absorb absolute Being within our relative being and, under the pretext of rendering man immanent to the absolute, to have rendered the absolute immanent in man.[1]

Thus in the evolution of idealism the two central ideas of Spinoza had been so intimately united little by little that they ended up in Hegel's doctrine by mutually determining each other and becoming interchanged.

If one reflects on the historical evolution of Spinoza's position, Blondel contends, the result of the inclusion of the moral problem was to doubly restrain the metaphysical problem to the conditions of knowledge, and to the conditions of specifically human knowledge. For two unacknowledged postulates lie behind Hegel's completion of Spinoza's theory. The first is the supposition that man carries within his conscious life all the secret of being. The second is the supposition that that secret within man can be understood by means of human reason alone. The result of this double postulate is that one attempts to resolve the problem of human destiny exclusively by speculative means.

> By proposing a *théogonie transcendentale* or by proposing to develop the evolution of a God who determines himself within history Schelling or Hegel do not describe in the end anything else but the effort of man to make his own thought itself the absolute and to justify the apotheosis

---

[1] *Ibid.*, 328-329.

of his own reason. Spinoza had sublimated the human into God; Hegel confides to man the role of constructing God with the human itself.[1]

In Blondel's opinion the most important idea of Spinoza was the idea of immanence: things carry in themselves their explanation and justification, in so far as they are reintegrated into that entire context in which they are included. In the field of moral philosophy this idea of immanence implies that man carries in himself the law of his destiny. He need not search for the norm of judgment on his thoughts and actions in that which they are not, because it is to be found precisely in that which they are. The idea of immanence was first presented under the form of an ontological affirmation. We have seen how in Blondel's view this metaphysical doctrine of immanence by a process of intrinsic logical evolution led to an identity of the absolute being with the evolving content of human thought and life. The moment when the monism of Spinoza or Hegel had restrained the metaphysical problem to the conditions of human knowledge, it was inevitable that what was presented as the real absolute and the becoming of being should appear less as the truth of substance or the history of the divine as the continuing play of our representations and the interrelations of phenomena. "The phenomena, if one reflects well, is the true object to which the Hegelian dialectic applies; this is the true scientific idea which that philosophy of the absolute elaborated."[2] Consequently, Blondel speaks of a "fruitful transformation" of Hegelianism from a metaphysical system to a scientific method for the study of phenomena. In dealing with the logic of action we have seen that Blondel considered Hegel's dialectical logic as a valid, if limited, expression of that necessary law which governs the synthetic development of living human action.

When he posed the idea of immanence as the norm of truth, Spinoza had in mind the abstract rational process of mathematical reasoning. The result of the evolution of Spinozism was to introduce into that logical process not only the intelligible essences of things considered under the form of abstract, static universality but also the apparently contingent facts and moving aspects of concrete reality.

> Hegel has left us ... an idea forever incorporated in human intelligence. By teaching us that what is real is rational he taught us to respect and understand the facts, to discover the absolute of scientific laws not in

---

[1] *Ibid.*, 329.
[2] *Ibid.*, 331.

abstract generalities ... but in each concrete detail. There is no question, according to Hegel, of reattaching the empirical facts to an essences which is their substrate or divine principle; the only problem is to understand that the internal necessary relations which govern the development of facts are the truth itself.[1]

Even when, however, the Hegelian dialectic is considered as a pure methodological procedure, if it is seen as the exclusive law of human action, it can lead to a new danger, that of moral relativism. In the beginning, Blondel tells us, Hegel's immanent dialectic seemed to exclude all qualification of things and acts in order to search out their pure intelligibility. The idea of the necessary was transformed; instead of being a pure identity, it became the identity of contradictories. It included even that which denied it and absorbed that which limited it. It introduced the contingent and accidental into the constitution of its order and power. From then on critical philosophy, instead of tending to exclude radically, seemed to reintegrate equally the most heterogeneous forms of life and thought within the framework of a universal philosophy. For Spinoza, to understand was to exclude everything which did not enter into Being; for Hegel to understand was to include within Being everything which seemingly was outside of it, but in reality constitutes and develops it. "For Spinoza truth is one; there is no way of judging that which is outside of it. For Hegel truth is never one; there is no way of judging that which it is in itself because it becomes; and in becoming it is its own measure of what ought to be."[2]

Both these positions, in Blondel's judgment, represent only a provisional stage in the development of a total method for philosophy.

> Spinoza posed an absolute difference between that which is and that which is not. Hegel posed an identity of contraries. However, in its natural evolution critical philosophy is led to draw together these two conceptions under a new form of thought. In place of believing that to understand everything is to include everything either in the absolute (Spinoza) or in the relative (Hegel), one begins to see that to understand is precisely *to be able to distinguish an absolute difference in the relative itself*.[3]

---

[1] *Ibid.*, 332.

[2] *Ibid.*, 335.

[3] *Ibid.* Parentheses and *underlining* added. This was one of Blondel's objectives from the very start. In the notes for the preparation of *Action* we find the following: "With Hegel reason received a form large enough to understand everything without excluding anything... (-go beyond, and recapture the right to exclude and to condemn!"). Confer *Notes for Action*, No. 998.

We have already seen how Blondel sought just such a method in his logic of action by uncovering a real function for the law of contradiction within the context of the Hegelian dialectic. If Hegel had succeeded in formalizing the dynamic material movement of life, he had failed to materialize the formal, that is, to discover the real or existential function of the absolute principle of formal thought.

This renewal of methodology, wherein by means of an immanent criticism one discovers within the relativity of human thought and action a principle of absolute differentiation which judges and separates them radically, involves, Blondel claimed, as a necessary corollary a progress in doctrine. If it is possible and necessary for us to judge, to approve and condemn, the reason is that it does not suffice to understand. Although the understanding is capable of penetrating everything, it itself is not everything. It does not supply for action, even at the moment when it renders action intelligible.

> It is action which justifies the basic difference in our destinies and the absolute qualification of our works as good or evil. By means of action a transcendent principle of truth and reality becomes immanent in us. And the thought which uncovers that immanence does not supply for its necessity, nor change anything in the character of its transcendence.[1]

Thus Blondel saw the normal evolution of philosophical thought after Hegel as leading naturally to a philosophy of action such as he proposed. However, there was in his estimation a "radical vice" in contemporary thought which tended to impede that normal process of evolution. That radical vice was the belief that "the speculative solution to the problem of life is the equivalent or even superior to the effective solution." This tendency to substitute speculation for practice is so great that even when the modern philosophers oppose practice to theory it is a theory of practice of which they speak. There was an ambiguity in Spinoza's avowed intention to resolve the moral problem by thought alone. Was it absolutely or merely relative to us that that purely intellectual solution was valid? However, both Schelling and Hegel tended to resolve that ambiguity by claiming that there is an "absolute knowledge." According to Delbos, Schelling held that "it is by knowledge that human life completes itself."[2] Hegel

---

[1] *Ibid.*, 337.

[2] Delbos, *op. cit.*, pp. 358-359. Delbos' reference to Schelling is to the *Vorrede* of *Vom Ich als Prinzip der Philosophie* (1795): "Gebt dem Menschen das Bewusstsein desser, was er *ist*, er wird bald auch lernen, zu seyn, was er *soll*: gebt ihn *theoretische* Achtung vor sich selbst, die *praktische* wird bald nachfolgen." Vol. I, p. 81.

went a step further, Blondel adds, when he stated: "Thought is the highest and the only form under which the eternal and absolute Being can be seized."[1]

But why this substitution of thought for practice? We must clarify the implicit aspiration in such an undertaking, Blondel claims, in order to open up the way for a true development of philosophy. At the heart of this undertaking is the desire, rather the need, to see the problem of life resolved absolutely by the *sole efforts of man alone.*

> If there is one idea common to the idealism of Kant or the pantheism of Spinoza, an idea which is the πρῶτον ωεύδος of all exclusive rationalism, it is that man alone can succeed in integrating himself into the absolute...[2]

Once we have accepted this norm for our philosophical effort, then we must necessarily turn exclusively to speculation for a final answer. For, in so far as concerns those things which do not pertain to us nor depend on us, it would seem that thought and only thought gives us at least a representation; and this representation does pertain to us and depend on us. Consequently, if it is necessary, philosophically speaking, that the problem be resolved by the sole effort of man, it follows necessarily that the solution must be the exclusive product of thought. The essential truth to be derived from the entire evolution of philosophical thought from Spinoza to Hegel, in Blondel's judgment, is the vanity of any such effort. "In vain does one pretend, as did Hegel, that the unity of the infinite and the finite does not suppose anything beyond the formula which expresses it, and that the entire truth can be absolutely understood in the dialectic ..."[3]

This awareness that "knowledge, even adequate knowledge, cannot supply for practice," is, in Blondel's opinion, the most important gain resulting from the whole period of the evolution of Spinozism. Christianity no doubt had always implied it; but the effort of philosophical reflection has finally succeeded for the first time in fully disengaging it and in clarifying it, with the result that the terms of the moral and metaphysical problem have been placed in a new and different light. The practical preoccupation which had originally inspired the author of *Ethics* reappears but with a new meaning, precision, and

---

[1] Blondel, *op. cit.*, p. 337. Blondel's reference for the quotation is to Vera's translation of Hegel's *Logique*, Tome I, p. 216.

[2] Blondel, *op. cit.*, II, 338.

[3] *Ibid.*, II, 339.

dignity. No speculative philosophical system can be considered as a closed, finished system; every speculative system is transcended by a progress of speculation. The only system which can contain definitive truth is one which does not search its completion in itself but, rather, concludes to the need of action and determines the practical exigencies. "The absolute error of Hegel was to try to fix the philosophy of the absolute."[1]

> What ought to be considered as the continually renewed stimulus for a speculative dialectic is not Spinoza's substance, nor Kant's thing-in-itself, nor Fichte's subject or pure reason, nor Schelling's subject-object, nor Hegel's identity of contraries, nor even the phenomenon; rather it is *action*.[2]

For this reason Blondel felt justified in claiming that his attempt to create a philosophy of action was not divorced from the contemporary current of thought, nor even contrary to that current, but the "natural outcome of over two centuries of speculation."

THE MORAL PROBLEM

The primary criticism which, as we have seen, Blondel made against the dialectic of Hegel, considered as a method for moral philosophy, was the absence of an absolute norm of judgment between true and false, right and wrong, within that system. This moral relativism was, in Blondel's judgment, a necessary result of the identity both Schelling and Hegel established between being and becoming, and their resulting tendency to mistake the dialectical development of human activity with a becoming of the absolute itself. The renewal of method and doctrine in the philosophy of action which Blondel envisaged was directed precisely towards a correction of that deficit; a true philosophy of life and being is one which permits us "to be able to distinguish an absolute difference in the relative itself." What we propose to consider at this point is where and how Blondel understood these systems to be defective in this respect, and how exactly he attempted to correct that deficiency, while preserving the valid progress contained in these systems.

Schelling saw as the central problem of all philosophy the problem

---

[1] *Ibid.*
[2] *Ibid.*, II, 340.

of the relation of the infinite and the finite.[1] In his *Exposition of my System of Philosophy* (Darstellung meines Systems der Philosophie) in 1801 he attempted to resolve that problem in terms of a system of pure identity. However, this theory of identity led to a new problem. If the absolute is pure identity then there is nothing outside of it. Consequently, we cannot conceive of the absolute as external cause of the universe. "The absolute identity is not cause of the universe but the universe itself. For everything which exists is the absolute identity itself and the universe is everything which is."[2] However, if the absolute is pure identity, somehow all distinctions must be outside of it. "Quantitative difference is possible only outside absolute totality."[3] Thus Schelling concluded that finite things are exterior to the absolute; and the problem he posed was how to explain that exteriority. It cannot be explained, Schelling tells us, by a process by which the absolute is understood as going outside of itself. "The fundamental error of all philosophy is the proposition that the absolute has really gone out of itself."[4] Only from the point of view of empirical consciousness, he concludes, is there a distinction between subject and object as subsistent finite things. Thus in *Bruno, or on the Divine and Natural Principle of Things* (Bruno, oder über das göttliche und natürliche Prinzip der Dinge) in 1802 Schelling states quite clearly that finite things are separate from the absolute only from man's finite empirical viewpoint.[5] This position led to a new problem: how explain the emergence of the point of view of empirical consciousness and its ontological status? How can empirical consciousness, together with the distinctions it involves, arise either within the absolute, if it is pure identity, or outside of it, if it is totality? In attempting to meet this difficulty Schelling made use of a variant of Fichte's theory: the absolute as unconscious identity achieves conscious identity in and through human consciousness.

However, this absolute considered as unconscious identity reveals itself to itself not exclusively through human consciousness, but also through nature. Thus Schelling distinguishes two series of "evolving potencies", the real —which is considered as Nature, and the ideal—

---

[1] For a brief exposition of Schelling's point of departure and his theory of the absolute confer Copleston, *op. cit.*, Vol. VII, pp. 123–125.

[2] Schelling, "Darstellung meines Systems der Philosophie," Vol. III, p. 25.

[3] *Ibid.*, p. 23.

[4] *Ibid.*, p. 16.

[5] *Ibid.*, "Bruno oder über das göttliche und natürliche Prinzip der Dinge," Vol. III, p. 155.

which is considered as the human ego. If however, we wish to transcend the standpoint of empirical consciousness from which distinction as such exists, and grasp the absolute as it is in itself rather than in appearances, we can conceive of it only as "indifference" or as the vanishing point of all difference and distinction. "The starting point of all philosophy," Schelling tells us, "and the indispensable condition for even arriving at it is to understand that the absolute in the ideal order is identical with the absolute in the real order."[1] If we wish to think this identity, Schelling explains, we must first think it away; and then we are faced with two possibilities. Either we can start with the objective and proceed towards the subjective, asking how unconscious nature comes to be represented. Or we can begin with the subjective and proceed towards the objective, asking how an object comes to exist for a subject.

Schelling developed the first possibility in his philosophy of nature. Contrary to Fichte's subjective idealist position he refused to consider nature as no more than an obstacle posited by the ego in order that it may have something to overcome. Rather, nature must be understood as the immediate objective manifestation of the absolute. And since the absolute in itself is a pure identity of subject and object, nature also must reflect both aspects of that identity. Nature, then, is "visible spirit"; whereas Spirit is "invisible Nature." The philosopher's task is to show that apparently purely objective nature is in fact ideal, in the sense that it is a unified, dynamic, and teleological system which develops upward to the point at which it returns upon itself in and through the human spirit. Thus man's life of conscious representation is to be understood as nature's knowledge of itself; it is the actualization of nature's potentiality whereby "slumbering spirit awakens to consciousness." Thus the first step Schelling undertook in the formation of his system was to create a philosophy of nature, showing how nature develops the conditions of its own self-reflection on the subjective level.

In his *System of Transcendental Idealism* in 1800 Schelling undertook the second possibility. Here he began with the subjective and moved towards the objective, asking how an object came to exist for a subject. The ultimate task of a transcendental idealism was to demonstrate how the ultimate immanent principle of consciousness produced the objective world as the condition of its attainment of perfect self-con-

---

[1] *Ibid.*, "Ideen zu einer Philosophie der Natur," Vol. I, p. 708.

sciousness. In this work Schelling covered more or less the same ground covered by Fichte in his theoretical and practical deductions of consciousness and in his works on the theory of rights and on ethics. But Schelling adds a third part which is his own particular contribution to transcendental idealism and which serves to underline the difference between his concept of the goal of human action and that of Fichte.

THE PHILOSOPHY OF ART

In the *System of Transcendental Idealism* Schelling presents conscious spirit objectifying itself as a "second nature." He saw as the ultimate goal and highest perfection of that process an intuition in which the identity of the unconscious and of the conscious, of the real and of the ideal, would be presented in a concrete way to the ego itself. He discovered what he was seeking in aesthetic intuition. Consequently, he concluded that a philosophy of conscious human action culminates in a philosophy of art. Thus in Schelling's system, as contrasted with Fichte's and, as we shall see, also with Blondel's, emphasis shifts from ethics to aesthetics, from the moral life to artistic creation, from action to aesthetic contemplation. "The objective world (nature) is only the original, still unconscious poetry of the Spirit: the universal organon of philosophy—and the keystone of the whole arch—is the philosophy of art."[1] Art, according to Schelling, is grounded in the power of productive intuition, which is the instrument of transcendental idealism. The task of productive intuition is to re-create the stages of the history of consciousness, and present them to the ego's vision as constituted objects for its contemplation. Aesthetic intuition's value lies in the fact that it represents the most perfect manifestation of the basic truth concerning the unity of the unconscious and the conscious, of the real and the ideal. The creative artist is, as it were, the conscious vehicle of an unconscious power which acts through him. That same power which acts without consciousness in producing nature, "the unconscious poetry of the spirit," acts with consciousness in producing the work of art. The work of art thereby illustrates the ultimate unity of the unconscious and the conscious, of the real and the ideal. The completed

---

[1] "Die objective Welt ist nur die ursprüngliche, noch bewusslose Poesie des Geistes; das allgemeine Organon der Philosophie—und der Schusstein ihres ganzen Gewalbes—*die Philosophie der Kunst.*" Confer Schelling, "System des transzendentalen Idealismus," Vol. II, p. 349.

work of art is the spirit's supreme conscious objectification of itself to itself.

In the lectures on *The Philosophy of Art* in 1802-1803 Schelling brought out the metaphysical significance of the work of art; it serves as the finite manifestation of the infinite absolute. The absolute in itself is the indifference of the ideal and the real; and this indifference as indifference is expressed most perfectly in the ideal world through art.[1] Schelling introduced the platonic notion of divine ideas, and held that things are beautiful in virtue of their participation in these ideas. "Beauty exists where the particular is so in accord with its idea that this idea itself, as infinite, enters into the finite and is intuited *in concreto*."[2] Aesthetic intuition can be defined, then, as the intuition of the infinite in a finite product of consciousness. This conformity of the object with its eternal idea is its truth; hence, beauty and truth are ultimately one.

It is significant that at the same point in the context of his *Action* where Schelling developed his philosophy of art, Blondel proceeds to discuss various superstitious efforts, art among others, whereby man tries to subordinate divine power to his own human will and intellect. There is a philosophy of art in *Action*. This aesthetic theory is introduced in the course of Blondel's discussion of the role the concrete sign as such plays in the expansion of will-activity into the exterior world.[3] Many features of Schelling's analysis of art can be found in Blondel's phenomenological description of a sign. All artistic works, in Blondel's opinion, have the power to convey the presence and the unique, singular action of their creator. One finds in a work of art a sort of inchoative subjective life. "It is ... a secondary subject, detached from its agent and, as it were, an intention which has taken on flesh and life."[4] In this respect a work of art can be considered as a "real-idea" which has in some way its own intentional activity.[5] After the "co-action" of the creator of a work of art with the "subjective forces" in nature has produced its effect, the result seems to be a self-sufficient organism and, as it were, a new creature in the midst of the

---

[1] "Die Indifferenz des Idealen und Realen als Indifferenz stellt sich in der Idealen Welt durch die Kunst dar." *Ibid.*, "Philosophie der Kunst," Vol. III, p. 400.

[2] *Ibid.*, p. 402.

[3] This analysis of the role of the sign occurs in the context of the fourth step of the development of the phenomenon of action. Confer *L'Action*, pp. 201-244.

[4] *Ibid.*, p. 208.

[5] *Ibid.*, p. 211.

phenomena. The artistic work, as a result, gives rise spontaneously to a sort of "inchoative mysticism."

> Art is ... the mythical résumé of all the future developments of the will in search of its perfect fulfillment. In the sensible work or phenomenon it fictitiously inserts the real, the living, the human, the divine; it seizes by instinct and uncovers by intuitions the symbolic equivalent of all the aspirations still implicit in the will.[1]

Art, then, has practically the same meaning for Blondel as it did for Schelling. It is one of the most perfect objective, sensible symbols of that perfect unity of the real and the ideal, the infinite and the finite; its power and value lie in its symbolic representation of that perfect unity which is the secret aspiration of the human will.

However, Blondel was not in favor of over-stressing an abstract theory or philosophy of art. In his opinion one of the values of art was precisely to free us from a tendency to overdo abstract reflection and to bring us back into contact with concrete thought and reality.

> Far from being itself submitted to the restraint of abstraction, artistic or literary activity ought to contribute to our liberation. For it is she who opens up for us one of the most penetrating approaches to being; and it is she who, by concurring with a "science of the concrete" and with the progress and safeguard of concrete thought, gives rise to a true metaphysics in place of being submitted to an ideology.[2]

Schelling was right, in Blondel's judgment, in his understanding of the value of a work of art as the symbol of the ideal union of the infinite and the finite. However, there is a serious danger in extolling that creative act as the supreme act of which man is capable.

> It is true that the beautiful is very close to the sanctuary, but one risks to mistakenly convince oneself that it gives direct access, while in fact it is only a passage which must be coordinated with or subordinated to other ways through which one must necessarily pass before reaching the goal. For example, I hold asceticism much more at heart than it.[3]

The romanticist stress on the contemplation of the beautiful as man's highest destiny represented, in Blondel's mind, a return to the pagan idea of conquering beatitude by the use of knowledge; a sort of restoration of the pagan *visio* for the Christian *vita*. Artistic beauty, in his opinion, represents not the living truth of our personal union with

---

[1] *Ibid.*, pp. 228-229.
[2] *Ibid.*, *L'Itinéraire Philosophique*, pp. 121-122.
[3] *Ibid.*, p. 120.

the absolute, but a "fictitious" symbol of that truth. It is not by means of a contemplation of a symbol but by living sacrificial action that we can realize in our lives what art symbolically portrays. Schelling's promotion of art as the keystone of philosophy represented a tendency in idealist thought to seek the fulfillment of man's destiny in a dialectical process which, although employing man's conscious powers, operates independently of personal, individual liberty. As we have seen, the "keystone" of philosophy in Blondel's theory lies in the free moral option for or against union with the absolute. On this option both personal fulfillment and a true progressive evolution of human society depends.

The Theory of Necessary Progress

Schelling was naturally at pains to correlate his development of the history of consciousness with his previously developed philosophy of nature. Thus he was inclined to see society as a "second or moral nature" and to seek in the development of this second nature a necessary tendency towards the ideal goal; just as there was a necessary progressive evolution in nature itself towards its ideal goal of the self-conscious organism. This desire for correlation led to Schelling's theory of a necessary, endless progress in history. "There lies in the concept of history the concept of endless *progress*."[1] This concept of necessary progress is closely connected with Schelling's theory of the absolute. "History as a whole is a continual revelation of the absolute, a revelation which gradually discloses itself."[2] Just as the absolute itself is a pure identity of the ideal and the real, so history must be a necessary movement towards the creation of a second nature which reveals such an identity. However, if the absolute were perfectly revealed in its true nature as identity of subject and object, the point of view of human consciousness which presupposes a distinction between subject and object would no longer exist. Hence the revelation of the absolute in human history must be in principle endless.

Schelling was aware that to understand human history as a progressive revelation which the absolute makes of itself, and to see in that history a necessary progress, seemed to imply a negation of individual human freedom. If one asserts that the human will is free, then one

---

[1] Schelling, "System der transzendentalen Idealismus," Vol. II, p. 592.
[2] *Ibid.*, p. 603.

must admit that man can thwart the ends of history. Thus individual freedom would seem to contradict the idea of a necessary progress towards an ideal goal. Schelling tried to escape this dilemma, while trying to preserve at the same time the universal determinism of the absolute which he inherited from Spinoza, and the freedom of the individual which he found in Fichte. In order to do so he had recourse to the idea of an "absolute synthesis." Individuals do act freely; and any given individual may act for a purely private and selfish end. But there is at the same time a hidden necessity which achieves an absolute synthesis of the apparently unconnected and often conflicting actions of human beings.[1] Thus, even when an individual man acts for purely selfish motives, he will nonetheless unconsciously contribute, even though against his will, to the fulfillment of the common end of human history.

The interesting point here for the future evolution of moral theory was the distinction Schelling was led to make, because of his theory of necessary progress, between the use man makes of his freedom—his own personal moral value—and the contribution he makes to the progressive revelation of the absolute in history. Although Schelling obviously wanted to retain freedom and moral responsibility, he effectively dissociated the progress of humanity in history towards a closer union with the absolute from the question of the moral value of human action. In this theory we find the same tendency to subordinate the interior moral value of the individual to a necessary objective manifestation of the absolute. Just as the artistic product, whose intrinsic value as a revelation of the absolute is independent of the artist's real moral worth, so the necessary progressive revelation of the absolute in history is independent of the moral value of the individual's actions within that history.

Whereas Schelling's philosophy of history tended towards a subordination of moral value to a necessary process, Hegel's philosophy of history seems to eliminate totally from consideration as irrelevant to historical judgment the moral quality of an individual's actions. It would seem that in Hegel's opinion history achieves its end not, as in Schelling's theory, despite moral evil, but on occasion by means of moral evil. This aspect of Hegel's philosophy is evident in his theory

---

[1] "... je freier das Individuum, desto mehr Widerspruch würde in Ganzen seyn, wenn nicht jenes Objective, allen Intelligenzen Gemeinshaftliche eine *absolute Synthesis* wäre, in welcher alle Widersprüche zum voraus aufgelöst und aufgehoben sind." *Ibid.*, p. 598.

concerning the world-historical individual (die weltgeschichtlichen Individuum).[1] The World-Spirit according to Hegel, uses certain individuals as its instruments in a signal way. These great individuals had their subjective passions and private motives, but these passions or motives are not of much importance or relevance for the philosopher of history, who is interested in such men for what they accomplished as necessary instruments of the World-Spirit. Nothing great is accomplished in this world without passion, Hegel claims; and the passions of the great figures of history are used as instruments by the World-Spirit and exhibit "the cunning of Reason."

Hegel did not profess the cynical theory that the only right is might. According to Copleston, what determined Hegel's theory was the exaggerated optimistic view that in history right, in the form of Reason, is the necessarily dominant factor.[2] Hegel's philosophy of history is a metaphysical interpretation of history. The Hegelian absolute was identical with the historical process itself; judgment had been made purely immanent to the historical process itself. Thus the final result of Hegel's theory was identical with a cynical theory; if right always prevails in history, then successful might is automatically justified.

Hegel did hold that moral judgments could be passed on the world-historical individuals; but such judgments possess only a "purely formal rectitude." Their validity depended on the adoption of the point of view of a given ethical system. But from the view of world-history morally evil deeds could be justified, if by them an individual accomplished what the universal spirit required. This amoral aspect of the development of the absolute in history goes hand in hand with Hegel's theory of war as a necessary rational phenomenon. War for Hegel is a necessary means in the dialectic of history. It prevents stagnation and preserves "the ethical health of the nation."[3] It is the

---

[1] Hegel, "Grundlinien der Philosophie des Rechts," *Samtliche Werke*, Vol. VII, p. 427. Unless otherwise stated, all references to Hegel's writings will be given according to volume and page of the jubilee edition of his collected works by Hermann Glockner (Stuttgart: Fr. Frommans Verlag, 1928).

[2] Copleston, *op. cit.*, Vol. VII, p. 224.

[3] Hegel, *op. cit.*, Vol. VII, p. 434. When Blondel posthumously edited his friend Delbos' notes on German philosophy, he called attention in an editor's note to his friend's awareness of this moral ambiguity in idealist thought. He cites Delbos as understanding "... that there is something monstrous (énorme) in German philosophical thought beginning with Kant himself, the idea of a deduction which is prepared and a creation which occurs *in and by the unconscious* under the pretext of idealism." Delbos realized, Blondel insists, "... what the value of

chief means by which a people's spirit acquires renewed vigor, or a decayed political organism gives place to a more vigorous manifestation of the spirit. The implication is that the victor in any war is morally justified by reason of his victory.

Hegel defended his theory of the "cunning of reason" as being in accord with the Christian doctrine of divine providence; for Christianity holds that God is capable of bringing good out of evil. However, such a justification begs the question. Is the God in question transcendent in any way to the historical process, or is he totally identical with it? If God is totally immanent in that process, then no escape is left from the conclusion that from the world-historical viewpoint all the events and actions which factually form moments in the self-manifestation of the absolute are justified; and any moral judgment on these facts is ultimately unfounded.

According to Delbos, Hegel's model in the development of his moral theory was Spinoza. Hegel maintained that Spinoza's great contribution to morality was to have proven that "in God as such ... difference of any sort does not exist; it is only for man that difference exists and, in particular, the difference between good and evil."[1] Spinoza did not deny the distinction of good and evil such as it is produced by our consciousness; he only refused to acknowledge that the distinction had absolute value. The absolute distinction of good and evil, according to Hegel has its foundation in the traditional idea of the principle of contradiction as a law which determines the real. But this world of the understanding is not the real world. The understanding, which necessarily thinks according to the principle of contradiction, can only give rise to a morality of exclusion.

Hegel maintained that the true source of evil is that very property of an idea to differentiate itself negatively before it reconstitutes itself affirmatively. The human will is capable of good or evil in so far as it is in a state of differentiation. It is evil not because it traverses a mo-

___

German ideology was; if it was not responsible itself for the unleashing of the terrible struggle (the first world war), still it did not possess either the authority to prevent it, or the rectitude necessary to condemn it; and it managed to discover without difficulty all the sophisms capable of absolving it." Confer Delbos, "Les Facteurs Kantiens de la Philosophie Allemande du Commencement du XIX Siècle," edited by M. Blondel, *Revue Métaphysique et Morale*, Tome XXVI (Septembre, 1919) 569-593; Tome XXVII (Janvier, 1920) 1-25.

[1] "Im Gott als solchem, ... ist der Unterschied nicht, aber für den Menschen ist dieser Unterschied, auch der zwischen Gutem and Bösem." Hegel, "Vorlesungen über die Philosophie der Religion," Vol. XV, pp. 112-113. Confer also Delbos, *op. cit.*, pp. 436-440.

ment of negation, but because it pretends to fix itself and find the entire absolute there. This is true of every doctrine which makes personal conscience based on a morality of contradiction the sovereign judge of all morality. The morality of the individual consciousness (moralität) is only a preparation for the total concrete morality (Sittlichkeit); the truth of man is not so much in his intentions as in the objective order of his acts. Moral life achieves its completion beyond the order of subjective will and ideal obligation.[1]

If intellectual understanding can only give rise to an exclusive act of morality, then, Hegel argues, it is better to permit oneself to be determined by the immediate instinct to preserve one's being than by the partial concepts of the understanding. This thesis led Hegel to praise the role of passion. Passion is a desire limited to a particular state; but as desire it aspires to an ensemble of satisfactions and contains an aspiration to the universal within itself. In it all the energies of the spirit: character, talent, and sensibility, concentrate on an object to the exclusion of all others. Since nothing great is accomplished without passion, it is only an abstract, moribund morality which condemns it. On the contrary Hegel maintains, passion is the exclusive form of interest which the individual ought to bring to his actions in order that they be vigorous and efficacious. For passion thus succeeds in achieving the unity of the particular will with its essence which is the absolute idea.[2] If, on the one hand, man seems to act only in virtue of his interests; on the other, the work which is accomplished has an objective significance infinitely superior to its particular expression. "The highest liberty of man consists in the knowledge that he is absolutely determined by the absolute idea."[3]

According to Delbos, the essential defect in Hegel's system lies in the fact that Hegel places the unity between the infinite and the finite in an objective idea.[4] Hence there is a tendency throughout Hegel's philosophy to elevate above subjective life its objective determined expression. In fact he seems to maintain that the moment of subjectivity as such is produced only to stop the world from stagnating and in order to put it back into movement. Hegel believed that objective social morality completes and includes all that there is of truth and

---

[1] Delbos, *op. cit.*, pp. 463-464. Delbos' reference to Hegel's writings is to "Grundlinien der Philosophie des Rechts," Vol. VII, pp. 199-220.

[2] Delbos, *op. cit.*, pp. 453-454.

[3] *Ibid.*, p. 482.

[4] *Ibid.*, p. 560-561.

value in subjective personal morality. However, Delbos claims, between these two forms of morality there ought to be not a relation of defined subordination but a relation of incessant communication. The unity of the infinite and the finite, such as Hegel affirmed it, is in adequate to the absolute, because it is too exclusively conceived under the objective form of an idea.

Blondel accepted this criticism of Delbos and took as his objective the task of redefining that "relation of incessant communication" between objective and subjective morality. By identifying the absolute with the totality of becoming, Blondel maintained, Hegel had effectively identified the absolute with the system of relations which unite the individuals among themselves and with the spirit which thinks them. He did not, it is true, deny the individual uniquenses or existential reality of the individual as such. On the contrary he emphasized it; but only as a necessary foundation for the establishment of a real universal.

> According to Hegel, although the relations of things among themselves or with the spirit which thinks them are accidental and exterior to those things, yet it is these relations which in their systematic grouping constitute all the true and all the real; this universal relativity is the absolute itself.[1]

Hegel, in Blondel's estimation, tended to consider the individual as such merely as a necessary means for the coming-to-be of the self-conscious absolute spirit. Absolute spirit is the infinite spirit knowing itself as infinite. This infinite spirit exists in and through finite spirits; it does so not at every level, but only at that level at which the individual is no longer a finite mind enclosed in its own private reality but has become a moment in the life of the infinite, which is an identity-in-difference and knows itself as such. The absolute spirit is one with the finite spirit only at the level of absolute knowledge.

As we have seen, Blondel understood the dialectical process in the human spirit as necessarily determining man to pose the idea of the absolute, and necessarily leading him to conceive of his destiny as a union with that absolute. Hegel was right to see an infinite potential present in the human spirit, an infinite spirit which is not yet that which it is but which becomes. He was right to conceive of that spirit as evolving according to a dialectical law of identity-in-difference. He was wrong, however, to objectify that infinite potentiality in the

---

[1] Blondel, "L'Evolution du Spinozisme," II, 328.

human spirit as the absolute, and to consider its progressive unfolding as necessarily true and good. Even if the idea of union with the absolute is necessary, the option by which man effectively realizes what he necessarily conceives remains free. In Blondel's opinion, once Hegel placed the effective solution of man's destiny in the order of knowledge, he inevitably confused the necessity man is under to arrive at an idea of his destiny as a union with the absolute with a necessity to arrive at an effective union. Man's individual freedom had no decisive role to play in that process. However, once we realize that the necessary dialectic within the human spirit, although directed towards union with the absolute, is not identical with the absolute, then man's personal freedom enters into the picture once again. There is room in the necessary evolution of individuals, and of human societies for a "discernment of spirits." Man is *capax omnia*; but everything that man does is not necessarily true and good solely because it gives expression to his infinite capacity. True, there is an identity of contraries within the infinite capacity of the human will; but these contraries are not of equal value. One can distinguish ,so to speak, a positive and a negative pole. It is true that the principle of contradiction contained in purely formal reasoning in one sense falsely absolutizes what is in reality only partial and relative. But the formal principle of contradiction is only a symbol of a real power of contradiction or identity within the human spirit.

THE RELATION BETWEEN PHILOSOPHY AND RELIGION

In the year 1800, before he had begun to develop his philosophy of the dialectic, Hegel wrote a series of notes which are called *Fragments of a System* (System Fragment).[1] These notes deal with the problem of overcoming the opposition of the infinite and the finite. The problem Hegel posed was: Are we able by conceptual thought so to unify the infinite and the finite that neither term is dissolved in the other, while at the same time they are truly united?[2] We can see the necessity, Hegel maintained, for a synthesis in which unity does not exclude distinction, but we cannot really think it. Consequently Hegel came to the con-

---

[1] These notes were first published by Hermann Nohl in his work *Hegels theologische Jugendschriften* (Tübingen, 1907). References will be to the English translation of this work by T. M. Knox *Early Theological Writings* (Chicago: The University of Chicago Press, 1948).

[2] Hegel, "Fragments of a System," *Early Theological Writings*, p. 311.

clusion that the unification of the many with the one without the
former's dissolution can only be achieved by living it, that is, by man's
self-elevation from finitude to infinite life. This living process he identifies as religion.

The consequence of this is that philosophy stops short of religion;
philosophy shows us what is demanded if the opposition between
finite and infinite is to be overcome, but it cannot fulfill that demand.
We must turn to religion and, in particular, to the Christian religion
for that fulfillment. Christ discovered the infinite life within himself
as source of his thought and action. This is the right idea of the infinite.
The infinite is not a being set over above and outside the finite. Rather,
it is immanent in the finite and comprises the finite within itself. But
this synthesis can only be lived and not thought; it is the life of love.
The organ of mediation between the finite and the infinite is love, not
reflection.[1]

At first sight this theory of the young Hegel concerning the priority
of the lived religious experience over philosophical reflection seems
to be identical with Blondel's position that only lived experience and,
in particular, the lived religious experience, can effectively resolve the
problem of man's union with the absolute. There is the same idea of
discovering the infinite in oneself as source of thought and action, yet
as transcending the finite self. There is the same role assigned to
philosophy; to show us what is demanded if the opposition between
finite and infinite is to be overcome. Finally, there is the same appeal
to a concrete, vital religious act of love in order to effectively achieve
that union. However, a second and closer study of Hegel's position
in relation to Blondel's manifests a totally different spirit and ultimate
meaning behind the apparently similar appeal to living action.

First of all, the problem which Hegel initially posed is a problem
concerning conceptual thought; the failure of thought as such to be
able to conceive of a union between the absolute and man led Hegel
to appeal to living action. The obvious influence here would seem to
be that of Fichte. Hegel discovers, as did Fichte before him, that such
a union is "necessary but unthinkable."[2] Consequently, once again as
did Fichte before him, he makes an appeal to a living act of love in
order to achieve in reality what he found from the point of view of
theory was basically an irrational, if necessary, solution to the problem

---

[1] *Ibid.*, p. 313.
[2] Confer above, Chapter VIII; pp. 144-149.

of man's destiny. What Hegel seems to realize better than Fichte is that an appeal to love cannot be made on a purely theoretical or rational level, since no clear idea corresponds to that word. Rather, the idea as such of a union between the infinite and finite by means of love encloses the same contradiction as any other theoretical solution, and remains a purely verbal solution. Thus love in this context must be understood as a symbolic reference to a vital religious act which transcends in its reality any idea which one can have of it. In our earlier analysis of the relation between Fichte and Blondel we called attention to the fact that the impossibility of which Blondel speaks is not one of conceiving a possible solution but of effectively producing that solution by human forces alone. Although the position of Hegel is not absolutely clear on this point, he seems to imply that, even if man cannot conceive of a solution, he can effectively produce that solution by his own power of action. For that act of love which resolves the problem Hegel calls an act of "self-elevation."[1]

In the same work, *Fragments of a System*, Hegel tells us that, despite his apparent failure, the philosopher must try to conceive and understand what religious practice effectively does.[2] In other words Hegel will attempt by reflection to accomplish what he had previously declared to be impossible. This impossibility to conceive of a union of man with the absolute is traced to the apparent necessity man is under to think of that relation according to the laws of contradiction or identity. What is needed then, Hegel announces, is a new form of logic, a logic which is able to follow the movement of living action and does not leave opposite concepts in irremediable opposition. The implication is clear; religion is superior to philosophy only because of a lack of development in philosophy. Once philosophy has developed all its potentialities, then speculative philosophy will be the supreme truth.

Whatever may have been the implications of Hegel's early position on the relation between religion and philosophy, it is certain that his final position, subsequent to his development of the logic of the dialectic, represents a clear-cut contradiction with Blondel's position concerning the same problem. Hegel's philosophy of religion occurs within the dialectical development of his philosophy of absolute spirit. The spirit in this context is understood as rising above finitude and

---

[1] "This self-elevation of man ... from finite life to infinite life, is religion." Hegel, *op. cit.*, p. 311.

[2] *Ibid.*, p. 312.

knowing itself as being or totality. This dialectic of the absolute spirit comprises three parts: art, religion and philosophy. Hegel insists, however, that there is no question of a transition from one subject-matter to another; in each one of the three stages of the philosophy of absolute spirit we are dealing with "*the eternal truth*, God and nothing but God, and the unfolding (Explication) of God."[1] The distinction between these three steps has only to do with form or, more precisely, with three different ways of conceiving God. Art represents the knowledge which the absolute has of itself under its "sensuous semblance (Sheinen)."[2] Hegel agrees with Schelling that the aesthetic experience represents an objective sensible intuition of the unity of the infinite and the finite. He does not agree, however, that this intuition represents man's supreme act; rather, it is only the first degree. When the mind perceives that no material embodiment is adequate to the expression of the spirit, it passes from the sphere of art to that of religion.[3]

Religious consciousness represents an internal way of apprehending the absolute spirit, a transposition into subjective consciousness of that which art expresses exteriorly. It is essentially "an interior sentiment which encloses the idea of the absolute." Religion in general essentially involves the self-manifestation of the absolute in the form of *Vorstellung*, that is, as figurative or pictorial thought.[4] Religious consciousness differs from aesthetic consciousness in that it *thinks* the absolute. However, the thought involved is not the pure conceptual thought found in philosophy. It is thought hidden in imagery, a union of thought and imagination. Hegel gives as examples of this figurative thought the Christian doctrines such as creation, incarnation, or the trinity. It is a mistake, Hegel claims, to separate religion from knowledge; for religion is nothing other than the knowledge of God and of the relation of man with God. However, it expresses that knowledge in images which necessarily remain exterior to one another, and whose heterogeneous multiplicity only translate imperfectly the internal accord of reason. Religion represents the divine spirit knowing itself by means of the finite spirit.[5]

The transition from religion to philosophy represents, then, a pro-

---

[1] Hegel, "Vorlesungen über die Philosophie der Religion," Vol. XV, p. 37.

[2] *Ibid.*, "Vorlesungen über die Aesthetik," Vol. XII, p. 160.

[3] *Ibid.*, p. 151.

[4] *Ibid.*

[5] Hegel, "Vorlesungen über die Philosophie der Religion," Vol. XV, pp. 267-268.

gress towards a different and more perfect way of conceiving God; it is a change from *Vorstellung* to pure thought. This change involves the replacement of the form of contingency present in religious knowledge by that of strict logical sequence. Philosophy, Hegel maintains, has no other object but religion. Religion is the thought of God; philosophy is "the thought of that thought" which frees itself from all that is pure symbol, literary expression, or sensible sign. Pure philosophy, then, is to be understood as the perfect act by which the absolute knows itself.[1]

This final theory concerning the supremacy of philosophy over religion is based on the premise that the most perfect act of man, the act which resolves his destiny, is an act of knowledge. As long as philosophical knowledge was ruled by the law of contradiction it was incapable of rising up above the point of view of the finite mind. In that condition the figurative insights contained in Christian dogmas, since they imaginatively portrayed a liberation from the law of contradiction, represented superior knowledge to that contained in traditional metaphysics. But once the logic of the dialectic had been developed and philosophy had been freed from its subservience to finite reason and its limitations, philosophical knowledge became the most perfect form of knowledge, superior to religion.

Blondel obviously understood his philosophy of action not as a return to Hegel's early theory but as an advance beyond his final position concerning the relation between thought and act, philosophy and religion. Any criticism of a philosophical system, Blondel tells us, must satisfy perfectly the exigencies which Hegel himself formulated.

> Science cannot be judged except according to the very idea on which it is based; and any judgment which one can bring to bear on that idea will not be so much a judgment as a development and progress which become one with the object it judges. Thus the last philosophy in time, if it is a true philosophy, is the result of all the earlier ones; nothing is lost; all principles are preserved.[2]

Blondel applies this critical principle to his friend Delbos' treatment of the evolution of the moral problem from Spinoza to Hegel. As we have seen, he understood Delbos' criticism to be based at least implicitly on the insights of a philosophy of action. Blondel's conscious role was to try to explicitate that philosophy of action, which would

---

[1] *Ibid.*, Vol. XV, pp. 41-43,
[2] Blondel, *op. cit.*, p. 336. Blondel's citation of Hegel is from Vera's translation of Hegel's *Logic* Tome I, pp. 173-200.,

retain all the principles of Hegel's position, yet by—pass it by "judging it according to the very idea on which it was based."

Hegel attributed a superiority to dialectical philosophy over religion because he understood the dialectic as the law intrinsic to the absolute spirit, and, as such, exclusive of all contradiction. Blondel was inclined to accept Hegel's criticism of traditional metaphysics as an attempt to comprehend the man-God relation within a finite, rational and formal pattern of exclusion. This traditional metaphysics represented that first metaphysics within Blondel's analysis of the phenomenon of action, which he relegated to the position of a moment in the dialectical development of the human spirit. Consequently, Blondel saw in Hegel's dialectic a true insight into the law of phenomena, that is, into the law governing the human spirit as such in its process of becoming. The dialectic is the law of the infinite, not the positive infinite or absolute, but the negative or potential infinite contained within the human will. Once this distinction is granted, Blondel concedes Hegel's thesis that the dialectic within the human spirit as such necessarily leads man to posit the absolute as idea, and necessarily determines man to conceive of his destiny as lying in a union with the absolute.

However, because of his initial mistaken identification of the negative infinite within the human spirit and the positive infinite of the absolute, Hegel, in Blondel's judgment, misunderstood his speculative solution for a real solution, and man's necessary idea of the absolute and his union with the absolute as God's idea of himself in which knowledge and reality, essence and existence, are one. Blondel believed that another dialectic began precisely at the point where Hegel's dialectic ended. This necessary idea of the absolute leads necessarily to a free option for or against union with the absolute. Man can be God with God, or he can be God against God. At this point the dialectical logic, which is the law of man's spirit, is transformed into a living, free dialogue between man and God. The principles of contradiction and identity are removed from their exclusive, static application to the phenomenal sphere where they are false, but applied to the real sphere of being where they are the true law. Beyond the philosophy of the dialectic there is a religion of living action by means of which man truly becomes what he has truly thought.

Summary

Blondel considered the metaphysical doctrine contained in Schelling's and Hegel's philosophies as a continuation and logical evolution of the *Ethics* of Spinoza. Spinoza had implicitly introduced the anthropomorphic idea of becoming into the absolute. Fichte made the becoming of the absolute explicit. Schelling attributed the value of a primary truth to that becoming. Hegel, according to Blondel, maintained that it was the only truth; absolute being in his doctrine was identified with the relativity of becoming.

Since Spinoza had proposed to resolve the ethical problem of human destiny within the context of his metaphysics, in direct correlation with this evolution of metaphysical doctrine there was an evolution in moral doctrine. This evolution expressed itself in a progressive tendency to identify the true and the good with the necessary process of becoming of the absolute and to refuse any ultimate value to man's exercise of individual liberty.

In Blondel's opinion this tendency to objectify the good in terms of the necessary self-manifestation of the absolute showed itself in Schelling's philosophy of art, which represented a shift of interest away from the values of subjective moral life and action to objective artistic creation and aesthetic contemplation. It was developed further in Schelling's theory of necessary progress in history, and reached its logical completion in Hegel's theory of a subordination of individual morality to an a-personal system of social ethics.

With Hegel's moral doctrine, Blondel maintains, we have arrived at the exact contrary of the position of Spinoza; but contraries are always members of the same species. For Spinoza, the true and the good were the exclusive properties of a static absolute substance; for Hegel, the true and the good became the exclusive properties of a dynamic absolute becoming. What Blondel found missing in the entire process of evolution from Spinoza to Hegel was a clear idea of a third possibility, namely, that the true and the good represent the presence of the absolute within the relative itself, that moral value represents not a pure transcendence nor a pure immanence, but the immanence in human action of the transcendent. In a word, what Blondel found missing was in his judgment a true understanding of the metaphysical value and moral import of free, synthetic human action.

This new effort to substitute the *visio* of an objective, necessary process as an object of intellectual contemplation for a free, vital, subjective commitment of self was reflected in a particularly striking way in Hegel's final effort to subordinate religion to philosophy. Hegel understood the distinction between true and false, the good and the evil, as being the properties of reality only in so far as it is understood in a state of differentiation. By means of the dialectic man can by his own powers achieve a vision of the universe which transcends that state of differentiation. The intellectual element in religion is, in Hegel's opinion, an imaginary anticipation of that philosophical vision. In Blondel's judgment, Hegel had mistaken the necessity which governs the formation of that philosophical vision with the necessity of a free vital commitment of himself which man must make if he would participate in the subjective existential reality which that intellectual vision indicates. In order to pass from vision to life, from speculative objective understanding to subjective practical participation, one must commit oneself in a decisive option. Consequently, beyond the philosophical vision there is still need for vital religious activity.

CHAPTER FIFTEEN

THE INFLUENCE OF SCHELLING'S FINAL PHILOSOPHY

INTRODUCTION

The influence of German idealism on Blondel's thought did not end with Hegel. There was a further and, in certain respects, a decisive influence which can be traced to the final philosophy of Schelling. After Hegel's death in 1831 Schelling proposed a new philosophy which he called "positive" in contrast with his own previous work and that of Hegel. This positive philosophy of Schelling formed the subject matter of Delbos' latin thesis entitled *Concerning the Posterior Philosophy of Schelling in so far as it differs from Hegelian Doctrine.*[1] From their correspondence there is reason to believe that, when Delbos urged Blondel to make an addition to the manuscript copy of *Action* treating of the final role of metaphysics, he had in mind a final stage in Blondel's thought analogous to the final positive metaphysics of Schelling.[2] Consequently, it is not surprising to find several key ideas in Delbos' interpretation of Schelling's final philosophy reflected in Blondel's thought. However, once again these ideas have been assimilated into a totally different context with the end-result that the differences are even more original and instructive than are the analogies. But these differences can be best understood and appreciated in contrast with their source.

THE PROBLEM OF THE REALITY OF EVIL

In his Latin thesis Delbos traced the origins of Schelling's final or positive philosophy back to his theory concerning the reality of evil which occurred in his work of 1809, *Philosophical Inquiries into the Nature*

---

[1] Delbos, *De Posteriore Schellingii Philosophia Quatenus Hegelianae Doctrinae Adversatur*, (Paris: Félix Alcan, 1902).
[2] Confer Blondel's letter to Delbos dated the 1st of October, 1894, *Lettres Philosophiques*, pp. 67-70. The letters from Delbos urging Blondel to add a last chapter concerning the role of metaphysics are published in the *Archives de Philosophie*, Tome XXIV, Chapter I (Janvier-Mars, 1961), 59-63.

of Human Freedom.[1] The central problem of all Schelling's philosophical inquiry had to do with the relation between the infinite and the finite. Beginning as he did with the principle of absolute identity the problem became more specifically the problem of the existence of the world of finite things. As we have seen, Schelling's system of identity implied that the universe must be considered as the actualization of the absolute. He also asserted, however, that the distinction between potency and act falls outside the absolute itself. Consequently, he was obliged to search for a more satisfactory account of the relation between the infinite and the finite. Schelling seems to have had a much keener sensitivity to the reality of evil in the finite world than did Hegel. In the course of time his problem centered more and more on the question of the possibility and the reality of evil. Within the context of a system of identity how can man be really free and capable of evil, if the absolute is totality? If one grants a real possibility of evil, must it not have a ground in the absolute itself?

While he was considering this problem Schelling read the works of Jakob Boehme.[2] Boehme attributed the origin of the world to a falling-away (Abbrechen, Sprung) from God. Thus in his work of 1804, *Philosophy and Religion*, we find Schelling seeking an explanation of the possibility of evil in terms of this cosmic fall.[3] Since there is no continuous transition from the absolute to the world, the cosmic fall cannot be explained. "The origin of the world must be ascribed to freedom."[4]

This appeal to freedom created a new problem for Schelling. If it is true that the "ground of possibility" for a cosmic fall lies in freedom, where is it one can locate this freedom? It cannot be a freedom exercised by the world or, rather, man in the world, since the existence of

---

[1] Delbos, *op. cit.*, pp. 11-12. Delbos' analysis of Schelling's treatment of the problem of evil occurs in his *Le Problème Moral dans la Philosophie de Spinoza*, pp. 416-435. This particular work of Schelling appears to have been the object of a special study of Blondel. We have already noted the use Blondel made of Schelling's criticism of Spinoza's *Ethics*. Confer Part I, Chapter II, prge 45, footnote 2.

[2] Delbos, *Le Problème Moral dans la Philosophie de Spinoza*, p. 148. In discussing the influence of Boehme on Schelling Delbos calls attention in a footnote to a study on Boehme by Boutroux, *Le Philosophe allemand Jakob Boehme* (Compte-rendu de l'Académie des Sciences Morales et Politiques, 1888). It is not surprising, then, to find Blondel studying "the theological writings of Boehme" in 1890, at the same time that he undertook his study of Schelling. (Confer *Lettres Philosophiques*, p. 20).

[3] *Schelling* "Philosophie und Religion," Vol. IV, p. 28.

[4] *Ibid.*, p. 30.

the world depends on it; and if one appeals to a free creative act of God or the Word, how can one describe the origin of the world as a fall? Or to pose the problem in another way, if there is a real possibility of evil must it not have its ultimate foundation in the absolute itself? This is the problem which Schelling attempted to answer in his *Philosophical Inquiry into the Nature of Human Freedom*. In attempting to solve this problem Schelling introduces the concept of the relation which exists between antecedent and consequence. God is *causa sui*; but God as cause has a distinct but inseparable reality from God as effect. Since God must be understood as a self-revealing life, the manifestation which God makes of himself must be understood as remaining immanent in God, yet distinguishable from him, just as a consequence is immanent in its antecedent but is not identical with it. Both God and man are free, Schelling tells us and he also maintains: "The real and living concept (of freedom) is that it is a power of good and evil."[1]

Schelling was aware that in granting that this power is present in man, the consequence, it would seem to follow that it is also present in God, the antecedent. In order to answer this problem Schelling began to develop a philosophy of will and a theory of potencies. "In the last analysis," Schelling claims, "there is no other being but Will. The will is primitive being; and all the attributes of being belong to it."[2] Consequently, Schelling undertakes an analysis of the structure of the human will. The perfect act of freedom, Schelling claims, is the highest perfection of the will and constitutes man as a person. But human freedom and personality is not something which is given, but must be won. "All birth is birth out of darkness into light."[3] In man there is a dark foundation, the unconscious life of natural impulse, on which personality is built. Man is free to follow his natural impulses; he can affirm himself as a particular finite being to the exclusion of the moral law. Or man can subordinate selfish desire or impulse to the rational will and develop a true human personality.

Delbos understood Schelling as holding that the two will-principles in man were directly attached to their corresponding principles in God.

---

[1] "Der reale und lebendige Begriff aber ist, dass sie (die Freiheit) ein Vermögen des Guten und des Bösen sey." Schelling, "Philosophische Untersuchungen über das Wesen der menschlichen Freiheit" (1809), Vol. IV, p. 244.

[2] "Es gibt in der letzten und höchsten Instanz gar kein anderes Seyn als Wollen. Wollen ist urseyn, und auf dieses allein passen alle Prädicate desselben..." Schelling, *op. cit.*, Vol. IV, p. 242.

[3] *Ibid.*, p. 252.

"The natural principle, by which a being reattaches itself to the un-conscious cause in God, is the blind desire to be for oneself. The divine principle, by which a being reattaches itself to the perfection of God, is the rational will."[1] Thus we can also distinguish in God a natural and a divine principle. The natural principle in God is the ground of his personal existence, which is itself impersonal. This ground is the will understood as an unconscious desire or yearning for personal existence. Delbos describes it as a "blind power of an un-conscious will to be."[2] This unconscious will Schelling calls "the egoism of God."[3] The divine principle in God is the conscious, rational will; this will is the will of love, a self-communicating, expansive will.

This theory of a double principle within the absolute will permitted Schelling to develop a theory in which he could find a foundation for the possibility of evil in the absolute without at the same time being obliged to attribute actual evil to God. He was obliged in the process, however, to enlarge his original theory of identity. The *Urgrund* or *Urkraft* of the divine being, the natural principle of will, is a pure un-conscious identity. However, this absolute undifferentiated identity does not exist as such. "A division or difference must be posited; that is if we wish to pass from essence to existence."[4] Consequently, Schelling understood the possibility of a philosophy of freedom based on the absolute as personal being as necessarily involving this theory of a double principle in the divine will.

Although the foundation of the possibility of evil is to be found in the double principle of the divine will, God cannot do evil. The divine conquest of personality is not a temporal affair. In God "both acts are one act; and both are absolutely simultaneous."[5] In all external mani-festations, however, the two principles are and must be separable.

> If the identity of the two principles were as indissoluble in the human spirit as in God, there would be no distinction; that is to say, God would not manifest himself. Therefore, the unity, which is indissoluble in God, must be dissolved in man. And this is the possibility of good and evil.[6]

---

[1] Delbos, *op. cit.*, p. 425.

[2] *Ibid.*, p. 424.

[3] Schelling, "Stuttgarter Privatvorlesungen" (1810), Vol. IV, p. 330.

[4] *Ibid.*, p. 331. "... eine Trennung, eine Differenz gesetzt werden muss, wenn wir nämlich vom Wesen zur Existenz kommen wollen." *Ibid.*, p. 316.

[5] *Ibid.*, p. 326.

[6] Schelling "Philosophische Untersuchungen über das Wesen der menschlichen Freiheit," Vol. IV, p. 256.

Despite his insistence on the reality of man's freedom Schelling was equally anxious to preserve a necessary pattern for the progressive revelation of the divine spirit in history. Thus he proposed a theory of determinism in human action. He found the determining ground for man's successive choices in his "moral character," or "intellectual essence." Man's free acts stand to his character in a relation analogous to consequent and ground or antecedent. However, although this character or essence predetermines acts, it does not destroy freedom, because it itself is due to an original self-positing of the ego as a result of an original choice of the ego itself.[1] Thus a man's actions in principle are both predictable and they are free. The necessity is an inner necessity imposed by the ego's own choice and not a necessity externally imposed by God. "This inner necessity is itself freedom; the essence of man is essentially *his own act*. Necessity and freedom are mutually immanent as one reality, which appears as one or the other only when looked at from different sides."[2]

What is of particular interest to us here in relation to Blondel is Schelling's analysis of the structure of the human will. Blondel was aware of this theory of Schelling, both from his own reading of Schelling and from his study of Delbos' book. Once we eliminate the idealist and monist metaphysical context in which this theory of the will was elaborated and consider it as a phenomenological analysis of the structure of the human will as such, we find a theory remarkably identical to that which we find in Blondel's thought. The resemblance is even closer when we consider the presentation Delbos made of Schelling's later development of this theory in his work of 1858, *The Philosophy of Revelation*. According to Schelling, Delbos claims, the primary task of philosophy is to define what is before being itself comes to be. That is nothing other than the will considered as an infinite potentiality for existence.

> This potency must be considered κατ'ἐξοχήν. Thus whatever exists is a participation of will, which is itself the ground of all reality. ... We must not forget, however, that this type of being, even when complete, is not full or integral being. Rather, there is a certain στέρησις in it.[3]

---

[1] *Ibid.*, pp. 277-281.
[2] *Ibid.*, p. 277.
[3] "Porro hanc infinitam existendi potentiam nihil melius repraesentat quam voluntas; quae ita concepta potentia est κατ'ἐξοχήν. Inde fit, ut quidquid existit voluntatis sit particeps. ... Sed ne nos fugiat illud entis ita finitum genus non id esse quod plenum sit et integram; nempe in eo inest στέρησις quaedam." Delbos,

The exact opposite of this pure potency is pure act, that which lacks any potentiality whatsoever. Whereas the pure potency represents pure possibility; pure act represents certain and absolute necessity. Schelling names the will in a state of pure potency "the willing" (der Wille); whereas the will in a state of pure act is called "the willed" (das Wollen).[1] Both pure potency and pure act must be considered not as being, but as aspects of being. The most important problem, Schelling maintains, is to understand what is the *Verknüpfung* or *Copula*, the third element which represents the unity of the first two.[2] This *Vinculum* is precisely that living process of becoming, that spirit or activity which Fichte designated as the "ego."[3] The ego at every moment of its becoming is a synthesis of act and potency. But this potency must be considered as a privation of act and not non-being.[4] The world of thought or ideas is a projection outward by the will-spirit of its unfulfilled potentiality as an object of action or choice.[5] As such the world of ideas represents the world of essences, the world of *Wass*, which can be best defined as "that which becomes being."[6]

These few indications of the many striking parallels between the thought in Blondel's *Action* and Schelling's philosophy of freedom would seem to indicate that perhaps the closest and most direct historical influence on Blondel's thought, especially as concerns his theory of will, is to be found in Schelling's thought, especially as it developed

---

De Posteriori Schellingii Philosophia, pp. 14-15. Delbos refers the reader to Schelling's "Philosophie der Offenbarung," Vol. VI (Ergänzungsband), pp. 204-217. It is to be noted that the same key Greek words are employed here by Delbos, and can be found in the references he gives to Schelling's works on mythology and revelation which, as we have seen, Blondel employed in the description of his real dialectic of the human will. Confer above, Chapter VIII, p. 231.

[1] The text which Delbos evidently has in mind is the following: "Nun kennen wir keinen andern Uebergang *a potentia ad actum* als im Wollen. Der Wolle an sich ist die Potenz κατ'ἐξοχήν, das Wollen der Actus κατ'ἐξοχήν. Der Uebergang *a potentia ad actum* ist überal nur Uebergang vom nicht-wollen zum Wollen. *Ibid.*, pp. 205-206.

[2] *Ibid.*, p. 217. Delbos translates the word *Verknüpfung* or *Copula* as *Vinculum*, *op. cit.*, p. 16.

[3] *Ibid.*, Delbos' reference here is to Schelling's "Einleitung in die Philosophie der Mythologie," Vol. V, pp. 644-648.

[4] Schelling, *op. cit.*, Vol. V, pp. 592-593. Schelling also attributes the origin of all distinctions, especially the distinction between subject and object, to the will-activity. Confer Vol. VI (E), p. 206, We find in this context the same criticism as Blondel's of Parmenides' formulation of the idea of contradiction. Confer Schelling, *Ibid.*, pp. 223-224.

[5] *Ibid.*, pp. 216-217.

[6] "Das, was sein wird, ist also der Begriff *par excellence*." *Ibid.*

in his final philosophy. For here we find the same idea of the will-act as a composite being, and practically the same identification of the elements of that composition as will-willing and will-willed. Further we find the same concept of the real dialectic of will as an infinite potency which at every moment of its development is a dynamic synthesis of actuality and privation. We find the same role assigned to thought as the product of past will-activity and the source of new will-activity. We find, finally, the idea of the ultimate identity of freedom and necessity in terms of an intrinsic essence within the will itself, which man freely ratifies.[1]

Even if, however, Schelling's theory of will resembles closely many fundamental features of Blondel's thought, yet it is evident that we are dealing with two totally different concepts of philosophy. Schelling's doctrine remains an absolute monism. Beginning with the assumption that man as "consequence" is an immediate revelation of the absolute, Schelling applies all the factors of his analysis of the human will directly to the absolute will. In Blondel's words he constructs God with the human. This a priori refusal to grant man any true reality apart from the absolute explains the ultimate ambiguity in Schelling's theory of liberty and the reality of evil. Once he had traced the real cause of evil to human freedom as such, Schelling equivalently denied the reality of the effect by denying the reality of the cause. For his theory that the reality of human freedom can be assigned to an unconscious, original self-positing, and that all consequent conscious actions are determined by that unconscious choice, would seem to be an ultimately meaningless doctrine. Freedom, Blondel maintains, is the synthesis of the power of the infinite contained in the will with the *conscious* awareness of that infinite power contained in the intellect. Schelling's refusal to grant conscious freedom of choice to the human will was probably determined by his a priori monism. Man in his philosophy remains the locus of a progressive manifestation of the absolute. Consequently, Blondel could find no equivalent in Schelling's philosophy for what he called the real function of the principle of contradiction. Within Schelling's theory of will there is no ground for an absolute judgment within the relative itself.

This theory of will, which Schelling developed in his treatment of the problem of evil, served as a basis for the distinction he made in

---

[1] Confer above pp. 86-93 for Blondel's theory concerning the relation of necessity and liberty in terms of an intrinsic essence or determination within man's will.

his final philosophy between a negative and positive philosophy, and for his effort to by—pass Hegelianism by means of a positive philosophy of existence. This positive philosophy of Schelling represents the final stage of that evolution of philosophical thought which Blondel acknowledges as the historical background of his philosophy of action.

Negative and Positive Philosophy

All philosophy, Schelling maintains, is concerned with the first principle of reality. Negative philosophy, with Hegel's doctrine as its supreme example, discovers this principle only as a supreme essence or absolute idea.[1] But from an essence we can deduce only other essences, from the idea only other ideas. From a what (Was) we cannot deduce a that (Dass). In other words negative philosophy is incapable of explaining the existent world precisely as existing. But the fundamental problem which philosophy must answer, Schelling tells us, is: Why is there something, rather than nothing? Negative philosophy is incapable of responding to that problem; it is obliged by its method to presuppose the existence of the world as an hypothesis, and to rest content with the deduction of what things must be, if they exist. "*If* it exists, it can exist only in this way and only as such and such."[2] This is especially true, Schelling claims, of the Hegelian system which by-passes the order of existence.

Positive philosophy does not start simply with the absolute as idea, as a what or essence, but with the absolute "as a pure That" (als reines Dass), that is, as a pure act or being in an existential sense.[3] And from this supreme existential act it passes to the concept or nature of God, showing that he is not an impersonal idea or essence but a creative personal Being. Positive philosophy, then, represents a complete reversal of the method of procedure in negative philosophy.

But how do we make the transition from negative to positive philosophy? The transition cannot be made merely by thinking because conceptual thought by its very nature is concerned only with essences

---

[1] For a brief, clear presentation of Schelling's distinction between negative and positive philosophy confer Copleston, *op. cit.*, Vol. VII, pp. 135-138.

[2] "Sie (Negative Philosophie) sagt nicht: das aussergöttliche Seyn existirt, sondern: *nur so ist es möglich*, wo also immer stillschweigend das Hypothetische zu Grunde liegt: *wenn es* existiert, so wird es nur auf diese Weise, und nur ein solches oder solches." Schelling, "Einleitung in die Philosophie der Mythologie," Vol. V, p. 558.

[3] *Ibid.*, p. 746.

and logical deductions. Hence we must have recourse to the will, "a will which demands with inner necessity that God should not be a mere idea."[1] The initial affirmation of the divine existence is based on an act of faith demanded by the will. The ego becomes conscious of its fallen condition, of its state of alienation; and it is aware that this alienation can be overcome only by God's activity. It demands, therefore, that God should be not simply an ideal but an existing personal God, through whom man can be redeemed. Consequently, this faith is not in Fichte's ideal moral order; what the will demands is not a pure becoming, a doing, but a personal, creative God, a Doer (Thätiger). Nor is it a faith in Hegel's absolute idea; Hegel's primary error, Schelling judges, was to have believed in "the autorealization of Reason." Nor are we dealing with Kant's theory of practical or moral faith. Kant's affirmation of God on faith was, in Schelling's judgment, simply a postulate and, as it were, an instrument for synthesizing virtue and happiness. The truly religious man is aware of his profound need of God, and he is brought by this consciousness to a personal Deity. "For the person seeks a person."[2] The ego, Schelling claims, "demands God himself. *Him, Him,* will it have, the God who acts, who exercises providence, who as being himself real can meet the reality of the fall... In this God alone does the ego see the *real* supreme good."[3]

This transition from negative to positive philosophy is accomplished by what Schelling calls an "ecstasy of reason." Reason having exhausted its resources arrives at the "*Gott am Ende,*" that is, God as a pure object of thought or pure possibility. Thus reason is forced to realize that it is not its own foundation; it becomes aware of the finite character of its own self-determination. Thus it is obliged to forego the immediate will to capture the absolute within itself; it must convert itself from an "absolute will to a will of the absolute." "Reason can only locate Being outside itself ... Thus reason itself is transposed outside of itself as absolute ecstasy."[4] Schelling's description of this "death of Reason to itself" recalls many features of Fichte's description of the transition from reason to faith.[5] This going out of itself must

---

[1] "Ein Wille, der mit innern Nothwendigkeit verlangt, dass Gott nicht blosse Idee sey." *Ibid.*, p. 747.

[2] *Ibid.*, p. 748.

[3] *Ibid.*

[4] "Die Vernunft kann das Seyende ... nur als *Ausser-sich* setzen. ... Die Vernunft ist daher in diesem Setzen ausser sich gesetzt, absolut ekstatisch." Schelling, "Philosophie der Offenbarung," Vol. VI (E), pp. 162-163.

[5] Confer above, Chapter IX, pp. 161-165.

also represent a rejection of the idea of God within pure reason. "He who wishes to place himself at the point of departure of this truthful and free philosophy must also abandon his idea of God."[1] Consequently, reason realizes that all its constructions, even its idea of God, are merely hypothetical. It has attempted to construct the real with the possible. But such an attempt necessarily ends in an impasse; for there is no passage from the absolute considered as a non-existing essence to the existence of a real God from within reason itself. Thus reason dissociates the pure activity of the will from itself, and we have as a result an inversion of correlatives; reason understands itself not as containing but as the contained.

The major difficulty in the interpretation of Schelling's final philosophy has to do with understanding exactly what he understood as the relation of negative and positive philosophy. Evidently he did not intend that negative philosophy should be simply rejected. Rather, it would seem that the question is one of emphasis and priority. Therefore, Schelling tells us, "we must assert the connection, yes the unity, between the two."[2] As X. Tilliette points out there are at present two major schools of interpretation concerning this relation.[3] The central question of this controversy has to do with whether Schelling's final philosophy should be understood either as a rejection of idealism and the acceptance of a new type of realism, or as a further development of idealist thought. In the realist interpretation Schelling is understood to have asserted the primacy of being over thought, and of existence over ideas, while retaining the dialectic.[4] However, as the title of his book implies, *The Fulfillment of German Idealism in Schelling's Late Philosophy*, Walter Schulz accepts almost a contradictory interpretation.[5] Schelling's point of departure in his final philosophy, according to

---

[1] Schelling, "Erlanger Vorträge," Vol. V, p. 217.

[2] *Ibid.*, "Einleitung in die Philosophie der Mythologie," Vol. V, p. 746.

[3] X. Tilliette, "Une nouvelle interprétation de Schelling," *Archives de Philosophie*, Tome XXI, Cahier III, (Juillet-Septembre, 1958), 423-456; Cahier IV (Octobre-Décembre, 1958), 564-599.

[4] One of the primary proponents of the realist hypothesis is Horst Fuhrmans in his work, *Schellings letzte Philosophie: Die negative und positive Philosophie im Einsatz die Spätidealismus* (Berlin: Junker und Dünnkaupt Verlag, 1940). Fuhrmans somewhat corrected his earlier judgment in his more recent book, *Schellings Philosophie der Weltalter* (Düsseldorf: L. Schwann Verlag, 1954). Here Fuhrmans sees the final philosophy of Schelling in its deepest essence as a penetrating effort, united to idealism, to arrive at a new theism by means of the *Potenzlehre*.

[5] Walter Schulz, *Die Vollendung des Deutschen Idealismus in der Spätphilosophie Schellings*, (Stuttgart: W. Kohlhammer Verlag, 1955).

Schulz, was not in reality but in reason. The existing personal God, which Schelling postulates as the point of departure, does not represent so much an existential truth of faith as a necessity of reason resulting precisely from the previous construction of the potencies. Consequently, this late philosophy is in reality the completion of the basic inspiration of all idealism, which was to transcend and contain being within thought.[1] Schelling's effort was directed towards maintaining God immanent in reason, while at the same time erecting him as transcendent person. Schulz calls attention especially to the texts where, speaking of the ecstasy of reason, Schelling remarks that if reason places God outside itself, it does so, "it must be granted, only so that afterwards, a posteriori, it can win him back again as its content and thus return again within itself."[2] Or again Schelling speaks of reason as affirming the transcendent "in order that it can be transposed into absolute immanence."[3] This divergence of interpretation will be important, as we shall see, in the interpretation of the relation of religion and philosophy in Schelling's thought.

Corresponding to Schelling's new point of departure, he proposed a new method. Since positive philosophy has as its object the free acts of a personal existential absolute, its method, Schelling tells us, must be experimental and, in a sense, empirical. Empirical, here, does not have its usual pejorative meaning. It is not a question of ascertaining sensible facts. Rather, what we are dealing with is a "metaphysical empiricism." It is an empiricism of freedom. "For a free act is always something more than what can be grasped by pure thought."[4] Existence itself is the a priori ground (tragender Grund) of all reasoning; and all the a priori of reason suppose existence as an all-embracing and dominating a priori. Positive philosophy begins by removing the hypothesis of existence. This starting point reflects itself in method by use of an "experimental or a posteriori method." A posteriori, Schelling tells us, "in this context signifies by means of the posterior (per posterius), through (durch) its consequence the Prius can be known."[5]

---

[1] Tilliette, op. cit., p. 456.

[2] "... freilich nur, um es hinternach, a posteriori, wieder als ihren Inhalt zu gewinnen, und so zugleich selbst in sich zurückzukehren. ..." Schelling, "Philosophie der Offenbarung," Vol. VI (E), p. 163. Confer Schulz, op. cit., pp. 62-67.

[3] "Sie setzt das Transzendente, um es in das absolute Immanente zu verwandeln." Schelling, op. cit., p. 170.

[4] Ibid., p. 114.

[5] "A posteriori heisst hier per posterius, durch seine Folge wird das Prius erkannt." Ibid., p. 129.

Schelling illustrates what he means in terms of an empirical study of free human actions. "Nobody knows what is in a man, unless he gives outward expression to himself. His intellectual and moral character are knowable only a posteriori, that is, only through this self-expression and activity."[1] Although he seems to be suggesting an a posteriori study of man's activity Schelling makes it quite clear, however, that this a posteriori study applies only to the free actions of the absolute as such. Man, as belonging to the world, is capable of being understood, in so far as that is of interest to a philosopher, a priori. "In regard to the world positive philosophy is a priori science, yet a science derived from an absolute *Prius*; in regard to God, however, it is an a posteriori science and knowledge."[2] Within Schelling's system there is no need to apply an a posteriori method to the study of man's actions because, as we have seen, despite man's freedom his actions are necessary.

SCHELLING'S PHILOSOPHY OF RELIGION

Positive philosophy is, in Schelling's estimation, a philosophy which can assimilate the religious consciousness of man and its demands.

> The longing for the real God and for redemption through him is, as you see, nothing else but the expression of the need of religion ... Without an active God ... there can be no religion, for religion presupposes an actual, real relationship of man to God. ... At the end of negative philosophy I have only possible and not actual religion, religion only "within the limits of bare reason". ... It is with the transition to positive philosophy that we first enter the sphere of religion.[3]

This transition within philosophy to the study of real religion implies, as we have seen, first of all an act of faith in a real, personal God capable of free action. Schelling's philosophy of revelation is an application of his a posteriori or empirical method as a proof for the rationality of that initial act of faith. The demand of religious consciousness is for a God who reveals himself and accomplishes man's redemption. The proof takes the form of showing the historical development of

---

[1] "Denn niemand weiss, was in einem Menschen ist, er äussere sich denn, seinem intellektuellen und moralischen Charakter nach ist er nur *a posteriori*, nämlich durch seine ausserungen und Handlungen erkennbar." *Ibid.*, p. 129. Delbos calls attention to this text at two points in his latin thesis. Confer *op. cit.*, p. 47 and p. 58.

[2] Schelling, *op. cit.*, p. 130.

[3] Schelling, "Einleitung in die Philosophie der Mythologie," Vol. V, p. 750,

religious consciousness —the history of man's demand for God and God's answer to that demand. "Positive philosophy is historical philosophy."[1] Schelling explicitly rejects a study based on individual self-consciousness; only in the objective history of mankind as such can we find the evidence of this progressive revelation of God.[2] Consequently, Schelling develops a philosophy of mythology and revelation as an attempt to exhibit God's progressive self-revelation to man and the progressive work of divine redemption.

But Schelling insists that he is not abandoning his earlier negative philosophy. In his work of 1841, *Another Deduction of the Principles of Positive Philosophy*, he begins with a rational deduction of the moments or phases of God's inner life. Thus he retains the general scheme of his earlier religious philosophy. In Copleston's judgment he never really freed himself from the idealist tendency to interpret the relation of God and the world as a relation of ground or antecedent to consequent.[3] He obviously presupposes that the necessary nature of absolute being will be progressively revealed, and that in his theory of will he already possessed the metaphysical scheme of that revelation. His philosophy of religion is empirical in the sense that its matter is provided by the actual history of religion as known through empirical investigation. However, the framework of interpretation is provided by the supposedly necessary deductions of metaphysics.

The problem Schelling poses in his philosophy of religion is: How can we think the passage outside itself of an absolute subject? Or to rephrase the problem: How can we think creation? This first part of his philosophy of religion Schelling calls a "Mitwissenschaft mit der Schöpfung," a co-comprehension with the creative act itself. Schulz interprets this first stage of Schelling's philosophy of religion as "reason following the pure movement of thought as the essential constructing of being (Wesenkonstruktion des Seienden), while God as absolute represents the possibility of that development transcendent to reason."[4]

This first stage or reconstruction of God's creative act is followed by a study of myths. The development of mythological religion in history is understood as an unconscious and necessary process corresponding to the dark or lower principle in the divine will. "In mythological religion we have blind (because produced by a necessary

---

[1] *Ibid.*, p. 753.
[2] *Ibid.*
[3] Copleston, *op. cit.*, Vol. VII, pp. 138-139.
[4] Schulz, *op. cit.*, p. 143.

process) *unfree* and *unspiritual* religion."[1] Revelation, on the other hand, represents "something which exists only as a result of an absolutely free will."[2] The concept of revelation thus presupposes an act whereby God "freely gives or has given himself to mankind."[3] Hence the manifestation of God in time corresponds to the moments of the timeless theogony in God.

The final stage in this process, according to Schelling, is that of reason understanding both mythology and revelation. This is the stage of positive philosophy. However, this final stage must be understood not, as in Hegel's system, as a rationalist interpretation of religion from outside, but as an activity of religious consciousness whereby it understands itself from within. This will be "the *free* religion, the religion of spirit, which, although its nature can only be sought and found by means of freedom, can reach its full development only as philosophy." This philosophy of religion presupposes Christianity and will be a synthesis of philosophy and religion. "Philosophical religion is, therefore, *historically* mediated through revealed religion."[4] Hence it cannot be simply identified with Christian belief and life as facts. These facts serve as the subject matter for free reflective understanding. This philosophical religion is free because it is based on understanding and not on the simple acceptance of revelation on authority. "The free religion is only *mediated* through Christianity; it is not immediately posited by it."[5]

BLONDEL'S PHILOSOPHY OF RELIGION

The major acquisition for philosophy resulting from the evolution of modern thought, Blondel claimed in his *Letter of 1896*, was the realization that both subjective religious consciousness and objective historical religion can and, in some way, should be included within the legitimate domain of philosophical analysis and investigation.[6]

---

[1] *Ibid.*, Vol. V, p. 437.

[2] *Ibid.*, "Philosophie der Offenbarung," Vol. VI, p. 396.

[3] *Ibid.*, p. 345. This free revelation of God was historically mediated in Schelling's opinion by Christ. However, man's assimilation of that revelation follows a new dialectical pattern: a petrine period of law and authority, a pauline period of freedom represented by the protestant revolt, and a final johannine period of synthesis which had yet to be achieved.

[4] *Ibid.*, "Einleitung in die Philosophie der Mythologie," Vol. V, p. 437.

[5] *Ibid.*, p. 440.

[6] Confer above Chapter I, pp. 10-15.

There is a rightful place for a philosophy of religion which will not be a substitution of philosophy for religion.

> A slow and laborious evolution of thought was necessary in order to disengage the true perspective, to give birth to the only method which permits the erection of an integral philosophy within the context of an integral Christianity.[1]

The final and decisive step in that evolution, which led to a philosophy of action, can be traced primarily to Schelling's concept of positive philosophy as a philosophy capable of assimilating the religious consciousness of man and its demands. As we have seen, Schelling was led to affirm the existence of a personal God capable of free initiative by reason of the need inherent in man's will for such a God. This postulate opened the way for an a posteriori search in history for that free revelation God makes of himself in the evolution of religious consciousness. The a priori scheme of that philosophy of revelation is to be found in Schelling's previously metaphysical reconstruction of the absolute will.

Blondel also claims that there is a valid sense in which revelation belongs within the domain of philosophy. The idea of a possible divine revelation is a necessary, spontaneous idea which has its a priori source in the human will. "The role of philosophy is to follow out to its term the will of man by continually searching within human action what is truly in conformity with its primitive aspiration."[2] As we have seen, Blondel traced the determinism within the human will to pose the necessary idea of God as a person who is both immanent in and transcendent to man's will-activity, and the consequent necessity to place an option for or against a union of wills with God. However, the problem remains: by what concrete action can that union of wills between man and God, which is man's end, be accomplished? This is the problem which Blondel poses in the subsequent fifth part of his analysis of the phenomenon of action, after he had dealt with the necessity of option. "The human will senses the irremediable insufficiency of its act, as well as the invincible need of fulfilling it. And, since the act cannot be completed unless God give himself to us, how substitute in some way his action for ours?"[3]

In dealing with this problem, Blondel claims, there is a legitimate

---

[1] Blondel, *Lettre* (1896), p. 92.
[2] *Ibid., L'Action*, p. 393.
[3] *Ibid.*, p. 395.

use the philosopher can make of revealed religion. He can undertake to search in history for the a posteriori evidence of a divine revelation and accept the evidence of such a revelation as an hypothesis; not, as did Schelling, in order to confirm a rational reconstruction of the absolute will, but as revelatory of the need intrinsic in the human will and the necessary means of its fulfillment.

> It would not be legitimate to pretend to discover by reason alone what must be revealed in order to be known. But it is legitimate to continue to push on in our search up to the point where we realize we ought to desire intimately something analogous to that which from without the dogmas propose to us. It is legitimate to consider these dogmas not indeed at first as revealed but as revealing (révélateurs): that is to say, to confront them with the profound exigencies of the will and to discover, if it is to be found there, the image of our real needs and the answer we attend. It is legitimate to accept them as hypotheses as do those geometricians who suppose that a problem is resolved and then verify the fictional solution by means of an analysis.[1]

The problem, as Blondel poses it initially, is to understand how the idea itself of a possible revelation is necessarily engendered in man; and how that possible revelation seems necessary for the human will in order that man's action can reach its fulfillment in consciousness. There is no question of trying to determine the content itself of revelation: "In its principle, its object and its end, revelation, in order to be what it ought to be, must escape reason; and no effort of man precisely as man can penetrate its essence."[2]

The first step in Blondel's philosophy of revelation is a genetic study of the idea of a possible revelation. There is, he argues, an intrinsic contradiction in the very idea of a purely exterior revelation without any a priori foundation in human will-activity whatsoever. "If it is necessary to consider revelation itself as something which arrives completely from without as an entirely empirical given, then the very idea itself of a revealed dogma or precept would be totally unintelligible."[3] For by hypothesis and by definition, Blondel argues, revelation does not make use of sensible or natural intermediaries except as a vehicle for the supernatural. However, the sole means we have to judge the meaning and value of purely external empirical facts are our senses and the objective sciences; and a priori our senses and the

---

[1] *Ibid.*, p. 391.
[2] *Ibid.*, pp. 406-407.
[3] *Ibid.*, p. 394.

objective sciences are totally incompetent in relation to the supernatural.

> Whether supernatural in their principle or not ... it is scarcely in the
> sensible signs themselves that we ought to place the origin of our idea
> (of a possible revelation). It is by the development of practical activity
> and by reason of the effort of the will to become adequate to its own
> *élan* that a need is born, we have seen how, of an exterior correspond-
> ence and a necessary complement to our interior action.[1]

However, even if we grant that the idea of a possible revelation
arises from an initiative interior to our will-activity, the question
remains: By what traits can we recognize outside of ourselves an
authentic response to the need of our will, granting that such a
response has actually been given? The second stage of Blondel's
phenomenological investigation into the idea of a possible revelation
is an effort to establish the a priori characteristics any possible revelation must possess in order that from without it offer those qualities
appropriate to the exigencies of the will. If a given hypothetical revelation is to correspond to the exigencies of the human will, then the first
and essential necessity is that it must be offered to man by a mediator.
"There is no revelation, given or received, except by a *mediator*, the
first and essential exigency."[2] The very notion of revelation contains
within itself the idea that what is revealed must be presented as independent of our human initiative. Where is God to be found, Blondel
asks, if not there where the will by a sort of self-dispossession goes
outside of itself? "If a revelation exists ... it is necessary that it requires
an act of submission, a substitution of thought and will."[3] Employing
Schelling's terminology, the first requirement for an authentic revelation capable of meeting our need is that it demand an ecstasy not only
of reason but of both reason and will together; and that movement
itself of self-dispossession must have its source in the initiative and
free gift of a mediator.

The free gift in question is not only, then, a question of light for the
intellect but also of force for the will. Thus the second and even more
essential exigency for any authentic revelation is that it be both "*via et
veritas*, but first of all *via*."

> What we cannot even conceive without help, much less can we accom-
> plish alone. Nothing which man can do, nothing in the natural order

---

[1] *Ibid.*
[2] *Ibid.*, p. 398.
[3] *Ibid.*

of action can bring man to his perfection or lead him to God. In order to constitute God as the destiny of man, according to the imperious need of our will, in order to become his cooperator and to introduce into our life what is its source and its destiny, we need a helper, an intercessor, a pontiff who will be, as it were, the act of our acts.[1]

But this aspiration of our will seems to involve a contradiction; it seems inconceivable that such an active mediation could remain supernatural while at the same time it becomes our activity. This living revelation must come from a source completely exterior to us and at the same time be completely immanent in us. How then, Blondel asks can we introduce and cause to live within ourselves another thought and another life other than our own? How can this superior life be introduced into our life, especially if it is true that in its source it must be absolutely independent of our initiative? It is precisely at this point, he answers, that the sovereign efficacy and the supreme mediating power of action manifests itself. Just as the necessary idea of God springs from action and leads to action, so too the necessary idea of a possible revelation.

> On the one hand, it is by means of the mediation of action that revealed truth penetrates into our thought without losing anything of its supernatural integrity. And on the other hand, if believing thought ... has a meaning and a value, it is because it leads to action and finds in literal practice its commentary and living reality.[2]

A revelation as such cannot find entrance into our interior life either by means of our own proper thought, nor by means of an action which springs from our proper initiative. Any attempt to assimilate a revelation from without by thought would be once again to reduce what is by definition above our powers of comprehension to the measure of our thought. Any effort to lift ourselves by our own efforts up to a participation in absolute life would be only to fall back again into that frustration which was the very reason for desiring a revelation. There is only one means, Blondel maintains, by which man is capable of receiving the divine gift of life without denaturing or destroying that gift; that means is action.

> If there ought to be a synthesis of man with God in order that the will find its equilibrium, one must not forget that the mutual act which consecrates every alliance is, in a sense, entirely the work of each co-operator. Now man is capable of those actions which by hypothesis are

---

[1] *Ibid.*, p. 399.
[2] *Ibid.*, p. 400.

purely of faith, actions whose imposition no natural reason can explain
and which go against man's proper instinct, because they demand a sort
of disappropriation from oneself.[1]

Thus Blondel believed that the necessity of action based in faith could
be philosophically established as the only possible means of a vital
knowledge of the value and meaning of that hypothetical revelation
which is necessary for the fulfillment of human destiny. "One can
never know what is contained in it except by an effective experimentation ... *Fac ut videbis*."[2] Only by means of action can we hope to
introduce the divine light into our spirit, on the condition that God
acts within our action. "For that reason the thought which follows on
the action is infinitely richer than that which precedes. It has entered
into a new world where no purely speculative philosophy can either
lead it or follow it."[3]

The final step of Blondel's analysis of the phenomenon of revelation
is an attempt to define the necessary conditions for man's natural cooperation which the religious act as such requires. "One cannot insist
too much that even on the supposition that a *théandrique* action is entirely founded in the divine will, yet the human will remains co-
extensive with it."[4] The same movement which led us necessarily to
conceive the idea of a religious action, leads us also to determine the
exigencies and requisites of that inevitable cooperation.

Action, Blondel maintains, is not only a transient means necessary
only to arrive at faith; rather its mediation is permanent. The act of
faith introduces into us not so much a vision as a life, a power of new
activity and the source of a new dialectic. The necessary communion
of wills between God and man can only be achieved, maintained, and
developed by continual action. "Just as by reason of the dynamism of
reflection, thought, which is the fruit of the experience of life, becomes
itself a motive and point of departure for further experience; in the
same way faith, which one can call the divine experience in us, is the
origin of an activity."[5]

Throughout the entire course of the science of action, Blondel
points out, action has constantly appeared as a new synthesis, heterogeneous in relation to its proper conditions. This scientific truth is con-

---

[1] *Ibid.*, p. 402.
[2] *Ibid.*, pp. 402-403.
[3] *Ibid.*, p. 403.
[4] *Ibid.*
[5] *Ibid.*, p. 411.

firmed once again here in relation to the religious act as such. "In order for a religious act to be truly such it must contain the real presence of the transcendent and be its immanent truth."[1] Consequently, this act cannot spring, anymore than faith itself, from purely human initiative. A religious act which springs from purely human initiative would be an idolatrous fiction. "All religious practice which is not given as a supernatural order is superstitious."[2] The essential condition for all valid religious activity is that it have its source in the divine will.

> It is necessary that the secret principle of all action offer itself to us under the form by means of which we can enter into communion with it, receive it, and possess it in our finitude. We need a finite infinite. But it is not our right to limit it; for if we do, we lower it to our level. The infinite itself must place itself within our reach and condescend to our littleness in order to exalt and enlarge us to its immensity.[3]

Consequently, Blondel concludes, within the context of a philosophy of religion the ordinary relation between thought and action, which has been analyzed throughout the entire dialectic of the development of human life, must be at the same time conserved, complemented, and reversed. It must be conserved; for it remains true that religious belief, as all truth, in order to be living and sincere, has need to manifest itself in action. It must be complemented; for it is only by means of a positive precept that there can be a possible harmony between the infinite spirit and the finite literal form which expresses it. But finally, and most important, this relation between thought and action as concerns a possible religious action must be reversed. In contrast with ordinary natural activity in which thought precedes sensible operations here it is the sensible sign which contains obscurely the light whose invisible presence thought gradually searches to uncover. What one cannot see clearly, one can do fully. Religious action must be prescribed, Blondel argues, because within what one must do is contained the reality which one must believe. "While in the natural order the material operation which gives expression to the intention extends the domain of the will but does not profit thought ..., here it is the operation itself which becomes nourishment and light for the spirit; for it is the divine will which shines through the obscurity of sensible signs."[3]

---

[1] *Ibid.*, p. 415.
[2] *Ibid.*, p. 416.
[3] *Ibid.*, p. 418.
[4] *Ibid.*, p. 419.

There can never be a question in Blondel's estimation of a substitution of philosophy for religion, of vision for life. The necessity for the mediation of action is an absolute and permanent necessity. "The true infinite is much less in knowledge, than in life itself; it is not in the facts, nor in the sentiments, nor in ideas; it is found in action."[1] The true infinite can only be known in so far as it is vitally present in a living action which synthesized the divine and human wills. Any effort which tries to transcend the need of action and substitute thought in its place, having destroyed that synthesis, has lost possession of the object which it tries to comprehend.

One final problem concerning the relation between Blondel's philosophy of action and Schelling's positive philosophy remains to be discussed. Blondel's original manuscript did not include his idea of a "metaphysics to the second power," which is found in the final chapter of his published work. This idea, as we shall see, was added before publication under the influence of Delbos, who proposed Schelling's concept of a positive philosophy to Blondel as his model. At first sight there is a close resemblance between these two ideas. Schelling understood the final stage of his positive philosophy, in Copleston's words, as "an activity of religious consciousness whereby it understands itself from within."[2] Blondel understood his metaphysics to the second power as presupposing "the real possession of the living truth" within our consciousness of our religious activity.[3] What remains to be determined, then, is what Blondel himself understood as the relation between his final metaphysics and Schelling's concept of philosophical religion.

METAPHYSICS TO THE SECOND POWER

When Delbos first read the manuscript-copy of *Action*, he wrote to Blondel to congratulate him. However, he mentioned one reservation which, he said, "results evidently from my own studies."[4] That reservation had to do with the limited, secondary role that Blondel assigned to metaphysics. "It comes, according to you, as a moment in the development of action and you consider it more in terms of its

---

[1] *Ibid.*, p. 422.
[2] Copleston, *op. cit.*, Vol. VII, p. 141.
[3] Blondel, *Lettres Philosophiques*, pp. 126-127.
[4] The text of the letter can be found in the periodical *Archives de Philosophie*, Tome XXIV, Cahier I (Janvier-Mars), p. 60.

efficiency than in terms of its intrinsic nature.[1] Delbos agrees with the rejection of a metaphysics which would erect itself as a religion. However, he objects, metaphysics ought to have the role "of *rationally justifying* (rationaliser) that dialectic of action." Metaphysics should establish with absolute validity the necessity for mediating action.

> Should you not have established it (the mediation of action) as a truth in itself and not only for us? Before expressing itself entirely by means of religious faith the subordination of human action to God can and ought to be metaphysically affirmed: Religion renders efficacious what reason affirms.
> Metaphysics is not only the substance of the will in action, it is ... *in itself* its justification. In my opinion truth is primary and action derived, especially that concrete human action such as you conceive of it.[2]

Blondel granted a certain validity in his friend's criticism. In his eagerness to establish the role of action he acknowledged that perhaps he tended to subordinate truth to action, whereas his real objective was to coordinate the two.

> I acknowledge that, if I have an excessive "tendency", it is analogous to that of those heretics who would have the Spirit proceed exclusively from the Father; and you call attention quite justly to the necessary consubstantiality of thought; *Filioque procedit*. Action has no supremacy over the word; metaphysics is total and divine also, and I am too inclined to forget it.[3]

As a result of Delbos' criticism Blondel revised the final chapter and introduced the idea of a metaphysics to the second power:

> ... that metaphysics which, following the study of the total determinism of our thoughts, and accepting the fact that we invincibly affirm the objective reality of what we have invincibly conceived and thought, searches out the conditions under which these truths ... can be real independently of our thoughts, absolutely real. ...[4]

Evidently, Delbos remained dissatisfied with Blondel's concept of metaphysics. Instead of a clear subordination of action to truth, as he desired, Blondel granted only their equality and compenetration in being from the absolute viewpoint, but the necessary subordination of thought to action from man's viewpoint. In his further critique of

---

[1] *Ibid.*
[2] *Ibid.*
[3] Blondel, *Lettres Philosophiques*, p. 69.
[4] *Ibid.*, p. 126. Confer above pages 97-103 for a description of Blondel's concept of metaphysics.

Blondel's revised final chapter, Delbos spoke of the necessity of maintaining a "rational and practical dualism," using Schelling's distinction between negative and positive philosophy as his model. In his response Blondel indicates where and why his position differs from Schelling's concept of positive philosophy. He insists that in his opinion the idea behind traditional metaphysics, the idea of a complete system which encloses the total content of thought and reality, is justified ,but only as an *idea*.

> In place of juxtaposing the philosophy of essence and the philosopoy of existence, as you would do according to Schelling, I have tried to show that they mingle and compenetrate everywhere without being confused or replacing each other anywhere. ... If one limits oneself to juxtaposing reason and practice, one leaves outside of metaphysics an irreducible and irrational element.[1]

That irreducible element, which in Blondel's judgment had escaped Schelling's distinction between positive and negative philosophy, is the same element which he had found missing in Kant's distinction of pure and practical reason; in Fichte's original distinction between the theoretical and practical developments of consciousness, and his later distinction between reason and faith; in the early Schelling's distinction between a philosophy of nature and a philosophy of the ego; and, finally, in Hegel's distinction between a material dialectic and formal logic. Once again the real synthesis between the ideal and the real found in free human action as such has been ignored by reason of a methodological postulate. In Blondel's judgment, every dogmatic absolute monism is forced to adopt a system of philosophical dualism in order to try to explain reality.

Schelling's concept of negative philosophy represented, in Blondel's mind, a pure rationalism, an abstraction of pure reason from its organic role in human action and its erection as an absolute. Once again, as Fichte had done before him, Schelling acknowledged the failure of that pure rationalism and turned to the will and to faith in order to escape its limits. By proposing a positive philosophy of existence Schelling posited all the elements previously missing from tradition necessary for a philosophy of action as such. He recognized the will as a living power which reason presupposes and serves; he developed the experimental a posteriori method necessary for a philosophical

---

[1] *Ibid.*, p. 69.

study of the progressive synthesis of thought and reality contained in free action. But Schelling did not develop a philosophy of action as such. He was satisfied to note that necessity inherent in the human will "which demands that God should not be a pure idea." This observation justified, in his opinion, an act of faith understood as an ecstasy of reason outside of itself in order to postulate the existential reality of the absolute as a pure that or existence. However, reason immediately reenters the picture as a perfect mirror of the intrinsic constitutive process whereby that pure existence arrives at its essence in an historical process of self-constitution and self-manifestation.

Blondel believed that all the same presuppositions could be found in Schelling's positive philosophy which could be found in his idealist predecessors. Philosophy remains a monist system which begins with the absolute and deduces the finite. True, the absolute is now considered as an existing person who manifests himself freely. However, once this existential factor has been acknowledged by an act of faith, the absolute reason of dogmatic idealism takes over, and one attempts to deduce the necessary pattern contained in that free self-manifestation of the absolute. The reason involved in Schelling's ecstasy of reason is absolute reason; and the will whose mediation that reason acknowledges is absolute will. There is an immediate inverse correlation, according to Schelling, between the ecstasy of reason and the ecstasy of the absolute will in its creative act.

There is an equivalent of Schelling's ecstasy of reason in Blondel's philosophy of action; it is that Copernican revolution at the point of departure whereby man recognizes the a priori relation of the act of thinking to thought. There is also an ecstasy of will and reason combined; it occurs at the end of the phenomenological analysis of human action, when man recognizes that he cannot fulfill his destiny by his own forces alone; yet he finds within his own conscious activity the evidence for the presence of a person who is both immanent in and transcendent to the combined forces of his intellect and will. This second ecstasy, as a result, takes the form of that option or sacrifice by which one chooses to supplant self-will by the will of the absolute.

These two ecstasies remained one in Schelling's thought; more accurately, Blondel understood him to mistake the first for the second. Consequently, there is a confusion of the evolution of the human will with an evolution proper to the divine will. Hence, in Blondel's judgment, Schelling was guilty of the same basic error as Hegel, but with the difference that, whereas Hegel had tried to construct the absolute with human reason, Schelling tried to construct the absolute with the human will.

Schelling's distinction between a philosophy of essence and a philosophy of existence carried with it the seeds of the radical rift in contemporary philosophical thought into rival essentialist and existentialist camps. Sören Kierkegaard, after attending the Berlin lectures of Schelling in 1841, expressed disappointment that after making his distinction between negative and positive philosophy, Schelling failed to rethink radically his philosophy in the light of that distinction. Blondel's philosophy of action represents just such an attempt to rethink radically not only Schelling's positive philosophy but the whole evolution of philosophical thought from Spinoza to the final Schelling. However, his concern was not to exploit the division between a philosophy of essence and a philosophy of existence; rather, it was to attempt to heal that rift by going back to the point of departure and finding the true synthetic source of unity which would permit him to develop an integral philosophy at the same time both rational and existential, a philosophy which would maintain the same synthetic union between thought and action in theory as they manifest in life, a philosophy, finally, which would be open to an understanding of religion without trying to substitute itself for religion. He found that point of departure in action.

CONCLUSION

Our purpose in this study was to try to understand Blondel's method and thought and to clarify the exact nature of his originality in terms of the primary philosophical sources which influenced his thought at the time he composed his major work, *Action*. On several occasions after the publication of *Action*, as we have seen, Blondel himself claimed that his work "had been prepared and even demanded by a speculative effort which was thoroughly in accord with the exigencies of reason," and that it was "an extension and utilization of philosophical tradition." Thus Blondel himself considered his philosophy of action as an integral part of an "evolution of modern thought" and, as it were, the most recent logical step in the intrinsic development of that evolution. Further, on several occasions, especially in his article "The Evolution of Spinozism," Blondel identified that evolution as a development of moral philosophy within modern thought which had its beginning in Spinoza's *Ethics* and, passing through Kant's *Critique of Practical Reason*, Fichte's *Theory of Science*, Schelling's *Transcendental Idealism*, reached its logical completion in Hegel's dialectical philosophy and began its transformation into a philosophy of action with Schelling's final positive philosophy.

As the evidence we have seen proves, this claim of a relation between *Action* and this specific German tradition was by no means an afterthought on Blondel's part, nor an accidental relation. From the very beginning of his philosophical career, when the young Blondel was merely at the stage of jotting down seminal notes for his projected work on the philosophy of action, he already had a definite idea of the nature and importance of that specific tradition. He understood Spinoza to have developed the realist thesis of moral philosophy in his *Ethics* and Kant, the critical antithesis in his *Critique of Practical Reason*. He saw the efforts of the three great German idealists, Fichte, Schelling and Hegel, as three major efforts to achieve a valid synthesis of these two positions. These three efforts at synthesis, each in its turn, marked a definite progress, but each in its turn failed to achieve its ultimate objective. Blondel's philosophy of action would represent then the most recent effort to achieve that synthesis, benefiting from all the partial achievements of his predecessors, while at the same time avoiding their defects by means of a new intuition and a new method. Thus we find Blondel announcing his project as an effort to redefine the relation of the speculative and the practical orders in such a way as to transcend the antithetical relation of Spinoza's realism and Kantian criticism. He would do so, his notes declare, by "going back to the starting point of Fichte and Hegel, the concept of mediator," and redoing what they had done in a different context. By so doing it was his avowed intention from the very beginning to "go beyond Hegel," and win back for the philosopher the right to pronounce absolute moral judgments within the context of the relative itself. Consequently from the very beginning Blondel understood his philosophy of action as a post-Hegelian work, and even as a post-existentialist work in Schelling's sense of the word. However, it was so not in the sense of a refutation but, rather, in the sense of an assimilation and transformation of all that he found valuable in that evolution into a new and original philosophical synthesis.

As we have noted on several occasions, Blondel did not consider himself in any sense an historian of philosophy; he had no personal interest in the task of reconstituting objectively the thought of his predecessors. He was completely preoccupied by his personal effort to create an original philosophical synthesis commanded by his own starting point and intuition into the synthetic function of will-activity. During the period in which he composed the various redactions of *Action* he undertook a rather intensive program of reading and reflection on the evolution of moral philosophy in recent German thought under the guidence of his director Emile Boutroux, and in collaboration with his friend, Victor Delbos. The extent of his study, as we have seen, was indicated by the fact that not only, for example, did Blondel read those works of Schelling available in French translations such as his *Transcendental Idealism* and his *Philosophical Inquiries into the Nature of Human Freedom*, but he even began a study of Schelling's sources such as Jakob Boehme and Master Eckhart.

But, as we have noted throughout this study, even more essential for an accurate understanding of the influence of German philosophical thought on *Action* is the relation which existed between Blondel and Delbos. Their correspondence reveals the fact that these two young men worked together in a close collaboration during the period when Blondel composed *Action*. Blondel himself considered Delbos' book

The Moral Problem in the Philosophy of Spinoza and the History of Spinozism, which was the fruit of their collaboration, as a companion work to *Action*. For in Blondel's judgment Delbos in this work has accurately portrayed that tradition which he had "employed and utilised" in *Action*.

However, Blondel's purpose in these readings and in the dialogue with Delbos was "to find the various levels of his own intellectual evolution and the sources of his own synthesis." Since he had begun his own personal project from a completely different intuition and centre of perspective, he was quite aware that the ideas and terminology of his predecessors took on a new and different meaning within the context of his philosophy of action. He made use of the past primarily as a means of stimulating his own thought. Therefore he did not wish that his ideas should be judged according to a norm of fidelity to historical tradition.

However, if Blondel insisted that his philosophy was not to bl judged in terms of past systems, he insisted with even greater force that what he attempted in his philosophy of action could not be propere ly understood without an adequate knowledge of that philosophica tradition to which it belonged. He was aware of the debt he owed to those philosophers who had prepared the way for a philosophy of action and provided him with a frame of reference within which he could construct his system. It is evident a priori that if Blondel's thought in *Action* represents an effort to assimilate and transform into a new synthesis the idealist tradition in German thought, then no profound and accurate understanding of what he has accomplished is possible without some understanding of that tradition and his relation to it. Blondel himself attributed the general misunderstanding and misinterpretation with which his work was originally received to this lack of knowledge of the development of modern philosophical thought after Kant. The fact remains that until the present almost no effort has been made to understand Blondel's thought within that context.

THE ROLE OF THE CHRISTIAN IDEA

There is a tendency in nearly all the commentaries written on Blondel's thought to treat his work as if its primary value was apologetic. Blondel is considered as a religious man who undertook a philosophical defence of his faith; and for many commentators the only important problem would seem to be that of the orthodoxy from a theological viewpoint of his defence. But even those who recognize the originality of his philosophical position seem to assume that it has no major roots in a specific historical tradition and is capable of being understood adequately by an independent study of the text of *Action*. Blondel himself on several occasions before his death deplored this tendency to overlook his philosophical contribution and its relation to modern thought. He considered himself to be a philosopher in the strict sense of the term and his *Action* as an autonomous work of philosophical research. He believed that his originality lay not so much in his apologetics, which were an application of his philosophy, but in the philosophy itself—his intuition into the synthetic function of action, and the phenomenological method, the concept of a real dialectic, the logic of action, all of which resulted from that intuition. As far as he was concerned all the true originality and value of his *Action* belonged more properly to the first one hundred pages rather than to the last, which represented an application of his original method to the specific problems of religious belief.

Certainly, it was Blondel's intention from the start to attempt a new philosophical solution to the problem of human destiny. This objective made it obligatory that he deal with the apologetic questions of the role of faith and religious belief in so far as they enter into the domain of philosophical research. Blondel is also quite explicit that one of the inspirations and, perhaps, the most important, which led him to undertake the construction of an original philosophical synthesis was the desire to redefine the relation of philosophy to religion. He intended in his own words to establish "an integral philosophy wholly appropriate to Christian belief, but only in so far as that philosophy would be autonomous." But he felt this inspiration did not distinguish his work from the autonomous philosophical tradition in which he participated. Rather, it helped to identify him with that tradition. For, Blondel claimed, it was the presence of the Christian idea of human destiny which inspired the entire evolution of that tradition.

Each new stage in the evolution of modern thought from Spinoza to the final Schelling had as its aim to create a philosophy adequate to the Christian concept of human destiny. The failure of each stage and the renewed effort to create a more adequate philosophical system was due to the frequently explicit desire to create a philosophy compatible with Christianity.

The transformation of the idea of God in Spinoza's *Ethics* between the first book, where he appears as a static object or thing, and the fifth book, where he becomes an active, personal being with whom man can unite himself by an act of intellectual love, was inspired in Blondel's opinion, by the secret presence of the Christian idea of human destiny. The entire critical effort of Kant to establish the limits of human thought and action, was also inspired, in Blondel's opinion, by the desire of Kant to destroy the absolutist pretensions of human reason and, thus, to restore within philosophy the Christian idea of the relation of man to God. Fichte's avowed objective in his first *Theory of Science* was to synthezise "heart and head," his religious beliefs with his philosophical convictions; and the evolution of Fichte's thought in his final philosophy of love was expressly an attempt to formulate philosophically the johannine Christian idea of a union of man with God through love. Hegel's express objective in his search for a dialectical philosophy was an attempt to save the truth contained in Christian dogmas against the rationalist attack of the *Aufklarung*. The primary reason Schelling gives for his attack on Hegelianism, and his attempt to create a positive existential philosophy was, he maintained, to find a place in philosophy for the real, personal God of Christianity and his free revelation of himself in Christ. But despite these implicit or avowed "apologetic" inspirations no one questions the genuine contribution each of these men made to philosophical tradition as such. So too Blondel himself undertook to create a new and original philosophical synthesis. He too found his inspiration for his autonomous philosophical research in the Christian idea. As he himself wrote to Delbos, he found implicit in St. Paul's epistles a real dialectic of life which admitted the dialectic of contradiction of Hegel as well as a dialectic of non-contradiction. Since that Pauline dialectic comprehended both traditional concepts of the dialectic in a higher synthesis, it was superior to both; and the task Blondel set himself was to explicitate the philosophical truth contained in that higher synthesis. If he succeeded as a result in establishing a different, and as he believed, more adequate relation between philosophy and religion, this was the result of the working out of his philosophical dialectic. Consequently, he felt that his real contribution was essentially philosophical; and it is in terms of the value of that philosophical contribution and its originality that he ought to be judged.

BLONDEL'S PHILOSOPHICAL ORIGINALITY

Blondel believed that his primary original contribution to philosophical method lay in his attempt to transpose the point of departure or center of perspective of philosophical research from either reason or will as such into the synthetic reality of living, human action. In a sense the whole of Blondel's effort can be summarised as a systematic thematization of the truth contained in the ancient adage *solvitur ambulando*. In the actual lived experience as such there is no division or conflict between thought and reality but rather a mutual compenetration. It is only in reflection that the distinction and conflict arises. Blondel's philosophy of action represented an attempt to find a philosophical method which would permit the retention and expression of that synthesis of thought and reality in philosophy, just as it is to be found a priori in life.

In his study of the evolution of modern philosophy from Spinoza to Hegel what impressed Blondel in that entire history was the constant search for a means of integrating thought and reality within a philosophical system. Although each philosopher, benefiting from the advances and failures of his predecessors, came closer to that goal, yet Blondel felt the entire movement ended in an impasse. In terms of his intuition of the synthetic a priori function of action he believed he had found the basic reason for that failure and the means of correcting it. Spinoza had limited the center of perspective of philosophy to the objective pole of reason. Hence he was led to identify reality with the object as such and to attempt to absorb the subject and the whole process of becoming into the objective reality of that static absolute. Kant in his *Critique of Practical Reason* had, in Blondel's opinion, limited that perspective to the subjective pole of reason and, thus, he was led to establish a dichotomy between the subjective a priori nature of thought, and the objective reality of the thing-in-itself. Fichte, it is true, had an intuition into the synthetic role of vital will-activity and the corresponding necessity of a phenomenological descriptive method. But his desire to systematise philosophy on a mathematical model resulted in the loss of that perspective. Hegel, in turn, grasped the dialectical nature of the law which governs the vital evolution of human action. But he remained within the center of perspective of reason and as a result identified the logical necessity contained in a rational reconstruction of that dialectic with the total free dialectical evolution of life of which that rational reconstruction is only a partial aspect.

Both Fichte and Schelling in their final philosophies realized that as long as the center of perspective of philosophy remained exclusively within reason, it could never achieve its objective of understanding life. So both attempted to shift the center of perspective outside of reason into will. But once again, Blondel held, they only succeeded in substituting a partial aspect of the real dialectic for the whole. If it is precisely the role of free human action to synthesize thought and reality into the being of a living act, then, Blondel claimed, the philosopher must develop a method whereby he can grasp the secret of that synthetic process. This method must be such that it does not necessarily destroy the very synthesis which it seeks to understand. Consequently a philosophy of action must drop the pretension of being a strict analytical and deductive science. Since such a philosophical endeavor necessarily presupposes the free exercise of the synthetic function of action, it must take the form of a sort of experimental science or, as Schelling called it, an a posteriori science. The philosopher of action must develop a new type of reflection whereby he can place himself at that point in consciousness where thought arises spontaneously out of life and enters synthetically into it. From this center of perspective he must carry out a purely phenomenological description of that dual process of genesis and subsequent dialectical evolution. His primary concern must be never to isolate and consequently to absolutise any aspect of that process but to remain scrupulously faithful to the progressive unfolding of that synthetic bond which unites all the factors of life in an organic synthesis. Only by means of such a method can he hope to arrive at a true understanding of the bond itself which exists between thought and life and of the dialectical laws which govern its progressive evolution.

As we have seen, Blondel made use of this new center of perspective and this new methodology throughout *Action*. One after another he confronted all the traditional philosophical problems as these problems arose in the progressive unfolding of the synthetic power of human action. In each of these problem areas he attempted by means of his new method to uncover the truth contained within the synthetic function of action as such. By this means he arrived at his final objective—an understanding of the structure and laws of the real, total dialectic within human life itself.

Nowhere is Blondel's originality and genius more evident than in this idea of the total dialectic. However, with the exception of Henrici's work *Hegel and Blondel*, none of Blondel's commentators have given serious consideration to his "logic of action." Yet, as we have seen, Blondel's objective from the start was to discover a new total logic whereby he could pass beyond the Hegelian dialectic and win back for man a legitimate right to judge absolutely within the relative itself. He understood Hegel to have succeeded in formalizing the material aspect of the total dialectic in life, but to have failed to materialize at the same time what is necessarily and constitutively formal in that dialectic. In the course of his phenomenological genetic study of the synthetic relation of thought and action Blondel uncovered the paradoxical truth of the simultaneous compatibility and exclusion of the principle of contradiction within the total dialectic of living action. He concluded that the understanding of that total dialectic depended on a clarification of the paradoxical double material and formal role of the principle of contradiction. He found the answer to this problem once again in the synthetic function of action.

Even as thought arises spontaneously out of action in order to re-enter synthetically into union with it, so too, the law of contradiction, which is the spontaneous formal law of thought, although it is not immediately and directly the material law of action, yet has its spontaneous origin in action and has a real, mediate function in the synthetic development of action. Because of the presence of the law of contradiction in his thought, man can by his conscious acts introduce the absolute of being into the phenomena without suppressing the relativity of the phenomena. Action, serving as the source of unity between the opposed forms of thought and life, insinuates the law of contradiction, formally present in thought, into the heart of the fact, while at the same time perpetually operating an experimental synthesis of the contraries. Within the total dialectic it is the spontaneous function of thought to project ahead, as it were, whatever remains privative in the relatively infinite potentiality of the human will. And it is the function of the law of contradiction within thought to make possible that option by which man can freely unite himself with being and transform privation into real possession. It was this understanding of the logical structure of the real dialectic which provided the key, as we have seen, for a true understanding of Blondel's originality in relation to his sources in Kant, Fichte, Schelling, and Hegel, as concerns his solution to such problems as the relation of morality to metaphysics. If one wishes to avoid a false metaphysics which absolutises a relative aspect of being, such as pure thought or pure will, then, Blondel maintains, one must presuppose and include within metaphysics that "moral option" which introduces the absolute of being into the phenomena. Man's destiny is not to think or will absolutely but to think and will the insertion of the absolute into the relativity of his acts and by willing it, to know it. This idea of the total dialectic provides also the key for a proper understanding of the relation Blondel establishes between philosophy and religion. A philosophical study of the synthetic function of action, such as Blondel conceived of it, necessarily leads man to the realization that the only means of achieving the total actualisation of the infinite potential in his will is by an active synthesis of his will with the Divine will. The absolute must become the "act of his acts." Philosophy as such can make clear the necessity of such a synthesis; it can even establish the necessary a priori conditions of such a synthesis, but it can by no means supply it. Nothing which man can do or think, nothing in the natural order of action can bring man to his perfection; yet it is only by means of action that we can hope to introduce the divine life and light into our spirit. Consequently, at this point the initiative of man must give way to the initiative of the absolute will. A purely autonomous philosophical process, having clarified what is necessary for man to achieve his destiny, must give way to a true religious activity.

Within the context of this study we have only been able to indicate the essential relation of resemblance and difference between Blondel's thought and that of his German sources. What we have wished to establish above all else is that Blondel's position was consciously thought out in relation to the position of such philosophers as Fichte, Schelling and Hegel, and was proposed precisely as a means of assimilating all that was positive in the German idealist tradition, while transforming, and as he believed, perfecting that tradition in terms of his new method and his concept of the total dialectic. But we believe that the evidence contained in this study imposes the conclusion that the Blondelian synthesis represents an original contribution to philosophical tradition which merits to be studied in its own right as a unique philosophical system of the first order.

SELECTIVE BIBLIOGRAPHY

I. BLONDEL'S WORKS

Only those books and articles are listed in this Bibliography which were employed or referred to in the writing of this work. An exhaustive General Bibliography concerning Blondel covering the years 1888-1951, and 1952-1962 is provided by André Hayen S.J. and Antonio Costa respectively (see below).

A. BOOKS

Blondel, Maurice. *L'Action: Essai d'une Critique de la Vie et d'une Science de la Pratique*. Paris: Bibliothèque de Philosophie Contemporaine, Félix Alcan, 1893.

— *L'Action: Essai d'une Critique de la Vie et d'une Science de la Pratique*. "Les Premiers Ecrits de Maurice Blondel", Paris: Presses Universitaires de France, 1950. Reedition.

— *Carnets Intimes* (1883-1894). Paris: Les Editions du Cerf, 1961.

— *Correspondance M. Blondel - Auguste Valensin*. "Editions Montaigne" Paris: Aubier, 1956. II Volumes.

— *De Vinculo Substantiale et de Substantia Composita apud Leibnitium*. Paris: Félix Alcan, 1903.

— *L'Itinéraire Philosophique*. Collections "La NEF," Ed. Frédéric Lefèvre, Paris: Editions Spes, 1928.

— *Lettres Philosophiques*. "Editions Montaigne," Paris: Aubier, 1961.

— *Léon Ollé-Laprune* (1839-1898). "Les Maitres d'une Génération," Paris: Librarie Bloud et Gay, 1932.

— *Une Enigme Historique: Le "Vinculum Substantiale" d'après Leibnitz et l'Ebauche d'un Realisme Superieur*. Paris: Bibliothèque des Archives de Philosophie, Gabriel Beauchesne Ed., 1930.

— (Mallet, F, pseud.) *Qu'est-ce que la Foi?* "Questions Théologiques," Paris: Librarie Bloud et Gay, 1907.

B. ARTICLES

Blondel, Maurice. "Action," *Vocabulaire Technique et Critique de la Philosophie*. André Lalande, Editeur, I. (1926), 17. I. (1947), 21.

— L'Anti-Cartésianisme de Malebranche," *Revue de Metaphysique et de Morale*. T. XXIII (Janvier, 1916) I-26.

— "La Clef de Voûte du Système Cartésien," *Revista di Filosofia Neoscholastica*. Supplemento, Vol. XXIX (Juglio, 1937) 69-77.

Blondel, Maurice. "Le Christianisme de Descartes," *Revue de Metaphysique et de Morale*. No. 4 (Juillet, 1896) 6-9.

— "Ebauche de Logique Générale," *Revue de Metaphysique et de Morale*. T. 65, No. I (Janviers-Mars, 1960) 7-18.

— "L'Evolution du Spinozisme et l'Accès qu'elle ouvre à la Transcendance," *L'Archivo di Filosofia*. Anno XI, Fasc. IV (Decembre, 1932) I-2.3-12.

— "Histoire et Dogme," *Les Premiers Ecrits de Maurice Blondel*. "Bibliothèque de Philosophie Contemporaine," Paris: Presses Universitaires de France, 1956. Republished from *La Quinzaine*. T. 56. 1904, 145-167; 349-373; 433-458.

— "L'Illusion Idéaliste," *Les Premiers Ecrits de Maurice Blondel*. "Bibliothèque de Philosophie Contemporaine," Paris: Presses Universitaires de France, 1956. 97-122. This article was republished from the *Revue de Metaphysique et de Morale*. T. 6. Novembre, 1898, 727-746.

— "Lettre concernant le rapport A. Lalande: "Constitution d'un Vocabulaire Philosophique," *Bulletin de la Société Française de Philosophie*. T. 2. 1902. Discussion of May 1902.

— "Lettre sur les Exigences de la Pensée Contemporaine en Matière d'Apologétique et sur la Méthode de la Philosophie dans l'Etude du Problème Religieux", *Les Premiers Ecrits de Maurice Blondel*. "Blibiothèque de Philosophie Contemporaine," Paris: Presses Universitaires de France, 1956. This letter appeared originally in the *Annales de Philosophie Chrétienne*, in January and July of 1896.

— "Reason," *Vocabulaire Technique et Critique de la Philosophie*. Ed. André Lalande, II (1926) 669-670. II (1947) 858-859.

— "Notes pour la seconde édition de l'Action," *Etudes Blondéliennes*. Fasc. 2. Paris: Presses Universitaires de France, 1952.

— "Le Point de Départ de la Recherche Philosophique," *Annales de Philosophie Chrétienne*. T. 151. (Janvier, 1905) 337-360; T. 152. (Juin, 1906) 225-250.

— "Principe Elémentaire d'une Logique de la Vie Morale," *Les Premiers Ecrits de Maurice Blondel*. Paris: Presses Universitaires de France, 123-128.

— "Un Interprète de Spinoza: Victor Delbos, 1862-1916," *Chronicon Spinozanum*. Tomus Primus (Hague Comitis, 1921) 290-300.

— "Une Association Inséparable: L'Agrandissement des Astres à l'Horizon," *Revue Philosophique de la France et de l'Etranger*. T. 26. (1888) 489-497; T. 27. (1889) 197-199.

— (Aimant, Bernard pseud.). "Une des Sources de la Pensée Moderne: l'Evolution du Spinozisme," *Annales de Philosophie Chrétienne*. 64è. année (Juin, 1894) 261; (Juillet, 1894).

— (Mallet, F. pseud.). "La Philosophie de l'Action," *Revue de Philosophie*. Vol. 6. No. 9. (September, 1906) 227-252.

C. Unedited Manuscripts

The unedited manuscripts and notes referred to here can be found in the Blondel Archives at Aix-en-Provence.

Blondel, Maurice. *L'Action. Etude sur la Metaphysique de la Science et de la Morale, et sur la Nature de la Pratique Religieuse*. This redaction was written between October 1888 and January 1890, and is referred to by Blondel as "Premier brouillon."

— *La Science de l'Action* (1890). Version dictated between 12 March and 2 April 1890.

— *L. Action* (1891).
This redaction was written between 14 June 1890 and 19 April 1891, and is referred to as "Projet de Thèse."

— *L'Action* (1892).
This redaction was begun 14 November 1891, presented to Emile Boutroux, and deposed at the Sorbonne in May 1892.

— *Pour la Conclusion de l'Action*. (1892).
Manuscript rewritten during 1892.

— *Correspondance Delbos - Blondel*. (1888-1910).

II. OTHER WORKS CITED

We have limited our reference to Blondel's major sources, Kant Hegel, etc., to the collected edition of their works used in this study.

A. Books

Boutroux, Emile. *La Contingence des Lois de la Nature*. Paris: 1874.
— *L'Idée de Loi Naturelle*. Paris: 2è Edition, 1901.
Brehier, Emile. *Histoire de la Philosophie*. Paris: Librairie Félix Alcan, 1932.
Brunschwicg, Léon. "Sur la Philosophie Religieuse au XVIIè Siècle," *Pour un Cinquantenaire Hommage a Maurice Blondel*. "La Nouvelle Journée, 12," Paris: Bloud et Gay, 1945.
Cartier, Albert. *Existence et Vérité; Philosophie Blondélienne de l'Action et Problématique Existentielle*. Nouvelle Recherche, Paris: Presses Universitaires de France, 1955.
Copleston, Fredrick. *A History of Philosophy*. London: Burns and Oates, Volume VI (1959), Volume VII (1963).
Cramer, Thomas. *Le Problème Religieux dans la Philosophie de l'Action*. Preface by Victor Delbos. Paris: Félix Alcan, 1912.
Delbos, Victor. *De Kant aux Post-Kantiens*. Editions Montaigne, Paris: Aubier, 1940. This work was originally published as "Les Facteurs Kantiens de la Philosophie Allemande du Commencement du XIXè Siècle" Ed. Maurice Blondel, in *Revue de Metaphysique et de Morale*. T. XXVI. (September, 1919) 569-593; T. XXVII (Janvier, 1920) 125ff.
— *De Posteriore Schellingii Philosophia quatenus Hegelianae doctrinae adversatur*. Paris: Félix Alcan, 1902.
— *La Philosophie Pratique de Kant*. Paris: Félix Alcan, 1905.
— *Le Problème Morale dans la Philosophie de Spinoza et dans l'Histoire du Spinozisme*. Paris: Félix Alcan, 1893.
Descartes, René. *Oeuvres Complètes*. Publiées par Victor Cousin. Paris: Leurault, 1824. 11 Volumes.
Duméry, Henri. *Raison et Religion dans la Philosophie de l'Action*. Paris: Editions du Seuil, 1963.
Fessard, Gaston. *La Dialectique des Exercices Spirituels de Saint Ignace de Loyola*. "Théologie," Lyon-Fourvière: 1956.
Fichte, J. G. *Doctrine de la Science, Principes Fondamentaux de la Science de la Connaissance*, trad. par Grimblot, Paris: Ladrange, 1843.
— *Fichtes sämmtliche Werke*, edited by J. H. Fichte, Berlin: Verlag von Veit und Comp. 1845. 8 Volumes.
— *Leben und Briefwechsel*, edited by J. H. Fichte, Leipzig: F. A. Brockhaus, 1862. 3 Volumes.
— *Méthode pour arriver à la Vie Bienheureuse*, trad. par M. Bouillier, Paris: Ladrange, 1845.
Fuhrmans, Horst. *Schellings Letzte Philosophie: die Negativa und Positiva Philosophie im Einsatz die Spätidealismus*. Berlin: Junker und Dünnkaupt Verlag, 1940.
— *Schellings Philosophie der Weltalter*. Düsseldorf: L. Schwann Verlag 1954.
Geuroult, Maurice. *L'Evolution et la Structure de la Doctrine de la Science chez Fichte*. Paris: Société des Editeurs, "Les belles Lettres," 1930.
Hegel, *Sämmtliche Werke*. Ed. Hermann Glockner, Stuttgart: Fr. Frommans Verlag, 1928. 20 Volumes.
Henrici, Peter. *Hegel und Blondel*. Pullach: Verlag Berchmanskolleg, 1958.

Jodl, Friedrich. *Geschichte der Ethik in der neueren Philosophie*. Stuttgart: 1889.
Kant, Emmanuel. *Kants gesammelte Schriften*, critical edition sponsored by the Prussian Academy of Science. Berlin: Georg Reimer, 1911. 22 Volumes.
Knox, M. T. *Hegel. Early Theological Writings*. Chicago: The University of Chicago Press, 1948.
Lachelier, Jules. *Du Fondement de l'Induction*. Paris: Félix Alcan, 1871.
Lacroix, Jean. *Maurice Blondel. Sa Vie, son Oeuvre*. "Philosophe," Paris: Presses Universitaires de France, 1963.
Léon, Xavier. *Fichte et son Temps*. Paris: Librarie Armand Colin, 1924.
— *La Philosophie de Fichte*, Preface by Emile Boutroux. Paris: Félix Alcan, 1902.
Maine de Biran. *Oeuvres*. avec notes et appendix. Publiées par Pierre Tisserand. Paris: Félix Alcan, 1920-22. 14 Volumes.
Marechal, Joseph. *Le Point de Départ de la Métaphysique*. "L'édition Universelle," Bruxelles: Desclée et Brouer, 1947.
Maritain, Raïssa. *Les Grandes Amitiés*. Bruges: Desclée et Brouwer, s.d.
Nabert, Jean. *Elements pour une Ethique*. "Bibliothèque de Philosophie Contemporaine," Paris: Presses Universitaires de France, 1943.
Nohl, Hermann. *Hegels Theologische Jugenschriften*. Tubingen, 1907.
Schelling. *Schellings Werke*. Munich: Beck und Oldenburg, edited by Manfred Schröter. 6 Volumes, 1927; 6 supplementary Volumes, 1956.
Schulz, Walter. *Die Vollendung des Deutschen Idealismus in der Spätphilosophie Schellings*. Stuttgart: W. Kohlhammer Verlag, 1955.
Spinoza. *Opera*. Carl Gebhardt editor. Heidelberg: Carl Winters 1924. 4 Volumes.
Windelband, Wilhelm. *Geschichte der neueren Philosophie*. Leipzig: 1880.
Weil, Eric. *Problèmes Kantiens*. Paris: Vrin, 1963.

B. ARTICLES

Bouillard, Henri. "Le Dernier Chapitre de l'Action," Edition Critique établie par Henri Bouillard, *Archives de Philosophie*. (Janvier-Mars, 1961) 65.
Boutroux, Emile. "Le Philosophe Allemand Jakob Boehme," Compter endu de l'Académie des Sciences Morales et Politiques, 1888.
Cartier, Albert. "Condition de la Présence à Soi et aux Autres d'après L'Action (1893) de Maurice Blondel," *L'Homme et son Prochain*. (Actes du VIIIè Congrès des Sociétés de Philosophie de Langue Française; Toulouse: 6-9 Septembre, 1956). Paris: Presses Universitaires de France, 1956.
Coreth, E. "Le Developpement de la Théologie de Fichte," *Archives de Philosophie*. T. XXV. Cahiers III-IV (Juillet-Décembre, 1962).
Costa, Antonio. "Un Decennio di Bibliographia Blondeliana 1951-1961," *Theoresi. Rivista di Cultura Filosofica*. Anno XVII. 1962. 295-320.
Delbos, Victor. "Compte-rendu de L'Action," *Revue Philosophique de la France et de l'Etranger*. T. 38. Décembre, 1894. 634-641.
Dhotel, D. C. "Action et Dialectique. Les Preuves de Dieu dans "L'Action" de 1893, *Archives de Philosophie*. T. XXVI. Cahier I. (Janvier-Mars, 1963).
Hayen, André. "Bibliographie Blondélienne (1888-1951)," *Theoresi. Rivista di Cultura Filosofica*. Anno VII N. 1-2 (Gennaio-Giugno, 1952) I-93. Published separately: Museum Lessinaum, Sect. Phil. No. 38, Desclée de Brouwer, 1953.
— "Un Texte Inédit du P. Maréchal "L'Action" de Maurice Blondel, présenté et commenté par André Hayen S.J. *Convivium Estudios Filosoficos*. Num. 4 Ano II. Fasc. 2. Julio-Diciembre 1957. 5-41.
Julia, D. "Le Savoir Absolu chez Fichte," *Archives de Philosophie*. T. XXV. Cahier III-IV (Juillet-Décembre, 1962).

— "Phenoménologie, Ontologie, ou Logique? A propos de la Théorie de la Science de Fichte," *Revue Philosophique de Louvin.* T. 57 (Troisième série, No. 54, Mai, 1959) 190-195.

Lauth, R. "Le Problème de l'Interpersonalité chez J. G. Fichte," *Archives de Philosophie.* T. XXV. Cahier III-IV (Juillet-Décembre, 1962).

Noël, G. "La Logique de Hegel," *Revue de Métaphysique et de Morale.* T. II. (1894) 36-57; 270-298; 644-675; T. III. (1895) 184-210; 503-526; T. IV (1896) 62-85; 585-614.

Tilliette, X. "Une Interpretation de Schelling," *Archives de Philosophie.* T. XXI. Cahier III. (Juillet-Septembre, 1958) 423-456. Cahier IV. (Oct-Dec, 1958) 564-599.

Since the preparation of this work all the unedited manuscripts of Blondel's works, originally to be found at his home in Aix-en-Provence, have been sent to the University of Louvain in Belgium, where under the able direction of Professor Van Riet and Abbé Troisfontaine they are in the process of being cataloged and photocopied.

The author also wishes to call the attention of the English speaking public to two works in English concerning Blondel. The first is a translation of two of Blondel's shorter works, The *Letter on Apologetics* and *History and Dogma*, texts presented and translated by Alexander Dru and Illtyd Trethowan, published by Holt, Rinehart and Winston. The second, to be published shortly, is entitled, *Maurice Blondel and the Drama of Human Action*, A Companion to the Thesis of 1893, by J. M. Sommerville, S.J.

INDEX

The complexity of both the problematic and the interrelations of ideas and philosophers with which the foregoing study deals makes it difficult to compose an adequate index and impossible to compose a complete one. We thought it best to provide the reader with a name index and, under the names of the principal philosophers whom Blondel used as sources, as well as Blondel himself, we have provided an index of the principal ideas and terms used in this study.

250; as approach to true metaphysics, 250; as secondary subject, 250; as form of superstition, 249; as symbol of unity of real and ideal, 250

Blondel, M.

Asceticism, preferred to aesthetics, 250-251, (*see also* sacrifice)

Autonomy, see Freedom

Being, relation to ethics, 32-33; and privation, 233, (*see also* Privation); as relation, 217-218, (*see also* Relation); as unity of opposites, 217-218; *see also* Substance, Realism

Categorical imperative, critique of, 87-88; as a priori structure of will-willing, 88-89, (*see also* will-willing)

Center of perspective, *see* Point of departure

Christian idea, of human destiny, 108, (*see also* Destiny); influence on Fichte, 120; influence on evolution of logic, 203; role in modern philosophy, 13, 244-245, 292-294; as transcending Hegelian dialectic, 203, (*see also* Dialectic); influence on Spinoza, 24-26

Concrete, science of, 159, 250, (*see also* Science)

Consciousness, idealist identity with being, 109; formation of moral consciousness 227-228; formation of psychological consciousness, 227; phenomenological study of, 61, (*see also* Phenomenology); self-consciousness as multipersonal, 191, (*see also* Interpersonal)

Contingent, characteristic of, 170; role in cosmological argument, 170-171, (*see also* Cosmological); relative necessity of, 170-171; restoration of role, 196-197

Contradiction, absence in order of real, 216-217, 223-224; action as solution to role of principle of, 222-223, (*see also* Action); Aristotelian transformation of Parmenides' principle of, 221; simultaneous compatability and exclusion of, 219; conflict between real and formal role of principle of, 218-219, 222-223; defined as "sentiment of irreparability of past", 225; extension of law to all categories, 226-227; genesis of principle of, 225, (*see also* Genesis); immoral act as self-contradictory, 90; insertion into relativity of phenomena by option, 225-226, (*see also* Option); inversion of role in moral option, 218-219; isolation of principle from origin in action, 226-227; role in moral choice, 232-233; role in development of moral consciousness, 227-228; role in total logic, 216-222; role in development of psychological consciousness, 227; real meaning as privation, 226, (*see also* Privation); role in option, 228, (*see also* Option); role of principle of, 216-219, 222-223, 297; substance as only true basis for, 226, (*see also* Substance); *see* Antibolie, Logic

Copernican revolution, 62-64, 81-82; role in philosophy of religion, 288-289, (*see also*, Religion, philosophy of)

Cosmological argument, 170-172; based on relative necessity of contingent, 170-171, (*see also* Contingent); *see also* Absolute

Criticism, acceptance of, XIII, 44; epistemological norm of, 52 n; gains of critical philosophy, 44 n; failure of exclusive critical philosophy, 53; criticism of Kantian critique, 57-72, 93-94; illusion of, 52-55; ultra-Kantian critique, 57; necessity of critique of totality of knowledge, 60; necessary moment in philosophical reflection, 58; role of, 57-60; Spinoza's contribution to, 32

Deduction, Fichte's mysterious process of, 113; *see also* Logic

Departure, *see* Point of

Destiny, absolute as man's, 182-183, (*see also* Absolute); Christian idea of, 13, 108, 120, (*see also* Christian idea); in Fichte's thought, 120-121; as consent to presence of absolute subject within, 183, (*see also* Subject); problem of